We are living in an important
and eventful age—*we are almost home!*

From the Heart

Ellen G. White

REVIEW AND HERALD® PUBLISHING ASSOCIATION
Since 1861 | www.reviewandherald.com

Daily texts are from the New King James Version. Copyright © 1979, 1980, 1982 by Thomas Nelson, Inc. Used by permission. All rights reserved.
Bible texts used by Ellen G. White are from the King James Version.

Cover design copyright © 2010
by Review and Herald® Publishing Association, Hagerstown, MD

This book was
Copyedited by Jan Schleifer
Cover designed by Trent Truman
Interior designed by Tina M. Ivany
Cover art by 123rf
Typeset: Bembo 11/12.5

PRINTED IN U.S.A.

14   13   12   11   10   5   4   3   2   1

Library of Congress Cataloging-in-Publication Data

White, Ellen Gould Harmon, 1827-1915.
  From the heart : daily devotionals / Ellen G. White.
     p. cm.
1. Seventh-Day Adventists—Prayers and devotions. 2. Devotional calendars—Seventh-Day Adventists. I. Title.
  BV4811.W4765 2010
  242'.2—dc22
                                  2009047900

ISBN 978-0-8280-2512-6

To order additional copies of *From the Heart,* or other books
by Ellen G. White, call 1-800-765-6955.

Visit us at **www.reviewandherald.com** for information on other
Review and Herald® products.

Foreword

In Ephesians 4:11 the apostle Paul lists five major gifts of the Holy Spirit: apostles, prophets, evangelists, pastors, and teachers. Seventh-day Adventists believe that Ellen G. White had the prophetic gift, but her life and ministry gave evidence of other gifts as well. It should be no surprise, then, that she chose not to limit the identification of her work to that of being a prophet. She once wrote, "My commission embraces the work of a prophet, but it does not end there" (*Selected Messages*, book 1, p. 36).

Mrs. White's writings may be classified into four general areas. First, there were her topical books, covering themes such as the great controversy story, education, health, evangelism, and other important subjects. Second, there were the published *Testimonies for the Church* that began in 1855 and continued until 1909, each addressing assorted topics. Third, there were letters, more than 5,000 of them. But this devotional book draws on material from the fourth area—her 5,000 articles in the various church journals. She wrote for all the major periodicals, starting with *The Present Truth,* then the *Review and Herald* and *The Youth's Instructor,* followed by *Signs of the Times* as well as other journals in North America. During her missionary service in Europe and Australia, her articles appeared regularly in publications in those places.

Throughout her prophetic service, particularly in its middle and later years, almost every week an article from her was published in one or more periodicals. These articles became her regular contact with church members. For many years they were printed on the covers of these journals. Her articles are the material of this devotional book, *From the Heart.*

Many of these articles were written specifically for publication. Some were transcriptions of sermons she preached. Others were notes of travel. Still others were accounts of her writing, especially of the controversy story. Some were letters. Some were drawn from her books, while others provided material for her books. That she was a prolific writer cannot be questioned. Her overall writing can easily be calculated at 100,000 pages. What a legacy to the church and the world!

Drawing on the 5,000 articles that appeared in church journals, this devotional book is evidence of the diversity of her counsel. She spoke and wrote to church leadership. She was often present when major decisions were made at General Conference sessions. She had a special burden for the ministry of the church. Her articles about Bible characters are rich with lessons for today. She also felt a deep interest in every church member. She often spoke about the use of talents, time, and money. She had a strong and supportive word for the doctrinal beliefs of the church, too. The Bible was always the foundation of what she wrote. Her rich knowledge of the Bible is evident in her articles. She strongly advocated study of the Bible, prayer, and other elements of a devotional life. Financial support in tithes and offerings was a high priority as well. And her major delight was to present the life of Christ in all its variety, including the parables.

Ellen White's lifetime ministry spanned more than 70 years from her first vision at age 17, in 1844, to her death at the age of 87, in 1915. There is not enough space in this book for every subject that might be covered. The topics here provide only a sampling.

From the Heart is the *twentieth* in the series of devotional books. When Ellen White prepared her final will, she instructed the appointed trustees who had care of her writings to prepare compilations from her manuscripts. Readers will be aware of many other compilations that have been prepared since her death. Without this provision in her will, much that is appropriate and helpful would not be available. Ellen White issued a number of compilations from her writings during her lifetime. The controversy theme went through several expansions. *Steps to Christ* was compiled by Ellen White and her staff. The *Testimonies* volumes represent her compiling work as well. Many other books might also be noted. And so, this book is a continuation of her practice while she lived.

As in other recent devotional volumes, most of Mrs. White's many generic masculine references (such as the generic "man," "men," and "he") have been changed to forms that are less likely to stand out to modern readers. Some of the punctuation has been updated as well, and except in quotes from the King James Version, this book consistently uses the American form "Savior" rather than the British spelling "Saviour." In a few instances, where a word's common meaning has changed, we have substituted an appropriate synonym.

Ellen White's periodical articles have been in facsimile reprint for several decades. They can be found in many private Adventist libraries as well as in churches, schools, and other facilities. Today they are also online and on CD-ROM. But never before have selections from them been brought together exclusively in a devotional book. It is our prayer that the messages in *From the Heart* may lead the reader closer to Jesus day by day.

—*The Ellen G. White Estate Board of Trustees*

The Author

Ellen Gould (Harmon) White, cofounder of the Seventh-day Adventist Church, writer, lecturer, and counselor, and one upon whom Seventh-day Adventists believe the gift of prophecy was bestowed, was born in Gorham, Maine, November 26, 1827, one of eight children of Robert and Eunice Harmon.

During her 70 years of active service to the church, she found time to write voluminously. She is credited with having written 100,000 manuscript pages. This remarkable legacy to the church could alone have occupied Ellen White's entire life, had she dedicated her time to little else but writing.

However, her service for the church embraces much more than writing. Her diaries tell of her public work, her travels, her personal labor, hostessing, contacts with neighbors, as well as of her being a mother and housewife. God blessed her abundantly in these activities. Her ambitions and concerns, her satisfactions and joys, her sorrows—her whole life—were for the advancement of the cause she loved.

Ellen G. White is reputed to be the most translated woman author and the most translated author in American history. For example, her little book *Steps to Christ* is available in more than 100 languages.

After a full life dedicated to the service of God and others, she died on July 16, 1915, confidently trusting in Him whom she had believed.

Biographical Notes

Ellen G. White, 1827-1915

The Early Years, 1827-1860

Born on a late fall day in a farmhouse near Gorham, Maine, Ellen Harmon spent her childhood and youth in nearby Portland. She married James White in 1846, and the struggling young couple lived in a variety of New England locations as they sought to encourage and instruct fellow Advent believers by their preaching, visiting, and publishing. After eleven irregular issues of *The Present Truth,* they launched the *Second Advent Review and Sabbath Herald*★ in Paris, Maine, in 1850. Thereafter they followed a steadily westward course—to Saratoga Springs, New York, and then Rochester, New York, in the early 1850s, and finally, in 1855, to Battle Creek, Michigan, where they resided for the next 20 years.

1827, November 26	Born at Gorham, Maine.
1836 (c.)	Broken nose and concussion at Portland, Maine.
1840, March	First heard William Miller present the Advent message.
1842, June 26	Baptized and accepted into Methodist Church.
1844, October 22	Disappointed when Christ did not come.
1844, December	First vision.
1845, Spring	Trip to eastern Maine to visit believers; met James White.
1846, August 30	Married James White.
1846, Autumn	Accepted seventh-day Sabbath.
1847-1848	Set up housekeeping at Topsham, Maine.
1847, August 26	Birth of first son, Henry Nichols.
1848, April 20-24	Attended first conference of Sabbathkeeping Adventists at Rocky Hill, Connecticut.
1848, November 18	Vision to begin publishing work—"Streams of Light."
1849, July	First of eleven numbers of *The Present Truth,* published as a result of the vision of November, 1848.
1849, July 28	Birth of James Edson, second son.
1849-1852	Moved from place to place with her publisher-husband.
1851, July	First book published, A *Sketch of Experience and Views.*
1852-1855	In Rochester, New York, where husband published *Review and Herald* and *Youth's Instructor.*
1854, August 29	Third son, William Clarence, born.
1855, November	Moved with the publishing plant to Battle Creek, Michigan.
1855, December	"Testimony for the Church," number 1, a 16-page pam-

phlet, published.

1856, Spring	Moved into their own cottage on Wood Street.
1858, March 14	"Great Controversy" vision at Lovett's Grove, Ohio.
1860, September 20	Fourth son, John Herbert, born.
1860, December 14	Death of John Herbert at three months.

Years of Church Development, 1860-1868

The 1860s saw Ellen White and her husband in the forefront of the struggle to organize the Seventh-day Adventist Church into a stable institution. The decade was also crucial in that it encompassed the beginnings of Adventist health emphasis. Responding to Mrs. White's appeal, the church as a body began to see the importance of healthful living in the Christian life. In response to her "Christmas Vision" of 1865, our first health institution, the Western Health Reform Institute, was opened in 1866. The institute later grew into the Battle Creek Sanitarium.

1860, September 29	Name Seventh-day Adventist chosen.
1861, October 8	Michigan Conference organized.
1863, May	Organization of General Conference of Seventh-day Adventists.
1863, June 6	Health reform vision at Otsego, Michigan.
1863, December 8	Death of eldest son, Henry Nichols, at Topsham, Maine.
1864, Summer	Publication of *Spiritual Gifts,* volume 4, with 30-page article on health.
1864, August- September	Visit to James C. Jackson's medical institution, Our Home on the Hillside, Dansville, New York, en route to Boston, Massachusetts.
1865	Publication of six pamphlets, *Health: or How to Live.*
1865, August 16	James White stricken with paralysis.
1865, December 25	Vision calling for a medical institution.
1865, December	Mrs. White takes James White to northern Michigan as an aid to his recovery.
1866, September 5	Opening of Western Health Reform Institute, forerunner of Battle Creek Sanitarium.
1867	Purchased a farm at Greenville, Michigan, and built a home and engaged in farming and writing.

The Camp Meeting Years, 1868-1881

Residing at Greenville and Battle Creek, Michigan, respectively, until late 1872, and then dividing her time between Michigan and California, Ellen White spent her winters writing and publishing. During the summer she attended camp meetings, some years as many as 28! *Testimonies,* numbers 14-30, now found in *Testimonies,* volumes 2-4, were published during these years.

1868, September 1-7	Attended first SDA camp meeting, held in Brother Root's maple grove at Wright, Michigan.
1870, July 28	Second son, James Edson, married on his twenty-first birthday.
1870	*The Spirit of Prophecy,* volume 1, published; forerunner of *Patriarchs and Prophets.*
1872, July-September	In Rocky Mountains resting and writing en route to California.
1873-1874	Divided time between Battle Creek and California, attended camp meetings, and spent some months in 1873 in Colorado resting and writing.
1874, April 1	Comprehensive vision of the advance of the cause in California, Oregon, and overseas.
1874, June	With James White in Oakland, California, as he founded the Pacific Press Publishing Association and the *Signs of the Times.*
1875, January 3	At Battle Creek for dedication of Battle Creek College. Vision of publishing houses in other countries.
1876, February 11	William Clarence, third son and manager of the Pacific Press, married at the age of 21.
1876, August	Spoke to 20,000 at Groveland, Massachusetts, camp meeting.
1877	*The Spirit of Prophecy*, volume 2, published; forerunner of *The Desire of Ages.*
1877, July 1	Spoke to 5,000 at Battle Creek on temperance.
1878	*The Spirit of Prophecy,* volume 3, published; forerunner of last part of *The Desire of Ages,* and *The Acts of the Apostles.*
1878, November	Spent the winter in Texas.
1879, April	Left Texas to engage in the summer camp meeting work.
1881, August 1	With husband in Battle Creek when he was taken ill.
1881, August 6	Death of James White.
1881, August 13	Spoke for ten minutes at James White's funeral at Battle Creek.

The 1880s, 1881-1891

Following James White's death in August 1881, Ellen White resided in California, at times in Healdsburg and at times in Oakland. She labored there, writing and speaking, until she left for Europe in August 1885, in response to the call of the General Conference. During the two years in Europe she resided in Basel, Switzerland, except for three extended visits to the Scandinavian countries, England, and Italy. Returning to the United States in August 1887, she soon made her way west to her Healdsburg home. She attended the 1888 General Conference session at Minneapolis in October and November; following the conference, while residing in Battle Creek, she worked among the churches in the Midwest and the East. After a year in the East she returned to California, but was called back to attend the General Conference session at Battle Creek in October 1889. She remained in the vicinity of Battle Creek until she left for Australia in September 1891.

1881, November	Attended the California camp meeting at Sacramento and participated in planning for a college in the West, which opened in 1882 at Healdsburg.
1882	*Early Writings* published, incorporating three of her early books.
1884	Last recorded public vision, at Portland, Oregon, camp meeting.
1884	*The Spirit of Prophecy,* volume 4, published; forerunner of *The Great Controversy.*
1885, Summer	Left California for trip to Europe.
1887, Summer	*The Great Controversy* published.
1888, October–November	Attended Minneapolis General Conference.
1889	*Testimonies,* volume 5, published, embodying *Testimonies,* numbers 31-33—746 pages.
1890	*Patriarchs and Prophets* published.
1891, September 12	Sailed to Australia via Honolulu.

The Australian Years, 1891-1900

Responding to the call of the General Conference to visit Australia to aid in establishing an educational work, Ellen White arrived in Sydney, December 8, 1891. She accepted the invitation somewhat reluctantly, for she had wanted to get on with her writing of a larger book on the life of Christ. Soon after her arrival she was stricken with inflammatory rheumatism, which confined her to her bed for some eight months. Although suffering intensely, she persisted in writing. In early 1893 she went to New Zealand, where she worked until the end of the year. Returning to Australia in late December, she attended the first Australian camp meeting. At this camp meeting, plans for a rural school were developed that resulted in the establishment of what became Avondale College at Cooranbong, 90 miles north of Sydney. Ellen White purchased land nearby and built her Sunnyside home late in 1895. Here she resided, giving her attention to her writing and traveling among the churches until she returned to the United States in August 1900.

1892, June	Spoke at opening of Australian Bible School in two rented buildings in Melbourne.
1892	Steps to Christ and Gospel Workers published.
1894, January	Joined in planning for a permanent school in Australia.
1894, May 23	Visited the Cooranbong site.
1895, December	Moved to her Sunnyside home at Cooranbong, where much of The Desire of Ages was written.
1896	Thoughts From the Mount of Blessing published.
1898	The Desire of Ages published.
1899–1900	Encouraged the establishment of Sydney Sanitarium.
1900	Christ's Object Lessons published.
1900, August	Left Australia and returned to United States.

The Elmshaven Years, 1900-1915

When Ellen White settled at Elmshaven, her new home near St. Helena in northern California, she hoped to give most of her time to writing her books. She was 72 and still had a number of volumes that she wished to complete. She little realized how much traveling, counseling, and speaking she would also be called upon to do. The crisis created by the controversies in Battle Creek would also make heavy demands on her time and strength. Even so, by writing early in the morning, she was able to produce nine books during her Elmshaven years.

1900, October	Settled at Elmshaven.
1901, April	Attended the General Conference session at Battle Creek.
1902, February 18	Battle Creek Sanitarium fire.
1902, December 30	Review and Herald fire.
1903, October	Met the pantheism crisis.
1904, April–September	Journeyed east to assist in the beginning of the work in Washington, D.C., to visit her son Edson in Nashville, and to attend important meetings.
1904, November–December	Involved in securing and establishing Paradise Valley Sanitarium.
1905, May	Attended General Conference session in Washington, D.C.
1905	The Ministry of Healing published.
1905, June–December	Involved in securing and starting Loma Linda Sanitarium.
1906-1908	Busy at Elmshaven with literary work.
1909, April–	At the age of 81 traveled to Washington, D. C., to

September	attend the General Conference session. This was her last trip east.
1910, January	Took a prominent part in the establishment of the College of Medical Evangelists at Loma Linda.
1910	Gave attention to finishing *The Acts of the Apostles* and the reissuance of *The Great Controversy*, a work extending into 1911.
1911-1915	With advancing age, made only a few trips to southern California. At Elmshaven engaged in her book work, finishing *Prophets and Kings* and *Counsels to Parents and Teachers*.
1915, February 13	Fell in her Elmshaven home and broke her hip.
1915, July 16	Closed her fruitful life at the age of 87. Her last words were "I know in whom I have believed." *Testimonies*, volumes 6-9, were also published in the Elmshaven years.

★ Now, known as the *Adventist Review,* it is one of the oldest continuously published religious journals in the United States.

The Old Year and the New

Examine yourselves as to whether you are in the faith. Test yourselves.
2 Cor. 13:5.

Already has the new year been ushered in; yet before we greet its coming, we pause to ask, What has been the history of the year that with its burden of records has now passed into eternity? . . . God forbid that at this important hour we should be so engrossed with other matters as to give no time to serious, candid, critical self-examination! Let things of minor consequence be put in the background, and let us now bring to the front the things which concern our eternal interests. . . .

No one of us can in our own strength represent the character of Christ, but if Jesus lives in the heart, the spirit dwelling in Him will be revealed in us. All our lack will be supplied. Who will seek at the beginning of this new year to obtain a new and genuine experience in the things of God? Make your wrongs right as far as possible. Confess your errors and sins to one another. Let all bitterness and wrath and malice be put away. Let patience, long-suffering, kindness, and love become a part of your very being; then whatsoever things are pure and lovely and of good report will mature in your experience. . . .

It behooves us individually to cultivate the grace of Christ, to be meek and lowly of heart, to be firm, unwavering, steadfast in the truth; for thus only can we advance in holiness and be made fit for the inheritance of the saints in light. Let us begin the year with an entire renunciation of self. Let us pray for clear discernment, . . . that we may always and everywhere be witnesses for Christ.

Our time and talents belong to God, to be used for His honor and glory. It should be our earnest, anxious effort to let the light shine through our life and character to illumine the pathway heavenward, that souls may be attracted from the broad road to the narrow way of holiness. . . .

Strong men and women are needed in the church, successful workers in the Lord's vineyard, men and women who will labor that the church may be transformed to the image of Christ rather than conformed to the customs and practices of the world. We have everything to gain or to lose. Let us see that we are on the side of Christ—the gaining side; that we are making sure work for Heaven.—*Signs of the Times,* Jan. 4, 1883.

Watch and Pray

But the end of all things is at hand; therefore be serious and
watchful in your prayers. 1 Peter 4:7.

Our Redeemer perfectly understood the wants of humanity. He who condescended to take upon Himself human nature was acquainted with our weakness. Christ lived as our example. He was tempted in all points as we are, that He might know how to succor all who should be tempted. . . .

Christ took upon Himself our infirmities, and in the weakness of humanity He needed to seek strength from His Father. He was often to be found in earnest prayer, in the grove, by the lakeside, and in the mountains. He has enjoined upon us to watch and pray. It is the neglect of watchfulness and close searching of heart that leads to self-sufficiency and spiritual pride. Without a deep sense of our need of help from God, there will be but little earnest, heartfelt prayer for divine aid. . . .

Unceasing watchfulness is a great help to prayer. . . . The one whose mind loves to dwell upon God has a strong defense. Such a one will be quick to perceive the dangers that threaten the spiritual life, and a sense of danger will lead that person to call upon God for help and protection.

There are times when the Christian life seems beset by dangers, and duty seems hard to perform. But the clouds that gather about our way, and the perils that surround us, will never disappear before a halting, doubting, prayerless spirit. At such times unbelief says, We can never surmount these obstructions; let us wait until we can see our way clearly." But faith courageously urges an advance, hoping all things, believing all things. . . .

The prayer may well be offered daily by those who have the fear of God before them, that He will preserve their hearts from evil desires, and strengthen their souls to resist temptation. . . .

The Word of God exhorts us to be found "praying always with all prayer and supplication in the Spirit, and watching thereunto with all perseverance"; and again, "Be ye therefore sober, and watch unto prayer." Here is the Christians' safeguard, their protection amid the perils that surround their pathway.—*Review and Herald,* Oct. 11, 1881.

Understanding for All

The entrance of Your words gives light; it gives understanding to the simple.
Ps. 119:130.

The Word of God presents the most potent means of education, as well as the most valuable source of knowledge, within the reach of humanity. The understanding adapts itself to the dimensions of the subjects with which it is required to deal. If occupied with trivial, commonplace matters only, never summoned to earnest effort to comprehend great and eternal truths, it becomes dwarfed and enfeebled. Hence the value of the Scriptures as a means of intellectual culture. Their perusal in a reverent and teachable spirit will expand and strengthen the mind as no other study can. They lead directly to the contemplation of the most exalted, the most ennobling, and the most stupendous truths that are presented to the human mind. They direct our thoughts to the infinite Author of all things.

We see revealed the character of the Eternal and listen to His voice as He communes with patriarchs and prophets. We see explained the mysteries of His providence, the great problems which have engaged the attention of every thoughtful mind, but which, without the aid of revelation, human intellect seeks in vain to solve. They open to our understanding a simple yet sublime system of theology, presenting truths which a child may grasp but which are yet so far reaching as to baffle the powers of the strongest mind. . . .

Our Savior did not ignore learning or despise education, yet He chose unlearned fishermen for the work of the gospel because they had not been schooled in the false customs and traditions of the world. They were men of good natural ability and of a humble, teachable spirit; men whom He could educate for His great work. . . .

The learned lawyers, priests, and scribes scorned to be taught by Christ. They desired to teach Him, and frequently made the attempt, only to be defeated by the wisdom that laid bare their ignorance and rebuked their folly. In their pride and bigotry, they would not accept the words of Christ, yet they were surprised at the wisdom with which He spake. . . . But the words and deeds of the humble Teacher, recorded by the unlettered companions of His daily life, have exerted a living power upon the minds of men and women from that day to the present.—*Review and Herald,* Sept. 25, 1883.

Fervent Prayer

The effective, fervent prayer of a righteous man avails much. James 5:16.

Jesus is our Savior today. He is pleading for us in the most holy place of the heavenly sanctuary, and He will forgive our sins. It makes all the difference in the world with us spiritually whether we rely upon God without doubt, as upon a sure foundation, or whether we are seeking to find some righteousness in ourselves before we come to Him. . . .

The Lord loves us, and bears with us, even when we are ungrateful to Him, forgetful of His mercies, wickedly unbelieving. . . . Let us make a complete change. Let us cultivate the precious plant of love, and delight to help one another. . . .

There are rich promises for us in the Word of God. The plan of salvation is ample. It is no narrow, limited provision that has been made for us. We are not obliged to trust the evidence that we had a year or a month ago, but we may have the assurance today that Jesus lives and is making intercession for us. . . .

If we would refresh others, we must ourselves drink of the Fountain that never becomes dry. It is our privilege to become acquainted with the Source of our strength, to have hold of the arm of God. If we would have spiritual life and energy, we must commune with God. We can speak to Him of our real wants; and our earnest petitions will show that we realize our needs and will do what we can to answer our own prayers. We must obey the injunction of Paul, "Arise from the dead, and Christ shall give you light."

[Martin] Luther was a man of prayer. He worked and prayed as though something must be done. . . . His prayers were followed up by venturing something on the promises of God; and through divine aid, he was enabled to shake the vast power of Rome, so that in every country the foundations of the church trembled.

The Spirit of God cooperates with the humble worker that abides in Christ and communes with Him. Pray. . . . When you are desponding, close the lips firmly to others; keep all the darkness within, lest you shadow the path of another, but tell it to Jesus. Ask for humility, wisdom, courage, increase of faith, that you may see light in His light and rejoice in His love. Only believe, and you shall surely see the salvation of God.—*Review and Herald,* Apr. 22, 1884.

The Importance of Prayer

Daniel purposed in his heart that he would not defile himself with the portion of the king's delicacies, nor with the wine which he drank. Dan. 1:8.

Prayer is not understood as it should be. Our prayers are not to inform God of something He does not know. The Lord is acquainted with the secrets of every soul. Our prayers need not be long and loud. God reads the hidden thought. We may pray in secret, and He who sees in secret will hear and will reward us openly. . . .

Prayer is not intended to work any change in God; it brings us into harmony with God. It does not take the place of duty. . . . Prayer will not pay our debts to God. The servants of Christ are to rely upon God as did Daniel in the courts of Babylon. Daniel knew the value of prayer, its aim, and its object; and the prayers which he and his three companions offered to God after being chosen by the king for the courts of Babylon, were answered.

There was another class of captives carried into Babylon. These the Lord permitted to be torn from their homes and carried into a land of idolaters because they were themselves continually going into idolatry. The Lord let them have all they desired of the idolatrous practices of Babylon. . . .

As the wisdom of the world viewed the matter, Daniel and his three companions had every advantage secured to them in the courts of Babylon, but it was here that their first great test was to come. Their principles were to come into collision with the regulations and appointments of the king. . . .

Daniel and his three companions did not take the position that because their food and drink were of the king's appointment it was their duty to partake of it. They prayed over the matter and studied the Scriptures. Their education had been of such a character that they felt even in their captivity that God was their dependence. . . . The appearance of Daniel and his companions was like what every youth's should be. They were courteous, kind, respectful, possessing the grace of meekness and modesty. . . .

When we are surrounded by influences calculated to lead us away from God, our petitions for help and strength must be unwearied. Unless this is so, we shall never be successful in breaking down pride and overcoming the power of temptation to sinful indulgences which keep us from the Savior.—*Youth's Instructor,* Aug. 18, 1898.

Prayer Lessons From Elijah

Elijah was a man with a nature like ours, and he prayed earnestly that it would not rain; and it did not rain on the land for three years and six months. And he prayed again, and the heaven gave rain, and the earth produced its fruit. James 5:17, 18.

Important lessons are presented to us in the experience of Elijah. When upon Mount Carmel he offered the prayer for rain, his faith was tested, but he persevered in making known his request unto God. Six times he prayed earnestly, and yet there was no sign that his petition was granted, but with strong faith he urged his plea to the throne of grace. Had he given up in discouragement at the sixth time, his prayer would not have been answered. . . . We have a God whose ear is not closed to our petitions; and if we prove His word, He will honor our faith. He wants us to have all our interests interwoven with His interests, and then He can safely bless us; for we shall not then take glory to self when the blessing is ours, but shall render all the praise to God.

God does not always answer our prayers the first time we call upon Him; for should He do this, we might take it for granted that we had a right to all the blessings and favors He bestowed upon us. Instead of searching our hearts to see if any evil was entertained by us, any sin indulged, we would become careless, and fail to realize our dependence upon Him, and our need of His help.

Elijah humbled himself until he was in a condition where he would not take the glory to himself. This is the condition upon which the Lord hears prayer; for then we shall give the praise to Him. . . .

We are to believe the Word of God whether we have any manifestation of feeling or not. I used to ask God for a flight of feeling, but I do not do this now. . . . Like Elijah, again and again I press my petition to the throne of grace; and when the Lord sees that I realize my inefficiency and weakness, the blessing comes. . . .

I have committed the keeping of my soul unto God as unto a faithful Creator, and I know that He will keep that which I have committed to Him until that day. . . .

Let us praise Him with heart and soul and voice. If any have lost faith, let them seek God today. The Lord has promised that if we seek Him with the whole heart, He will be found of us.—*Review and Herald,* June 9, 1891.

January

7

The Model Prayer

Lord, teach us to pray. Luke 11:1.

The world's Redeemer frequently went away alone to pray. On one occasion His disciples were not so far away but that they could hear His words. They were deeply impressed by His prayer, for it was charged with vital power that reached their hearts. It was very unlike the prayers which they themselves had offered, and unlike any prayers which they had heard from human lips. After Jesus had joined them again, they said to Him: "Lord, teach us to pray, as John also taught his disciples." . . .

It means much to pray to our Heavenly Father. We come to lay our imperfect tribute of thanksgiving at His feet in acknowledgment of His love and mercy, of which we are wholly undeserving. We come to make known our wants, to confess our sins, and to present to Him His own promises. . . .

Jesus has given to us a prayer in which every expression is full of meaning, to be studied and brought into practical life. . . . It is a prayer that expresses the essential subjects that we need to present to our heavenly Father. . . .

In the Lord's Prayer, solidity, strength, and earnestness are united with meekness and reverence. It is an expression of the divine character of its Author. . . .

Long prayers in a congregation are tedious to those who listen, and do not prepare the hearts of the people for the sermon which is to follow. The prayer of Christ was in marked contrast to these long prayers with their many repetitions. The Pharisees thought that they would be heard for their much speaking, and they made long, tedious, drawn-out prayers. . . .

The model prayer of Christ is in marked contrast to the prayers of the heathen. In all false religions, ceremonies and forms have been substituted for genuine piety and for practical godliness. . . .

Christ reproved the scribes and the Pharisees because of their self-righteous prayers. . . . Prayers of this order, that are made to be heard of men, call down no blessing from God. . . . But humility is always recognized by Him who has said, "Ask, and it shall be given you; seek, and ye shall find; knock, and it shall be opened unto you."—*Review and Herald,* May 28, 1895.

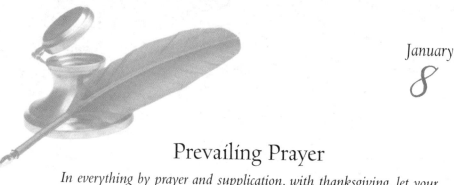

Prevailing Prayer

*In everything by prayer and supplication, with thanksgiving, let your
requests be made known to God. Phil. 4:6.*

God has made it our duty to pray. The riches of the universe belong to
Him. He has all temporal and spiritual treasures at His command and
can supply every want from His abundant fullness. We receive our breath
from Him; every temporal blessing that we enjoy is His gift. We are dependent upon Him not only for temporal blessings but for grace and strength to
keep us from falling under the power of temptation. We daily need the
Bread of Life to give us spiritual strength and vigor, just as much as we need
food to sustain our physical strength and give us firm muscles. We are com-
passed with weakness and infirmities, doubts and temptations; but we can
come to Jesus in our need, and He will not turn us away empty. We must
accustom ourselves to seek divine guidance through prayer; we must learn
to trust in Him from whom our help cometh. . . .

We must have a deep, earnest sense of our needs. We must feel our weakness and our dependence upon God, and come to Him with contrition of
soul and brokenness of heart. Our petitions must be offered in perfect submission; every desire must be brought into harmony with the will of God,
and His will must be done in us. . . .

If we walk in the light as Christ is in the light, we may come to the
throne of grace with holy boldness. We may present the promises of God
in living faith and urge our petitions. Although we are weak and erring and
unworthy, "the Spirit also helpeth our infirmities." . . . When we have offered our petition once, we must not then abandon it, but say, as did Jacob
when he wrestled all night with the angel, "I will not let thee go, except
thou bless me," and like him we shall prevail. . . .

It is only by watching unto prayer, and the exercise of living faith, that
Christians can preserve integrity in the midst of the temptations that Satan
brings to bear upon them. . . . Talk to your heart constantly the language of
faith: "Jesus said He would receive me, and I believe His word. I will praise
Him; I will glorify His name." Satan will be close by your side to suggest
that you do not feel any joy. Answer him, . . . "I have everything to be glad
of, for I am a child of God. I am trusting in Jesus."—*Signs of the Times,* May
15, 1884.

Rooted and Grounded in Christ

The righteous shall flourish like a palm tree. Ps. 92:12.
He shall be like a tree planted by the rivers of water, that brings forth its
fruit in its season, whose leaf also shall not wither; and whatever he does
shall prosper. Ps. 1:3.

These texts describe the happy state of the man or woman whose soul is rooted and grounded in Christ. But there is always danger of being satisfied with a superficial work; there is always danger that souls will not anchor themselves in God, but be content to drift hither and thither, the sport of Satan's temptations.

Are you beginning to see the defects in your character? Do not feel helpless and discouraged. Look to Jesus, who knows your every weakness and pities your every infirmity. . . . It is no disgrace to confess our sins and forsake them. The disgrace rests upon those who know their sins but continue in them and grieve the dear Savior by their crooked paths. A knowledge of our wrongs should be more highly prized than a happy flight of feeling, for it is evidence that the Spirit of God is striving with us and that angels are round about us. . . .

In true contrition for sin, come to the foot of the cross, and there leave your burdens. Come exercising repentance toward God because you have broken His law, and faith in our Lord Jesus Christ to pardon your transgressions and reconcile you to the Father. Believe what God says; take His promises to your heart. . . .

See the weary traveler toiling over the hot sands of the desert, with no shelter to protect him from the rays of a tropical sun. His water supply fails, and he has nothing to slake his burning thirst. His tongue becomes swollen; he staggers like a drunken man. Visions of home and friends pass before his mind as he believes himself ready to perish in the terrible desert. Suddenly those in advance send forth a shout of joy. In the distance, looming up out of the dreary, sandy waste, is a palm tree, green and flourishing. . . .

As the palm tree, drawing nourishment from fountains of living water, is green and flourishing in the midst of the desert, so the Christian may draw rich supplies of grace from the fountain of God's love and may guide weary souls, that are full of unrest and ready to perish in the desert of sin, to those waters of which they may drink, and live.—*Signs of the Times,* June 26, 1884.

Striking Examples of Prayer

If you abide in Me, and My words abide in you, you will ask what you desire, and it shall be done for you. John 15:7.

Prayer has been made the means of obtaining blessings that would not otherwise be received. The patriarchs were men of prayer, and God did great things for them. When Jacob left his father's house for a strange land, he prayed in humble contrition, and in the night season the Lord answered him through vision. He saw a ladder, bright and shining, its base resting on earth, and its topmost round reaching to the highest heaven. . . . Afterward, while on his return to his father's house, he wrestled with the Son of God all night, even till break of day, and prevailed. The assurance was given him, "Thy name shall be called no more Jacob, but Israel: for as a prince hast thou power with God and with men."

Joseph prayed, and he was preserved from sin amid influences that were calculated to lead him away from God. When tempted to leave the path of purity and uprightness, he said, "How then can I do this great wickedness, and sin against God?"

Moses, who was much in prayer, was known as the meekest man on the face of the earth. For his meekness and humility he was honored of God, and he discharged with fidelity the high, noble, and sacred responsibilities intrusted to him. While leading the children of Israel through the wilderness, again and again it seemed that they must be exterminated on account of their murmuring and rebellion. But Moses went to the true Source of power; he laid the case before the Lord. . . .

Daniel was a man of prayer, and God gave him wisdom and firmness to resist every influence that conspired to draw him into the snare of intemperance. Even in his youth he was a moral giant in the strength of the Mighty One. . . .

In the prison at Philippi, while suffering from the cruel stripes they had received, their feet fast in the stocks, Paul and Silas prayed and sang praise to God, and angels were sent from heaven to deliver them. The earth shook under the tread of these heavenly messengers, and the prison doors flew open, setting the prisoners free. . . . We should be continually loosening our hold upon earth, and fastening it upon heaven.—*Signs of the Times,* Aug. 14, 1884.

Prayers of Form and Prayers of Faith

When you pray, do not use vain repetitions as the heathen do. For they think that they will be heard for their many words. Matt. 6:7.

There are two kinds of prayer—the prayer of form and the prayer of faith. The repetition of set, customary phrases when the heart feels no need of God, is formal prayer. . . . We should be extremely careful in all our prayers to speak the wants of the heart and to say only what we mean. All the flowery words at our command are not equivalent to one holy desire. The most eloquent prayers are but vain repetitions if they do not express the true sentiments of the heart. But the prayer that comes from an earnest heart, when the simple wants of the soul are expressed just as we would ask an earthly friend for a favor, expecting that it would be granted—this is the prayer of faith. The publican who went up to the temple to pray is a good example of a sincere, devoted worshipper. He felt that he was a sinner, and his great need led to an outburst of passionate desire, "God be merciful to me a sinner." . . .

To commune with God we must have something to say to Him concerning our actual life. The long, black catalogue of our delinquencies is before the eye of the Infinite. The register is complete; none of our offenses are forgotten. But He who wrought wonderfully for His servants of old will listen to the prayer of faith and pardon our transgressions. He has promised, and He will fulfill His word. . . .

After we have offered our petitions, we are to answer them ourselves as far as possible, and not wait for God to do for us what we can do for ourselves. . . . Divine help is to be combined with human effort, aspiration, and energy. . . . We cannot be borne up by the prayers of others when we ourselves neglect to pray, for God has made no such provision for us. Not even divine power can lift one soul to heaven that is unwilling to put forth efforts in his own behalf. . . .

As thus step by step we ascend the shining ladder that leads to the city of God, oh how many times we shall be discouraged and come to weep at the feet of Jesus over our failures and our defeats. . . . Yet let us not cease our efforts. Heaven can be attained by every one of us if we will strive lawfully, doing the will of Jesus and growing into His image. Temporary failure should make us lean more heavily on Christ, and we should press on with brave heart, determined will, and unfaltering purpose.—*Signs of the Times,* Aug. 14, 1884.

Bible Religion Is Practical

*Pure and undefiled religion before God and the Father is this: to visit
orphans and widows in their trouble, and to keep oneself unspotted
from the world. James 1:27.*

Bible religion is not a garment which can be put on and taken off at
pleasure. It is an all-pervading influence which leads us to be patient,
self-denying followers of Christ, doing as He did, walking as He walked. . . .
This religion teaches us to exercise patience and long-suffering when
brought into places where we receive treatment that is hard and unjust. . . .

But if the word of God is made an abiding principle in our lives, everything with which we have to do, each word, each trivial act, will reveal that
we are subject to Jesus Christ, that even our thoughts have been brought
into captivity to Him. If the word of God is received into the heart, it will
empty the soul of self-sufficiency and self-dependence. Our lives will be a
power for good, because the Holy Spirit will fill our minds with the things
of God. The religion of Christ will be practiced by us, for our wills are in
perfect conformity to the will of God. . . .

"Search the scriptures." No other book will give you such pure, elevating, ennobling thoughts; from no other book can you obtain a deep religious experience. When you devote time to self-examination, to humble
prayer, to earnest study of God's Word, the Holy Spirit is near to apply the
truth to your heart. . . .

The Bible, and the Bible alone, is to be the rule of our faith. It is a leaf
from the tree of life, and by eating it, by receiving it into our minds, we shall
grow strong to do the will of God. . . .

If we do not receive the religion of Christ by feeding upon the Word of
God, we shall not be entitled to an entrance into the city of God. Having lived
on earthly food, having educated our tastes to love worldly things, . . . we could
not appreciate the pure, heavenly current that circulates in heaven. . . .

Jesus says, "Without me ye can do nothing." Living in Christ, adhering to
Christ, supported by Christ, drawing nourishment from Christ, we bear fruit
after the similitude of Christ. We live and move in Him; we are one with Him
and one with the Father. The name of Christ is glorified in the believing
child of God. This is Bible religion.—*Review and Herald*, May 4, 1897.

Be Conformed to the Word

*In vain they worship Me, teaching as doctrines the commandments of men.
Matt. 15:9.*

Those who desire to know the truth have nothing to fear from the investigation of the Word of God. But upon the threshold of investigation of the Word of God, inquirers after truth should lay aside all prejudice and hold in abeyance all preconceived opinion, and open the ear to hear the voice of God from His messenger. Cherished opinions, long-practiced customs and habits, are to be brought to the test of the Scriptures; and if the Word of God opposes your views, then, for your soul's sake, do not wrest the Scriptures, as many do to their soul's destruction in order to make them seem to bear a testimony in favor of their errors. Let your inquiry be, What is truth? Not, What have I hitherto believed to be truth? Do not interpret the Scriptures in the light of your former belief, and assert that some doctrine of finite humanity is truth. Let your inquiry be, What saith the Scriptures? . . .

Make up your mind that your former theories must change if they are not in harmony with the doctrines of the Bible. You are called upon to put forth diligent effort to discover what is truth. This should not be thought a hard requirement; for we are called upon to toil for our temporal and earthly blessings, and it is not to be expected that we shall find the heavenly treasure unless we are willing to dig in the mines of truth and exercise all our powers of mind and heart to understand. . . .

Beware lest you read the Word of God in the light of erroneous teaching. It was on this very ground that the Jews made their fatal mistake. They declared that there must be no different interpretation placed upon the Scriptures than that which had been given by the rabbis in former years; and as they had multiplied their traditions and maxims and had clothed them with sacredness, the Word of God was made of no effect through their traditions; and if Jesus Christ, the Word of God, had not come into the world, humanity would have lost all knowledge of the true God. . . .

It is Satan's studied plan to pervert the Scriptures and to lead us to put a false construction on the Word of God. . . . All articles of faith, all doctrines and creeds, however sacred they have been regarded, are to be rejected if they contradict the plain statements of the Word of God.—*Review and Herald,* Mar. 25, 1902.

God Hears Prayers

The eyes of the Lord are on the righteous,
and His ears are open to their cry. Ps. 34:15.

When Jesus was upon earth, and walked a man among the children of humanity, He prayed, and oh, how earnest were His prayers! How often He spent the whole night upon the damp, cold ground, in agonizing supplication! And yet He was the beloved and sinless Son of God. If Jesus felt the necessity of communion with His Father and manifested so much earnestness in calling upon Him, how much more should we, whom He has called to be heirs of salvation, who are subject to the fiery temptations of the wily foe and dependent upon divine grace for strength to overcome, have our whole souls stirred to wrestle with God. . . .

Satan is ever ready to insinuate that prayer is a mere form and avails us nothing. He cannot bear to have his powerful rival appealed to. At the sound of fervent prayer, the hosts of darkness tremble. Fearing that their captives may escape, they form a wall around them, that Heaven's light may not reach their souls. But if in their distress and helplessness they look to Jesus, pleading the merits of His blood, their compassionate Redeemer listens to the earnest, persevering prayer of faith and sends to their deliverance a reinforcement of angels that excel in strength. And when these angels, all-powerful, clothed with the armory of heaven, come to the help of the fainting, pursued souls, the angels of darkness fall back, well knowing that their battle is lost, and that more souls are escaping from the power of their influence. . . .

If you expect salvation, you must pray. Take time. Be not hurried and careless in your prayers. Intercede with God to work in you a thorough reformation, that the fruits of the Spirit may dwell in you, and that, by your godly life, you may shine as a light in the world. . . .

Take time to pray. And as you pray, believe that God hears you; have faith mixed with your prayers. Let faith take hold of the blessing, and it is yours. . . .

Every petition that is offered to God in faith and with a true heart will be answered. Such prayer is never lost; but to claim that it will always be answered in the very way and for the particular thing that we desire is presumption. God is too wise to err and too good to withhold any good thing from them that walk uprightly.—*Signs of the Times,* Nov. 18, 1886.

Pray Without Ceasing

Praying always with all prayer and supplication in the Spirit. Eph. 6:18.

We are not always so situated that we can enter into our closets to seek God in prayer, but there is no time or place in which it is inappropriate to offer up a petition to God. There is nothing that can hinder us from lifting up our hearts in the spirit of earnest prayer. In the crowds of the street, in the midst of a business engagement, we may send up a petition to God and plead for divine guidance, as did Nehemiah when he made his request before the king Artaxerxes. A closet of communion may be found wherever we are. We should have the door of the heart open continually and our invitation going up that Jesus may come and abide as a heavenly guest in our souls.

Although there may be a tainted, corrupted atmosphere around us, we need not breathe its miasma but may live in the pure atmosphere of heaven. We may close every door to impure imaginings and unholy thoughts by lifting the soul into the presence of God through sincere prayer. Those whose hearts are open to receive the support and blessing of God will walk in a holier atmosphere than that of earth and will have constant communion with God. . . . The heart is to be continually going out in desire for the presence and grace of Jesus, that the soul may have divine enlightenment and heavenly wisdom.

We need to have more distinct views of Jesus, and a fuller comprehension of the value of eternal realities. The beauty of holiness is to fill the hearts of God's people, and that this may be accomplished, we should seek for divine disclosures of heavenly things. . . .

We may keep so near to God that in every unexpected trial our thoughts may turn to God as naturally as the flower turns to the sun. The sunflower keeps its face sunward. If it is turned from the light, it will twist itself on the stem until it lifts up its petals to the bright beams of the sun. So let everyone who has given the heart to God turn to the Sun of Righteousness and eagerly look up to receive the bright beams of the glory that shine in the face of Jesus. . . .

The Lord is under no obligation to grant us His favors, yet He has pledged His word that if we will comply with the conditions stated in the Scriptures, He will fulfill His part of the contract. Men and women often make promises but do not live up to them. Often we have found that in trusting others we have leaned upon broken reeds; but the Lord will never disappoint the soul that believes in Him.—*Signs of the Times,* Dec. 16, 1889.

The Power of Prayer

You will keep him in perfect peace, whose mind is stayed on You,
because he trusts in You. Isa. 26:3.

Prayer to the Great Physician for the healing of the soul brings the bless-ing of God. Prayer unites us one to another and to God. Prayer brings Jesus to our side and gives new strength and fresh grace to the fainting, per-plexed soul. By prayer the sick have been encouraged to believe that God will look with compassion upon them. A ray of light penetrates to the hopeless soul and becomes a savor of life unto life. Prayer has "subdued kingdoms, wrought righteousness, obtained promises, stopped the mouths of lions, quenched the violence of fire"—we shall know what this means when we hear the reports of the martyrs who died for their faith—"turned to flight the armies of the aliens."

We shall hear about these victories when the Captain of our salvation, the glorious King of heaven, opens the record before those of whom John writes, "These are they which came out of great tribulation, and have washed their robes, and made them white in the blood of the Lamb." . . .

Christ our Savior was tempted in all points like as we are, yet He was without sin. He took human nature, being made in fashion as a man, and His necessities were the necessities of mankind. . . .

Prayer went before and sanctified every act of His ministry. He com-muned with His Father till the close of His life; and when He hung upon the cross, there arose from His lips the bitter cry, "My God, my God, why hast thou forsaken me?" Then in a voice which has reached to the very ends of the earth, He exclaimed, "Father, into thy hands I commend my spirit." . . . The night seasons of prayer which the Savior spent in the moun-tain or in the desert were essential to prepare Him for the trials He must meet in the days to follow. . . .

All things are possible to those that believe. No one coming to the Lord in sincerity of heart will be disappointed. How wonderful it is that we can pray effectually, that unworthy, erring mortals possess the power of offering their requests to God! . . . We utter words that reach the throne of the Monarch of the universe.—*Review and Herald,* Oct. 30, 1900.

God Speaks to Us

*Did not our heart burn within us while He talked with us on the road,
and while He opened the Scriptures to us? Luke 24:32.*

After Christ's death two disciples, on their way to Emmaus from Jerusalem, were talking over the scenes of the crucifixion. Christ Himself drew near, unrecognized by the sorrowing travelers. Their faith had died with their Lord, and their eyes, blinded by unbelief, did not recognize their risen Savior. Jesus, walking by their side, longed to reveal Himself to them, but He accosted them merely as fellow travelers, saying "What manner of communications are these that ye have one to another, as ye walk, and are sad?" Astonished at the question, they asked if He were a stranger in Jerusalem and had not heard that a prophet, mighty in word and deed, had been crucified. "We trusted that it had been He which should have redeemed Israel," they said, sadly.

"O fools, and slow of heart to believe all that the prophets have spoken," Christ said; "ought not Christ to have suffered these things, and to enter into his glory? And beginning at Moses and all the prophets, he expounded unto them in all the scriptures the things concerning himself." . . .

The disciples had lost sight of the precious promises linked with the prophecies of Christ's death, but when these were brought to their remembrance, faith revived; and after Christ had revealed Himself to them, they exclaimed, "Did not our heart burn within us, while he talked with us by the way, and while he opened to us the scriptures?" . . .

If we would search the Scriptures, our hearts would burn within us as the truths revealed therein are opened to our understanding. Our hopes would brighten as we claim the precious promises strewn like pearls through the Sacred Writings. As we study the history of patriarchs and prophets, men who loved and feared God, walking with Him, our souls would glow with the spirit that animated them. . . .

The question is asked, What is the cause of the dearth of spiritual power in the churches? The answer is, We allow our minds to be drawn away from the Word. . . . The Word of the living God is not merely written, but spoken. It is God's voice speaking to us, just as surely as if we could hear it with our ears. If we realized this, with what awe we would open God's Word, and with what earnestness we would search its pages.—*Review and Herald,* Mar. 31, 1903.

Bible Study Strengthens Intellect

Behold, I long for Your precepts; revive me in Your righteousness.
Ps. 119:40.

Given by inspiration of God," "able to make thee wise unto salvation," rendering "the man of God . . . perfect, thoroughly furnished unto all good works"—the Book of books has the highest claims to our reverent attention. Superficial study of the Word of God cannot meet the claims it has upon us nor furnish us with the benefit that is promised. . . . To read daily a certain number of chapters, or to commit to memory a stipulated amount of Scripture, without careful thought as to the meaning of the text, will profit but little.

To study one passage until its significance is clear to the mind and its relation to the plan of salvation is evident is of more value than the perusal of many chapters with no definite purpose in view and no positive instruction gained. We cannot obtain wisdom from the Word of God without giving earnest and prayerful attention to its study. It is true that some portions of Scripture are, indeed, too plain to be misunderstood, but there are many portions whose meaning cannot be seen at a glance, for the truth does not lie upon the surface. . . .

No study is better to give energy to the mind, to strengthen the intellect, than the study of the Word of God. No other book is so potent in elevating the thoughts, in giving vigor to the faculties, as is the Bible, which contains the most ennobling truths. If God's Word were studied as it should be, we would see breadth of mind, stability of purpose, nobility of character, such as is rarely seen in these times. . . .

Of all the books that flood the world, however valuable, the Bible is the Book of books, most deserving of our study and admiration. It gives not only the history of this world but a description of the world to come. It contains instruction concerning the wonders of the universe; it reveals to our understanding the character of the Author of the heavens and the earth. . . .

The one who studies the Bible holds converse with patriarchs and prophets. Contact is made with truth clothed in elevated language, which exerts a fascinating power over the mind and lifts the thoughts from the things of earth to the glory of the future immortal life. What human wisdom can compare with the revelation of the grandeur of God?—*Signs of the Times,* Jan. 30, 1893.

Personal Study Is Essential

Make me understand the way of Your precepts; so shall I meditate on Your wonderful works. Ps. 119:27.

The Bible is not exalted to its place among the books of the world, although its study is of infinite importance to the souls of men and women. In searching its pages the imagination beholds scenes majestic and eternal. We behold Jesus, the Son of God, coming to our world, and engaging in the mysterious conflict that discomfited the powers of darkness. Oh, how wonderful, how almost incredible it is, that the infinite God would consent to the humiliation of His own Son that we might be elevated to a place with Him upon His throne! Let all students of the Scriptures contemplate this great fact, and they will not come from a study of the Bible without being purified, elevated, and ennobled. . . .

All over the field of revelation are scattered glad springs of heavenly truth, of peace and joy. These glad springs of truth are within the reach of every seeker. The words of inspiration, pondered in the heart, will be as living streams flowing from the river of the water of life. . . . Whenever we study the Bible with a prayerful heart, the Holy Spirit is near to open to us the meaning of the words we read. . . .

The opening of God's Word is always followed by a remarkable opening and strengthening of human faculties, for the entrance of God's words giveth light. . . .

If the pillars of our faith will not stand the test of investigation, it is time that we knew it, for it is foolish to become set in our ideas and think that no one should interfere with our opinions. Let everything be brought to the Bible, for it is the only rule of faith and doctrine.

We must study the truth for ourselves; no living person should be relied upon to think for us, no matter who that person may be or in what position he or she may be placed. We are not to look upon any human being as a perfect criterion for us. We are to counsel together, and be subject one to another, but at the same time we are to exercise the ability God has given us to learn what is truth.

Each one of us must look to God for divine enlightenment, that we may individually develop a character that will stand the test of the day of God.— *Signs of the Times*, Feb. 6, 1893.

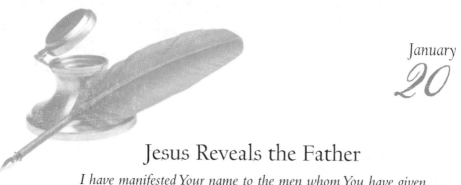

Jesus Reveals the Father

*I have manifested Your name to the men whom You have given
Me out of the world. John 17:6.*

If the poor and unlearned are not capable of understanding the Bible, then the mission of Christ to our world was useless, for He says, "The Spirit of the Lord is upon me, because he hath anointed me to preach the gospel to the poor; he hath sent me to heal the brokenhearted, to preach deliverance to the captives, and recovering of sight to the blind, to set at liberty them that are bruised." The command to search the Scriptures Christ addressed not only to the Pharisees and scribes but to the great multitude of the common people who crowded about them.

If the Bible is not to be understood by every class of people, whether they be rich or poor, what would be the need of the Savior's charge to search the Scriptures? What profit would there be in searching that which could never be understood? . . .

The duty of every intelligent person is to search the Scriptures. Each one should know for certainty the conditions upon which salvation is provided. . . . .

The Pharisees and the religious teachers so misrepresented the character of God that it was necessary for Christ to come to the world to represent the Father. Through the subtlety of Satan, men and women were led to charge upon God satanic attributes; but the Savior swept back the thick darkness which Satan had rolled before the throne of God in order that he might intercept the bright rays of mercy and love which came from God to us. . . .

Christ took upon Him humanity in order that the light and radiance of divine love should not extinguish the human race. When Moses pleaded, "I beseech thee, shew me thy glory," he was placed in the cleft of the rock, and the Lord passed by before him. When Philip asked Christ to show them the Father, He said, "He that hath seen me hath seen the Father." . . .

In plain language the Savior taught the world that the tenderness, the compassion, the love that He manifested toward humanity, were the very attributes of His Father in heaven. Whatever doctrine of grace He presented, whatever promise of joy, whatever deed of love, whatever divine attraction He exhibited, had its source in the Father of all. In the person of Christ we behold the eternal God engaged in an enterprise of boundless mercy toward the fallen race.—*Signs of the Times,* Aug. 20, 1894.

A Steward's Duty

He who gives, [let him do it] with liberality. Rom. 12:8.

Liberality is a duty on no account to be neglected; but let not rich or poor for a moment entertain the thought that their offerings to God can atone for their defects of Christian character. Says the great apostle, "Though I bestow all my goods to feed the poor, and though I give my body to be burned, and have not charity, it profiteth me nothing." . . .

It is to cultivate a spirit of benevolence in us that the Lord calls for our gifts and offerings. He is not dependent upon us for means to sustain His cause. He declares by the prophet, "Every beast of the forest is mine, and the cattle upon a thousand hills." . . .

God might have made angels the ambassadors of His truth. He might have made known His will, as He proclaimed the law from Sinai, with His own voice. But He has chosen to employ men and women to do this work. And it is only as we fulfill the divine purpose in our creation that life can be a blessing to us. All the riches intrusted to us will prove only a curse unless we employ them to relieve our own daily wants and the wants of the needy around us, and to glorify God by advancing His cause in the earth.

The Majesty of heaven yielded up His high command, His glory with the Father, and even His own life to save us. And now what will we do for Him? God forbid that His professed children should live for themselves! . . . The first and best of everything rightfully belongs to Him. . . . It is in this life that He requires all our talents to be put out to the exchangers. . . .

We should not look upon the tithe as the limit of our liberality. The Jews were required to bring to God numerous offerings besides the tithe; and shall not we, who enjoy the blessings of the gospel, do as much to sustain God's cause as was done in the former, less-favored dispensation? As the work for this time is extending in the earth, the calls for help are constantly increasing. . . .

Not till we wish the infinite Father to cease bestowing His gifts on us should we impatiently exclaim, Is there no end of giving? Not only should we faithfully render to God our tithes, which He claims as His own, but we should bring a tribute to His treasury as an offering of gratitude. Let us with joyful hearts bring to our Creator the firstfruits of all His bounties—our choicest possessions, our best and holiest service.—*Review and Herald,* Feb. 9, 1886.

Lay Up Treasure in Heaven

Lay up for yourselves treasures in heaven, where neither moth nor rust destroys and where thieves do not break in and steal. For where your treasure is, there your heart will be also. Matt. 6:20, 21.

What shall I eat? and what shall I drink? and wherewithal shall I be clothed? are the questions which are occupying the minds of men and women, while eternity is dropped out of their reckoning. There are some who do not look upon the Lord Jesus Christ as the only hope of the world.... Those for whom He died are absorbed in providing themselves with temporal things that are not required. At the same time they are neglecting the preparation of character which would fit them for an abode in the mansions which He has purchased for them at an infinite price....

When temporal matters absorb the mind and engage the attention, the whole strength of the being is engaged in the service of self, and we look upon the worship due to God as a trifling matter. Religious interests are made subservient to the world. But Jesus, who has paid the ransom for the souls of the human family, requires that they shall subordinate temporal interests to the heavenly interests. He would have them cease to indulge in hoarding up earthly treasures, in spending money upon luxuries, and in surrounding themselves with those things which they do not need....

By choosing to lay up treasure in heaven, our characters will be molded after the likeness of Christ. The world will see that our hopes and plans are made in reference to the advancement of the truth and the salvation of perishing souls....

In securing treasure in heaven, we place ourselves in living connection with God, who owns all the treasures of the earth and supplies all temporal mercies that are essential for life. Every soul may secure the eternal inheritance.... It is the highest wisdom to live in such a way as to secure eternal life. This may be done by not living in the world for ourselves but by living for God, by passing our property on to a world where it will never perish. By using our property to advance the cause of God, our uncertain riches are placed in an unfailing bank.... Every sacrifice made for the purpose of blessing others, every appropriation of means for the service of God, will be treasure laid up in heaven.— *Review and Herald,* Apr. 7, 1896.

A New Mind Will I Give You

I will give you a new heart. Eze. 36:26.

In the Bible the will of God is revealed. Through all time this book is to stand as a revelation of Jehovah. To human beings the divine oracles have been committed to be the power of God. The truths of the Word of God are not mere sentiment but the utterances of the Most High. Those who make these truths a part of their lives become in every sense new creatures. They are not given new mental powers, but the darkness that through ignorance and sin has clouded their understanding is removed.

The words, "A new heart also will I give you," mean, A new mind will I give you. This change of heart is always attended by a clear conception of Christian duty, an understanding of truth. The clearness of our views of truth will be proportionate to our understanding of the Word of God. Those who give the Scriptures close, prayerful attention will gain clear comprehension and sound judgment, as if in turning to God they had reached a higher grade of intelligence.

The Word of God, studied and obeyed as it should be, will give light and knowledge. Its perusal will strengthen the understanding. By contact with the purest, most lofty truths, the mind will be enlarged, the taste refined.

We are dependent on the Bible for a knowledge of the early history of our world, of the creation of human life, and of the fall. Remove the Word of God, and what can we expect but to be left to fables and conjectures and to that enfeebling of the intellect which is the sure result of entertaining error.

We need the authentic history of the origin of the earth, of the fall of Lucifer, and of the introduction of sin into the world. Without the Bible, we should be bewildered by false theories.

The mind would be subjected to the tyranny of superstition and falsehood. . . . Wherever Christians are, they may hold communion with God. And they may enjoy the intelligence of sanctified science. . . .

Cleave to the word, "It is written." Cast out of the mind the dangerous, obtrusive theories which, if entertained, will hold the mind in bondage so that we shall not become new creatures in Christ.—*Review and Herald,* Nov. 10, 1904.

A Time for Prevailing Prayer

It is time for You to act, O Lord, for they have regarded Your law as void.
Ps. 119:126.

The Lord is soon to come. Wickedness and rebellion, violence and crime, are filling the world. The cries of the suffering and the oppressed rise to God for justice. In the place of being softened by the patience and forbearance of God, the wicked are growing stronger in stubborn rebellion. The time in which we live is one of marked depravity. Religious restraint is thrown off, and people reject the law of God as unworthy of their attention. A more than common contempt is placed upon this holy law.

A moment of respite has been graciously given us of God. Every power lent us of heaven is to be used in doing the work assigned us by the Lord for those who are perishing in ignorance. The warning message is to be sounded in all parts of the world. There must be no delay. The truth must be proclaimed in the dark places of the earth. Obstacles must be met and surmounted. A great work is to be done, and this work is entrusted to those who know the truth for this time.

Now is the time for us to lay hold of the arm of our strength. The prayer of David should be the prayer of pastors and laymen: "It is time for thee, Lord, to work: for they have made void thy law." Let the servants of God weep between the porch and the altar, crying, "Spare thy people, O Lord, and give not Thine heritage to reproach." God has always wrought in behalf of His truth. The designs of the wicked, the enemies of the church, are subject to His power and His overruling providence. He can move upon the hearts of statesmen; the wrath of the haters of His truth and His people can be turned aside, even as the waters of a river could be turned, if thus He ordered it.

Prayer moves the arm of Omnipotence. He who marshals the stars in order in the heavens, whose word controls the waves of the great deep—the same infinite Creator will work in behalf of His people if they will call upon Him in faith. He will restrain all the forces of darkness until the warning is given to the world, and all who will heed it are prepared for His coming.—*Review and Herald,* Dec. 14, 1905.

God's Word Our Light

Your word is a lamp to my feet and a light to my path. Ps. 119:105.

I have a decided message from the Lord for the people who claim to believe the truth for this time. . . .

The Bible is the voice of God to His people. As we study the living oracles, we are to remember that God is speaking to His people out of His Word. We are to make this Word the man of our counsel. . . . If we realized the importance of searching the Scriptures, how much more diligently we would study them! . . . The Scriptures would be read and studied as the sure evidence of God's will concerning us.

The Bible is to be studied with special interest, for it contains the most valuable information that finite beings can have, pointing out the way in which we are to prepare for the coming of the Son of man in the clouds of heaven, putting away sin, and putting on the white robes of character that will give us entrance into the mansions that Christ told His disciples He was going to prepare for them. . . .

If we do not receive the Word of God as food for the soul, we shall miss the greatest treasure that has been prepared for men and women, for the Word is a message to each and every soul. . . . If obeyed, it gives spiritual life and strength. The pure, spiritual current that enters the life in a living experience is eternal life to the receiver.

God's Word is our light. It is Christ's message to His heritage, who have been bought with the price of His blood. It was written for our guidance, and if we make this Word our counselor, we shall never walk in strange paths. . . .

The spiritual life is built up from the food given to the mind, and if we eat the food provided in the Word of God, spiritual and mental health will be the result. . . .

We are each deciding our eternal destiny, and it rests wholly with us whether we shall gain eternal life. Shall we live the lessons given in the Word of God, Christ's great lesson book? It is the grandest and yet most simply arranged and easily understood study book ever provided for human beings. It is the only book that will prepare men and women for the life that measures with the life of God.—*Review and Herald,* Mar. 22, 1906.

The Word in Human Form

He taught them as one having authority, and not as the scribes. Matt. 7:29.

Clad in the vestments of humanity, the Son of God came down to the level of those He wished to save. In Him was no guile or sinfulness; He was ever pure and undefiled; yet He took upon Him our sinful nature. Clothing His divinity with humanity that He might associate with fallen humanity, He sought to redeem for humanity that which by disobedience Adam had lost, for himself and for the world. In His own character Jesus manifested to the world the character of God; He pleased not Himself, but went about doing good. His whole history for more than thirty years was of pure, disinterested benevolence.

Can we wonder that those who heard Him were astonished at His teaching? "He taught them as one having authority, and not as the scribes." The teaching of the scribes and the Pharisees was a continuous repetition of fables and childish traditions. Their opinions and ceremonies rested on the authority of ancient maxims and rabbinical sayings, which were frivolous and worthless. Christ did not dwell on weak, insipid sayings and human theories. As one possessing higher authority He addressed His hearers, presenting before them momentous subjects, and His appeals carried conviction to their hearts. The opinion of all, expressed by many who were not able to keep silent, was, "Never man spake like this man."

The Bible teaches the whole will of God concerning us.... The teaching of this Word is exactly that needed in all circumstances in which we may be placed. It is a sufficient rule of faith and practice, for it is the voice of God speaking to the soul, giving the members of His family directions for keeping the heart with all diligence. If this Word is studied, not merely read, but studied, it furnishes us with a storehouse of knowledge which enables us to improve every God-given endowment....

All who come to the Word of God for guidance, with humble, inquiring minds, determined to know the terms of salvation, will understand what saith the Scripture....

We need to humble our hearts and with sincerity and reverence search the Word of life; for that mind alone that is humble and contrite can see light.... The Lord speaks to the heart that humbles itself before Him.—*Review and Herald*, Aug. 22, 1907.

What the Word Is to Us

Be diligent to present yourself approved to God, a worker who does not need to be ashamed, rightly dividing the word of truth. 2 Tim. 2:15.

The Bible contains a simple and complete system of theology and philosophy. It is the book that makes us wise unto salvation. It tells us how to reach the abode of eternal happiness. It tells us of the love of God as shown in the plan of redemption, imparting the knowledge essential for all—the knowledge of Christ. He is the Sent of God; He is the Author of our salvation. But apart from the Word of God we could have no knowledge that such a person as the Lord Jesus Christ ever visited our world, nor any knowledge of His divinity, as indicated by His previous existence with the Father.

The Bible is not written for the scholar alone; on the contrary, it was designed for the common people. The great truths necessary for our salvation are made as clear as noonday, and none will mistake and lose their way except those who follow their own judgment instead of the plainly revealed will of God.

The Word of God strikes at every wrong trait of character, molding the whole person, internally and externally, abasing pride and self-exaltation, leading that person to bring the spirit of Christ into the smaller as well as the larger duties of life. It teaches all to be unswerving in their allegiance to justice and purity, and at the same time always to be kind and compassionate.

The appreciation of the Bible grows with its study. Whichever way the student may turn, the infinite wisdom and love of God is displayed. To all who are truly converted, the Word of God is the joy and consolation of the life. The Spirit of God speaks to them, and their heart becomes like a watered garden. . . .

No knowledge is so firm, so consistent, so far-reaching, as that obtained from a study of the Word of God. If there were not another book in the wide world, the Word of God, lived out through the grace of Christ, would make us perfect in this world, with a character fitted for the future, immortal life. Those who study the Word, taking it in faith as the truth and receiving it into the character, will be complete in Him who is all in all. Thank God for the possibilities set before humanity.—*Review and Herald,* June 11, 1908.

In My Name

If you ask anything in My name, I will do it. John 14:14.

The disciples were unacquainted with the Savior's unlimited resources and power. He said to them, "Hitherto have ye asked nothing in my name." John 16:24. He explained that the secret of their success would be in asking for strength and grace in His name. He would be present before the Father to make requests for them. The prayer of the humble suppliant He presents as His own desire in that soul's behalf. Every sincere prayer is heard in heaven. It may not be fluently expressed, but if the heart is in it, it will ascend to the sanctuary where Jesus ministers, and He will present it to the Father without one awkward, stammering word, beautiful and fragrant with the incense of His own perfection. . . .

"In my name" Christ bade His disciples to pray. In Christ's name His followers are to stand before God. Through the value of the sacrifice made for them, they are of value in the Lord's sight. . . .

The Lord is disappointed when His people place a low estimate upon themselves. He desires His chosen heritage to value themselves according to the price He has placed upon them. God wanted them, else He would not have sent His Son on such an expensive errand to redeem them. He has a use for them, and He is well pleased when they make the very highest demands upon Him, that they may glorify His name. They may expect large things if they have faith in His promises.

But to pray in Christ's name means much. It means that we are to accept His character, manifest His spirit, and work His works. The Savior's promise is given on condition. "If ye love me," He says, "keep my commandments." He saves us, not in sin, but from sin; and those who love Him will show their love by obedience.

All true obedience comes from the heart. It was heart-work with Christ. And if we consent, He will so identify Himself with our thoughts and aims, so blend our hearts and minds into conformity to His will, that when obeying Him we shall be but carrying out our own impulses. The will, refined and sanctified, will find its highest delight in doing His service.—*Review and Herald,* July 14, 1910.

God Will Not Turn Away From You

All that the Father gives Me will come to Me, and the one who comes to Me I will by no means cast out. John 6:37.

Jesus Himself, while He dwelt among us, was often in prayer. Prayer went before and sanctified every act of His ministry. . . .

He found comfort and joy in communion with His Father. And if our Savior, the Son of God, felt the need of prayer, how much more should feeble, sinful mortals feel the necessity of fervent, constant prayer. . . .

Do not entertain the thought that because you have made mistakes, because your life has been darkened by errors, your Heavenly Father does not love you and will not hear you when you pray. . . . His heart of love is touched by our sorrows, and even by our utterance of them. . . . Nothing is too great for Him to bear, for He holds up worlds, He rules over the affairs of the universe. Nothing that in any way concerns our peace is too small for Him to notice. There is no chapter in our experience too dark for Him to read; there is no perplexity too difficult for Him to unravel. None have fallen so low, none are so vile, that they cannot find deliverance in Christ. . . .

If we keep the Lord ever before us, allowing our hearts to go out in thanksgiving and praise to Him, we shall have a continual freshness in our religious life. Our prayers will take the form of conversation with God, as we would talk with a friend. He will speak His mysteries to us personally. Often there will come to us a sweet, joyful sense of the presence of Jesus. . . .

How wonderful it is that we can pray effectually, that unworthy, erring mortals possess the power of offering their requests to God. What higher power can we require than this—to be linked with the infinite God? Feeble, sinful people have the privilege of speaking to their Maker. They utter words that reach the throne of the Monarch of the universe. . . .

The rainbow about the throne is an assurance that God is true, that in Him is no variableness, neither shadow of turning. . . . When we come to Him confessing our unworthiness and sin, He has pledged Himself to give heed to our cry. The honor of His throne is staked for the fulfillment of His Word unto us.—*Signs of the Times,* June 18, 1902.

Cheerful Giving

*Let each one give as he purposes in his heart, not grudgingly or of necessity;
for God loves a cheerful giver. 2 Cor. 9:7.*

All our offerings should be presented with cheerfulness, for they come from the fund which the Lord has seen fit to place in our hands for the purpose of carrying forward His work in the world, in order that the banner of truth may be unfurled in the highways and byways of the earth. If all who profess the truth would give to the Lord His own in tithes and gifts and offerings, there would be meat in the house of the Lord. The cause of benevolence would no longer be dependent on the uncertain gifts of impulse, and vary according to people's changing feelings. God's claims would be welcomed, and His cause would be considered as justly entitled to a portion of the funds entrusted to our hands. The Lord is our divine Creditor, and He has made us promises through the prophet Malachi that are very plain, positive, and important. It means very much to us whether or not we are rendering to God His own. He allows His stewards a certain portion for their own use, and if they will trade upon that which He claims, He will divinely bless the means in their hands. . . .

The only plan which the gospel has marked out for sustaining the work of God is one that leaves the support of His cause to the honor of men and women. . . .

Those who are recipients of His grace, who contemplate the cross of Calvary, will not question concerning the proportion to be given, but will feel that the richest offering is all too meager, all disproportionate to the great gift of the only begotten Son of the infinite God. . . . Through self-denial, the poorest will find ways of obtaining something to give back to God. . . .

The rich are not to feel that they can be content in giving of their money merely. . . . Parents and children are not to regard themselves as their own, and feel that they can dispose of their time and property as shall please themselves. They are God's purchased possession, and the Lord calls for the profit of their physical powers, which are to be employed in bringing a revenue to the treasury of the Lord. . . .

Will every soul consider the fact that Christian discipleship includes self-denial, selfsacrifice, even to the laying down of life itself if need be, for the sake of Him who has given His life for the life of the world?—*Review and Herald,* July 14, 1896.

The Prophetic Messenger Prays

*So the Lord spoke to Moses face to face, as a man speaks to his friend.
Ex. 33:11.*

Prayer offered by Ellen White at the 1903 General Conference session.]
Our heavenly Father, we come to Thee this morning just as we are, needy
and wholly dependent upon Thee. Help us to have a clear knowledge of what
we must be, and of the characters that we must form, in order that we may be
prepared to unite with the heavenly family in the city of our God. . . .

O my Father, how can we proclaim Thy goodness, and Thy mercy, and
Thy love, unless we cherish them in our own hearts and reveal them in our
own experiences? Thou knowest how Thou hast presented this matter to
Thy servant. . . .

Here are Thy ministers, whose work it is to proclaim Bible truth. I ask
Thee that they may have a clear realization of the responsibilities that rest
upon them as guardians and as shepherds of Thy flock. . . . Let them understand their own weakness, and may the sanctification of the Spirit come to
them. . . .

Here are those who bear responsibilities in our institutions. . . . They have
not in their dealings given a right example to the world. They did not realize that others were taking knowledge of them, to see whether they were
sanctified by the truth.

Oh, pardon our transgressions and forgive our sins! Show us where we have
come short. Let Thy Holy Spirit descend upon us. The world is perishing in
sin, and we ask Thee to roll the burden upon us at this meeting. . . .

Thou hast opened these things before me, and Thou alone canst prepare
minds and hearts to hear the message that unless those who have left their
first love shall return to recognize the work that needs to be done in their
individual hearts, Thou wilt come quickly and remove the candlestick out
of his place. . . .

We must be reconverted, sanctified, and made fit to bear the message of
the Lord. . . .

My Father, break down the barriers, that confessions may be made, from
heart to heart, from brother to brother. May the Spirit of God come in; and
Thy blessed name shall have all the glory. Amen.—*General Conference
Bulletin,* Apr. 2, 1903.

Holiness in the Lord

This is a hard saying; who can understand it? John 6:60.

Some professed followers of Christ may be inclined to say, as did the disciples at a certain time as they listened to the earnest truths which fell from the lips of the divine Teacher, "This is an hard saying; who can hear it?" Many may think that the way is made too straight. When we talk of self-denial and sacrifice for Christ's sake, they think we dwell too much on these points. You would prefer to hear us speak of the Christian's reward. We know that those who are faithful will inherit all things, but the great question with us should be, "Who may abide the day of his coming? and who shall stand when he appeareth?" Who shall be counted worthy to receive the exceeding great and precious reward that shall be given to the overcomers? Those who shall be partakers of Christ's sufferings will be sharers with Him of His glory.

Without holiness, the Word of God tells us, no one can see the Lord. Without purity of life it is impossible for us to be fitted and prepared to dwell with the holy and sinless angels in a pure and holy heaven. No sin can be there. No impurity can enter the pearly gates of the golden city of God. And the question for us to settle is whether we will turn from all sin and comply with the conditions God has given us, that we may become His sons and daughters. Separation from the world He requires of us in order to become members of the royal family. . . .

We believe without a doubt that Christ is soon to come, and believing this we feel a necessity upon us to plead with men and women to prepare for the coming of the Son of man. . . . We want you to be of that company that shall bow before the throne of God crying, "Worthy, worthy, worthy, is the Lamb that was slain for us." . . .

When you are all ready, having overcome your sins, having put away all your iniquity from you, you are in a condition to receive the finishing touch of immortality. . . .

It will not be safe for you to wait for a better time to come. It is while it is called today. If anyone will hear His voice, harden not your hearts. It is to listen today to the invitation of mercy. It is to yield your pride, your folly, your vanity, and make an entire surrender of your heart to God. Come to Him with your talents and all the influence you have, and lay all these without reserve at the feet of Him who died on Calvary's cross to redeem you.—*Review and Herald,* Apr. 12, 1870.

What Do We Sacrifice for Heaven?

You shall love the Lord your God with all your heart, with all your soul, with all your mind, and with all your strength. . . .You shall love your neighbor as yourself. Mark 12:30, 31.

We see beauty and loveliness and glory in Jesus. We behold in Him matchless charms. He was the majesty of heaven. . . .Angels bowed in adoration before Him and readily obeyed His commands. Our Savior gave up all. He laid aside His glory, His majesty and splendor, and came down to this earth and died for a race of rebels who were transgressors against His Father's commandments. Christ condescended to humble Himself that He might save the fallen race. He drank the cup of suffering, and in its place offers us the cup of blessing; yes, that cup was drained for us; and although many know all this, yet they choose to go on in sin and folly; and still Jesus invites them. . . .The truths of God's Word must be brought to bear upon us, and we must lay hold upon them. If we do this, they will have a sanctifying influence upon our lives; they will fit us that we may have a preparation for the kingdom of glory, that when our probation shall close, we may see the King in His beauty and dwell in His presence forevermore.

And now the question is, Are we willing to make the sacrifice? . . . "Come out from among them, and be ye separate, saith the Lord, and touch not the unclean thing; and I will receive you, and will be a father unto you, and ye shall be my sons and daughters, saith the Lord Almighty." What a promise is this!

And do you think that by embracing the truth of God you are degrading yourself? . . .The truth elevates the receiver every time. . . . It brings purity of character and purity of life and gives a fitness that we may join the heavenly company in the kingdom of glory. Without this fitness we can never see the heavenly abode. . . .

Does the truth require you to stand alone in your position to serve God, because others around you are not willing to yield to the claims that Christ has upon them? Does it require a separation in feeling from them? Yes; and this is the cross which you must bear, which leads many to say, I cannot yield to the claims of the truth. But says Christ, If anyone love father, or mother, or brother, or sister, more than me, he is not worthy of me. . . . Is this too great a sacrifice to make for Him who sacrificed all for you?—*Review and Herald,* Apr. 19, 1870.

Grow in Grace

You therefore, my son, be strong in the grace that is in Christ Jesus. 2 Tim. 2:1.

The seeking of the kingdom of God and His righteousness is to be the object and aim of our lives. It is no child's play to fulfill this injunction, but whatever self-denial it calls for, it is still for our interest in this life and the life to come to obey this command. We are to have an eye single to the glory of God, and thus grow in grace and in the knowledge of our Lord and Savior Jesus Christ. The more earnestly and diligently we seek for divine wisdom, the more firmly established we shall be in the truth....

We are not always to remain children in our knowledge and experience in spiritual things. We are not always to express ourselves in the language of one who has just received Christ, but our prayers and exhortations are to grow in intelligence as we advance in experience in the truth. The language of a child of 6 in a child of 10 years of age would not be pleasing to us, and how painful would it be to hear expressions of childish intelligence in one who had arrived at years of maturity....

The youth who has had several years of experience in the Christian life ought not to have the hesitating language of one who is a babe in Christ. There is a want of growth in professed Christians. Those who are not growing up unto the full stature of men and women in Christ Jesus manifest this in the way they speak of the things of the kingdom of God....

The testimonies that are borne by many of the professed followers of Christ are those of persons who have become dwarfs in the Christian life. The language of true, deep, intelligent experience is wanting....

We are not to cultivate the language of the earthy, and be so familiar with human conversation that the language of Canaan will be new and unfamiliar to us....

Christians are to be faithful students in the school of Christ, ever learning more of heaven, more of the words and will of God, more of the truth, and how to use faithfully the knowledge that they have gained to instruct others and to lead them to seek first the kingdom of God and His righteousness. We are to have an intelligent knowledge of the Scriptures, for how can we know God's will and way without searching for the treasures of God's righteousness in His Holy Word? We should know the truth for ourselves and understand both the prophecies and the practical teachings of our Lord.—*Youth's Instructor,* June 28, 1894.

Counterfeit Sanctification

Because you say, "I am rich, have become wealthy, and have need of nothing"—and do not know that you are wretched, miserable, poor, blind, and naked. Rev. 3:17.

*D*ear Brother: We are pained to learn the condition of Brother B [A. W. Bartlett], and to know that Satan is pushing him on to cause disaffection in the Indiana Conference under the pious guise of Christian holiness. Both you and ourselves fully believe that holiness of life is necessary to fit us for the inheritance of saints in light. We contend that this state must be reached in a Bible way. Christ prayed that His disciples might be sanctified through the truth, and the apostles preached of purifying our hearts by obeying the truth.

The professed church of Christ is full of the spurious article, and one distinct feature of it is the more the members drink into the spirit of popular sanctification, the less they prize the present truth. Many of those who are the open opponents of God's Sabbath, the third angel's message, and the health reform are among the sanctified ones. Some of them have even reached the almost hopeless position that they cannot sin. These, of course, have no further use for the *Lord's Prayer,* which teaches us to pray that our sins may be forgiven, and but very little use for the Bible, as they profess to be led by the Spirit. . . .

What a terrible deception! They think they are complete in Christ, and know not that they are wretched, blind, miserable, poor, and naked. . . .

We warn our brethren of the Indiana Conference and elsewhere. Our position has ever been that true sanctification, which will stand the test of the judgment, is that which comes through obedience of the truth and of God. . . .

God is leading out a people, but it has been Satan's effort all the way to induce certain ones to set up their judgment against that of the body, and thus lead them away from the body to certain ruin. Thus have self-deceived souls fallen all the way along during the history of the third angel's message. Those who are led by fanaticism will gradually feel in harmony with those who fully reject the truth, and unless they can be arrested in their course will, sooner or later, be in the ranks of our bitterest opponents. (Signed by both James and Ellen White.)—*Review and Herald,* June 6, 1878.

Winning Back the Erring

If your brother sins against you, go and tell him his fault between you and him alone. If he hears you, you have gained your brother. Matt. 18:15.

If you are grieved because your neighbors or friends are doing wrong to their own hurt, if they are overtaken in fault, follow the Bible rule. "Tell him his fault between thee and him alone." As you go to the one you suppose to be in error, see that you speak in a meek and lowly spirit, for the wrath of man worketh not the righteousness of God. The erring can in no other way be restored than in the spirit of meekness and gentleness and tender love. Be careful in your manner. Avoid anything in look or gesture, word or tone of voice, that savors of pride or self-sufficiency. Guard yourself against a word or look that would exalt self or present your goodness and righteousness in contrast with their failings. Beware of the most distant approach to disdain, overbearing, or contempt. With care avoid every appearance of anger, and though you use plainness of speech, yet let there be no reproach, no railing accusation, no token of warmth, but that of earnest love. Above all, let there be no shadow of hate or ill will, no bitterness nor sourness of expression. . . .

Bear in mind that the success of reproof depends greatly upon the spirit in which it is given. Do not neglect earnest prayer that you may possess a lowly mind and that angels of God may work upon the hearts you are trying to reach, before you, and so soften them by heavenly impressions, that your efforts may avail. . . .

You may have excused yourself for speaking evil of your brother or sister or neighbor to others before going to them, and taking the steps God has absolutely commanded. Perhaps you say, "I did not speak to anyone until I was so burdened that I could not refrain." What burdened you? Was it a plain neglect of your own duty, a thus saith the Lord? You were under the guilt of sin because you did not go tell him his fault between thee and him alone. . . .

Sometimes the mildest and tenderest reproof will have no good effect. In that case, the blessing you wanted another to receive by pursuing a course of righteousness, ceasing to do evil and learning to do well, will return into your own bosom. If the erring persist in sin, treat them kindly and leave them with your Heavenly Father.—*Review and Herald,* July 17, 1879.

The Secret of Spiritual Life

Unless one is born of water and the Spirit, he cannot enter the kingdom of God. John 3:5.

The question is often asked, Why is there not more power in the church? Why not more vital godliness? The reason is, the requirements of God's Word are not complied with in verity and in truth; God is not loved supremely, and our neighbor as ourselves. This covers the entire ground. Upon these two commandments hang all the law and the prophets. Let these two requirements of God be obeyed explicitly, and there would be no discord in the church, no inharmonious notes in the family. With many the work is too superficial. Outward forms take the place of the inner work of grace. . . . The theory of the truth has converted the head, but the soul temple has not been cleansed from its idols.

When the commandment came home to the mind and heart of Paul, he says, "Sin revived and I died." In these days of pretense there are many sham conversions. True conviction of sin, real heart sorrow because of wickedness, death to self, the daily overcoming of defects of character, and the new birth—these, represented as old things, Paul says had passed away, and all things had become new. Such a work many know nothing of. They grafted the truth into their natural hearts, and then went on as before, manifesting the same unhappy traits of character. . . .

Make the tree good, and good fruit will be the result. The work of the Spirit of God upon the heart is essential to godliness. It must be received into the hearts of those who accept the truth, and create in them clean hearts, before one of them can keep His commandments and be doers of the Word. . . .

The Bible is not studied as much as it should be; it is not made the rule of life. Were its precepts conscientiously followed and made the basis of character, there would be steadfastness of purpose that no business speculations or worldly pursuits could seriously influence. A character thus formed, and supported by the Word of God, will abide the day of trial, of difficulties and dangers. The conscience must be enlightened, and the life sanctified by the love of the truth received into the heart, before the influence will be saving upon the world.—*Review and Herald,* Aug. 28, 1879.

A Living Church

You turned to God from idols to serve the living and true God, and to wait for His Son from heaven. 1 Thess. 1:9, 10.

A living church will be a working church. Practical Christianity will develop earnest workers for the advancement of the cause of truth. . . . We long to see the true Christian character manifested in the church. We long to see its members free from a light, irreverent spirit; and we earnestly desire that they may realize their high calling in Christ Jesus. Some who profess Christ are exerting themselves to the utmost to so live and act that their religious faith may commend itself to people of moral worth, that they may be induced to accept the truth. But there are many who feel no responsibility even to keep their own souls in the love of God, and who, instead of blessing others by their influence, are a burden to those who would work and watch and pray. . . .

Those who are seeking in humbleness of mind to exalt the truth of Christ by their exemplary course are represented in the Word of God as fine gold, while the class whose chief thought and study is to exhibit themselves are as sounding brass and a tinkling cymbal. . . .

We entreat those who have a connection with God to pray earnestly and in faith, and not to stop here, but to work as well as pray, for the purification of the church. The present time calls for men and women who have a moral fixedness of purpose, men and women who will not be molded or subdued by any unsanctified influences. . . .

No man or woman can succeed in the service of God without putting the whole soul in the work and counting all things but loss for the excellency of the knowledge of Christ. Those who make any reserve, who refuse to give all that they have, cannot be disciples of Christ; much less can they be His colaborers. The consecration must be complete. . . .

Jesus has gone to prepare mansions for those who are waiting and watching for His appearing. There they will meet the pure angels and the redeemed host and will join their songs of praise and triumph. There the Savior's love surrounds His people, and the city of God is irradiated with the light of His countenance—a city whose walls, great and high, are garnished with all manner of precious stones, whose gates are pearls, and whose streets are pure gold, as it were transparent glass.—*Review and Herald,* June 3, 1880.

The Christian Race

Let us lay aside every weight, and the sin which so easily ensnares us, and let us run with endurance the race that is set before us. Heb. 12:1.

In this text one of the public games so famous in Paul's time is used to illustrate the Christian race. The competitors in the race submitted to a painful training process, practicing the most rigid self-denial that their physical powers might be in the most favorable condition, and then they taxed these powers to the utmost to win the honor of a perishable wreath. Some never recovered from the effects. In consequence of the terrible strain, men would sometimes fall by the racecourse, bleeding at the mouth and nose. Others breathed out their life, firmly grasping the poor bauble that had cost them so dear.

Paul compares the followers of Christ to the competitors in a race. "Now," says the apostle, "*they* do it to obtain a *corruptible* crown; but *we* an *incorruptible.*" Here Paul makes a sharp contrast, to put to shame the feeble efforts of professed Christians who plead for their selfish indulgences and refuse to place themselves, by self-denial and strictly temperate habits, in a position that they will make a success of overcoming. All who entered the list in the public games were animated and excited by the hope of a prize if they were successful. In like manner a prize is held out before Christians, the reward of faithfulness to the end of the race. If the prize is won, their future welfare is assured; an exceeding and eternal weight of glory is in reserve for the overcomers. . . .

In the races, the crown of honor was placed in sight of the competitors, that if any were tempted for a moment to relax their efforts, the eye would rest on the prize, and they would be inspired with new vigor. So the heavenly goal is presented to the view of the Christian, that it may have its just influence and inspire all with zeal and ardor. . . .

All ran in the race, but only one received the prize. . . . It is not so with the Christian race. None who are earnest and persevering will fail of success. The race is not to the swift nor the battle to the strong. The weakest saint as well as the strongest may obtain the crown of immortal glory, if they are thoroughly in earnest and will submit to privation and loss for Christ's sake.—*Review and Herald,* Oct. 18, 1881.

Faith Is the Victory

I press toward the goal for the prize of the upward call of God in Christ Jesus. Phil. 3:14.

The greatest blessing we can have is a correct knowledge of ourselves, that we may see our defects of character and by divine grace remedy them. . . .

Are we nearer to God today than we were a year ago? What a change there would be in our religious experience, what a transformation in our characters, if day by day we carried out the principle that we are not our own, but that our time and talents belong to God, and every faculty should be used to do His will and advance His glory. . . .

We may be shut in by the promises of God, which will be as a wall of fire about us. We want to know how to exercise faith. Faith "is the gift of God," but the power to exercise it is ours. If faith lies dormant, it is no advantage to us; but in exercise it holds all blessings in its grasp. It is the hand by which the soul takes hold of the strength of the Infinite. It is the medium by which human hearts, renewed by the grace of Christ, are made to beat in harmony with the great Heart of love. Faith plants itself on the promises of God and claims them as surety that He will do just as He said He would. Jesus comes to the sinful, helpless, needy soul and says, "What things soever ye desire, when ye pray, believe that ye receive them, and ye shall have them." Believe, claim the promises, and praise God that you do receive the things you have asked of Him, and when your need is greatest, you will experience His blessing and receive special help. . . .

The inquiry in many hearts is, How shall I find happiness? We are not to make it our object to live for happiness, but we shall surely find it in the path of humble obedience. Paul was happy. He affirms repeatedly that notwithstanding the sufferings, conflicts, and trials that he was called to bear, he enjoyed great consolation. He says, "I am filled with comfort, I am exceeding joyful in all our tribulation." All the energies of the chiefest of the apostles were bent to a preparation for the future, immortal life, and when the time of his departure was at hand, he could exclaim in holy triumph, "I have fought a good fight, I have finished my course, I have kept the faith: Henceforth there is laid up for me a crown of righteousness, which the Lord, the righteous judge, shall give me at that day."—*Signs of the Times,* May 22, 1884.

Giving, a Habit Born of Love

Let each one of you lay something aside, storing up as he may prosper. 1 Cor. 16:2.

Giving is a part of gospel religion. The foundation of the plan of salvation was laid in sacrifice. Jesus left the royal courts of heaven and became poor, that we through His poverty might be made rich. His life on earth was unselfish, marked with humiliation and sacrifice. And is the servant greater than his Lord? Shall we, partakers of the great salvation which He wrought out for us, refuse to follow our Lord, and to share in His self-denial? When the world's Redeemer has suffered so much for us, shall we, the members of His body, live in thoughtless self-indulgence? No; self-denial is an essential condition of discipleship. . . .

Christ, as our head, led out in the great work of salvation, but He has entrusted that work to His followers upon earth. It cannot be carried on without means, and He has given His people a plan for raising means sufficient to make His cause prosperous. The tithing system, instituted for this purpose, reaches back to the time of Moses. Even as far back as the days of Adam, long before the definite system was given, men were required to offer to God gifts for religious purposes. . . .

God does not compel us to give to His cause. Our action must be voluntary. He will not have His treasury replenished with unwilling offerings. His design in the plan of systematic giving was to bring us into close relationship with our Creator and in sympathy and love with our fellow human beings, thus placing upon us responsibilities that would counteract selfishness and strengthen disinterested, generous impulses. We are inclined to be selfish and to close our hearts to generous deeds. The Lord, by requiring gifts to be made at stated times, designed that giving should become a habit and be looked upon as a Christian duty. The heart, opened by one gift, was not to have time to close and become selfishly cold, before another offering was bestowed. . . .

Every man, woman, and child may become a treasurer for the Lord. . . .

It is for our own good that He has planned to have us bear some part in the advancement of His cause. He has honored us by making us coworkers with Himself. He has ordained that there should be a necessity for the cooperation of His people, that they may cultivate and keep in exercise their benevolent affections.—*Signs of the Times,* Mar. 18, 1886.

The Christian's Rest

Come to Me, all you who labor and are heavy laden, and I will give you rest. Take My yoke upon you and learn from Me, for I am gentle and lowly in heart, and you will find rest for your souls. For My yoke is easy and My burden is light. Matt. 11:28-30.

The world is full of unrest, trials, and difficulties. It is an enemy's land, and on every hand we are beset by temptations. "In the world," says Jesus, "ye shall have tribulation: but be of good cheer; I have overcome the world"; and "my peace I give unto you."

Our Savior represents His requirements as a yoke, and the Christian life as one of burden-bearing. Yet, contrasting these with the cruel power of Satan and with the burdens imposed by sin, He declares: "My yoke is easy, and my burden is light." When we try to live the life of a Christian, to bear its responsibilities and perform its duties without Christ as a helper, the yoke is galling, the burden intolerably heavy. But Jesus does not desire us to do this. . . .

Many profess to come to Christ, while they yet cling to their own ways, which are a painful yoke. Selfishness, covetousness, ambition, love of the world, or some other cherished sin, destroys their peace and joy. . . .

In every act the Christian should seek to represent his Master, to make His service appear attractive. Let none make religion repulsive by persistent gloominess, and by relating their trials and their difficulties, their self-denials and their sacrifices. . . .

Let it be seen that with you the love of Christ is an abiding motive; that your religion is not like a garment that may be put off and resumed again, as the circumstances demand, but a principle, calm, steady, unvarying—one that rules your whole life. . . .

Whatever your lot in life may be, remember that you are in the service of Christ, and manifest a contented, grateful spirit. Whatever your burden or cross, lift it in the name of Jesus; bear it in His strength. . . .

Love to Jesus cannot be hidden, but will make itself seen and felt. . . . It makes the timid bold, the slothful diligent, the ignorant wise. It makes the stammering tongue eloquent, and rouses the dormant intellect into new life and vigor. . . . Peace in Christ is of more value than all the treasures of earth.—*Signs of the Times,* Dec. 17, 1885.

Developing a Godlike Character

The fruit of the Spirit is love, joy, peace, longsuffering, kindness, goodness, faithfulness, gentleness, self-control. Gal. 5:22, 23.

People can be just what they choose to be. Character is not obtained by receiving an education. Character is not obtained by amassing wealth or by gaining worldly honor. Character is not obtained by trying to have others fight the battle of life for us. It must be sought, worked for, fought for; and it requires a purpose, a will, a determination. To form a character which God will approve requires persevering effort. It will take a continual resisting of the powers of darkness to stand under the bloodstained banner of Prince Immanuel, to be approved in the day of judgment, and have our names retained in the book of life. Is it not worth more to have our names registered in that book, have them immortalized among the heavenly angels, than to have them sounded in praise throughout the whole earth? Let me know that Jesus smiles upon me; let me know that He approves my actions and my course, and then let come what may, let afflictions be ever so great, I will be resigned to my lot and rejoice in the Lord. . . .

Have you kindled your fire from the altar? Then let it shine forth in good works to those around you. Gather yourselves together, and by your divine influence and earnest efforts scatter the light. . . .

We must work for God, and we must work for heaven, with all the might and faith there is in us. Be not deceived by the temporary things of this life. Consider the things of eternal interest. I want a closer connection with God. I want to sing the song of redemption in the kingdom of glory. I want the crown of immortality to be placed upon my brow. With an immortal tongue I want to sing praises to Him who left glory and came to earth to save those that were lost. I want to praise Him. I want to magnify Him. I want to glorify Him. I want the immortal inheritance and the eternal substance. And what care I, I ask you, what care I for the things of the world if I lose or if I gain heaven at last? Or what advantage will they be to me? But if I have a hold on Heaven, I can have a right hold on my fellow human beings; I can have an influence that will constantly press against the tide of evil that there is in the world, and lead souls into the ark of safety.—*Review and Herald,* Dec. 21, 1886.

Led by the Spirit

See, I have inscribed you on the palms of my hands. Isa. 49:16.

There are two courses of action which we may pursue. One leads us away from God, and shuts us out of His kingdom; and in this path are envying, strife, murder, and all evil deeds. The other course of action we are to follow, and in its pursuance will be found joy, peace, harmony, and love. . . . It is the love that glowed in the bosom of Jesus which we most need; and when it is in the heart, it will reveal itself. Can we have the love of Jesus Christ in the heart, and that love not go out to others? It cannot be there without testifying that it is there. It will reveal itself in the words, in the very expression of the countenance. . . .

When our eldest son, in whom we had the brightest hopes, and upon whom we expected to lean, and whom we had solemnly dedicated to God, was taken from us, when we had closed his eyes in death,★ and mourned in great sorrow because of our affliction, then there came a peace into my soul that was beyond description, that was past understanding. I could think of the morn of the resurrection; I could think of the future, when the great Life-giver will come and break the fetters of the tomb, and call forth the righteous dead from their dusty beds; when He will release the captives from their prison houses; that then our son will be among the living ones again. In this there was a peace, there was a joy, there was a consolation, that was beyond description. . . .

When Christ left the world He committed a work into our hands. While here He Himself carried His work forward; but when He ascended to heaven His followers were left to take it up where He left it. Others took up the work where the disciples left it; and so it has been carried on until now we have the work to do in our own time. . . .

We do not have to walk alone. We can carry all our sorrows and griefs, troubles and trials, afflictions and cares, and pour them into the ear that is open to hear, of One who is pleading before the Father the merits of His own blood. He is pleading His wounds—My hands, My hands! "I have graven thee upon the palms of my hands." He offers the wounded hands to God, and His petitions are heard, and swift angels are sent to minister to fallen men and women, to lift up and to sustain.—*Review and Herald*, Jan. 4, 1887.

★Henry Nichols White (1847-1863).

Adding and Multiplying

Grace and peace be multiplied to you in the knowledge of God and of Jesus our Lord. 2 Peter 1:2.

We are not to trust in our faith, but in the promises of God. When we repent of our past transgressions of His law, and resolve to render obedience in the future, we should believe that God for Christ's sake accepts us and forgives our sins.

Darkness and discouragement will sometimes come upon the soul and threaten to overwhelm us, but we should not cast away our confidence. We must keep the eye fixed on Jesus, feeling or no feeling. We should seek to faithfully perform every known duty, and then calmly rest in the promises of God. . . .

We may not feel today the peace and joy which we felt yesterday, but we should by faith grasp the hand of Christ, and trust Him as fully in the darkness as in the light.

Satan may whisper, "You are too great a sinner for Christ to save." While you acknowledge that you are indeed sinful and unworthy, you may meet the tempter with the cry, "By virtue of the atonement, I claim Christ as my Savior." . . .

If we would permit our minds to dwell more upon Christ and the heavenly world, we should find a powerful stimulus and support in fighting the battles of the Lord. . . . When the mind has been long permitted to dwell only on earthly things, it is a difficult matter to change the habits of thought. That which the eye sees and the ear hears, too often attracts the attention and absorbs the interest. But if we would enter the city of God, and look upon Jesus in His glory, we must become accustomed to beholding Him with the eye of faith here. . . .

Sanctification is a progressive work. The successive steps are set before us in the words of Peter: "Giving all diligence, add to your faith virtue; and to virtue knowledge; and to knowledge temperance; and to temperance patience; and to patience godliness; and to godliness brotherly kindness; and to brotherly kindness charity." . . . Here is a course by which we may be assured that we shall never fall. Those who are thus working upon the plan of addition in obtaining the Christian graces, have the assurance that God will work upon the plan of multiplication in granting them the gifts of His Spirit.—*Review and Herald,* Nov. 15, 1887.

February

15

United With Our Maker

He who says he abides in Him ought himself also to walk just as He walked. 1 John 2:6.

There is a great work for us to do if we would inherit eternal life. We are to deny ungodliness and worldly lusts, and live a life of righteousness. Many teach that all that is necessary to salvation is to believe in Jesus; but what saith the word of truth? "Faith without works is dead." We are to "fight the good fight of faith, lay hold on eternal life," take up the cross, deny self, war against the flesh, and follow daily in the footsteps of the Redeemer. There is no salvation for us except in Jesus, for it is through faith in Him that we receive power to become the sons and daughters of God; but it is not merely a passing faith; it is faith that works the works of Christ. . . .

Living faith makes itself manifest by exhibiting a spirit of sacrifice and devotion toward the cause of God. Those who possess it stand under the banner of Prince Emmanuel, and wage a successful warfare against the powers of darkness. . . .

Genuine faith in Jesus leads to denial of self, but however high the profession may be, if self is exalted and indulged, the faith of Jesus is not in the heart. True Christians manifest by a life of daily consecration that they are bought with a price and are not their own. . . .

Whoever takes the position that it makes no difference whether or not we keep the commandments of God, is not acquainted with Christ. . . . It is a fatal mistake to think that there is nothing for you to do in obtaining salvation. You are to cooperate with the agencies of heaven. . . .

Those who are connected with Jesus are in union with the Maker and Upholder of all things. They have a power that the world cannot give nor take away. But while great and exalted privileges are given to them, they are not simply to rejoice in their blessings. As stewards of the manifold grace of God, they are to become a blessing to others. . . .

We are our brother's keeper. Christ "gave himself for us, that he might redeem us from all iniquity, and purify unto himself a peculiar people, zealous of good works." And that faith which accomplishes this zeal in us is the only genuine faith. If the branch is abiding in the True Vine, its union is made manifest by the fruit that appears, for "by their fruits ye shall know them."—*Review and Herald,* Mar. 6, 1888.

Heavenly Attributes

Sanctify them by Your truth. Your word is truth. John 17:17.

Every moment of our probationary time is precious, for it is our time for characterbuilding. We should give most diligent heed to the culture of our spiritual nature. We should watch our hearts, guarding our thoughts lest impurity tarnish the soul. We should seek to keep every faculty of the mind in the very best condition, that we serve God to the extent of our ability. Nothing should be permitted to interrupt our communion with God. . . .

We have a work to do in this world, and we must not allow ourselves to become self-absorbed, and so forget the claims of God and humanity upon us. If we seek God with earnestness, He will impress us by His Holy Spirit. He knows what we need, for He is acquainted with our every weakness, and He would have us work away from self, that we may become kind in thought and word and deed. We must cease to think and talk of self, making our needs and wants the sole object of our thoughts. God would have us cultivate the attributes of heaven. . . .

How patiently should we bear with the faults and errors of our brethren, when we remember how great are our own failings in the sight of God. How can we pray to our Heavenly Father, "Forgive us our debts, as we forgive our debtors," if we are denunciatory, resentful, exacting in our treatment of others? God would have us more kind, more loving and lovable, less critical and suspicious. Oh, that we all might have the Spirit of Christ, and know how to deal with our brethren and neighbors! . . .

There are too many among those who profess to be followers of Christ who seek to excuse their own defects by magnifying the errors of others. We should copy the example of Jesus, for when He was reviled, He reviled not again, but committed Himself to Him that judgeth righteously. . . . He was the Majesty of heaven, and in His pure breast there dwelt no room for the spirit of retaliation, but only for pity and love. . . .

We may not remember some act of kindness which we do, it may fade from our memory; but eternity will bring out in all its brightness every act done for the salvation of souls, every word spoken for the comfort of God's children; and these deeds done for Christ's sake will be a part of our joy through all eternity.—*Review and Herald,* Feb. 24, 1891.

God's Blessings and Our Responsibility

"Return to Me, and I will return to you," says the Lord of hosts.
Mal. 3:7.

S atan constantly presents the sins and wrongs of those who claim to be
the children of God, and he taunts the angels of God with their defects.
What will bring the Lord's people into a right position before Him? The
Lord answers the question in Malachi, saying, "Return unto me, and I will
return unto you, saith the Lord of hosts." When we seek the Lord with full
purpose of heart, He will be found of us.

Daniel purposed in his heart that he would be true to the God of heaven.
He determined that he would not eat of the king's meat, or drink of his
wine; and his three companions determined that they would not dishonor
God by bowing down before the golden image that Nebuchadnezzar set
up in the plain of Dura. When we purpose to serve the Lord with a determination like that of these faithful servants of God, the Lord will take our
part and enable us to lay hold of His strength. . . .

Angels look with amazement upon the ingratitude of those for whom God
has done so much in continually bestowing His favors and gifts. People forget
the claims of God, and indulge in selfishness and worldliness. . . .

God cannot bless us in lands and flocks when we do not use His blessings
for His glory. He cannot trust His treasure to those who misapply it. In the
simplest language the Lord has told His children what He requires of them.
They are to pay tithes of all they possess, and to make offerings of that
which He bestows upon them. His mercies and blessings have been abundant and systematic. He sends down His rain and sunshine, and causes vegetation to flourish. He gives the seasons; sowing and reaping-time come in
their order; and the unfailing goodness of God calls for something better
than the ingratitude and forgetfulness that many render to Him.

Shall we not return to God, and with grateful hearts present our tithes
and offerings? The Lord has made duty so plain that if we neglect to fulfill
His requirements we shall be without excuse. The Lord has left His goods
in the hands of His servants to be handled with equity, that the gospel may
be preached in all the world. The arrangement and provision for the spread
of His truth in the world has not been left to chance.—*Signs of the Times*,
Jan. 13, 1890.

Let Your Light Shine

But he who does the truth comes to the light, that his deeds may be clearly seen, that they have been done in God. John 3:21.

In His sermon on the mount, Christ presented to the people the fact that personal piety was their strength. They were to surrender themselves to God, working with Him with unreserved cooperation. High pretensions, forms, and ceremonies, however imposing, do not make the heart good and the character pure. True love for God is an active principle, a purifying agency. . . .

The Jewish nation had occupied the highest position; they had built walls great and high to enclose themselves from association with the heathen world; they had represented themselves as the special, loyal people who were favored of God. But Christ presented their religion as devoid of saving faith. It was a combination of dry, hard doctrines, intermingled with sacrifices and offerings. They were very particular to practice circumcision, but they did not teach the necessity of having a pure heart. They exalted the commandments of God in words, but refused to exalt them in practice, and their religion was only a stumbling block to others. . . .

Although they had hitherto held undisputed authority in religious matters, they must now give place to the great Teacher, and to a religion which knew no bounds and made no distinction of caste or position in society, or of race among nations. But the truth taught by Christ was designed for the whole human family. The only true faith is that which works by love and purifies the soul. It is as leaven that transforms human character. . . .

The gospel of Christ means practical godliness, a religion which lifts the receiver out of his natural depravity. The one who beholds the Lamb of God knows that He takes away the sins of the world. True religion would result in an entirely different development of life and character than that seen in the lives of the scribes and Pharisees. . . .

God does not give light that it may be hidden selfishly, and not penetrate to those who sit in darkness. Human agents are God's appointed channel to the world. Instead of being instructed to hide their light, the Savior says to His people, "Let your light so shine before men, that they may see your good works, and glorify your Father which is in heaven."—*Review and Herald,* Apr. 30, 1895.

Our Need of the Holy Spirit

If we live in the Spirit, let us also walk in the Spirit. Gal. 5:25.

The Holy Spirit is not only to sanctify but to convict. We cannot repent of our sins until we are convicted of our guilt. How necessary, then, it is that we should have the Holy Spirit with us as we labor to reach fallen souls. Our human abilities will be exercised in vain unless they are united with this heavenly agency. . . .

In the work of saving sinners, we and angels are to work in harmony, teaching the truth of God to those who are unlearned therein, in order that they may be set free from the bonds of sin. Truth alone can make us free. The liberty that comes through a knowledge of truth is to be proclaimed to every creature. Our heavenly Father, Jesus Christ, and the angels of heaven are all interested in this grand and holy work. To us has been given the exalted privilege of revealing the divine character by unselfishly seeking to rescue sinners from the pit of ruin into which they have been plunged. Every human being who will submit to be enlightened by the Holy Spirit is to be used for the accomplishment of this divinely conceived purpose. . . .

Our Savior is to be more distinctly recognized and acknowledged as the all-sufficiency of His church. He alone can perfect the faith of His people. . . .

We need to leave more room for the working of the Holy Spirit in order that laborers may be bound together and may move forward in the strength of the united body of soldiers. . . . Entire consecration to the service of God will reveal the molding influence of the Holy Spirit at every step along the way. . . .

God desires that His church shall lay hold by faith upon His promises, and ask for the power of the Holy Spirit to help them in every place. . . .

Oh, that frail mankind would realize that it is the General of the armies of heaven that is leading and directing the movements of His allies on earth. Christ Himself is the renewing power, working in and through every soldier by the agency of the Holy Spirit. Every individual is to become an instrument in His hands to work for the salvation of souls. Not one who desires to labor for the Master is to be refused a place, if he is a true follower of Christ. Every one has an *individual* responsibility to bear in the cause of Christ. The efficiency of the Spirit of God will make effective the labors of all who are willing to submit to His guidance.—*Review and Herald,* July 16, 1895.

Dare to Be a Daniel

Go away for now; when I have a convenient time I will call for you. Acts 24:25.

No matter how sinful we have been, no matter what our position may be, if we will repent and believe, coming unto Christ, and trusting Him as our personal Savior, we may be saved to the uttermost. But how dangerous is the position of the one who knows truth but delays to practice it. How perilous it is for men and women to seek to amuse the mind, to gratify the taste and satisfy the reason, by neglecting what has been revealed as duty, and rambling off in search of something they do not know. . . .

Jesus says, "Walk while ye have the light, lest darkness come upon you." . . . Practice every precept of truth presented to you. Live by every word that proceedeth out of the mouth of God, and you will then follow Jesus wherever He goeth. . . . The Lord does not refuse to give His Holy Spirit to them that ask Him. When conviction comes home to the conscience, why not listen, and heed the voice of the Spirit of God? By every hesitation and delay we place ourselves where it is more and more difficult for us to accept the light of heaven, and at last it seems impossible to be impressed by admonitions and warnings. The sinner says, more and more easily, "Go thy way for this time; when I have a more convenient season, I will call for thee." . . .

The souls that at first delay and hesitate, resisting light and pressing against all knowledge, have excellent intentions of making a square turnabout when a convenient season shall come; but the wily foe that is upon their track makes his plans to bind them by the imperceptible threads of evil habits. Character is formed by habits, and one step in the downward road is a preparation for the second step, and the second for those that shall follow. . . .

The children of God are to shine as lights in the midst of a perverse and crooked generation. But if right habits are not cultivated, they will give way to natural tendencies, and will become self-sufficient, self-indulgent, reckless, covetous, revengeful, independent, self-willed, heady, high-minded, lovers of pleasures more than lovers of God. . . .

The character of Daniel is an illustration of what a sinner may become through the grace of Christ. He was strong in intellectual and spiritual power. . . . The Holy Spirit is to be in us a divine indweller. Then let gratitude and love abound in your heart to God.—*Review and Herald,* June 29, 1897.

Becoming a Child of God

But as many as received Him, to them He gave the right to become children of God, to those who believe in His name. John 1:12.

If we could appreciate this great blessing, what an advantage it would be to us! We are given the privilege of being laborers together with God in the saving of our souls. Receiving and believing is our part of the contract. We are to receive Christ as our personal Savior, and are to continue to believe in Him. This means abiding in Christ, showing in Him, at all times and under all circumstances, a faith that is a representation of His character—a faith that works by love, and purifies the soul from all defilement. . . .

We must each obtain an experience for ourselves. No one can depend for salvation on the experience or practice of any other individual. We must each become acquainted with Christ in order properly to represent Him to the world. . . . None of us need to excuse our hasty temper, our misshapen character, our selfishness, envy, jealousy, or any impurity of soul, body, or spirit. God has called us to glory and virtue. We are to obey the call. . . .

How can we escape the power of one who was once an exalted angel in the heavenly courts? He was a being full of beauty and personal charm, blessed with a powerful intellect. Because of his exaltation he thought himself equal with God. . . . How can we discern his false theories and resist his temptations? Only through the individual experience gained by receiving a knowledge of Jesus Christ our Lord. Without divine aid we could not possibly escape the temptations and snares that Satan has prepared to deceive human minds. . . .

We are to walk as He walked, following closely in His footsteps, manifesting His meekness and lowliness. . . . The service of Christ is pure and elevated. The path He traveled is not one of self-pleasing, self-gratification. He speaks to His children, saying, "If any man will come after me, let him deny himself, and take up his cross, and follow me." The price of heaven is submission to Christ. The way to heaven is obedience to the command, Deny thyself, take up thy cross, and follow Me. As Jesus journeyed, so we must journey. The path He followed, we must follow; for that path leads to the mansions He is preparing for us.—*Review and Herald,* Apr. 24, 1900.

Godliness With Contentment

How hard it is for those who have riches to enter the kingdom of God!
Luke 18:24.

These words of the Savior are deeply significant and call for our earnest study. . . . Many who possess great wealth have obtained their riches by close dealing, by benefiting themselves at the expense of their fellow human beings; and they glory in their shrewdness in closing a bargain. Every dollar thus obtained, and the increase of every such dollar, has upon it the curse of God. . . .

Wealthy men and women are to be more closely tested than they have ever yet been. If they stand the test, and remove the blemishes of dishonesty and injustice from their characters, and as faithful stewards render to God the things that are God's, to them it will be said, "Well done, thou good and faithful servant: . . . enter thou into the joy of thy Lord." . . .

"No man can serve two masters," Christ said, "for either he will hate the one, and love the other; or else he will hold to the one, and despise the other." . . . When the Pharisees, who were covetous, heard these things, they derided Him. But turning to them, Christ said, "Ye are they which justify yourselves before men; but God knoweth your hearts: for that which is highly esteemed among men is abomination in the sight of God." . . .

Writing to his son in the gospel, Paul says, "Godliness with contentment is great gain. For we brought nothing into this world, and it is certain we can carry nothing out. And having food and raiment let us be therewith content. But they that will be rich fall into temptation and a snare, and into many foolish and hurtful lusts, which drown men in destruction and perdition. For the love of money is the root of all evil: which while some coveted after, they have erred from the faith, and pierced themselves through with many sorrows." . . .

Paul would impress upon the mind of Timothy the necessity of giving such instruction as would remove the deception which so easily steals upon the rich, that because of their wealth they are superior to others who do not have such large possessions as themselves. They suppose their gain to be godliness. . . .

There are high and holy interests which call for our money, and the money invested in these will yield to the giver more elevated and permanent enjoyment than if it were expended for personal gratification or selfishly hoarded for greed of gain.—*Review and Herald,* Dec. 19, 1899.

What Is Faith?

Now faith is the substance of things hoped for, the evidence of things not seen. Heb. 11:1.

The thought that the righteousness of Christ is imputed to us, not because of any merit on our part, but as a free gift from God, is a precious thought. The enemy of God and humanity is not willing that this truth should be clearly presented, for he knows that if the people receive it fully, his power will be broken. If he can control minds, so that doubt and unbelief and darkness shall compose the experience of those who claim to be the children of God, he can overcome them with temptation. The simple faith that takes God at His word should be encouraged. God's people must have that faith which will lay hold of divine power; "for by grace are ye saved through faith; and that not of yourselves: it is the gift of God." Those who believe that God for Christ's sake has forgiven their sins should not, through temptation, fail to press on to fight the good fight of faith. Their faith should grow stronger until their Christian life, as well as their words, shall declare, "The blood of Jesus Christ his Son cleanseth us from all sin."

Faith is trusting God—believing that He loves us and knows best what is for our good. Thus instead of our own way, it leads us to choose His way. In place of our ignorance, it accepts His wisdom; in place of our weakness, His strength; in place of our sinfulness, His righteousness. Our lives, ourselves, are already His; faith acknowledges His ownership and accepts its blessing. Truth, uprightness, purity, have been pointed out as secrets of life's success. . . . Every good impulse or aspiration is the gift of God; faith receives from God the life that alone can produce true growth and efficiency.

How to exercise faith should be made very plain. To every promise of God there are conditions. If we are willing to do His will, all His strength is ours. Whatever gift He promises is in the promise itself. . . . As surely as the oak is in the acorn, so surely is the gift of God in His promise. . . .

Faith that enables us to receive God's gifts is itself a gift. . . . It grows as it is exercised in appropriating the Word of God. In order to strengthen faith, we must often bring it in contact with the Word.

How often those who trusted the Word of God, though in themselves utterly helpless, have withstood the power of the whole world. . . . These are the world's true noblemen. They are its royal line.—*Review and Herald,* Dec. 24, 1908.

The Only Treasure

For we are His workmanship, created in Christ Jesus for good works, which God prepared beforehand that we should walk in them. Eph. 2:10.

A character formed after the divine likeness is the only treasure that we can take from this world to the next. . . . Regard every moment of time as golden. Do not waste it in indolence, do not spend it in folly, but use it in grasping higher treasures. Cultivate the thoughts and expand the soul by refusing to allow the mind to be filled with unimportant matters. Secure every advantage within your reach for strengthening the intellect. Do not rest satisfied with a low standard. Be not content until, by faithful endeavor, watchfulness, and earnest prayer, you have secured the wisdom that is from above. . . .

Cherish every ray of light you can obtain by searching the Word of God. Take up your God-given work today, and see how much good you can accomplish in the strength of Christ. Make God your counselor. . . .

Christ remembered our nature in the requirements He made. He took our nature upon Himself, and brought to us moral power to combine with human effort. . . . Our spirit may be so identified with His Spirit that in thought and aim we shall be one with Him. . . .

The intellectual, moral, and physical faculties are to be equally cultivated and improved, that we may reach the highest standard in the attainment of knowledge. . . .

Daniel of sacred history was but a youth when with his friends he was taken captive to Babylon. But he stands before the heavenly universe, before the worlds unfallen, and before a rebellious world, as a bright example of what the grace of God can do for sinners. . . . It was not his choice to be exposed to the profligacy, the gluttony, and the spendthrift habits of that heathen nation. But he set his heart, while there, to serve the Lord. He cooperated with God. He stood under Christ's banner as a loyal subject of the heavenly King. . . .

The character formed in this world determines the destiny for eternity. The element of value in the life in this world will be of value in the world to come. Our future is determined by the way in which we now allow ourselves to be influenced. . . . We take Christ's yoke upon us, and learn His way.—*Youth's Instructor*, Aug. 17, 1899.

God's Way, Not My Way

Show me Your ways, O Lord; teach me Your paths. Ps. 25:4.

S ometimes one who professes to be a follower of Christ is heard saying, "You must not be surprised if I am rough, if I speak bluntly, if I manifest temper; it is my way."

You ask us not to be surprised! Is not Heaven surprised at such manifestations, since the plan of salvation has been devised, since an infinite sacrifice has been made on Calvary's cross, that you might reflect the image of Jesus? Will "your way" enter heaven? Suppose someone comes up to the pearly gates, and says, "I know that I have been rude and unkind, and that it is my disposition to lie and steal; but I want an entrance to the heavenly mansions." Will such a disposition find entrance through the portals of the heavenly city? No, no! Only those who keep God's way will enter there.

The manifestation of natural and cultivated tendencies to wrongdoing cannot be excused by the plea, "It is my way." Christians realize that in order to bring the principles of Christianity into the daily life, they need much of the grace of Christ.

The youth who cooperate with Christ will find that their way is full of errors needing to be corrected. Brought into the character-building, these errors are as rotten timbers. Let none allow them to remain. Let none plead for the privilege of clinging to their imperfections, excusing themselves by saying, "It is my way." Those who please self, refusing to give up their way for Christ's way, will suffer the sure result. . . .

Are you striving to walk in the way of truth and righteousness? Then be not discouraged by temptation. True, you will be tempted, but remember that temptation is not sin; it is no indication of the Lord's displeasure. He suffers you to be tempted, but He measures the temptation by the power which He imparts to enable you to resist and overcome. It is in the time of temptation and trial that you are to measure the degree of your faith in God, and to estimate the stability of your Christian character.

Do not say, "It is impossible for me to overcome." . . . In your own strength you cannot overcome, but help has been laid upon One that is mighty. Breathe the prayer, "Shew me thy ways, O Lord; teach me thy paths."—*Youth's Instructor,* Oct. 2, 1902.

Unquestioning Faith

The man believed the word that Jesus spoke to him, and he went his way.
John 4:50.

In the city of Capernaum a nobleman's son lies sick unto death. In vain his father has tried to save him. A messenger comes with hurried steps to the mansion, and asks to see the nobleman. He tells him that he has just come from Jerusalem, and that there is in Galilee a prophet of God, declared by some to be the long-expected Messiah.... It may be that He can heal the child.

As the nobleman listens, the expression of his countenance changes from despair to hope.... The hope born in his soul strengthens as he prepares for his journey. Before the day dawns, he is on his way to Cana of Galilee, where Jesus is supposed to have gone....

Finding Jesus, he beseeches Him to come to Capernaum and heal his son. "Except ye see signs and wonders, ye will not believe," Jesus answers. To a certain extent the nobleman did believe, else he would not have taken the long journey at that critical time. But Christ desired to increase his faith.

With heartbroken entreaty the father cries, "Sir, come down ere my child die." He fears that each passing moment will place his son beyond the power of the Healer.... Desiring to lead him to perfect faith, the Savior replies, "Go thy way; thy son liveth."

"And the man believed the word that Jesus had spoken unto him, and he went his way." Assured that the death he has dreaded will not come to his son, the nobleman does not ask any question nor seek any explanation. He *believes.* Over and over again he repeats the words, "Thy son liveth"

And the power of the words of the Redeemer flashes like lightning from Cana to Capernaum, and the child is healed.... The watchers by the bedside mark with bated breath the conflict between life and death. And when in an instant the burning fever disappears, they are filled with amazement. Knowing the anxiety of the father, they go to greet him with the joyful tidings. He has only one question to ask, When did the child begin to mend? They tell him and he is satisfied.... Now his faith is crowned with assurance....

In our work for Christ, we need more of the unquestioning faith of the nobleman.... The one who trusts the Savior implicitly finds the gates of heaven ajar and flooded with glory from the throne of God.—*Youth's Instructor,* Dec. 4, 1902.

The Power of Song

He will make her wilderness like Eden,
and her desert like the garden of the Lord;
joy and gladness will be found in it,
thanksgiving and the voice of melody. Isa. 51:3.

The melody of praise is the atmosphere of heaven; and when heaven comes in touch with the earth, there is music and song—"thanksgiving and the voice of melody."

Above the new-created earth, as it lay, fair and unblemished under the smile of God, "the morning stars sang together, and all the sons of God shouted for joy." So human hearts, in sympathy with heaven, have responded to God's goodness in notes of praise. Many of the events of human history have been linked with sacred song.

The history of the songs of the Bible is full of suggestion as to the uses and benefits of music and song. Music is often perverted to serve purposes of evil, and it thus becomes one of the most alluring agencies of temptation. But rightly employed, it is a precious gift of God, designed to uplift the thoughts to high and noble themes, to inspire and elevate the soul. As the children of Israel, journeying through the wilderness, cheered their way by the music of sacred song, so God bids His children today gladden their pilgrim life. There are few means more effective for fixing His Word in the memory than repeating them in song. And such song has wonderful power. It has power to subdue rude and uncultivated natures, power to quicken thought and to awaken sympathy, to promote harmony of action, and to banish the gloom and foreboding that destroy courage and weaken effort.

It is one of the most effective means of impressing the heart with spiritual truth. How often to the soul hard-pressed and ready to despair, memory recalls some word of God's—the long-forgotten burden of a childhood song—and temptations lose their power, and courage and gladness are imparted to other souls! . . .

Let there be singing in the home of songs that are sweet and pure, and there will be fewer words of censure, and more of cheerfulness and hope and joy. Let there be singing in the schools, and the pupils will be drawn closer to God, to their teachers, and to one another.

As a part of religious service, singing is as much an act of worship as is prayer.—*Youth's Instructor,* Mar. 29, 1904.

Truth Conquers Evil

Do not think that I came to bring peace on earth.
I did not come to bring peace but a sword. Matt. 10:34.

The question has been asked, How can there be agreement between the statement, "I came not to send peace, but a sword," and the song sung by the angels when Christ was born in the manger at Bethlehem, "Glory to God in the highest, and on earth peace, good will toward men"? The song of the angels is in harmony with the words of the prophet Isaiah, who, when he predicted the birth of Christ, declared Him to be the Prince of peace. The gospel is a glorious message of peace and goodwill to men; the blessing that Christ came to bring was that of harmony and peace. He left His throne of glory, and clothed His divinity with humanity, that He might bring back from apostasy to loyalty to God the children of men, and bind their hearts together and to the heart of Infinite Love. He came to present to a fallen world the remedy for sin, so that whosoever should believe on Him should not perish, but by becoming one with Him and the Father should have everlasting life. . . .

The condition of the world at the time when Christ came into the walks of humanity was no exceptional condition. At that time the Scriptures had been buried beneath human traditions, and Christ declared that those who professed to interpret the Word of God were ignorant both of the Scriptures and of the power of God. . . .

Christ presented to His countrymen and to the world brightness, beauty, and holiness, the divine nature, by which they might be bound close to the heart of Infinite Love. He brought light into the world to dispel spiritual darkness and to reveal truth. . . . The truth, which was to restore and renew, is a destroyer of evil; and when evil is persistently cherished, it becomes a destroyer of the sinner also. . . .

Sinners' perversity, their resistance of the truth, makes the mission of Christ appear to be what He announced to His disciples—the sending of a sword upon the earth; but the strife is not the effect of Christianity, but the result of opposition in the hearts of those who will not receive its blessings.

From the first presentation of Christianity to the world, there has been a deadly warfare instituted against it. . . . Those who suffer for the truth know the value of a pure gospel, a free Bible, and liberty of conscience.—*Bible Echo* (Australia), Mar. 12, 1894.

Sacrifice for the Cause of God

If you want to be perfect, go, sell what you have and give to the poor, and you will have treasure in heaven; and come, follow Me. Matt. 19:21.

Said Jesus [to the rich young ruler], "Give to the poor." . . . In this direct reference He pointed out his idol. His love of riches was supreme, therefore it was impossible for him to love God with all his heart, with all his soul, with all his mind. And this supreme love for his riches shut his eyes to the wants of his fellow human beings. He did not love his neighbor as himself, therefore he failed to keep the last six commandments. . . .

I saw that if men and women love their riches better than their fellow human beings, better than God or the truth of His Word, and their hearts are on their riches, they cannot have eternal life. They would rather yield the truth than sell and give to the poor. Here they are proved to see how much God is loved, how much the truth is loved, and like the young man in the Bible, many go away sorrowful, because they cannot have their riches and a treasure in heaven too. . . . The love of Jesus and riches cannot dwell in the same heart. . . .

I saw that God could send means from heaven to carry on His work; but this is out of His order. He has ordained that men and women should be His instruments, that as a great sacrifice was made to redeem them, they should act a part in this work of salvation by making a sacrifice for each other, and by thus doing show how highly they prize the sacrifice that has been made for them. . . .

I have seen that some give of their abundance, but yet they feel no lack. They do not particularly deny themselves of anything for the cause of Christ. They still have all that heart can wish. They give liberally and heartily. God regards it, and the action and motive is known, and strictly marked by Him. They will not lose their reward. You that cannot bestow so liberally must not excuse yourselves because you cannot do as much as some others. Do what you can. Deny yourself of some article that you can do without, and sacrifice for the cause of God. Like the widow, cast in your two mites. You will actually give more than all those who have given of their abundance. And you will know how sweet it is to give to the needy, to deny self, and sacrifice for the truth, and lay up treasure in heaven.—*Review and Herald,* Nov. 26, 1857.

God Uses Us to Help Others

Honor the Lord with your possessions, and with the firstfruits of all your increase; so your barns will be filled with plenty, and your vats will overflow with new wine. Prov. 3:9, 10.

God is abundantly able to fulfill His promises. Every earthly good comes from His hand. The resources of the Lord are infinite, and He employs them all in accomplishing His purposes. Faithful stewards, who wisely use the goods which God has entrusted to them to advance the truth and bless suffering humanity, will be rewarded for so doing. God will pour into their hands while they dispense to others. He is advancing His cause in the earth through stewards entrusted with His capital. Some there are who, notwithstanding they greatly desire wealth, would be ruined by its possession. God has tested individuals by lending them talents of means. It was in their power to abuse the gift or use it to the glory of God. . . . They have been tested and proved and found unfaithful in using that which was another's as though it was their own. God will not entrust such with the eternal riches.

Those who make a judicious and unselfish disposition of the Lord's goods, thus identifying their interest with that of suffering humanity, will be advanced, for they act the part which God designed they should in His own system of beneficence. . . .

Every good thing upon the earth was given to us as an expression of the love of God. He makes people His stewards and gives them talents of influence and means to use for the accomplishment of His work in the earth. Our heavenly Father proposes to connect finite human beings with Himself. As laborers they may be His instruments in the salvation of souls. . . .

Those who walk in the light of truth will emit light to those around them. They are living witnesses for Christ. They will not be like the world, living in moral darkness, loving themselves and the things of the world, and seeking for earthly treasures. . . .

God has made us our brother's keeper and will hold us responsible for this great trust. God has taken us into union with Himself, and He has planned that we shall work in harmony with Him. He has provided the system of beneficence, that we whom He has made in His image may be self-denying in character, like Him whose infinite nature is love.—*Review and Herald*, Oct. 31, 1878.

Deceitfulness of Riches

For the love of money is a root of all kinds of evil, for which some have strayed from the faith in their greediness, and pierced themselves through with many sorrows. 1 Tim. 6:10.

Many who profess the special truths for our time have not a proper discernment of character. They fail to appreciate moral worth. They may boast much of their fidelity to the cause of God and their knowledge of the Scriptures, but they are not humble in heart. They have a special regard for those who are wealthy and prosperous, forgetting that riches do not give us favor with God. True excellence of character is frequently overlooked if possessed by the poor. Money sways a mighty influence. But does God care for money—for property? The cattle upon a thousand hills are His, the world and all that is therein. . . .

God has committed to His stewards means to be used in doing good, and thus securing a treasure in heaven. But if, like the man who had one talent, they hide their means, fearing that God will receive that which belongs to Him, they will not only lose the increase which will finally be awarded the faithful steward, but also the principal which God gave them to work upon. . . .

The great apostle, in his letter to Timothy, would impress upon his mind the necessity of giving such instruction as should remove the deception which so easily steals upon the rich—that because of their ability to acquire wealth they are superior in wisdom and judgment to those who are in poverty, that gain is godliness. . . .

Individuals may devote their whole lives to the one object of acquiring riches, yet as they brought nothing into the world, they can carry nothing out. . . . They have sacrificed noble, elevated principles, given up their faith for riches, and if not disappointed in their object, they are disappointed in the happiness they supposed wealth would bring. . . .

The apostle shows the only true use for riches, and bids Timothy charge the rich to do good, to be rich in good works, ready to distribute, willing to communicate, for in so doing they are laying up in store for themselves a good foundation against the time to come—referring to the close of time—that they may lay hold on eternal life. . . . Godliness with contentment is great gain. Here is the true secret of happiness, and real prosperity of soul and body.—*Review and Herald,* Mar. 4, 1880.

Give to God What Is His

The world is Mine, and all its fullness. Ps. 50:12.

The end of all things is at hand, and what is done for the salvation of souls must be done quickly. For this reason we are establishing institutions for the dissemination of the truth through the press, for the education of the young, and for the recovery of the sick. But the selfish and money-loving inquire, "What is the use of all this, when time is so short? Is it not a contradiction of our faith to spend so much in publishing houses, schools, and health institutions?" We ask in reply, If time is to continue but a few years, why invest so much in houses and lands, or in needless and extravagant display, while so meager a sum is devoted to the work of preparation for the great event before us? . . .

With God's blessing, the power of the press can hardly be overestimated. . . . Let the publishing houses be sustained, and the message of truth be sent out to all the nations of the earth.

Schools have been established that our youth and children may receive the education and discipline needed to prepare them for the searching test so soon to come to every soul. In these schools the Bible should be made one of the principal subjects of study. Attention should be given to the development of both the moral and intellectual powers. We hope that in these schools many earnest workers may be prepared to carry the light of truth to those who sit in darkness.

In a health institution we provide a place where the sick can enjoy the benefit of nature's remedial agents, instead of depending upon deadly drugs. And many who thus find relief will be ready to yield to the influence of the truth. . . .

Wealth is a great blessing if used according to the will of God. But the selfish heart can make the possession of wealth a heavy curse. . . . The ones who obtain the most real enjoyment in this life are those who use God's bounty and do not abuse it. . . .

God is the rightful owner of the universe. All things belong to Him. Every blessing which men and women enjoy is the result of divine beneficence. . . . He justly bids us consecrate to Him the first and best of His entrusted capital. If we thus acknowledge His rightful sovereignty and gracious providence, He has pledged His word that He will bless the remainder.—*Review and Herald,* May 16, 1882.

Liberality and Love for God's Work

"Let neither man nor woman do any more work for the offering of the sanctuary." And the people were restrained from bringing. Ex. 36:6.

Under the Jewish system, the people were required to cherish a spirit of liberality, both in sustaining the cause of God and in supplying the wants of the needy. At the harvest and the vintage, the firstfruits of the fields—corn, wine, and oil—were to be consecrated as an offering to the Lord. The gleanings and the corners of the fields were reserved for the poor. The firstfruits of the wool when the sheep were shorn, of the grain when the wheat was threshed, were to be offered to the Lord; and at the feast it was commanded that the poor, the widows, the orphans, and the strangers should be invited. At the close of every year all were required to make solemn oath whether or not they had done according to the command of God.

This arrangement was made by the Lord to impress upon the people that in every matter He must be first. They were, by this system of benevolence, reminded that their gracious Master was the true proprietor of their fields, their flocks, and their herds, that the God of heaven sent them sunshine and rain for their seed-time and harvest, and that everything which they possessed was of His creation. All was the Lord's, and He had made them stewards of His goods.

The liberality of the Jews in the construction of the tabernacle evinced a spirit of benevolence which has not been equaled by the people of God at any later date. The Hebrews had just been freed from their long bondage in Egypt, they were wanderers in the wilderness; yet scarcely were they delivered from the armies of the Egyptians who pursued them in their hasty journey, when the word of the Lord came to Moses, "Speak unto the children of Israel, that they bring me an offering: of every man that giveth it willingly with his heart ye shall take my offering." . . .

All gave with a willing hand, not a certain amount of their increase, but a large portion of their actual possessions. They devoted it gladly and heartily to the Lord. They honored Him by so doing. Was it not all His? Had He not given them all that they possessed? If He called for it, was it not their duty to give back to the lender His own? No urging was needed. The people brought even more than was required; and they were told to desist, for there was already more than could be appropriated.—*Review and Herald,* Oct. 17, 1882.

The Joy of Advancing God's Work

O Lord our God, all this abundance that we have prepared to build You a house for Your holy name is from Your hand, and is all Your own.
1 Chron. 29:16.

In building the temple, the call for means met with a hearty response. The people did not give reluctantly; they rejoiced in the prospect of a building being erected for the worship of God. They donated more than enough for the purpose. David blessed the Lord before all the congregation, and said, "But who am I, and what is my people, that we should be able to offer so willingly after this sort? for all things come of thee, and of thine own have we given thee." . . .

David well understood from whom came all his bounties. Would that those of this day who rejoice in a Savior's love could realize that their silver and gold is the Lord's, and should be used to promote His glory, not grudgingly retained to enrich and gratify themselves. He has an indisputable right to all that He has lent His creatures. All that they possess is His.

There are high and holy objects that require means; thus invested, it will yield to the giver more elevated and permanent enjoyment than if expended in personal gratification or selfishly hoarded for the greed of gain. . . .

Many selfishly retain their means and soothe their conscience with a plan for doing some great thing for the cause of God after their death. They make a will donating a large sum to the church and its various interests, and then settle down with a feeling that they have done all that is required of them. Wherein have they denied self by this act? They have, on the contrary, exhibited only selfishness. When they have no further use for their money, they propose to give it to God. But they will retain it as long as they can, till they are compelled to relinquish it by a messenger that cannot be turned down.

God has made us all His stewards, and in no case authorized us to neglect our duty or leave it for others to do. The call for means to advance the cause of truth will never be more urgent than now. Our money will never do a greater amount of good than at the present time. . . . If we leave others to accomplish that which God has left for as to do, we wrong ourselves and Him who gave us all we have. . . . God would have all be executors of their own will in this matter, during their lifetime.—*Review and Herald,* Oct. 17, 1882.

What God Values

There is one who scatters, yet increases more; and there is one who with-holds more than is right, but it leads to poverty. Prov. 11:24.

Experience shows that a spirit of benevolence is more often to be found with those of limited means than among the more wealthy. The most liberal donations for the cause of God or the relief of the needy come from the poor person's purse, while many to whom the Lord has committed an abundance for this very purpose see not the necessity for means to advance the truth, and hear not the cries of the poor among them. . . .

The gift of the poor, the fruit of self-denial to extend the precious light of truth, is as fragrant incense before God. And every act of self-sacrifice for the good of others will strengthen the spirit of beneficence in the giver's heart, allying the donor more closely to the Redeemer of the world, who "was rich, yet for your sakes he became poor, that ye through his poverty might be rich."

The smallest sum given cheerfully as the result of self-denial is of more value in God's sight than the offerings of those who could give thousands and yet feel no lack. The poor widow who cast two mites into the treasury of the Lord showed love, faith, and benevolence. She gave all that she had, trusting to God's care for the uncertain future. Her little gift was pronounced by our Savior the greatest that day cast into the treasury. Its value was measured not by the worth of the coin, but by the purity of the motive which prompted her sacrifice.

God's blessing upon that sincere offering has made it the source of great results. The widow's mite has been like a tiny stream flowing down through the ages, widening and deepening in its course, and contributing in a thousand directions to the extension of the truth and the relief of the needy. The influence of that small gift has acted and reacted upon thousands of hearts in every age and in every country upon the globe. As the result, unnumbered gifts have flowed into the treasury of the Lord from the liberal, self-denying poor. And again, her example has stimulated to good works thousands of ease-loving, selfish, and doubting ones, and their gifts also have gone to swell the value of her offering.

Liberality is a duty on no account to be neglected. . . .

It is to cultivate a spirit of benevolence in us that the Lord calls for our gifts and offerings.—*Review and Herald,* Feb. 9, 1886.

Trust the Word, Not Feelings

Let the word of Christ dwell in you richly in all wisdom. Col. 3:16.

The Word of God is the foundation of our faith, and therefore it is by the Word of God that we may obtain evidence of our standing before God. We are not to make our feelings a test by which to discern whether we are in or out of favor with God, whether they be what we consider encouraging or not. As soon as we begin to contemplate feelings, we are on dangerous ground. If we feel joyous, we are confident we are in a favorable condition, but when a change comes, as it will, for circumstances will be so arranged that feelings of depression will make the heart sad, then we will be naturally led to doubt that God has accepted us. . . .

Satan will not be slow in presenting to the repentant soul suggestions and difficulties to weaken faith and destroy courage. He has manifold temptations that he can send trooping into the mind, one in succession of another, but Christians must not study their emotions, and give way to their feelings, or they will soon entertain the evil guest, doubt, and become entangled in the perplexities of despair. . . .

Do not exalt your feelings and be swayed by them, whether they be good, bad, sad, or joyful. . . . It is the Word of God that is to be your assurance. . . . There is a warfare in which every soul must engage who would have the crown of life. Inch by inch the overcomer must fight the good fight of faith, using the weapons of God's Word. We must meet the foe with "It is written." . . .

When the enemy begins to draw away the mind from Jesus, to shut away His mercy, His love, His all-sufficiency, do not devote precious time to the consideration of your feelings, but flee to the Word. In the Scriptures Christ is presented as the one by whom God made the worlds. He is the light of the world, and, as we seekers for light study the Word, we find heavenly illumination. . . .

What do we hope to accomplish by longing to have the whole world converted to Jesus by believing in His pardoning love, when we do not ourselves believe in His love or find rest in His grace? How can we possibly lead others to a full assurance, to simple, childlike faith in our heavenly Father, when we are measuring and judging our love to Him by our feelings?—*Signs of the Times,* Dec. 3, 1894.

The Word Became Flesh

Sacrifice and offering You did not desire, but a body You have prepared for Me. . . . Behold, I have come . . . to do Your will, O God. Heb. 10:5-7.

Should the angel Gabriel be sent to this world to take upon himself human nature and to teach the knowledge of God, how eagerly people would listen to his instruction. Supposing that he were able to set us a perfect example of purity and holiness, sympathizing with us in all our sorrows, bereavements, and afflictions, and suffering the punishment of our sins, how eagerly we would follow him. . . .

If, when this heavenly being returned to his home, he should leave behind him a book containing the history of his mission, with revelations regarding the history of the world, how eagerly would its seal be broken! How anxiously men and women would seek to obtain a copy! . . . But One surpassing all that imagination can present came from heaven to this world. . . . Of Himself Christ declares, "Before Abraham was, I am." "I and my Father are one." . . .

As Paul beheld Christ in His power, he broke out into exclamations of admiration and amazement: "Without controversy great is the mystery of godliness: God was manifest in the flesh, justified in the Spirit, seen of angels, preached unto the Gentiles, believed on in the world, received up into glory." . . . "And he is before all things, and by him all things consist."

The Bible is God's voice speaking to us, just as surely as if we could hear it with our ears. If we realized this, . . . with what earnestness we would search its precepts. The reading and contemplation of the Scriptures would be regarded as an audience with the Infinite One. . . .

Christ's words are the bread of life. As the disciples ate the words of Christ, their understanding was quickened. . . . In their comprehension of these teachings they stepped from the obscurity of dawn to the radiance of noonday.

So will it be with us as we study God's Word. Our minds will be quickened and our understanding enlarged. Those who receive and assimilate this Word, making it a part of every act, of every attribute of character, grow strong in the strength of God. It gives vigor to the soul, perfecting the experience, and bringing joys that abide forever.—*Signs of the Times,* Apr. 4, 1906.

What Are We Reading?

Give attention to reading. 1 Tim. 4:13.

The enemy knows that to a great degree the mind is affected by that upon which it feeds. He is seeking to lead both the youth and those of mature age to read story books, tales, and other literature. Those who yield to this temptation soon lose their relish for solid reading. They have no interest in Bible study. Their moral powers become enfeebled. Sin appears less and less repulsive. There is manifest an increasing unfaithfulness, a growing distaste for life's practical duties. As the mind becomes perverted, it is ready to grasp any reading of a stimulating character. . . .

Works that do not so decidedly mislead and corrupt are yet to be shunned, if they impart a disrelish for the study of the Bible. This Word is the true manna. Let all repress the desire for reading matter that is not food for the mind. You cannot possibly do the work of God with clear perception while the mind is occupied with this class of reading. . . .

Question your own experience as to the influence of light reading. Can you, after spending time in such reading, open the Bible and read with interest the words of life? Do you not find the Book of God uninteresting? . . .

In order to have a healthy tone of mind and sound religious principles, we must live in communion with God through His Word. Pointing out the way of salvation, the Bible is our guide to a higher, better life. It contains the most interesting and most instructive history and biography that were ever written. Those whose imaginations have not been perverted by the reading of fiction will find the Bible the most interesting of all books.

Resolutely discard all worthless reading. Such reading will not strengthen your spirituality, but will introduce into the mind sentiments that will pervert the imagination, causing you to think less of Jesus and to dwell less upon His precious lessons. . . .

The Bible is the Book of books. If you love the Word, searching it as you have opportunity, that you may come into the possession of the rich treasure that it contains and be thoroughly furnished unto all good works, then you may be assured that Jesus is drawing you to Himself.—*Signs of the Times,* June 13, 1906.

True and False Sanctification

By their fruits you will know them. Matt. 7:20.

Jesus came into the world because the human race were under sentence of death for their transgressions. His work was to bring them back to allegiance to the law of God, which Paul declares is "holy, and just, and good." He kept His Father's commandments. Those who by repentance and obedience testify their appreciation of the salvation He came to bring will show the work of the Spirit on their hearts. And the test is the life. "By their fruits ye shall know them." "He that saith, I know Him," says John, "and keepeth not his commandments, is a liar, and the truth is not in him."

Yet notwithstanding these inspired testimonies as to the nature of sin, many claim to be sanctified and incapable of sin, while they are constantly transgressing the law of God. . . .

No one who claims holiness is really holy. Those who are registered as holy in the books of heaven are not aware of the fact and are the last ones to boast of their own goodness. None of the prophets and apostles ever professed holiness, not even Daniel, Paul, or John. The righteous never make such a claim. The more nearly they resemble Christ, the more they lament their unlikeness to Him, for their consciences are sensitive, and they regard sin more as God regards it. . . .

The only safe position for any of us to take is to consider ourselves sinners, daily needing divine grace. Mercy through the atoning blood of Christ is our only plea. . . . Those who have the truth as it is revealed in that Holy Word must stand fast on the platform of truth, relying on, "It is written." . . .

God has great blessings to bestow upon His people. They may have the "peace of God, which passeth all understanding." They "may be able to comprehend with all saints" . . . "what is the breadth, and length, and depth, and height" of the love of Christ, being "filled with all the fulness of God." But it is only to those who are meek and lowly of heart that Christ will thus manifest Himself. The ones whom God justifies are represented by the publican rather than the self-righteous Pharisee. Humility is heaven-born, and none can enter the pearly gates without it. All unconsciously, it shines in the church and in the world, and it will shine in the courts of heaven.—*Signs of the Times*, Feb. 26, 1885.

The Royal Family

He who believes in the Son has everlasting life. John 3:36.

Those who are truly children of God are believers, not doubters and chronic grumblers. . . . Through all ages and in every nation those that believe that Jesus can and will save them personally from sin, are the elect and chosen of God; they are His peculiar treasure. . . .

The Lord has graciously opened out to our understanding by the Holy Spirit rich truth, and we should respond to this by corresponding works of piety and devotion, in harmony with the superior privileges and advantages that have been bestowed upon us. The Lord is waiting to be gracious to His people, to give them an increased knowledge of His paternal character, of His goodness, mercy, and love. He waits to show them His glory; and if they follow on to know the Lord, they shall know that His goings forth are prepared as the morning.

The people of God are not to stand upon common ground, but upon the holy ground of gospel truth. They are to keep step with their Leader, looking continually to Jesus, the Author and Finisher of their faith, marching onward and upward, and having no fellowship with the unfruitful works of darkness. . . .

It is the privilege of the children of God to be delivered from the control of the lusts of the flesh, and to preserve their peculiar, heavenly character, which distinguishes them from the lovers of the world. In their moral taste, in their habits and customs, they are separate from the world. Who are the children of God? They are members of the royal family, and a royal nation, a peculiar people, showing forth the praises of Him who hath called them out of darkness into His marvelous light. . . .

Will not those to whom have been committed the treasures of truth, consider the superior advantages of light and privilege that have been purchased for us by the sacrifice of the Son of God on Calvary's cross? We are to be judged by the light that has been given us, and we can find no excuse by which to extenuate our course. The Way, the Truth, and the Life has been set before us. . . .

We are to place our will on the side of the Lord's will, and firmly determine that by His grace we will be free from sin.—*Review and Herald*, Aug. 1, 1893.

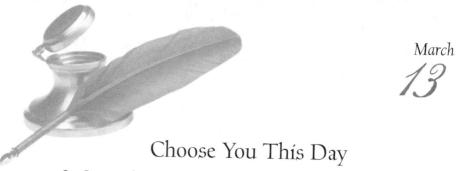

Choose You This Day

Lo, I am with you always, even to the end of the age. Matt. 28:20.

For many months I have been troubled as I have seen that some of our brethren whom God has used in His cause are now perplexed over the scientific theology which has come in to lead men away from a true faith in God. Sabbath night, a week ago, after I had been prayerfully studying over these things, I had a vision in which I was speaking before a large company where many questions were asked concerning my work and writings.

I was directed by a messenger from heaven not to take the burden of picking up and answering all the sayings and doubts that are being put into many minds. "Stand as the messenger of God anywhere, in any place," I was bidden, "and bear the testimony I shall give you. Be free. Bear the testimony that the Lord has for you to bear in reproof, in rebuke, in the work of encouraging and lifting up the soul; 'teaching them to observe all things whatsoever I have commanded you: and, lo, I am with you alway, even unto the end of the world.' "

After the vision I prayed aloud with great fervor and earnestness. My soul was strengthened, for the words had been spoken: "Be strong, yea, be strong. Let none of the misleading words of ministers or physicians distress your mind. Tell them to take the light given them in publications. Truth will always bear away the victory. Go straight forward with your work.

"If the Holy Spirit is rejected, all My words will not help to remove, even for the time being, the false representations that have been made, and Satan stands ready to invent more. If the evidence already given is rejected, all other evidence will be useless until there is seen the converting power of God upon minds. If the convincing impressions of the Holy Spirit made in the past will not be accepted as trustworthy evidence, nothing that can be presented hereafter will reach them, because the bewitching guile of Satan has perverted their discernment." . . .

God now calls for all who choose to serve Him to stand firmly on the platform of eternal truth. Let those who have brought about the present state of confusion by making the division that exists, stop to consider seriously before going any further. "Choose you this day whom ye will serve." "If the Lord be God, follow him: but if Baal, then follow him."—*Review and Herald,* Aug. 9, 1906.

The Example of Liberality

He who sows sparingly will also reap sparingly, and he who sows
bountifully will also reap bountifully. 2 Cor. 9:6.

Liberality is one of the directions of the Holy Spirit, and when the professed people of God withhold from the Lord His own in gifts and offerings, they meet with spiritual loss. . . .

It were better not to give at all than to give grudgingly, for if we impart of our means when we have not the spirit to give freely, we mock God. Let us bear in mind that we are dealing with One upon whom we depend for every blessing, One who reads every thought of the heart, every purpose of the mind.

The apostle Paul had a special work to present before his Corinthian brethren. There was a famine in Jerusalem, and the disciples, "every man according to his ability, determined to send relief unto the brethren which dwelt in Judaea." They presented the need to the churches, expecting to receive a small sum for the relief of the needy saints; and in prayer they presented before the Lord the necessity.

But the Macedonian believers, moved by the Spirit of God, first made an entire consecration of themselves to God, and then gave all that they had. They felt it a privilege thus to give expression to their trust in God. The Macedonian believers were poor, but they did not have to be urged to give. They rejoiced that they had opportunity to contribute of their means. Of themselves they came forward and made the offering, in their Christlike simplicity, their integrity and love for their brethren, denying themselves of food and clothing in cases where they had no money. And when the apostles would have restrained them, they pleaded with them to receive the contribution and carry it to the afflicted saints.

This self-denial and self-sacrifice far exceeded Paul's expectations, and he was filled with thanksgiving; and taking courage by this example, by epistle he exhorted Titus to stir up the church in Corinth to the same good works. . . .

"We desired Titus, that as he had begun, so he would also finish in you the same grace also. Therefore, as ye abound in everything, in faith, and utterance, and knowledge, and in all diligence, and in your love to us, see that ye abound in this grace also."

This movement on the part of the Macedonians was inspired of God to arouse in the Corinthian church the spirit of liberality.—*Review and Herald,* May 15, 1900.

In Christ's Steps

Let this mind be in you which was also in Christ Jesus, . . .
who made Himself of no reputation, taking the form of a bondservant,
and coming in the likeness of men. Phil. 2:5-7.

The Son of God . . . left His riches and honor and glory, and clothed His divinity with humanity, that humanity might take hold of divinity and become a partaker of the divine nature. He came not to live in the palaces of kings, to live without care and labor and be supplied with all the conveniences which human nature naturally craves. The world never saw its Lord wealthy. In the council of heaven He had chosen to stand in the ranks of the poor and the oppressed, . . . to learn the trade of His earthly parent. He came to the world to be a reconstructor of character, and He brought into all His work the perfection which He desired to bring into the character He was transforming by His divine power.

Nor did He shun the social life of His countrymen. That all might become acquainted with God manifest in the flesh, He mingled with every class of society, and was called the friend of sinners. In Himself Christ possessed an absolute right to all things, but He gave Himself to a life of poverty that we might be rich in heavenly treasure. Commander in the heavenly courts, He took the lowest place on earth. Rich, yet for our sake He became poor. . . .

For a little time the Lord allows His people to be His stewards, that He may test their character. In that time they decide their eternal destiny. If they work in opposition to the will of God, they cannot belong to the royal family. . . .

Evidence of the work of grace in the heart is given when we do good to everyone as we have opportunity. The proof of our love is given in a Christlike spirit, a willingness to impart the good things God has given us, a readiness to practice self-denial and self-sacrifice in order to help advance the cause of God and suffering humanity. Never should we pass by the object that calls for our liberality. . . .

The Lord will use all who will give themselves to be used. But He requires heart service. . . . When the heart is given to God, our talents, our energy, our possessions, all we have and are, will be devoted to His service.—*Review and Herald,* May 15, 1900.

God Needs Our Talents

We are God's fellow workers. 1 Cor. 3:9.

Our indebtedness to God and our entire dependence upon Him should lead us to acknowledge Him as the giver of all our blessings, and by our offerings we acknowledge this. Of the bounties He has bestowed upon us, He requires that a portion be returned to Him. By giving to the Lord His due, we declare to the world that all our mercies are from Him, that all we possess belongs to Him. . . .

When the Jews held their services of thanksgiving after the ingathering of nature's treasure, they offered sacrifices to God. To us it might seem strange that sacrificial offerings should have formed so important a part of the universal rejoicing; and to outward appearances, it was a strange combination to mingle the sacrifice of beasts with the expressions of joy. But this was built upon the true foundation, for Christ Himself was the object of these ceremonial services. When, in these festal gatherings, blood was shed and offerings were made to God, the people were not only thanking Him for His present mercies, but they were thanking Him for the promise of a Savior, and by this expressing the truth that without the shedding of the blood of the Son of God there could be no forgiveness of sins. . . .

The Lord has committed talents to men and women, that they may be better fitted to honor and glorify Him. To some He has entrusted means; to others, special qualifications for service; to others, tact and influence. Some have five talents, others two, and others one. From the highest to the lowest each has been entrusted with some gift. These talents are not our own. They belong to God. He has given them to us for conscientious use, and He will one day ask for an account of them.

The great lesson we are daily to learn is that we are stewards of God's gifts— stewards of money, of reason, of intellect, of influence. As stewards of the Lord's gifts, we are to trade upon these talents, however small they may be. . . .

However small your talent may appear, use it in God's service, for He has need of it. If it is wisely used, you may bring to God one soul who also will dedicate his or her powers to the Master's service. That soul may win other souls, and thus one talent, faithfully used, may gain many talents.—*Review and Herald,* Nov. 24, 1896.

Receiving to Give

Jesus took the loaves, and when He had given thanks He distributed them to the disciples, and the disciples to those sitting down; and likewise of the fish, as much as they wanted. John 6:11.

By this miracle Christ has shown how missionary work is to be bound up with the ministry of the Word. Not only did the Master give the people spiritual food; by a miracle He also provided temporal food to satisfy their physical hunger. This merciful provision helped to fasten in the minds of the people the gracious words of truth which He had spoken. . . .

By this miracle Christ desires to teach us the truth of the words, "Without me ye can do nothing." He is the source of all power, the giver of all temporal and spiritual blessings. He employs human beings as coworkers, giving them a part to act with Him as His helping hand. We are to receive from Him, not to hoard for self-gratification, but to impart to others. As we do this work, let us not suppose that we are to receive the glory. All the glory is to be given to the great Master Worker. The disciples were not to receive the glory for feeding the five thousand. They were only the instruments used by the Lord. . . .

He, the great Master Worker, slumbers not. Constantly He is working for the harmonious accomplishment of His purposes. He entrusts talents to us that we may cooperate with Him. We are ever to remember that we are but instruments in His hands. "He that glorieth, let him glory in the Lord." . . .

All who have really accepted Christ will not be satisfied to enjoy the divine favor without giving to others the joy that cheers their souls. The purest and holiest devotion is that which leads to persevering, unselfish effort for the salvation of those outside the fold. . . .

Those who impart to others of the riches of the grace of heaven will themselves be enriched. The ministering angels are waiting, longing, for channels through which they can communicate the treasures of heaven. Men and women can reach the highest stage of mental and moral development only by cooperating with Jesus in unselfish effort for the good of others. We are never so truly enriched as when we are trying to enrich others. We cannot diminish our treasure by sharing it. The more we enlighten others, the brighter our light will shine.—*Review and Herald,* Apr. 4, 1907.

First Things First

You are the light of the world. Matt. 5:14.

Eternal things should awaken our interest and should be regarded, in comparison with temporal things, as of infinite importance. God requires of us to make it our first business to attend to the health and prosperity of the soul. We should know that we are enjoying the favor of God, that He smiles upon us, and that we are His children indeed, and in a position where He can commune with us and we with Him. We should not be at rest until we are in that position of lowliness and meekness that He can safely bless us, and we be brought into a sacred nearness with God, where His light may shine upon us, and we reflect that light to all around us. But we cannot do this unless we are earnestly striving ourselves to live in the light. This God requires of all His followers, not merely for their own good, but also for the benefit of others around them.

We cannot let our light shine out to others so as to attract their attention to heavenly things unless we have the light in us. We must be imbued with the Spirit of Jesus Christ, or we cannot manifest to others that Christ is in us the hope of glory. We must have an indwelling Savior, or we cannot exemplify in our lives His life of devotion, His love, His gentleness, His pity, His compassion, His self-denial, and purity. This is what we earnestly desire. This should be the study of our lives, How shall I conform my character to the Bible standard of holiness?. . .

Christ sacrificed His majesty, His splendor, His glory, and His honor, and for our sakes became poor, that we through His poverty might be made rich. He condescended to a life of humiliation. He was subjected to scorn. He was despised and rejected of men. He bore insult and mockery, and a most painful death in the most shameful manner, in order that He might exalt and save the fallen sons and daughters of Adam from hopeless misery. In view of this unparalleled sacrifice and mysterious love manifested for us by our Redeemer, shall we withhold from God our entire service, which at the best is so feeble? Shall we use selfishly, for business or pleasure, the time which is necessary for us to devote to religious exercises, to the study of the Scriptures, and to self-examination and prayer? . . .

We have not built our hopes here, in this world. Our actions have testified to our faith, that in heaven is our enduring substance.—*Review and Herald,* Mar. 29, 1870.

Christian Temperance

I beseech you therefore, brethren, by the mercies of God, that you present your bodies a living sacrifice, holy, acceptable to God, which is your reasonable service. Rom. 12:1.

We are living in an age of intemperance. Health and life are sacrificed, by very many, to gratify their appetite for hurtful indulgences. These last days are characterized by depreciated morals and physical debility, in consequence of these indulgences and the general unwillingness to engage in physical labor. Many are suffering today from inaction and wrong habits. . . .

When we pursue a course of eating and drinking that lessens physical and mental vigor, or become the prey of habits that tend to the same results, we dishonor God, for we rob Him of the service He claims from us. Those who acquire and indulge the unnatural appetite for tobacco do this at the expense of health. They are destroying nervous energy, lessening vital force, and sacrificing mental strength.

Those who profess to be the followers of Christ, yet have this terrible sin at their door, cannot have a high appreciation of the atonement and an elevated estimate of eternal things. Minds that are clouded and partially paralyzed by narcotics are easily overcome by temptation and cannot enjoy communion with God.

Those who use tobacco can make but a poor plea to the liquor inebriate. Two thirds of the drunkards in our land created an appetite for liquor by the use of tobacco. Those who claim that tobacco does not injure them can be convinced of their mistake by depriving themselves of it for a few days; the trembling nerves, the giddy head, the irritability they feel, will prove to them that this sinful indulgence has bound them in slavery. It has overcome will power. . . .

Means are thereby squandered that would aid in the good work of clothing the naked, feeding the hungry, and sending the truth to poor souls out of Christ. What a record will appear when the accounts of life are balanced in the book of God! It will then appear that vast sums of money have been expended for tobacco and alcoholic liquors! For what? To ensure health and prolong life? Oh, no! To aid in the perfection of Christian character and a fitness for the society of holy angels? Oh, no! But to minister to a depraved, unnatural appetite for that which poisons and kills not only the users but those to whom they transmit their legacy of disease and imbecility.—*Signs of the Times,* Jan. 6, 1876.

God's Innumerable Bounties

Jesus . . . said to her, "If you knew the gift of God, and who it is who says to you, 'Give Me a drink,' you would have asked Him, and He would have given you living water." John 4:10.

The gifts of God are on every hand, and all His gifts come to us through the merit of Jesus, whom He gave to the world. The apostle Paul breaks forth in an exclamation of gratitude, saying, "Thanks be unto God for his unspeakable gift." And with Christ God has given us all things. The opening bud, the blooming flowers in their variety and loveliness, delightful to the senses, are the work of the Master Artist's expressions of His love toward us. . . . The Lord has taken great care that everything should be grateful and pleasant to us, and yet how much greater effort He has made to provide us with that gift whereby we may perfect a Christian character, after the pattern of Christ.

Through the flowers of the field God would call our attention to the loveliness of Christlike character. . . . God is a lover of the beautiful. He desires that we shall consider the lovely flowers of the valley, and learn lessons of trust in Him. They are to be our teachers. . . . The Lord takes care of the flowers of the field, and clothes them with loveliness, and yet He has made it evident that He looks upon humanity as of greater value than the flowers for which He cares. . . .

Suppose that our benevolent Father should grow weary with our ingratitude, and for a few weeks should withhold His innumerable bounties. Suppose He should become discouraged in seeing His treasures applied to selfish ends, in hearing no response of praise and gratitude for His unmerited mercies, and should forbid the sun to shine, the dew to fall, the earth to yield her increase. What a sensation would be created! What dismay would fall upon the world! What a cry would be raised as to what we should do to supply our tables with food and our bodies with clothing! . . .

God has not only supplied us with temporal benefits, but has provided for our eternal welfare; "for God so loved the world, that he gave his only begotten son, that whosoever believeth in him should not perish, but have everlasting life." . . . Oh, if we did but know the gift of God, if we did but appreciate what this gift of God means to us, we would have been earnestly seeking for it with unwavering perseverance.—*Signs of the Times,* June 19, 1893.

Jesus' Love Seen in the Clouds

I set My rainbow in the cloud, and it shall be for the sign of the covenant between Me and the earth. . . . The waters shall never again become a flood to destroy all flesh. Gen. 9:13-15.

Some time ago, we were favored with a view of the most glorious rainbow we ever beheld. We have often visited galleries of art and have admired the skill displayed by the artist in paintings representing God's great bow of promise. . . .

As we look upon this bow, the seal and sign of God's promise to us that the tempest of His wrath should no more desolate our world by the waters of a flood, we contemplate that other than finite eyes are looking upon this glorious sight. Angels rejoice as they gaze upon this precious token of God's love to us. The world's Redeemer looks upon it, for it was through His instrumentality that this bow was made to appear in the heavens as a token or covenant of promise to us. God Himself looks upon the bow in the clouds and remembers His everlasting covenant between Himself and us.

After the fearful exhibition of God's avenging power in the destruction of the Old World by a flood had passed, He knew that those who had been saved from the general ruin would have their fears awakened whenever the clouds should gather, the thunders roll, and the lightnings flash, and that the sound of the tempest and the pouring out of the waters from the heavens would strike terror to their hearts, for fear that another flood was coming upon them. . . .

The family of Noah looked with admiration and reverential awe mingled with joy upon this sign of God's mercy which spanned the heavens. The bow represents Christ's love which encircles the earth and reaches unto the highest heavens, connecting humanity with God and linking earth with heaven.

As we gaze upon the beautiful sight, we may be joyful in God, assured that He Himself is looking upon this token of His covenant, and that as He looks upon it He remembers the children of earth, to whom it was given. Their afflictions, perils, and trials are not hidden from Him. We may rejoice in hope, for the bow of God's covenant is over us. He will never forget the children of His care. How difficult for the mind of finite human beings to take in the peculiar love and tenderness of God and His matchless condescension when He said, "I will look upon the bow in the cloud, and remember thee."—*Review and Herald,* Feb. 26, 1880.

God Revealed in Nature and Jesus

For since the creation of the world His invisible attributes are clearly seen, being understood by the things that are made, even His eternal power and Godhead. Rom. 1:20.

The created works of God are a pictured history of ministry. The sun is doing its appointed work in ministering to all animate and inanimate nature. It causes the trees to grow and yield their blessings in fruit. It causes vegetation to flourish for the benefit of all. The moon also has its mission. It makes light in the nighttime for our happiness, and the stars also are marshaled in the heavens to minister to the enjoyment of the world. None of us can fully understand the appointment of these silent watchers, but they all have their work of ministry.

The deep waters, too, have their place in God's great plan. The mountains and the rocks are subjects for meditation, and contain lessons for the student. Everything in nature—the humblest flower and the grass that carpets the earth with its covering of green—proclaims the goodness and love of God to us. . . .

His thoughts and works are so connected with one another that we can read in nature the great love of God for a fallen world. The universe contains one great masterpiece of infinite Wisdom in the innumerable diversities of His great works, which in their matchless variety form a perfect whole.

By close investigation, God's innumerable providences in the natural world are found to have connection one with another, and in tracing these links in the chain of Providence we are led to become better acquainted with the great Center. This is a truth worthy of our careful study. Jesus Christ is the one great Unity; He possesses the attributes that harmonize all diversities. And He, the Gift above all others, was given to our world to give expression to the mind and character of God, that every intelligent being who will may see God in the revelation of His Son.

All these things were given by God to the human family. . . . Have you looked upon God's created works as prepared by His hand to minister to the happiness of the human family? . . .

There is a precious reward awaiting those who are faithful in their ministry. They will have a home in the mansions that Christ has gone to prepare for them that love Him and wait for His appearing.—*Youth's Instructor,* Aug. 19, 1897.

Hidden Treasure

He who hears My word and believes in Him who sent Me has everlasting life, and shall not come into judgment, but has passed from death into life. John 5:24.

The sayings of Christ are to be valued not merely in accordance with the measure of our understanding; they are to be considered in the important bearing which Christ Himself gave them. He took the old truths, of which He Himself was the originator, and placed them before His hearers in heaven's own light. And how different was their representation! What a flood of meaning and brightness and spirituality was brought in by their explanation! . . .

The rich treasures of truth, opened before the people, attracted and charmed them. They were in marked contrast with the spiritless, lifeless expositions of the Old Testament Scriptures by the rabbis. And the miracles which Jesus wrought kept constantly before His hearers the honor and glory of God. He seemed to them a messenger direct from heaven, for He spoke not to their ears only, but to their hearts. As He stood forth in His humility, yet in dignity and majesty, as one born to command, a power attended Him; hearts were melted into tenderness. An earnest desire was created to be in His presence, to listen to the voice of Him who uttered truth with such solemn melody. . . .

Every miracle wrought by Christ convinced some of His true character. Had someone in the common walks of life done the same works that Christ did, all would have declared that person to be working by the power of God. But there were those who did not receive the light of heaven, and they set themselves more determinedly against this evidence. . . .

It was not the absence of external honor and riches and glory that caused the Jews to reject Jesus. The Sun of Righteousness, shining amid the moral darkness in such distinct rays, revealed the contrast between sin and holiness, purity and defilement, and such light was not welcome to them. . . .

The teachings of Christ, in precept and example, were the sowing of the seed afterward to be cultivated by His disciples. The testimony of these fishermen was to be referred to as the highest authority by all the nations of the world.—*Review and Herald,* July 12, 1898.

Christ Connects Heaven to Earth

As the Father gave Me commandment, so I do. John 14:31.

Those who have experienced the blessing of God should be the most grateful of persons.

They should send up to God words of thanksgiving because Christ came in the likeness of sinful flesh, clothing His divinity with humanity in order that He might bring before the world the perfection of God in His own character. He came to represent God, not as a stern judge, but as a loving father. . . .

The Lord Jesus is an example in all things. By the works which He did He made it plain that He was in council with the Father and that He was in every move fulfilling the eternal purposes of God. In spirit, in works, in His whole earthly history, He revealed the mind and purpose of God toward His heritage among humanity. In His obedience to the law of God, He exemplified in His human nature the fact that the law is a transcript of divine perfection. In the gift of Christ to the world God would overwhelm fallen men and women with a marvelous manifestation of His great love wherewith He has loved us; but while He would that all should come to repentance, the declaration no less expressed His character, that He will by no means clear the guilty. Should He give the least sanction to sin, His throne would be corrupted. . . .

All who receive Jesus Christ as their personal Savior also are provided with heavenly protection and heavenly light, for the angels of God are sent to minister to those who shall be heirs of salvation. The representation given to Jacob of a ladder whose base rested upon earth and whose top reached to the throne of God, whereon ascended and descended the angels of heaven, is a representation of the plan of salvation. Had the ladder failed to connect with earth by one inch, the connection between earth and heaven would have been broken, and all would have been hopelessly lost. But the ladder is planted firmly upon the earth, that heaven may connect with earth and that the fallen human family be redeemed and rescued. Christ is the ladder that Jacob saw, whose base is upon the earth and whose topmost round reaches the throne of God. . . . Through Christ heavenly intelligences may communicate with human agents.—*Signs of the Times,* Apr. 11, 1895.

God and Mammon

No one can serve two masters; for either he will hate the one and love the other, or else he will be loyal to the one and despise the other. You cannot serve God and mammon. Matt. 6:24.

Satan presents the same temptations today that he presented to Adam, and to Jesus, the second Adam, who overcame him and made it possible for us to overcome.... Our efforts and Christ's power will bring us off conquerors....

All heaven is watching with interest to see what use we are making of God's entrusted talents. If we lay up treasure in heaven, we shall use the Lord's goods to advance His cause, to save souls, and to bless humanity, and all that is so used the Lord will place to our account in the bank that never fails. When the heart loves God supremely, property is no hindrance to advancement in the Christian warfare, because the consecrated followers of Jesus will discern the best investments to make, and will use their wealth to bless the children of God.

The constant employment of the capabilities to amass wealth on earth binds us to earth. We become slaves to mammon. When wealth increases, the idolatrous heart becomes forgetful of God, and grows self-secure and satisfied. Religious duties are neglected. There is an impatience manifested under restraint, and we become self-sufficient.... The world comes in between the soul and heaven. Our eyes are blinded by the "god of this world," so that we cannot discern or appreciate the value of eternal things....

Motives stronger, and agencies more powerful, could never be brought into operation—the enjoyment of heaven, the exceeding rewards for right-doing, the society of angels, the communion and love of God and His Son, the elevation and extension of all our powers throughout eternal ages; and it hath not "entered into the heart of man, the things which God hath prepared for them that love him" (1 Cor. 2:9). Are these not mighty incentives and encouragements to urge us to give our heart's loving service to our Creator and Redeemer? ...

Shall we not regard the great mercy of God? Let us place ourselves in right relation to Him who has loved us with amazing love, and avail ourselves of the great privilege of becoming instruments in His hands, that we may cooperate with the ministering angels and be colaborers with God and Christ.—*Bible Echo* (Australia), Feb. 15, 1889.

What Must I Do to Be Saved?

*You did not choose Me, but I chose you and appointed you that you should
go and bear fruit, and that your fruit should remain. John 15:16.*

Christ ever rebuked the Pharisees for their self-righteousness. . . . They
were exalted to heaven in point of opportunity, in having the
Scriptures, in knowing the true God, but their hearts were not filled with
thankfulness to God for His great goodness toward them. They came forth
filled with spiritual pride, and their theme was self—"myself, my feelings,
my knowledge, my ways." Their own attainments became the standard by
which they measured others. . . .

Let every disciple of Christ inquire in all humility of mind, What must I
do to be saved? If we sincerely desire to understand, we shall know. It is not
because of our riches, our knowledge, our superiority of position, that Jesus
loves us and blesses us, but because we believe in Him as our personal
Savior. Jesus loved us while we were yet sinners, but having chosen us He
says He has ordained us to go and bring forth fruit. Has each one something to do? Certainly, everyone that is yoked up with Christ must bear His
burden, work in His lines. . . . The life of Christ's pardoning love in the soul
is as a well of water springing up unto eternal life. If the well of water is in
the heart, then the entire life will reveal the fact, and the refreshing grace
of God will be made manifest.

Religion is not simply to have joyous feelings, to be conscious of having
privileges and light, to have rapturous emotions, while expending all the
energies to keep a balance in the Christian life, while doing nothing for the
salvation of souls. Religion is doing the words of Christ; it is standing as
faithful sentinels, not doing to earn salvation, but doing because, all undeserving, you have received the heavenly gift. Religion is to work out God's
plans, to cooperate with the intelligences of heaven. . . .

If we will follow on to know the Lord, our views will broaden. They will
not be bound about by self. We should pray the Lord to enlarge our understanding, so that we may not only understand that Jesus Christ is our substitute and surety, but that we belong to Christ as His purchased possession.
Paul says, "Ye are bought with a price," and draws this conclusion,
"Therefore glorify God in your body, and in your spirit, which are
God's."—*Signs of the Times,* Dec. 17, 1894.

Gathering or Scattering

He who is not with Me is against Me, and he who does not gather with Me scatters abroad. Matt. 12:30.

Half-converted men and women make halfhearted Christians. They are fruitless trees. On them Christ looks in vain for fruit; He finds nothing but leaves. . . .

If Christ and self could be served at the same time, a large number would join the ranks of those who are journeying heavenward. But it is not for such as these that Jesus calls. His cause does not need such adherents.

Christ's true followers use their knowledge to make others the recipients of His grace. With their lamps filled with holy oil, they go forth to give light to those in darkness. Such workers see many souls turning to the Lord. New truths continually unfold to them, and as they receive, they impart.

Those for whom the fetters of sin have been broken, who have sought the Lord with brokenness of heart and have obtained answer to their yearning requests for righteousness, are never cold and spiritless. They realize that they have a part to act in the work of soul-saving. They watch and pray and work for the salvation of souls. Molded and fashioned by the Holy Spirit, they gain depth and breadth and stability of Christian character. They gain enduring spiritual happiness. Walking in Christ's footsteps, they become identified with Him in His self-sacrificing plans. Such Christians are not cold and unimpressible. Their hearts are filled with unselfish love for sinners. They put away from them all worldly ambition, all self-seeking. Contact with the deep things of God makes them more and more like their Savior. They exult in His triumphs; they are filled with His joy. Day by day they are growing up to the full stature of men and women in Christ Jesus. . . .

By the way in which we do the work Christ has given us to do in His absence, we decide our future destiny. . . . Christ, the Master of the household, has gone to prepare for us mansions in the heavenly city. We are waiting for His return. Let us honor Him in His absence by doing with faithfulness the work He has placed in our hands. Waiting, watching, working, we are to prepare for His return.—*Signs of the Times,* July 9, 1902.

Asking to Give

The Son of Man did not come to be served, but to serve. Mark 10:45.

Christ was continually receiving from the Father, that He might communicate to us. "The word which ye hear," He said, "is not mine, but the Father's which sent me." . . . Not for Himself, but for others, He lived and thought and prayed. From hours spent with God He came forth morning by morning to bring the light of heaven to those who heard Him. Daily He received a fresh baptism of the Holy Spirit. In the early hours of the new day the Lord awakened Him from His slumbers, and His soul and His lips were anointed with grace, that He might impart to others. His words were given Him fresh from the heavenly courts, words that He might speak in season to the weary and oppressed. . . .

Christ's disciples were much impressed by His prayers and by His habit of communion with God. One day after a short absence from their Lord, they found Him absorbed in supplication. Seemingly unconscious of their presence, He continued praying aloud. The hearts of the disciples were deeply moved. As He ceased praying, they exclaimed, "Lord, teach us to pray." In answer Christ repeated the Lord's Prayer, as He had given it in the Sermon on the Mount. . . .

"Which of you," He said, "shall have a friend, and shall go unto him at midnight, and say unto him, Friend, lend me three loaves; for a friend of mine in his journey is come to me, and I have nothing to set before him?" . . .

Here Christ represents the petitioner as asking that he may give again. . . . In like manner the disciples were to seek blessings from God. In the feeding of the multitude and in the sermon on the bread from heaven, Christ had opened to them their work as His representatives. They were to give the bread of life to the people. . . . Souls that were hungering for the bread of life would come to them, and they would feel themselves to be destitute and helpless. They must receive spiritual food, or they would have nothing to impart. But they were not to turn one soul away unfed. Christ directs them to the source of supply. . . . And would not God, who had sent His servants to feed the hungry, supply their need for His own work?—*Review and Herald,* Aug. 11, 1910.

For the Mission Fields

Go therefore and make disciples of all the nations, baptizing them.
Matt. 28:19.

Our churches are often appealed to for gifts and offerings to aid missionary enterprises in the home field and to sustain the missionary work abroad. . . . From every church prayers should ascend to God for an increase of devotion and liberality. Those whose hearts are knit with the heart of Christ will be glad to do what they can to help the cause of God. They will rejoice in the continual expansion and advancement, which means larger and more frequently given offerings.

We may well feel that it is a privilege to be laborers together with God by giving of our means to set in operation that which will carry out His purposes in the world. All who possess that Spirit of Christ will have a tender, sympathetic heart and an open, generous hand. Nothing can be really selfish that has Christ for its absorbing object. . . .

Consider the necessities of our mission fields throughout the world. Our missionaries labor hard and earnestly, but often they are greatly hindered in their work because the treasury is empty, and they cannot be given facilities necessary for the greatest success of their labor. May God help those who have been entrusted with this world's goods to awaken to His design and to their individual responsibilities. God says to them, I have put you in possession of My goods that you may trade upon them to carry forward the Christian missions that are to be established far and near. . . .

Not all can go as missionaries to foreign lands, but all can do the work waiting for them in their own neighborhood. All can give of their means for the carrying forward of foreign missionary work. . . .

God will encourage His faithful stewards who are ready to put all their energies and God-given endowments to the very best use. As all learn the lesson of faithfully rendering to God what is His due, He through His providence will enable some to bring princely offerings. He will enable others to make smaller offerings; and the small and the large gifts are acceptable to Him if given with an eye single to His glory. "He that ministereth seed to the sower both minister bread for your food, and multiply your seed sown, and increase the fruits of your righteousness; being enriched in every thing to all bountifulness, which causeth through us thanksgiving to God."—
Review and Herald, Apr. 18, 1912.

Privilege of Giving

As each one has received a gift, minister it to one another, as good stewards of the manifold grace of God. 1 Peter 4:10.

The Lord has made men and women His agents, and with hearts filled with the love of Jesus, they are to cooperate with Him in turning human beings from error to truth. God blesses the earth with sunshine and showers. He causes the earth to bring forth its plenteous treasures for the use of all. The Lord has made us His almoner to dispense His heavenly gifts by bringing souls to the truth. Will my brethren in America [written from Australia in 1895] inquire how the precious, saving truth reached them when they were in darkness? Men and women brought their tithes and offerings unto God, and as means filled the treasury, laborers were sent out to advance the work. This same process must be repeated if souls in darkness are reached in this day. . . .

The necessities of the work now demand a greater outlay than ever before. The Lord calls upon His people to make every effort to curtail their expenses. . . . Let the money that has been devoted to the gratification of self flow into the Lord's treasury to sustain those who are working to save perishing souls. . . .

The Lord is soon to come. We must work while the day lasts, for the night is coming in which no one can work. Oh, many, many have lost the spirit of self-denial and sacrifice. They have been burying their money in temporal possessions. There are souls whom God has blessed, whom He is testing to see what response they will make to His benefits. . . . Make haste, brethren, you now have opportunity to be honest with God; delay not. For your soul's sake no longer rob God in tithes and offerings. . . .

As the plan of redemption begins and ends with a gift, so it is to be carried forward. The same spirit of sacrifice which purchased salvation for us will dwell in the hearts of all who become partakers of the heavenly gift. Says Peter, "As every man hath received the gift, even so minister the same one to another, as good stewards of the manifold grace of God." Said Jesus to His disciples as He sent them forth, "Freely ye have received, freely give." . . .

Let all do everything in their power to help, both by their means and by their prayers, to carry the burden for souls for whom the ministers are laboring.—*General Conference Bulletin*, May 30, 1897.

They Shall See His Face

They shall see His face, and His name shall be on their foreheads.
Revelation 22:4.

When Moses pleaded with God, saying, "I beseech thee, shew me thy glory," God said, "Thou canst not see my face: for there shall no man see me, and live." . . . Moses could not behold the revelation of the glory of the face of God, and live; but there is a promise given to us, "They shall see his face."

When Moses came down from the mount where he had been given a view of the glory of God, his face was so lighted up that Aaron and all the children of Israel "were afraid to come nigh him." . . .

We cannot now see the glory of God; but it is only by receiving Him here that we shall be able by and by to see Him face to face. God would have us keep our eyes fixed on Him, that we may lose sight of the things of this world. . . .

Today by our associations, by our life, by our character, we are choosing whom we will have as our king. Heavenly intelligences are seeking to draw us to Christ. . . . Though we are transgressors of the law of God, if we repent in faith, God can work through us the works of Christ. . . .

When Christ ascended on high, He sent His representative as a Comforter. This Representative is by our side wherever we may be—a watcher and a witness to all that is said and done—standing ready to protect us from the assaults of the enemy if we will but place ourselves under His protection. But we must act our part, and then God will act His part. When we are brought into trial and affliction for His sake, the Comforter will stand by our side, bringing to our remembrance the words and teachings of Christ.

Is your name written in the book of life? Only by looking to Jesus, the Lamb of God, and following in His steps, can you prepare to meet God. Follow Him, and you will one day walk the golden streets of the city of God. . . .

Those who consecrate their lives to the service of God will live with Him through the ceaseless ages of eternity. . . .

He takes them as His children, saying, Enter ye into the joy of your Lord. The crown of immortality is placed on the brow of the overcomers.—*Youth's Instructor,* Aug. 20, 1896.

The Great Supper

A certain man gave a great supper and invited many, and sent his servant at supper time to say to those who were invited, "Come, for all things are now ready." Luke 14:16, 17. (Read Luke 14:16-24.)

This parable correctly represents the condition of many professing to believe the present truth. The Lord has sent them an invitation to come to the supper which He has prepared for them at great cost to Himself, but worldly interests look to them of greater importance than the heavenly treasure. They are invited to take part in the things of eternal value, but their farms, their cattle, and their home interest, seem of so much greater importance than obedience to the heavenly invitation that they overpower every divine attraction, and these earthly things are made the excuse for their disobedience to the heavenly command, "Come; for all things are now ready." . . .

The very blessings which God has given to these individuals, to prove them, to see if they will render "unto God the things that are God's," they use as an excuse that they cannot obey the claims of truth. They have grasped their earthly treasure in their arms and say, I must take care of these things; I must not neglect the things of this life; these things are mine. Thus the hearts of these people have become as unimpressible as the beaten highway. . . .

Their hearts are so overgrown with thorns and cares of this life that heavenly things can find no place. Jesus invites the weary and heavy laden with promises of rest if they will come to Him. . . . He would have them lay aside the heavy burdens of worldly cares and perplexities, and take His yoke, which is self-denial and sacrifice for others. This burden will prove to be light. Those who refuse to accept the relief Christ offers them, and will continue to wear the galling yoke of selfishness, tasking their souls to the utmost in plans to accumulate money for selfish gratification, have not experienced the peace and rest found in bearing the yoke of Christ and lifting the burdens of self-denial and disinterested benevolence which Christ has borne in their behalf. . . .

Souls for whom Christ died might be saved by their personal effort and godly example. . . . But the precious light is hid under a bushel, and it gives no light to those who are in the house.—*Review and Herald*, Aug. 25, 1874.

Two Sons

A man had two sons, and he came to the first and said, "Son, go, work today in my vineyard." He answered and said, "I will not," but afterward he regretted it and went. Then he came to the second and said likewise. And he answered and said, "I go, sir," but he did not go. Which of the two did the will of his father? Matt. 21:28-31.

In the parable the son who refused to go represented the Gentile world, and the class who said, "I go, sir" represented the Pharisees. Christ had just cleansed the temple of those who defiled it with forbidden traffic. Divinity had flashed through humanity, and the people had seen the glory and power of God manifested before them. . . . As He had traveled toward Jerusalem, the multitude had spread their garments in the way and had strewn His path with palm branches, and they had proclaimed His praises, singing, "Hosanna to the son of David." Though the rejoicing ones had not dared to carry their acclamations to the very gate of the temple, fearing the priests and rulers, the children had taken up the song, and were praising God in the temple, and shouting, "Hosanna to the son of David." . . .

The Gentile world would accept the truth; but those who had so great light and such wonderful privileges, to whom had been granted both temporal and spiritual blessings, refused the message of salvation. They had professed to be the people of God. They had said, "We go, sir," but they failed of doing their Father's will. . . .

When the invitation of heaven has been brought to your ears, have you said, "Yes, Lord, I believe the truth," yet by the actions of your life shown that you did not believe? Have you brought it into your heart? Has its transforming power taken hold upon your soul? Has its sanctifying grace been brought into your character? How is it with you? . . .

It is the privilege of everyone to say, "I will carry out my Captain's orders to the very letter, feeling or no feeling. . . . I will say, 'What are my orders? What is the line of my duty? What says the Master to me? . . . What is my position before God?'" Just as soon as we come into right relations to God, we shall understand our duty and do it, and we shall not think the good things we do entitle us to salvation. . . .

The question is not, How will you stand in the day of trouble, or at some future time, but how is it with your soul today? Will you go to work today?—*Review and Herald,* Apr. 9, 1889.

The Barren Fig Tree

Having a form of godliness but denying its power. 2 Tim. 3:5.
(Read Matt. 21:19-21.)

The treatment of the barren fig tree by the Savior of the world shows how all pretenders to godliness will be treated. . . . This tree represents the Jews, who refused to respond to the love of Christ. Despite all the privileges and opportunities granted them, they brought forth only briers and thorns—no fruit to the glory of God. This blighted tree was a parable to the house of Israel—a most impressive lesson. It is also a lesson to the professed followers of Christ in every age. Reaching through all time, it speaks in unmistakable language to all formalists and boasters of godliness who stand forth to the world with high profession but are utterly devoid of that vital piety which alone God recognizes as fruit. . . .

Like the barren fig tree, many flaunt their foliage-covered branches before the Lord, proudly claiming to be His commandment-keeping people, while the heart-searching God finds them destitute of fruit. . . .

We learn from the Sacred Record that this tree, upon which hung not a redeeming cluster of fruit, was clothed with green foliage. Notice the words, "Having a form of godliness, but denying the power thereof." The doom of the fruitless fig tree has an application to individual professors who manifest the natural tendencies of the unrenewed heart, and contradict their faith by their daily life. They do not represent to the world the character of Christ, because they have not Christ in them.

Our Savior never turned away from the truly penitent, no matter how great their guilt. But He hates all hypocrisy and vain display. . . .

Fruitless professors, sad indeed is your fate; for the open sinner stands in a more favorable position in the sight of God. The blight of God's curse is upon that class who hide the deformity of their lives under a profession of godliness. John, that bold, undaunted reprover of sin, who came to prepare the way for Christ's first advent, thus addressed the multitude that flocked to hear him: "Therefore every tree which bringeth not forth good fruit is hewn down, and cast into the fire."—*Review and Herald,* January 11, 1881.

I Have Many Things to Say Unto You

I still have many things to say to you, but you cannot bear them now.
However, when He, the Spirit of truth, has come, He will
guide you into all truth. John 16:12, 13.

The Lord Jesus had precious truth to open before His disciples, but He could not unfold it to their minds until they were in a condition to comprehend the significance of what He desired to teach. . . .

Though He unfolded great and wonderful things to the minds of His disciples, He left many things unsaid that could not be comprehended by them. At His last meeting with them before His death, He said, "I have yet many things to say unto you, but ye cannot bear them now." . . . Earthly ideas, temporal things, occupied so large a place in their minds, that they could not then understand the exalted nature, the holy character, of His kingdom, though He laid it out in clear lines before them. It was because of their former erroneous interpretation of the prophecies, because of human customs and traditions, presented and urged upon them by the priests, that their minds had become confused and were hardened to truth.

What was it that Jesus withheld because they could not comprehend it? It was the more spiritual, glorious truths concerning the plan of redemption. The words of Christ, which the Comforter would recall to their minds after His ascension, led them to more careful thought and earnest prayer that they might comprehend His words and give them to the world. Only the Holy Spirit could enable them to appreciate the significance of the plan of redemption. The lessons of Christ, coming to the world through the inspired testimony of the disciples, have a significance and value far beyond that which the casual reader of the Scriptures gives them. Christ sought to make plain His lessons by means of illustrations and parables. He spoke of the truths of the Bible as a treasure hid in a field, which, when a man had found, he went and sold all that he had, and bought the field. He represents the gems of truth, not as lying directly upon the surface, but as buried deep in the ground; as hidden treasures that must be searched for. We must dig for the precious jewels of truth, as a man would dig in a mine.

In presenting the truth to others, we should follow the example of Jesus.—*Review and Herald,* Oct. 14, 1890.

Wayside Hearers

A sower went out to sow his seed. And as he sowed,
some fell by the wayside. Luke 8:5.

The great controversy between Christ, the prince of light, and Satan, the prince of darkness, is presented before us in the parable of the sower. . . . The sower is the Son of God, or the one to whom He delegates His work, for by cooperating with Christ, we are to become laborers together with God. Those who by personal ministry open to others the Scriptures are sowing the good seed, for the good seed is the Word of God. . . .

The seed sown by the wayside represents the word of God as it falls upon the heart of those who are inattentive hearers, for those who are to bring the fruit forth must meditate much upon the word of God which has been presented to them. . . . As the birds of the air are ready to catch up the seed from the wayside, so Satan is represented as ready with his unseen agencies of evil to catch away the seeds of divine truth from the heart, lest it should find a lodgment there and bring forth fruit unto eternal life. . . .

Satan and his angels are in the assembly where the gospel of the kingdom is preached. While heavenly angels also are present to minister for those who shall be heirs of salvation, the enemy is ever on the alert that he may make of no effect the influence of the truth. With an earnestness that is only equaled by his malice, he seeks to thwart the operation of the Spirit of God on the heart of the hearer, for he sees that if the truth is accepted, he has lost control of his subject, and Christ has won the victory. . . .

There are many whose hearts are as hard as the beaten pathway, and apparently it is a useless effort to present the truth to them; but while logic may fail to move, and argument be worthless to convince, let the laborer for Christ come close to such in Christlike sympathy and compassion, and it may be that the love of Christ will subdue and melt the soul into tenderness and contrition. . . .

Through the years of probation, God is testing and proving the hearts of all, that it may be seen who will find room for Jesus. The question to be answered by every soul is, Will you accept the pardoning love of God, which is a remedy for the diseases of the soul, or will you choose the enmity of Satan, and reap the terrible doom of the lost?—*Review and Herald,* May 31, 1892.

Stony-ground Hearers

Some fell on stony places, where they did not have much earth; and they immediately sprang up because they had no depth of earth. Matt. 13:5.

The seed sown upon stony ground finds little depth of soil in which to take root. The plants spring up quickly, but the tender roots cannot penetrate into the rock and find nutriment to sustain the growing plant, and it soon perishes. A large number who make a profession of religion may be represented by the stony-ground hearers. They are a class that are easily convinced, but they have only a superficial religion. . . .

There are those who receive the precious truth with joy; they are exceedingly zealous, and express amazement that all cannot see the things that are so plain to them. They urge others to embrace the doctrine that they find so satisfying. They hastily condemn the hesitating and those who carefully weigh the evidences of the truth, and consider it in all its bearings. . . . But in the time of trial, these enthusiastic persons too often falter and fail. . . .

As the roots of a plant strike down into the soil, gathering moisture and nutriment from the ground, so Christians must abide in Christ, drawing sap and nourishment from Him, as does the branch from the vine, until they cannot be turned away from the Source of their strength by trials. . . .

Stony-ground hearers may rejoice for a season, for they think that religion is something that will free them from test and from all difficulty. They have not counted the cost. . . .

The class that Jesus represents as stony-ground hearers trusted in their good works, in their good impulses, and were strong in themselves, in their own righteousness. They were not "strong in the Lord, and in the power of his might." They did not feel that eternal vigilance was the price of safety. They might have put on the whole armor of God, and have been able to stand against the wiles of the enemy. The rich and abundant promises of God were spoken for their benefit, and believing the Word of God, they might have been clothed with a "Thus saith the Lord" and been able to meet every wily device of the adversary; for when the enemy should come in like a flood, the Spirit of the Lord would have lifted up a standard against him.—*Review and Herald*, June 7, 1892.

Thorny-ground Hearers

And some fell among thorns, and the thorns sprang up and choked them.
Matt. 13:7.

In the thorns that choke the good seed, the Great Teacher would depict the dangers that are around those who hear the Word of God; for there are foes on every hand to make of no effect the precious truth of God. All that draws the affections from God, all that fills the attention so that Christ has no room in the heart, must be renounced if the seed of truth is to flourish in the soul. Jesus specifies the things that are dangerous to the soul. He says the cares of the world, and the deceitfulness of riches, and the desire for other things, choke the word, the growing spiritual seed, so that the soul does not draw nourishment from Christ, as does the branch from the vine, and the spiritual life dies from the heart. Love of the world, love of its pleasures and display, and love of other things keep the soul away from God; for those who love the world do not depend upon God for their courage, their hope, their joy. They know not what it is to have the joy of Christ, for this is the joy of leading others to the Fountain of life, of winning souls from sin to righteousness. . . .

When those who have but a partial knowledge of the truth are called upon to study some point that cuts across their preconceived opinions, they are confused. Their preconceived opinions are as thorns that choke the Word of God, and when truth is sown, and it becomes necessary to root up the thorns to give it place, they feel that everything is going from them, and they are in trouble.

There are many who have but an imperfect understanding of the character of God. They think of Him as stern and arbitrary, and when the fact is presented that God is love, it is a difficult matter for these souls to lay aside their false conceptions of God. But if they do not let the Word of truth in, rooting out the thorns, the briers will start up afresh and choke out the good Word of God; their religious experience will be dwarfed, for the evil of their hearts will overtop the tender plant of truth, and shut away the spiritual atmosphere. . . .

The law of God is the rule of God's government, and through eternal ages it will be the standard of His kingdom. . . . If we do not yield to its requirements in this life, learning to love God with all our hearts and our neighbors as ourselves, we shall meet with no change in character at the appearing of Jesus.—*Review and Herald,* June 21, 1892.

Good-ground Hearers

But others fell on good ground and yielded a crop: some a hundredfold, some sixty, some thirty. Matt. 13:8.

What an encouragement it is that the sower is not always to meet with disappointment. The seed is sometimes received into honest hearts. The hearers comprehend the truth and do not resist the Holy Spirit or refuse to receive the impression of truth upon their hearts. . . . They receive the truth into the heart, and it accomplishes its transforming work upon the character. They are not able to change their own hearts, but the Holy Spirit, through their obedience to the truth, sanctifies the soul.

The good heart does not mean a heart without sin, for the gospel is to be preached to the lost. Jesus says, "I came not to call the righteous, but sinners to repentance." Convicted sinners see themselves as transgressors in the great moral mirror, God's holy law. They look upon the Savior upon the cross of Calvary and ask why this great sacrifice was made; and the cross points to the holy law of God, which has been transgressed. It was to save the transgressor from ruin that He who was coequal with God offered up His life on Calvary. . . . The law has no power to pardon the evil-doer; but Jesus has taken the sins of the transgressor upon Himself, and as a sinner exercises faith in Him as the sacrifice, Christ imputes His own righteousness to the guilty one. There has been but one way of salvation since the days of Adam. "There is none other name under heaven given among men, whereby we must be saved." We have no reason to fear while we are looking to Jesus, believing that He is able to save all who come unto Him.

As the result of active faith in Christ we are brought into the moral warfare with the world, the flesh, and the devil. If we undertake this warfare in our own wisdom, our human ability, we shall certainly be overcome; but if we exercise living faith in Jesus, and practice godliness, we shall understand what it means to be sanctified through the truth, and we shall not be overcome in the conflict, for heavenly angels encamp around about us. Christ is the captain of our salvation. He it is who strengthens His followers for the moral conflict which they are pledged to undertake. . . .

Those who open the Scriptures and feed upon the heavenly manna become partakers of the divine nature. They have no life or experience apart from Christ. . . . They know that in character they must be like Him with whom God is well pleased.—*Review and Herald*, June 28, 1892.

Opposition May Benefit Us

But the ones that fell on the good ground are those who, having heard the
word with a noble and good heart, keep it and bear fruit with patience.
Luke 8:15.

But if the love of the world, if self-esteem or any defiling thoughts or actions, obtain the victory over us, then shall we lose confidence in Jesus,
or in ourselves? Is it because Jesus failed us and did not supply us with His
grace? No; it is because we did not do what the Lord has told us to do,
"Watch unto prayer"; "Pray always"; "Pray without ceasing."

How can your soul be in health when you shut yourself away from prayer
and have no connection with Christ, the source of all spiritual light and life
and power? We must have a constant connection with Christ, for He is our
sustenance. He is that bread which came down from heaven. Then let us be
doers of His word, and we shall have spiritual life and power. We must place
ourselves often before God as suppliants, because prayer brings the soul into
immediate contact with God through Jesus Christ. He is the Way, the Truth,
and the Life. If Christians fail, it is because they do not obey the orders of
their Captain. They are off guard; they are not Christlike. It will work disaster to the soul to neglect prayer, for you will be led to yield carelessly to
temptation. But if you do yield, do not therefore cast away your confidence
in God; lose confidence in yourself, and press closer to the side of Christ.

Christ is not to be charged with the results of the negligence and indecision. He who gave His life to save fallen men and women appreciates the
value of the soul. He will never fail of doing His part nor become discouraged. He will never leave the erring one, tempted and tried in the conflict.
"My grace is sufficient for thee." "God is faithful, who will not suffer you
to be tempted above that ye are able." He weighs and measures every trial
before He permits it to come. . . .

The opposition we meet may prove a benefit to us in many ways. If it is
well borne, it will develop virtues which would never have appeared if the
Christian had nothing to endure. And faith, patience, forbearance, heavenly
mindedness, trust in Providence, and genuine sympathy with the erring, are
the results of trial well borne. . . .

If the word is received into good and honest hearts, the stubborn soul
will be subdued, and faith, grasping the promises and relying upon Jesus,
will prove triumphant.—*Review and Herald,* June 28, 1892.

The Rich Man

The ground of a certain rich man yielded plentifully. And he thought within himself, saying, "What shall I do, since I have no room to store my crops?" Luke 12:16, 17.

This man had received everything from God. The sun had been permitted to shine upon his land; for it falls on the just and on the unjust alike. The showers of heaven fall on the evil and the good. The Lord had caused vegetation to flourish, and the fields to yield fruit, and bring to perfection an abundant harvest. The rich man was in perplexity as to what he should do with all his produce. He regarded himself as favored above others and took credit to himself for his wisdom. He had great wealth, and could not reproach himself with the sins of which many were guilty. He had obtained his goods, not by gambling, not by taking advantage of another's misfortune who had been involved in financial embarrassment and who was obliged to sell his goods below cost; but his wealth had been obtained through the providence of God in causing his land to yield abundantly. But the man revealed his selfishness, and manifested that which he did not before suspect was in his character.

He did not think of God, the great giver of all his blessings. He did not consider his accountability to God. . . . Had he loved and feared God, he would have offered up thanksgiving and bowed before God, saying, "Instruct me how to use these goods." . . .

How many hungry could have been fed, how many naked clothed, how many hearts made glad, how many prayers answered for bread and clothing, and what a melody of praise could he have caused to ascend to heaven. The Lord was answering the prayers of the poor and needy and was making abundant provision for the supply of all their wants by the blessing He had bestowed upon the rich man. But the man made suddenly so rich closed the avenues of his soul to the cry of the needy; and in place of disposing of his superabundance of goods in supplying their needs, he said to his servants, "This will I do: I will pull down my barns, and build greater; and there will I bestow *all* my fruits and my goods." . . .

He said, "I will say to my soul, Soul, thou hast much goods laid up for many years; take thine ease, eat, drink, and be merry." . . . God said unto him, "Thou fool, this night thy soul shall be required of thee."—*Review and Herald,* June 19, 1894.

The Laborers

For the kingdom of heaven is like a landowner who went out early in the morning to hire laborers for his vineyard. Now when he had agreed with the laborers for a denarius a day, he sent them into his vineyard. Matt. 20:1, 2. (Read Matt. 20:1-16.)

Christ taught by means of figures and symbols. On one occasion He spoke a parable in regard to the hiring of laborers to illustrate the way in which God deals with those who devote themselves to His service. . . .

It was the custom in Judea for men to wait at the marketplaces for someone to come and employ them; and in Europe this custom is still in vogue. Those who need help go to the marketplace to find servants that they may employ. The man in the parable is represented as going out at different hours to engage workmen. Those he hired at the earliest hour agreed to work for him for a stated sum of money, while those who were hired later left the wages they were to receive wholly to the discretion of the householder.

"So when even was come, the lord of the vineyard saith unto his steward, Call the labourers, and give them their hire, beginning from the last unto the first. And when they came that were hired about the eleventh hour, they received every man a penny. But when the first came, they supposed that they should have received more; and they likewise received every man a penny." . . .

The lesson of the laborers had a bearing upon the question about which the disciples had disputed by the way—who should be greatest in the kingdom of heaven. The world's Redeemer saw the danger that would imperil His church, and sought to arouse His people to an understanding of their position; for this parable was but a continuation of the lesson taught when Peter asked, "Behold, we have forsaken all, and followed thee; what shall we have therefore?" . . .

With implicit trust we are to stay upon God, and let the heart rest in Him without a question as to what is to be our measure of reward. . . .

Jesus would have those who are engaged in His service not [be] eager for rewards nor feel that they must receive compensation for all that they do. . . . The Lord measures the spirit, and rewards accordingly, and the pure, humble, childlike spirit of love makes the offering precious in His sight.—*Review and Herald,* July 3, 1894.

A Teacher of Righteousness

If you abide in My word, you are My disciples indeed. And you shall know the truth, and the truth shall make you free. John 8:31, 32.

Jesus says, "Learn of me; for I am meek and lowly in heart: and ye shall find rest unto your souls." Jesus was the greatest teacher the world ever knew. He presented truth in clear, forcible statements, and the illustrations He used were of the purest and highest order. . . .

In His sermon on the mount, Christ gave the true interpretation to the Old Testament Scriptures, expounding the truth that had been perverted by the rulers, the scribes, and the Pharisees. What a vast meaning does He give to the law of God! He Himself had given the law when the morning stars sang together and all the sons of God shouted for joy. Christ Himself was the foundation of the whole Jewish economy, the end of types, symbols, and sacrifices. Enshrouded in the pillar of cloud, He Himself had given specific directions to Moses for the Jewish nation, and He was the only one who could disperse the multitude of errors that through human maxims and traditions had accumulated about the truth. . . .

He set the truth on high, in order that like a light it might illuminate the moral darkness of the world. He rescued every gem of truth from the rubbish of human maxims and traditions, and exalted the truth to the throne of God from whence it had issued. . . .

His course was in such marked contrast to the course of the scribes and Pharisees and the religious teachers of that day, that they were made manifest as whited sepulchers, hypocritical pretenders to religion, who sought to exalt themselves by a profession of holiness, while within they were full of ravening and all uncleanness. They could not tolerate true holiness, true zeal for God, which was the distinguishing feature of the character of Christ; for true religion cast a reflection upon their spirit and practices. . . .

In the heart of Jesus there was hatred of nothing save sin. They could have received Him as the Messiah had He simply manifested His miracle-working power and refrained from denouncing sin, from condemning their corrupt passions, and from pronouncing the curse of God upon their idolatry; but since He would give no license to evil, though He healed the sick, opened the eyes of the blind, and raised the dead, they had nothing for the divine Teacher but bitter abuse, jealousy, envy, evil-surmising, and hatred.—*Review and Herald,* Aug. 6, 1895.

Have You Oil in Your Lamps?

Then the kingdom of heaven shall be likened to ten virgins who took their lamps and went out to meet the bridegroom. Matt. 25:1. (Read Matt. 25:13.)

Though five of these virgins are represented as wise and five as foolish, all had lamps. They had all been convicted that they must prepare for the coming of the bridegroom, and all had gained a knowledge of the truth. There was no apparent difference between the wise and the foolish until the cry was made, "Behold, the bridegroom cometh; go ye out to meet Him," but the true state of things was then developed. The wise had taken precautions to carry oil with them in their vessels, so that their lamps that were beginning to burn dimly might be replenished with oil; but the foolish had not provided for this emergency, and now they made an earnest, distressed petition to those who were wise.... They had neglected to prepare themselves to meet the bridegroom, and now turned to those who had provided themselves with oil....

In reading this parable one cannot but pity the foolish virgins and ask the question, Why is it that the wise did not divide their supply of oil? But as we make the spiritual application of the parable, we can see the reason. It is not possible for those who have faith and grace to divide their supply with those who have not. It is not possible for those who have made a thorough heart work, to impart the benefit of this to those who have done but surface work. ...All the ten virgins appeared to be ready for the coming of the bridegroom, and yet the test brought out the fact that five were unready....

The foolish virgins do not represent those who are hypocritical. They had a regard for truth, they advocated the truth, they were intending to go forth to meet the bridegroom. They are attached to those who believe the truth, and go with them, having lamps, which represent a knowledge of the truth....

Many receive the truth readily, but they fail to assimilate truth, and its influence is not abiding. They are like the foolish virgins, who had no oil in their vessels with their lamps. Oil is a symbol of the Holy Spirit, which is brought into the soul through faith in Jesus Christ. Those who earnestly search the Scriptures with much prayer, who rely upon God with firm faith, who obey His commandments, will be among those who are represented as wise virgins.—*Review and Herald,* Sept. 17, 1895.

The Unfaithful Servant

Then he who had received the one talent came and said,
"Lord, I knew you to be a hard man, reaping where you have not sown,
and gathering where you have not scattered seed. And I was afraid, and
went and hid your talent in the ground." Matt. 25:24, 25.

The teaching of this parable is plain. All the gifts of intellect or of property which anyone has are entrusted to him. They are the Lord's goods, and are to be used to His honor and glory. They are to be improved and increased by use, that the Lord may receive returns from them. But the Lord receives no returns from many talents; for, like the unfaithful servant, those to whom they are entrusted put them where they are not increased.

All in whose hearts selfishness is cherished will listen to the temptations of Satan and will act the part of the unfaithful, slothful servant. They will hide their entrusted treasure, neglecting to use their talents for the Lord. . . . They have sown sparingly, or not at all, and they will reap sparingly. But although the Lord has told them this in words too plain to be honestly misconstrued, they cherish dissatisfaction in their hearts, and complain that the Lord is a hard master, that they are dealt hardly and unjustly with. . . .

Today this work is being done by many who claim to know God. They speak in a repining, complaining manner of the Lord's requirements. They do not directly charge God with being unjust, but they complain of everything touching the question of using their influence or their means in His service. Whoever they may be, if those to whom the Lord has entrusted His gifts do not make the best use of their endowments, if they do not cooperate with the heavenly angels by trying to be a blessing to their fellow human beings, they will receive the denunciation from the Lord, Thou wicked and slothful servant. You had My gifts to use, but you neglected to use them. . . . You, who thought you knew so much, wickedly misrepresented Me and led others to think that I was unjustly hard and exacting. "Cast ye the unprofitable servant into outer darkness; there shall be weeping and gnashing of teeth." In that day these unfaithful servants will see their mistake and will realize that by selfishly putting their talents where the Lord could receive no increase from them, they have not only lost all they had but have lost also the eternal riches.—*Review and Herald*, Jan. 5, 1897.

What Can Be

To everyone who has, more will be given, and he will have abundance;
but from him who does not have, even what he has will be taken away.
Matt. 25:29.

Those who accept Jesus as their personal Savior will live lives of humility, patience, and love. They did not give themselves to the Lord for the sake of the profit they should receive. They have become one with Christ, as Christ is one with the Father, and daily they receive their reward in being partakers of the humility, the reproach, the self-denial, and the self-sacrifice of Christ. They find their joy in keeping the Lord's ordinances. In true service they find hope, and peace, and comfort; and with faith and courage they go forward in the path of obedience, following Him who gave His life for them. By their consecration and devotion they reveal to the world the truth of the words, "I live; yet not I, but Christ liveth in me."

"They that feared the Lord," writes the prophet Malachi, "spake often one to another: and the Lord hearkened, and heard it, and a book of remembrance was written before him for them that feared the Lord, and that thought upon his name." Were the words spoken, words of complaint, of faultfinding, of self-sympathy? No; in contrast to those who speak against God, those who fear Him speak words of courage, of thankfulness, and of praise. They do not cover the altar of God with tears and lamentations; they come with faces lighted up with the beams of the Sun of Righteousness, and praise God for His goodness.

Such words make all heaven rejoice. Those who utter them may be poor in worldly possessions, but by faithfully giving to God the portion He claims, they acknowledge their indebtedness to Him. Self-serving does not make up the chapters of their life history. In love and gratitude, with songs of joy upon their lips, they bring their offerings to God, saying as did David, Of Thine own we freely give Thee. "And they shall be mine, saith the Lord of hosts, in that day when I make up my jewels; and I will spare them, as a man spareth his own son that serveth him." . . .

Those who truly serve God will fear Him, but not as did the unfaithful servant, who hid his talent in the earth because he was afraid the Lord would receive His own. They will fear to dishonor their Maker by failing to improve their talents.—*Review and Herald*, Jan. 5, 1897.

Captivating Words

No man ever spoke like this Man! John 7:46.

The educated were charmed with Christ's teaching, and the uneducated were always profited, for He appealed to their understanding. His illustrations were taken from the things of daily life, and although they were simple, they had in them a wonderful depth of meaning. The fowls of the air, the lilies of the field, the seed, the shepherd and his sheep—with these objects, Christ illustrated immortal truth; and ever afterward when His hearers chanced to see these things in nature, they recalled His words. Christ's illustrations constantly repeated His lessons.

Christ always used the most simple language, yet His words were received by deep, unprejudiced thinkers, for they were words that tested their wisdom. Spiritual things should always be presented in simple language even though learned men are being addressed, for such are generally ignorant regarding spiritual things. The simplest language is the most eloquent. . . . Christ's words, so comforting and cheering to those that listened to them, are for us today. As a faithful shepherd knows and cares for his sheep, so Christ cares for His children. . . . Christ knows His sheep intimately, and the suffering and helpless are objects of His special care. . . .

Christ did not design that His words should return to Him void. . . . He Himself wrote nothing; but the Holy Spirit brought all His words and acts to the remembrance of His disciples, that they might be recorded for our benefit. Christ's instruction was given with the greatest clearness. There was no need for anyone to misunderstand. But the scribes and Pharisees . . . misconstrued and misapplied His words. The utterances which were the bread of life to starving souls were bitterness to the Jewish rulers. . . .

In His sermon on the mount, Christ spoke as though He knew that the scribes and Pharisees believed the Old Testament. They were in that gathering, and the disciples were close beside their beloved Teacher. There Christ declared, "Except your righteousness shall exceed the righteousness of the scribes and Pharisees, ye shall in no case enter into the kingdom of heaven." By His words He condemned their formalism and hypocrisy. And though applying directly to those before Him, these words apply also to those of this age who do not the will of God. They are far-reaching, and come sounding down the ages to our time.—*Review and Herald,* May 18, 1897.

The Vine and the Branches

I am the true vine, and My Father is the vinedresser. John 15:1.

In His lessons, Christ did not aspire to high-flown, imaginary things. He came to teach, in the simplest manner, truths that were of vital importance, that even the class whom He called babes might understand them. And yet, in His simplest imagery there was a depth and beauty that the most educated minds could not exhaust. . . .

The vine had often been used as a symbol of Israel, and the lesson Christ now gave His disciples was drawn from this. He might have used the graceful palm to represent Himself. The lofty cedar that was towering toward the skies, or the strong oak that spreads its branches and lifts them heavenward, He might have used to represent the stability and integrity of those who are followers of Christ. But instead of this, He took the vine, with its clinging tendrils, to represent Himself and His relation to His true followers.

"I am the true vine, and my Father is the husbandman."

On the hills of Palestine our heavenly Father planted a goodly Vine, and He Himself was the Husbandman. It had no remarkable form that would at first sight give an impression of its value. It appeared to come up as a root out of dry ground, and attracted but little attention. But when attention was called to the plant, it was by some declared to be of heavenly origin. The people of Nazareth stood entranced as they saw its beauty; but when they received the idea that it would stand more gracefully and attract more attention than themselves, they wrestled to uproot the precious plant, and cast it over the wall. The people of Jerusalem took the plant, and bruised it, and trampled it under their unholy feet. Their thought was to destroy it forever. But the heavenly Husbandman never lost sight of His plant. After the people thought that they had killed it, He took it, and replanted it on the other side of the wall. He hid it from earthly view. . . .

Every branch that bears fruit is a living representative of the vine, for it bears the same fruit as the vine. . . . Every branch will show whether or not it has life; for where there is life, there is growth. There is a continual communication of the life-giving properties of the vine, and this is demonstrated by the fruit which the branches bear.

As the graft receives life when united to the vine, so the sinner partakes of the divine nature when in connection with Christ. Finite men and women are united with the infinite God.—*Review and Herald,* Nov. 2, 1897.

The Pearl of Great Price

*Again, the kingdom of heaven is like a merchant seeking beautiful
pearls, who, when he had found one pearl of great price, went and
sold all that he had and bought it. Matt. 13:45, 46.*

By comparing the kingdom of heaven to a pearl, Christ desired to lead
every soul to appreciate that pearl above all else. The possession of the
pearl, which means the possession of a personal Savior, is the symbol of true
riches. It is a treasure above every earthly treasure.

Christ is ready to receive all who come to Him in sincerity. He is our
only hope, our Alpha and Omega. He is our sun and shield, our wisdom,
our sanctification, our righteousness. Only by His power can our hearts be
kept in the love of God. . . .

On one occasion Christ warned His disciples to beware how they cast
their pearls before those who had not discernment to appreciate their
value. . . . "Give not that which is holy unto the dogs," He said, "neither
cast ye your pearls before swine, lest they trample them under their feet, and
turn again and rend you." . . .

When people show themselves unimpressionable, unable to appreciate the
pearl of great price; when they deal dishonestly with God and with others;
when they show that the fruit they bear is the fruit of the forbidden tree, beware lest, by connecting with them, you lose your connection with God. . . .

Truth as it is in Jesus sets us right and keeps us so. The truth is an anchor
to the soul, both sure and steadfast. But the truth is no truth to those who
do not obey it. When men and women drift away from the principles of
truth, they always betray sacred trust. Let every soul, in whatever sphere of
action, make sure that the truth is implanted in the heart by the power of
the Spirit of God. Unless this is made certain, those who preach the Word
will betray holy trusts. Physicians will make shipwreck of the faith. Lawyers,
judges, senators, will become corrupted, and yielding to bribery, will allow
themselves to be bought and sold. Those who do not walk in the light as
Christ is in the light are blind leaders of the blind, "Clouds they are without
water, carried about of winds; trees whose fruit withereth, without fruit,
twice dead, plucked up by the roots."—*Review and Herald*, Aug. 1, 1899.

How Often Shall I Forgive?

Jesus said to him, "I do not say to you, up to seven times, but up to seventy times seven." Matt. 18:22. (Read Matt. 18:15-35.)

Then came Peter to him, and said, Lord, how oft shall my brother sin against me, and I forgive him? till seven times? Jesus saith unto him, I say not unto thee, Until seven times: but, Until seventy times seven. . . .

"The kingdom of heaven [is] likened unto a certain king, which would take account of his servants. And when he had begun to reckon, one was brought unto him, which owed him ten thousand talents. But forasmuch as he had not to pay, his lord commanded him to be sold, and his wife, and children, and all that he had, and payment to be made. The servant therefore fell down, and worshipped him, saying, Lord, have patience with me, and I will pay thee all. Then the lord of that servant was moved with compassion, and loosed him, and forgave him the debt.

"But the same servant went out, and found one of his fellowservants, which owed him an hundred pence: and he laid hands on him, and took him by the throat, saying, Pay me that thou owest. And his fellowservant fell down at his feet, and besought him, saying, Have patience with me, and I will pay thee all. And he would not." . . .

This parable is designed to show the spirit of tenderness and compassion which we should manifest for others. The pardon of this king represents a pardon that is supernatural—a divine forgiveness of all sin. Christ is represented by the king who, moved with compassion, forgave the debt of his servant. . . .

When the debtor pleaded for delay with the promise, "Have patience with me, and I will pay thee all," the sentence was revoked; the whole debt was canceled, and he was soon given an opportunity to pattern after the master who had forgiven him. . . . But he who had been so mercifully treated dealt with his fellow laborer in an altogether different manner. . . .

The lesson to be learned is that we must have the spirit of true forgiveness, even as Christ forgives sinners, who can in no case pay their enormous debt. We are to bear in mind that Christ has paid an infinite price for erring human beings, and we are to treat them as Christ's purchased possession.—*Review and Herald,* Jan. 3, 1899.

The Marriage of the King's Son

The kingdom of heaven is like a certain king who arranged a marriage for his son, and sent out his servants to call those who were invited to the wedding; and they were not willing to come. Matt 22:2, 3. (Read Matt 22:1-14.)

The king sent his messengers first to those who were called his chosen people. But these, wholly intent on securing worldly gain, sent in their refusal, saying, "I pray thee have me excused." . . .

When the class that were first called refused the invitation, the king sent his messengers into the highways, where were found those who were not so deeply absorbed in the work of buying and selling, planting and building. . . .

"And when the king came in to see the guests, he saw there a man which had not on a wedding garment: and he saith unto him, Friend, how camest thou in hither not having a wedding garment? And he was speechless. Then said the king to the servants, Bind him hand and foot, and take him away, and cast him into outer darkness; for there shall be weeping and gnashing of teeth." . . .

There are those who come in to enjoy the privileges of the banquet of truth who have not eaten the flesh and drunk the blood of the Son of God. They claim to believe and teach the Word to others, but they work the works of unrighteousness. . . .

The invitation neglected by those who had first been bidden was sent to another class. It was given to the Gentile world. And it was first to be proclaimed in "the highways"—to those who had an active part in the world's work, to the leaders and teachers among humanity. . . .

Those who give the last message of mercy to a fallen world are not to pass by the ministers. God's servants are to approach them as those who have a deep interest in their welfare, and then plead for them in prayer. . . .

Lest we should think only of the great and gifted, to the neglect of the poorer classes, those who are in humble circumstances, Christ in the parable of the great supper instructs His messengers to go also to those in the byways and hedges, to the poor and lowly of this earth. . . . Labor is to be put forth for all classes.—*Review and Herald,* May 8, 1900.

The Wedding Garment

When the king came in to see the guests, he saw a man there who did not
have on a wedding garment. Matt. 22:11. (Read Matt. 22:1-14.)

By the help of the Holy Spirit, men and women can rise from commonness and live pure, holy lives. Those professed believers who do not do
this lie against the truth. . . . They do not show forth in word and deportment the transforming power that attends the truth. How can the Lord be
pleased with those who make no effort to rise to a high standard? Do they
not claim to have received a high, noble truth? . . .

God does not ask men and women to surrender anything that is for the
health of soul or body, but He does ask them to surrender debasing, enfeebling
vices which, if cherished, will exclude them from heaven. He leaves them
room for every pleasure that can be enjoyed without compunction of conscience, and remembered without remorse. He asks them, for their present and
eternal good, to cultivate those virtues that bring health to the body and
strength to the soul. Pure thoughts and correct habits are necessary to our happiness as human beings and as Christians. Everything of a debasing character
must be overcome if we would see the King in His beauty. . . .

The Lord can and will help everyone who seeks His help in the effort to
become pure and holy. . . . Have earnest efforts been made to overcome natural inclinations to wrong, to conquer the habits and practices that were a
part of the life before the acceptance of the truth? Are those who claim to
believe the truth as untidy and disorderly in the home and as un-Christlike
in the daily life as before they professed to accept Christ? If so, they are not
showing forth the praises of Him who hath called them out of darkness.
They have not put on Christ's righteousness.

Strive to make decided improvement. Cleanse yourselves from all filthiness of the flesh and of the spirit, perfecting holiness in the fear of the Lord.
Be neat and tidy in your dress, and kind and courteous in your manner. Be
pure and refined, for heaven is the very essence of purity and refinement.
As God is pure and holy in His sphere, so we are to be in our sphere.

Read carefully and critically the parable of the wedding garment, and
make a personal application of the lessons it teaches. . . . Those who make
a profession of faith, and yet remain unchanged in habit and practice, are
represented . . . by the man who came to the feast without a wedding garment.—*Review and Herald,* Feb. 26, 1901.

The Lord's Vineyard

There was a certain landowner who planted a vineyard and set a hedge around it. Matt. 21:33. (Read Matt. 21:33-41.)

A description of this vineyard is given in Isaiah: "Now will I sing to my well-beloved a song of my beloved touching his vineyard. My well-beloved hath a vineyard in a very fruitful hill: and he fenced it, and gathered out the stones thereof, and planted it with the choicest vine, and built a tower in the midst of it, and also made a winepress therein."

This figure represents the advantages and opportunities given to Israel. . . . Through Moses they received divine precepts and commandments. . . . God gave them riches and prosperity. They had every temporal and every spiritual advantage. They were hedged about by the law of ten commandments. This was what distinguished Israel from every other nation on the face of the earth.

The church is God's peculiar treasure, precious in His sight, and dear to His heart of infinite love. . . . The householder made every provision that the vineyard should receive the best of attention. Nothing was left undone that could be done to make the vineyard an honor to the one who owned it. . . .

With fire and tempest and death the great I AM redeemed His people, to make them glorious as His special representatives. He took them out of the land of bondage. He bore them as upon eagles' wings and brought them unto Himself, that they might dwell under the shadow of the Most High. Christ was the invisible leader of the children of Israel in their wilderness wanderings. . . . They witnessed a most wonderful manifestation of God's power when they passed through the Red Sea. And day by day they journeyed under the pillar of cloud, the symbol of the divine presence. . . .

With such a Leader, with such manifestations of His greatness and power, the children of Israel should have been inspired with faith and courage to go forward. . . . Only two of those who crossed the Red Sea lived to go over into the promised land. . . .

We need to beware lest we suffer the same fate as did ancient Israel. The history of their disobedience and downfall has been recorded for our instruction, that we may avoid doing as they did.—*Review and Herald,* July 10, 1900.

How Jesus Taught Truth

And this is eternal life, that they may know You, the only true God, and Jesus Christ whom You have sent. John 17:3.

If Christ had thought it necessary, He could have opened to His disciples mysteries which would have eclipsed and put far out of sight all the discoveries of the human mind. He could have presented facts concerning every subject that would have gone beyond human reasonings, and yet not misrepresented the truth in any particular. He could have revealed that which was unknown, that which would have put imagination to the stretch and attracted the thoughts of successive generations to the close of earth's history. He could have opened doors into the mysteries that the human mind had sought in vain to open. He could have presented to men and women a tree of knowledge from which they might have plucked from age to age; but this work was not essential to their soul's salvation, and the knowledge of the character of God was necessary to their eternal interests. . . .

Jesus, the Lord of life and glory, came to plant the tree of life for the human family and to invite the members of a fallen race to eat and be satisfied. He came to reveal to them what was their only hope, their only happiness, both in this world and in that which is to come. . . . He would allow nothing to divert His attention from the work which He came to do. . . .

Jesus saw that people needed to have their minds attracted to God, that they might become acquainted with His character and obtain the righteousness of Christ represented in His holy law. He knew that it was necessary that all should have a faithful representation of the divine character, that they might not be deceived by the misrepresentations of Satan, who had cast his hellish shadow athwart their pathway, and to their minds clothed God with his own satanic characteristics. . . .

However great and wise the teachers of the world might have been regarded in His day or may be regarded in our day, yet in comparison to Him they are not to be admired; for all the truth they uttered was but that which He originated, and all that came from any other source was foolishness. Even the truth they uttered, in His mouth was beautified and made glorious; for He presented it in simplicity and dignity.—*Signs of the Times,* May 1, 1893.

The Lost Sheep

*If a man has a hundred sheep, and one of them goes astray, does
he not leave the ninety-nine and go to the mountains to seek the
one that is straying? Matt. 18:12. (Read Matt. 18:11-14.)*

In the parable of the shepherd seeking for the lost sheep is a representation
of the tender patience, perseverance, and great love of God. As we contemplate the unselfish love of God, our hearts well up with gratitude, praise,
and thanksgiving. We praise Him for the priceless gift of His only begotten
Son. There is no animal so helpless and bewildered as is the sheep that has
strayed away from the fold. If the wanderer is not sought for by the compassionate shepherd, it will never find its way back to the fold. The shepherd
must take it in his arms himself, and bear it to the fold. . . .

The Pharisees were ready to accuse and condemn Jesus because He did not,
like themselves, repulse and condemn the publicans and sinners. . . . They
thought that the law would justify them, and they would not consider the
compassion and mercy that Jesus presented in His lessons as necessary to be
brought into their practical life. . . . Christ never invited the wicked to come
to Him to be saved in their sins, but to be saved from their sins. . . .

Christ did not ordain the plan of salvation for any one people or nation.
He said: "I lay down my life for the sheep. And other sheep I have, which
are not of this fold: them also I must bring, and they shall hear my voice;
and there shall be one fold, and one shepherd." . . .

Let every desponding, distrustful soul take courage, even though that individual may have done wickedly. . . . You are not to think that perhaps God
will pardon your transgressions and permit you to approach into His presence, but you are to remember that it is God who has made the first advance, that He has come forth to seek you while you were still in rebellion
against Him. . . .

If the ardor and enthusiasm encouraged as necessary to the success of attaining worldly things is not commendable in seeking the salvation of the
lost, which has a twofold object—to bless and to make us a blessing—what
is? Through conversion we are personally placed in vital connection with
Jesus Christ, who is made unto us wisdom, righteousness, sanctification, and
redemption.—*Signs of the Times,* Jan. 22, 1894.

The Prodigal Son

A certain man had two sons. And the younger of them said to his father, "Father, give me the portion of goods that falls to me." So he divided to them his livelihood. Luke 15:11, 12. (Read Luke 15:11-32.)

It was to answer the accusation of the scribes and Pharisees to the effect that Jesus chose the companionship of sinners that He spake the parables concerning the lost sheep, the lost silver, and the prodigal son, and in these presentations showed that His mission to the world was not to make miserable, not to condemn and destroy, but to recover that which was lost. . . . These were the very ones that needed a Savior. . . .

The prodigal son was not a dutiful son, not one who would please his father, but one who desired his own way. . . . The tender sympathy and love of his father were misinterpreted, and the more patient, kind, and benevolent the father acted, the more restless the son became. He thought his liberty was restricted, for his idea of liberty was wild license, and as he craved to be independent of all authority, he broke loose from all the restraint of his father's house, and soon spent his fortune in riotous living. A great famine arose in the country in which he sojourned, and in his hunger he would fain have filled himself with the husks that the swine did eat. . . .

He had no one now to say: "Do not do that, for you will do injury to yourself. Do this, because it is right." . . . Starvation stared him in the face, and he joined himself to a citizen of the place. He was sent to do the most menial of work—to feed the swine. Although this to a Jew was the most disreputable of callings, yet he was willing to do anything, so great was his need. . . .

He is suffering keen hunger, and cannot fill his want, and, under these circumstances he remembers that his father has bread enough and to spare, and resolves to go to his father. . . . Having made this decision, he does not wait to make himself more respectable. . . . "When he was yet a great way off, his father saw him, and had compassion, and ran, and fell on his neck, and kissed him." . . .

The home looks just as it did when he left it; but what a difference there is in himself. . . . The father does not give him a chance to say, "Make me as one of thy hired servants." The welcome he receives assures him that he is reinstated to the place of son.—*Signs of the Times, Jan. 29, 1894.*

The Older Brother

But he was angry and would not go in. Therefore his father came out and pleaded with him. Luke 15:28.

Mark the points in the parable. The elder brother coming from the field, hearing the sound of rejoicing, inquires what it all means, and is told of the return of his brother, and how the fatted calf has been killed to provide for the feast. Then is revealed in the elder brother selfishness, pride, envy, and malignity. He feels that favor to the prodigal is an insult to himself, and the father remonstrates with him, but he will not look upon the matter in the right light, nor will he unite with the father in rejoicing that the lost is found. He gives the father to understand that, had he been in the father's place, he would not have received the son back, and forgets that the poor prodigal is his own brother. He speaks with disrespect to his father, charging him with injustice to himself while he shows favor to one who has wasted his living. He speaks of the prodigal to his father as "this thy son." Yet notwithstanding all this unfilial conduct, his expressions of contempt and arrogance, the father deals patiently and tenderly with him. . . .

Did the elder son finally come to see his unworthiness of so kind and considerate a father? Did he come to see that, though his brother had done wickedly, he was his brother still, that their relationship had not altered? And did he repent of his jealousy, and ask his father's forgiveness for so misrepresenting him to his face?

How true a representation was the action of this elder son of unrepenting and unbelieving Israel, who refused to acknowledge that the publicans and sinners were their brethren, who should be forgiven and should be sought for, labored for, and not left to perish, but led to have everlasting life! How beautiful is this parable as it illustrates the welcome that every repentant soul will receive from the heavenly Father! With what joy will the heavenly intelligences rejoice to see souls returning to their Father's house! The sinners will meet with no reproach, no taunt, no reminder of their unworthiness. All that is required is penitence. The psalmist says, "For thou desirest not sacrifice; else I would give it: thou delightest not in burnt offering. The sacrifices of God are a broken spirit: a broken and a contrite heart, O God, thou wilt not despise."—*Signs of the Times,* Jan. 29, 1894.

The Good Samaritan, Part 1

A certain lawyer stood up and tested him, saying, "Teacher, what shall I do to inherit eternal life?" Luke 10:25. (Read Luke 10:30-37.)

With breathless attention the large congregation awaited Jesus' answer. . . . But Christ, the true searcher of hearts, understood the intents and purposes of His enemies. He turned the matter over to the lawyer who had asked the question, saying, "What is written in the law? how readest thou?". . . And the lawyer said, "Thou shalt love the Lord thy God with all thy heart, and with all thy soul, and with all thy strength, and with all thy mind; and thy neighbour as thyself." . . .

The lawyer had asked a plain, decided question, and the answer is equally plain and decided. . . . In answering the question, "What is written in the law?" the lawyer passed over all the mass of ceremonial and ritualistic ordinances as of no value, and presented only the two great principles on which hang all the law and the prophets, and Jesus commended his wisdom, and said, "This do, and thou shalt live." . . .

To answer the question, "Who is my neighbour?" Jesus presented the parable of the good Samaritan. He knew that the Jews included only those of their own nation under the title of neighbors, and looked upon the Gentiles with contempt, calling them dogs, uncircumcised, unclean, and polluted. But above all others they despised the Samaritans. . . . Yet Jesus said: "A certain man went down from Jerusalem to Jericho, and fell among thieves, which stripped him of his raiment, and wounded him, and departed, leaving him half dead." . . .

As the sufferer lies thus, a priest passes by, but merely glances at the wounded man; and, as he does not wish to be put to the trouble and expense of helping him, he passes by on the other side. Then a Levite passes. Curious to know what has happened, he stops and looks at the sufferer; but he has no feeling of compassion to prompt him to help the dying man. He does not like the work, and, as he thinks it is no concern of his, he too passes by. Both these men were in sacred office, and claimed to know and to expound the Scriptures. They had been trained in the school of national bigotry, and had become selfish, narrow, and exclusive, and they felt no sympathy for anyone unless that person was of the Jews. They look upon the wounded man, but cannot tell whether he is of their nation or not. He might be of the Samaritans—and they turn away.—*Signs of the Times,* July 16, 1894.

The Good Samaritan, Part 2

*So he went to him and bandaged his wounds, pouring on oil and wine;
and he set him on his own animal, brought him to an inn, and took
care of him. Luke 10:34.*

In this parable Jesus presented a stranger, a neighbor, a brother in suffering,
wounded and dying. . . . But though priests and scribes had read the law,
they had not brought it into their practical life. . . .

In speaking of the manner in which the priest and the Levite treated the
wounded man, the lawyer had heard nothing out of harmony with his own
ideas, nothing contrary to the forms and ceremonies that he had been
taught were all the law required. But Jesus presented another scene: "But a
certain Samaritan, as he journeyed, came where he was: and when he saw
him, he had compassion on him, and went to him, and bound up his
wounds, pouring in oil and wine, and set him on his own beast, and
brought him to an inn, and took care of him." . . .

After Christ had shown up the cruelty and selfishness manifested by the
representatives of the nation, he brought forward the Samaritan, who was
despised, hated, and cursed by the Jews, and set him before them as one
who possessed attributes of character far superior to those possessed by
those who claimed exalted righteousness. . . .

Everyone who claims to be a child of God should note every detail of this lesson. . . . The Samaritan realized that there was before him a human being in need
and suffering, and as soon as he sees him, he has compassion upon him. . . .

The Samaritan followed the impulse of a kind and loving heart. Christ so
presented the scene that the most severe rebuke was placed upon the unfeeling actions of priest and Levite. But this lesson is not only for them, but
for Christians of this day, and is a solemn warning to us that for humanity's
sake we may not fail to show mercy and pity to those who suffer. . . .

In the parable of the good Samaritan, Jesus presented His own love and
character. The life of Christ was filled with works of love toward the lost
and erring. In the man bruised and wounded and stripped of his possessions, the sinner is represented. The human family, the lost race, is pictured
in the sufferer, left naked, bleeding, and destitute. Jesus takes His own robe
of righteousness to cover the soul, and whosoever believeth in Him shall
not perish, but have everlasting life.—*Signs of the Times,* July 23, 1894.

The Unjust Judge

Though I do not fear God nor regard man, yet because this widow troubles
me I will avenge her, lest by her continual coming she weary me.
Luke 18:4, 5. (Read Luke 18:1-8.)

In this parable Christ draws a sharp contrast between the unjust judge and God. The judge, though fearing neither God nor man, listened to the widow because of her constant petitions. Although his heart remained like ice, yet the widow's persistence resulted in her success. He avenged her, though he felt no pity or compassion for her, though her misery was nothing to him. "And the Lord said, Hear what the unjust judge saith. And shall not God avenge his own elect, which cry day and night unto him, though he bear long with them? I tell you that he will avenge them speedily."

The judge yielded to the widow's request merely because of selfishness, that he might be relieved of her persistence. How different is God's attitude in regard to prayer! Our heavenly Father may not seem to respond immediately to the prayers and appeals of His people, but He never turns from them indifferently. In this parable and the parable of the man rising at midnight to supply his friend's necessity, that the friend might minister to a needy, wayfaring man, we are taught that God hears our prayers. Too often we think that our petitions are unheard, and we cherish unbelief, distrusting God when we should claim the promise, "Ask, and it shall be given you; seek, and ye shall find; knock, and it shall be opened unto you." . . .

What is prayer—merely the presentation of our soul hunger? No; the presentation of our perplexities and necessities, and of our need of God's help against our adversary the devil. . . . Prayer is to be offered for the preservation of life, for the preservation of every power and faculty, that we may render the highest service to our Maker. . . .

The just Judge repulses no one who comes to Him in contrition. He has more pleasure in His church, struggling with temptation here below, than in the imposing host of angels that surround His throne. Not one sincere prayer is lost. Amid the anthems of the celestial choir, God hears the cries of the weakest human being. You who feel most unworthy, commit your case to Him, for His ears are open to your cry. "He that spared not his own Son, but delivered him up for us all, how shall he not with him also freely give us all things?"—*Signs of the Times,* Sept. 15, 1898.

The Pharisee and the Publican

*God, I thank You that I am not like other men . . . or even as this
tax collector. Luke 18:11. (Read Luke 18:9-14.)*

Both these men are represented as resorting to the same place for prayer.
Both came to meet with God. But what a contrast there was between
them! One was full of self-praise. He looked it, he walked it, he prayed it;
the other realized fully his own nothingness. The Pharisee was looked upon
as righteous before God, and thus he was in his own estimation. The publican, in his humility, looked upon himself as having no claim to the mercy
or approval of God. . . .

The publican would not so much as lift his eyes to heaven, but smote
upon his breast, saying, "God be merciful to me a sinner." The Searcher of
hearts looked down upon both men, and He discerned the value of each
prayer. He looks not on the outward appearance; He judges not as humans
judge. He does not value us according to our rank, talent, education, or position. . . . He saw that the Pharisee was full of self-importance and self-
righteousness, and the record was made against his name, "Weighed in the
balances, and found wanting." . . .

The Majesty of heaven humbled Himself from the highest authority, from
the position of one equal with God, to the lowest place, that of a servant. . . .
His trade was that of a carpenter, and He labored with His hands to do His
part in sustaining the family. . . . His humility did not consist in a low estimate
of His own character and qualifications, but in humbling Himself to fallen
humanity, in order to raise them with Him to a higher life. . . .

That person is nearest God, and is the most honored of Him, who has
the least self-importance and self-righteousness, the least trust and confidence in self, who waits on God in humble, trusting faith. . . .

Pride and self-importance, when compared with humility and lowliness,
are indeed weakness. It was our Savior's gentleness, His plain, unassuming
manners, that made Him a conqueror of hearts. . . .

God looks down from heaven with pleasure on the trusting, believing
ones who have a full sense of their dependence on Him. To such He delights to give when they ask Him. "He satisfieth the longing soul, and filleth
the hungry soul with goodness."—*Signs of the Times,* Oct. 21, 1897.

Compare the Sinner and the Righteous

*Yea, though I walk through the valley of the shadow of death, I will fear
no evil; for You are with me; Your rod and Your staff, they comfort me.
Ps. 23:4.*

We often hear the life of Christians described as being filled with trials, sadness, and sorrow, with but little to cheer and comfort; and the
impression is too often given that if they should give up their faith and their
efforts for eternal life, the scene would be changed to pleasure and happiness. But I have been led to compare the life of the sinner with the life of
the righteous. Sinners do not have a desire to please God, therefore can
have no pleasing sense of His approval. They do not enjoy their state of sin
and worldly pleasure without trouble. They feel deeply the ills of this mortal
life. Oh yes, at times they are fearfully troubled. They fear God but do not
love Him.

Are sinners free from disappointment, perplexity, earthly losses, poverty,
and distress? Oh, no! In this respect they are no more secure than the righteous. They often suffer lingering sicknesses, yet have no strong and mighty
arm to lean upon, no strengthening grace from a higher power to support
them. In their weakness they must lean upon their own strength. They cannot look forward with any pleasure to the resurrection morn, for they have
no cheering hope that they will then have part with the blest. They obtain
no consolation by looking forward to the future. A fearful uncertainty tor-
ments them, and thus they close their eyes in death. This is the end of poor
sinners' lives of vain pleasures.

Christians are subject to sickness, disappointment, poverty, reproach, and
distress. Yet amid all this they love God, and love to do His will, and prize
nothing so highly as His approval. In the conflicts, trials, and changing
scenes of this life, they know that there is One who understands it all; One
who will bend His ear low to the cries of the sorrowful and distressed; One
who can sympathize with every sorrow and soothe the keenest anguish of
every heart. He has invited the sorrowing ones to come to Him and find
rest. Amid all their affliction Christians have strong consolation, and if they
suffer a lingering, distressing sickness, before they close their eyes in death,
they can with cheerfulness bear it all, for they hold communion with their
Redeemer.—*Review and Herald,* Apr. 28, 1859.

What Does the Christian Gain?

Seek first the kingdom of God and His righteousness, and all these things shall be added to you. Matt. 6:33.

Many speak of the life of the Christian taking away from us pleasure and worldly enjoyment. I say it takes away nothing worth having. Is there perplexity, poverty, and distress endured by the Christian? Oh, yes, this is expected in this life. But are the sinners of whom we speak as enjoying the pleasures of this world free from these ills of life? Do we not often see in them the pale cheek, the wracking cough, indicating a fatal disease? Are they not subject to burning fevers and contagious diseases? How often do you hear their complaints of meeting with heavy losses of worldly goods; and consider, this is their only treasure. They lose all. These troubles of sinners are overlooked.

Christians are too apt to think they are the only ones who have a hard time, and some seem to think that it is a condescension in them to embrace unpopular truth and profess to be Christ's followers. The road seems hard. They think they have many sacrifices to make, when in truth they make no real sacrifice. If they are adopted into the family of God, what sacrifices have they made? Their following Christ may have broken friendship with worldly relatives, but look at the exchange—their names written in the Lamb's book of life—elevated, yes, greatly exalted to be partakers of salvation—heirs of God and joint heirs with Jesus Christ to an imperishable inheritance. If the link which binds them to worldly relatives is weakened for Christ's sake, a stronger one is formed, a link which binds finite humanity to the infinite God. Shall we call this a sacrifice on our part because we yield error for truth, light for darkness, weakness for strength, sin for righteousness, and a perishable name and inheritance for honors that are lasting and an immortal treasure? . . .

If there is anyone who enjoys happiness even in this life, it is the faithful follower of Jesus Christ. . . . If Christians dwell too much upon the rough pathway, they make it harder than it really is. If they dwell upon the bright spots in the way and are grateful for every ray of light, and then dwell upon the rich reward that lies at the end of the race, instead of gloom, mourning, and complaints, they will bear a cheerful countenance.—*Review and Herald,* Apr. 28, 1859.

The Blessings of Benevolence

The generous soul will be made rich, and he who waters
will also be watered himself. Prov. 11:25.

Divine wisdom has appointed, in the plan of salvation, the law of action and reaction, making the work of beneficence, in all its branches, twice blessed. Those who give to the needy bless others, and are blessed themselves in a still greater degree. . . .

That we might not lose the blessed results of benevolence, our Redeemer formed the plan of enlisting us as His coworkers. By a chain of circumstances which would call forth our charities, He bestows upon us the best means of cultivating benevolence, and keeps us habitually giving to help the poor and to advance His cause. By their necessities, a ruined world are drawing forth from us talents of means and influence, to present to them the truth, of which they are in perishing need. . . . In bestowing, we bless others, and thus accumulate true riches. . . .

The cross of Christ appeals to the benevolence of every follower of the blessed Savior. The principle there illustrated is to give, give. This, carried out in actual benevolence and good works, is the true fruit of the Christian life. The principle of worldlings is to get, get, and thus they expect to secure happiness, but carried out in all its bearings, the fruit is misery and death. . . .

Christ assigned to human beings the work of spreading the gospel. But while some go forth to preach, He calls upon others to answer His claims upon them for offerings, with which to support His cause in the earth. This is one of God's ways of exalting us. It is just the work that we need, for it will stir the deepest sympathies of our heart and call into exercise the highest capabilities of the mind. . . .

God planned the system of beneficence in order that we might become, like our Creator, benevolent and unselfish in character. . . .

Christ's believing people are to perpetuate His love. . . . Meet around the cross of Calvary in self-sacrifice and self-denial. As you stand before the cross and see the Royal Prince of heaven dying for you, can you seal your heart, saying, "No; I have nothing to give"? God will bless you as you do your best.—*Review and Herald*, Oct. 3, 1907.

Does God Ask Too Much?

Do not love the world or the things in the world. 1 John 2:15.

We see beauty and loveliness and glory in Jesus. We behold in Him matchless charms. He was the Majesty of heaven. He filled all heaven with splendor. Angels bowed in adoration before Him and readily obeyed His commands. Our Savior gave up all. He laid aside His glory, His majesty, and splendor and came down to this earth and died for a race of rebels who were transgressors against His Father's commandments. Christ condescended to humble Himself that He might save the fallen race; He drank the cup of suffering, and in its place offers us the cup of blessing; yes, that cup was drained for us; and although many know all this, yet they choose to go on in sin and folly; and still Jesus invites them. He says, Whosoever will, let him come and take of the water of life freely....

The truths of God's Word must be brought to bear upon us, and we must lay hold upon them. If we do this, they will have a sanctifying influence upon our lives; they will fit us that we may have a preparation for the kingdom of glory; that when our probation shall close, we may see the King in His beauty and dwell in His presence forevermore....

It is the strength of the entire being that God requires. He requires of you a separation from the world and the things of the world. "Love not the world, neither the things that are in the world. If any man love the world, the love of the Father is not in him." It is separation from the love of the world that is required, and what is given you in its place? "I will be a father unto you." Do you have to separate in your affections from friends? Does the truth require you to stand alone in your position to serve God because others around you are not willing to yield to the claims that Christ has upon them? Does it require a separation in feeling from them? Yes, and this is the cross which you must bear, which leads many to say, I cannot yield to the claims of the truth. But says Christ, If anyone love father, or mother, or brother, or sister, more than Me, he is not worthy of Me. Whosoever will come after Me and will be My disciple, let him take up his cross and follow Me. Here is the cross of self-denial and sacrifice, to separate in your affections here from those who will not yield to the claims of truth. Is this too great a sacrifice to make for Him who sacrificed all for you?—*Review and Herald,* Apr. 19, 1870.

True Christians Are Happy

Blessed be the Lord, who daily loads us with benefits, the God of our salvation! Ps. 68:19.

Christians should be the most cheerful and happy people that live. They may have the consciousness that God is their father and their everlasting friend. But many professed Christians do not correctly represent the Christian religion. They appear gloomy, as if under a cloud. They often speak of the great sacrifices they have made to become Christians. They appeal to those who have not accepted Christ, representing by their own example and conversation that they must give up everything which would make life pleasant and joyful. They throw a pall of darkness over the blessed Christian hope. The impression is given that God's requirements are a burden even to the willing soul, and that everything that would give pleasure or that would delight the taste must be sacrificed.

We do not hesitate to say that this class of professed Christians have not the genuine article. God is love. Whoso dwelleth in God dwelleth in love. All who have indeed become acquainted, by experimental knowledge, with the love and tender compassion of our heavenly Father will impart light and joy wherever they may be. Their presence and influence will be to their associates as the fragrance of sweet flowers, because they are linked to God and heaven, and the purity and exalted loveliness of heaven are communicated through them to all that are brought within their influence. This constitutes them the light of the world, the salt of the earth. . . .

Where does the artist obtain his design? From nature. But the great Master Artist has painted upon heaven's shifting, changing canvas the glories of the setting sun. He has tinted and gilded the heavens with gold, silver, and crimson as though the portals of high heaven were thrown open that we might view its gleamings and our imagination take hold of the glory within. . . .

As we are attracted to the beautiful in nature and associate the things which God has created for the happiness of men and women with His character, we will regard God as a tender, loving Father rather than merely a stern judge. . . . The heart is quickened and throbs with new and deeper love mingled with awe and reverence as we contemplate God in nature.— *Review and Herald,* July 25, 1871.

The Laodicean Church

As many as I love, I rebuke and chasten. Therefore be zealous and repent.
Rev. 3:19.

The message to the church of the Laodiceans is a startling denunciation, and is applicable to the people of God at the present time. . . .

The Lord here shows us that the message to be borne to His people by ministers whom He has called to warn the people is not a peace-and-safety message. . . . The people of God are represented in the message to the Laodiceans in a position of carnal security. They are at ease, believing themselves in an exalted condition of spiritual attainments. . . .

The message of the True Witness finds the people of God in a sad deception, yet honest in that deception. They know not that their condition is deplorable in the sight of God. While those addressed are flattering themselves that they are in an exalted spiritual condition, the message of the True Witness breaks their security by the startling denunciation of their true situation of spiritual blindness, poverty, and wretchedness. . . .

The Christian life is a constant battle and a march. There is no rest from the warfare. It is by constant, unceasing effort that we maintain the victory over the temptations of Satan. . . . We are fully sustained in our positions by an overwhelming amount of plain scriptural testimony. But we are very much wanting in Bible humility, patience, faith, love, self-denial, watchfulness, and a spirit of sacrifice. We need to cultivate Bible holiness. Sin prevails among the people of God. . . . Many cling to their doubts and their darling sins, while they are in so great a deception as to talk and feel that they are in need of nothing. . . .

All the soldiers of the cross of Christ virtually obligate themselves to enter a crusade against the adversary of souls, to condemn wrong, and sustain righteousness. . . . Eternal life is of infinite value, and will cost us all that we have. . . .

It is not enough for ministers to present theoretical subjects. They need to study the practical lessons Christ gave His disciples, and make a close application of the same to their own souls and to the people. Because Christ bears this rebuking testimony, shall we suppose that He is destitute of tender love to His people? Oh, no! . . . He rebukes those He loves.—*Review and Herald,* Sept. 16, 1873.

The Creation

*Then God saw everything that He had made, and indeed it was very good.
Gen. 1:31.*

Adam and Eve came forth from the hand of their Creator in the perfection of every physical, mental, and spiritual endowment. God planted for them a garden and surrounded them with everything lovely and attractive to the eye and that which their physical necessities required. This holy pair looked out upon a world of unsurpassed loveliness and glory. A benevolent Creator had given them evidences of His goodness and love in providing them with fruits, vegetables, and grains, and had caused to grow out of the ground trees of every variety for usefulness and beauty.

The holy pair looked upon nature as a picture of unsurpassed loveliness. The brown earth was clothed with a carpet of living green diversified with an endless variety of self-propagating, self-perpetuating flowers. Shrubs, flowers, and trailing vines regaled the senses with their beauty and fragrance. The many varieties of lofty trees were laden with fruit of every kind and of delicious flavor adapted to please the taste and meet the wants of the happy Adam and Eve. This Eden home God provided for our first parents, giving them unmistakable evidences of His great love and care for them.

Adam was crowned as king in Eden. To him was given dominion over every living thing that God had created. The Lord blessed Adam and Eve with intelligence such as He had not given to the animal creation. He made Adam the rightful sovereign over all the works of His hands. Human beings made in the divine image could contemplate and appreciate the glorious works of God in nature. . . .

The natural loveliness which surrounded them, like a mirror reflected the wisdom, excellence, and love of their heavenly Father. And their songs of affection and praise rose sweetly and reverentially to heaven, harmonizing with the songs of the exalted angels and with the happy birds who were caroling forth their music without a care. There was no disease, decay, nor death anywhere. Life, life was in everything the eye rested upon. The atmosphere was impregnated with life. Life was in every leaf, in every flower, and in every tree.—*Review and Herald,* Feb. 24, 1874.

The Chance to Choose

But of the tree of the knowledge of good and evil you shall not eat, for in the day that you eat of it you shall surely die. Gen. 2:17.

The Lord knew that Adam and Eve could not be happy without labor; therefore He gave them the pleasant employment of dressing the garden. And, as they tended the things of beauty and usefulness around them, they could behold the goodness and glory of God in His created works. Adam and Eve had themes for contemplation in the works of God in Eden, which was heaven in miniature. God did not form them merely to contemplate His glorious works; therefore He gave them hands for labor, as well as minds and hearts for contemplation. If the happiness of His creatures consisted in doing nothing, the Creator would not have given them their appointed work. In labor, Adam and Eve were to find happiness as well as meditation. They could reflect that they were created in the image of God, to be like Him in righteousness and holiness. Their minds were capable of continual cultivation, expansion, refinement, and noble elevation; for God was their teacher, and angels were their companions.

The Lord placed Adam and Eve upon probation, that they might form characters of steadfast integrity for their own happiness and for the glory of their Creator. He had endowed the holy pair with powers of mind superior to any other living creature that He had made. Their mental powers were but little lower than those of the angels. They could become familiar with the sublimity and glory of nature, and understand the character of their heavenly Father in His created works. Everything that their eyes rested upon in the immensity of the Father's works, provided with a lavish hand, testified of His love and infinite power. . . .

The first great moral lesson given to Adam and Eve was that of self-denial. The reins of self-government were placed in their hands. Judgment, reason, and conscience were to bear sway. . . . Adam and Eve were permitted to partake of every tree in the garden save one. There was only a single prohibition. The forbidden tree was as attractive and lovely as any of the trees in the garden. It was called the tree of knowledge, because in partaking of that tree, of which God had said, "Thou shalt not eat of it," they would have a knowledge of sin, an experience in disobedience.—*Review and Herald,* Feb. 24, 1874.

The Fall

Of the fruit of the tree which is in the midst of the garden, God has said,
"You shall not eat it, nor shall you touch it, lest you die." Gen. 3:3.

Eve went from the side of her husband, viewing the beautiful things of nature in Gods creation, delighting her senses with the colors and fragrance of the flowers and the beauty of the trees and shrubs. She was thinking of the restrictions God had placed upon them in regard to the tree of knowledge. She was pleased with the beauties and bounties which the Lord had furnished for the gratification of every want. All these, said she, God has given us to enjoy. . . .

Eve had wandered near the forbidden tree, and her curiosity was aroused to know how death could be concealed in the fruit of this fair tree. She was surprised to hear her queries taken up and repeated by a strange voice. "Yea, hath God said, Ye shall not eat of every tree of the garden?" Eve was not aware that she had revealed her thoughts by conversing to herself aloud; therefore she was greatly astonished to hear her queries repeated by a serpent. She really thought the serpent had a knowledge of her thoughts and that he must be very wise.

She answered him, "We may eat of the fruit of the trees of the garden: but of the fruit of the tree which is in the midst of the garden, God hath said, Ye shall not eat of it, neither shall ye touch it, lest ye die. And the serpent said unto the woman, Ye shall not surely die: for God doth know that in the day ye eat thereof, then your eyes shall be opened, and ye shall be as gods, knowing good and evil." . . .

Eve had overstated the words of God's command. He had said to Adam and Eve, "But of the tree of the knowledge of good and evil, thou shalt not eat of it: for in the day that thou eatest thereof thou shalt surely die." In Eve's controversy with the serpent, she added the clause, *"Neither shall ye touch it,* lest ye die." . . . . This statement of Eve gave him advantage, and he plucked the fruit, and placed it in her hand, and used her own words, "He hath said, 'If ye touch it, ye shall die.' You see no harm comes to you from touching the fruit, neither will you receive any harm by eating it." . . . She ate the fruit, and realized no immediate harm. She then plucked the fruit for herself and for her husband. . . .

Adam and Eve should have been perfectly satisfied with the knowledge of God in His created works, and by the instruction of the holy angels. . . . It was for their happiness to be ignorant of sin.—*Review and Herald,* Feb. 24, 1874.

A Redeemer Is Promised

And I will put enmity between you and the woman, and between your seed and her Seed; He shall bruise your head, and you shall bruise His heel. Gen. 3:15.

Adam and Eve should have been perfectly satisfied with the knowledge of God in His created works, and by the instruction of the holy angels. ...The high state of knowledge to which they thought to attain by eating of the forbidden fruit plunged them into the degradation of sin and guilt.

The angels who had been appointed to guard Adam and Eve in their Eden home before their transgression and expulsion from paradise were now appointed to guard the gates of paradise and the way of the tree of life, lest they should return and gain access to the tree of life and sin be immortalized.

Sin drove Adam and Eve from paradise. And sin was the cause of paradise being removed from the earth. In consequence of transgression of God's law, they lost paradise. In obedience to the Father's law and through faith in the atoning blood of His Son, paradise may be regained....

Satan made his exulting boasts to Christ and to loyal angels that he had succeeded in gaining a portion of the angels in heaven to unite with him in his daring rebellion. And now that he had succeeded in overcoming Adam and Eve, he claimed that their Eden home was his. He proudly boasted that the world which God had made was his dominion. Having conquered Adam, the monarch of the world, he had gained the race as his subjects, and he should now possess Eden and make that his headquarters. And he would there establish his throne and be monarch of the world.

But measures were immediately taken in heaven to defeat Satan in his plans. Strong angels, with beams of light representing flaming swords turning in every direction, were placed as sentinels to guard the way of the tree of life from the approach of Satan and the guilty pair....

A council was held in heaven, which resulted in God's dear Son undertaking to redeem the human race from the curse and from the disgrace of Adam's failure, and to conquer Satan. Oh, wonderful condescension! The Majesty of heaven, through love and pity for fallen humanity, proposed to become their substitute and surety.—*Review and Herald,* Feb. 24, 1874.

God's Mirror

By the law is the knowledge of sin. Rom. 3:20.

The law of God is the mirror to show men and women the defects in their characters. But it is not pleasant to those who take pleasure in unrighteousness to see their moral deformity. They do not prize this faithful mirror because it reveals to them their sins. Therefore, instead of instituting a war against their carnal minds, they war against the true and faithful mirror, given them by Jehovah for the very purpose that they may not be deceived, but that they may have revealed to them the defects in their characters. Should the discovery of these defects lead them to hate the mirror, or to hate themselves? Should they put away the mirror which discovers these defects? No. The sins which they cherish, which the faithful mirror shows them as existing in their characters, will close before them the portals of heaven unless they are put away, and they become perfect before God.

Listen to the words of the faithful apostle, "By the law is the knowledge of sin." These people who are zealous to abolish the law had far better manifest their zeal in abolishing their sins. . . .

The Lord made humanity upright, but we have fallen and become degraded because we refuse to yield obedience to the sacred claims which the law of God has upon us. All our passions, if properly controlled and rightly directed, will contribute to our physical and moral health and insure to us a great amount of happiness. The adulterer, the fornicator, and the wanton do not enjoy life. There can be no true enjoyment for the transgressor of God's law. The Lord knew this; therefore He restricts us. He directs, commands, and He positively forbids. . . .

Sin does not appear as sinful unless viewed in the truthful mirror God has given us as a test of character. When men and women acknowledge the claims of the law of God and plant their feet upon the platform of eternal truth, they will stand where the Lord can give them moral power to let their light so shine before men that they may see their good works and glorify our Father who is in heaven.

Their course will be marked with consistency. They will not justly earn the charge of hypocrisy and sensualism. They can preach Christ with power, being imbued with His Spirit. They can utter truths which will melt and burn their way to the hearts of the people.—*Review and Herald,* Mar. 8, 1870.

Praise God!

Then all the people answered, "Amen, Amen!"
while lifting up their hands. Neh. 8:6.

God says by the psalmist, "Whoso offereth praise glorifieth me." The worship of God consists chiefly of praise and prayer. Every follower of Christ should engage in this worship. No one can sing by proxy, bear testimony by proxy, or pray by proxy. As a rule, too many dark testimonies are borne in social service [prayer meeting], savoring more of murmuring than of gratitude and praise.

When the word of God was spoken to the Hebrews anciently, the Lord said to Moses, "And let all the people say, Amen." This response, in the fervor of their souls, was required as evidence that they understood the word spoken and were interested in it.

When the ark of God was brought into the city of David and a psalm of joy and triumph was chanted, all the people said, Amen. And David felt that he was fully repaid for his labor and anxiety. . . .

There is too much formality in the church. . . . We should be so connected with the Source of all light that we can be channels of light to the world. The Lord would have His ministers who preach the Word energized by His Holy Spirit. And the people who hear should not sit in drowsy indifference or stare vacantly about, making no response to what is being said. The spirit of the world has paralyzed the spirituality of such, and they are not awake to the precious theme of redemption. The truth of God's Word is spoken to leaden ears, and hard, unimpressible hearts. . . . These dull, careless ones show ambition and zeal when engaged in the business of the world, but things of eternal importance do not engross the mind and interest them as do worldly things. . . .

Fruitful Christians will be connected with God and intelligent in the things of God. The truth and the love of God is their meditation. They have feasted upon the words of life, and when they hear it spoken from the desk, they can say, as did the two disciples who were traveling to Emmaus when Christ explained to them the prophecies in reference to Himself, "Did not our heart burn within us, while he talked with us by the way, and while he opened to us the scriptures?"

All who are connected with the light will let their light shine to the world, and will, in their testimonies, praise God, to whom their hearts will flow forth in gratitude.—*Review and Herald,* Jan. 1, 1880.

A New Song

And they sang a new song, saying: "You are worthy . . .
for You were slain, and have redeemed us to God by Your blood
out of every tribe and tongue and people and nation, and have made us
kings and priests to our God; and we shall reign on the earth."
Rev. 5:9, 10.

God has reposed confidence in us by making us stewards of means and of His rich grace; and He now points us to the poor and suffering and oppressed, to souls bound in chains of superstition and error, and assures us that if we do good to these, He will accept the deed as though done to Himself. "Inasmuch as ye have done it unto one of the least of these my brethren," He declares, "ye have done it unto me."

The poor are not excluded from the privilege of giving. They, as well as the wealthy, may act a part in this work. The lesson that Christ gave in regard to the widow's two mites shows us that the smallest willing offerings of the poor, if given from a heart of love, are as acceptable as the largest donations of the rich. . . .

All wise stewards of the means entrusted to them, will enter into the joy of their Lord. What is this joy? "Likewise, I say unto you, there is joy in the presence of the angels of God over one sinner that repenteth." There will be a blessed commendation, a holy benediction, on the faithful winners of souls. They will join the rejoicing ones in heaven who shout the harvest home. How great will be the joy when the redeemed of the Lord shall all meet—gathered into the mansions prepared for them! Oh, what rejoicing for all who have been impartial, unselfish laborers together with God in carrying forward His work in the earth! What satisfaction will every reaper have when the clear, musical voice of Jesus shall be heard, saying, "Come, ye blessed of my Father, inherit the kingdom prepared for you from the foundation of the world." . . .

With glad, rejoicing hearts, those who have been colaborers with God see of the travail of their soul for perishing, dying sinners, and are satisfied. . . . The self-denial they have practiced in order to support the work is remembered no more. As they look upon the souls they sought to win to Jesus, and see them saved, eternally saved—monuments of God's mercy and of a Redeemer's love—there ring through the arches of heaven shouts of praise and thanksgiving. —*Review and Herald,* Oct. 10, 1907.

A Short Time

Woe to the inhabitants of the earth . . . ! For the devil has come down to you, having great wrath, because he knows that he has a short time. Rev. 12:12.

Jesus Christ is the only refuge in these perilous times. Satan is at work in secrecy and darkness. Cunningly he draws away the followers of Christ from the cross and brings them into self-indulgence and wickedness.

Satan is opposed to everything that will strengthen the cause of Christ and weaken his own power. . . . He never rests for a moment when he sees that the right is gaining the ascendancy. He has legions of evil angels that he sends to every point where light from heaven is shining upon the people. Here he stations his pickets to seize every unguarded man, woman, or child, and pass them over to his service. . . .

God would have His work done intelligently, not in a haphazard manner. He would have it done with faith and careful exactitude, that He may place the sign of His approval upon it. Those who love Him and walk with fear and humility before Him, He will bless, and guide, and connect them with heaven. If the workers rely upon Him, He will give them wisdom and correct their infirmities, so that they will be able to do the work of the Lord with perfection.

Our good works alone will not save any of us, but we cannot be saved without good works. And after we have done all that we can do, in the name and strength of Jesus we are to say, "We are unprofitable servants." We are not to think we have made great sacrifices and should receive great reward for our feeble services.

We must put on the armor and be prepared to successfully resist all the attacks of Satan. His malignity and cruel power are not sufficiently estimated. When he finds himself foiled upon one point, he assumes new ground and fresh tactics, and tries again, working wonders in order to deceive and destroy humanity. . . .

Christ asks for all. It will not do to withhold anything. He has purchased us with an infinite price, and He requires that all we have shall be yielded to Him a willing offering. If we are fully consecrated to Him in heart and life, faith will take the place of doubts, and confidence the place of distrust and unbelief.—*Signs of the Times,* Apr. 20, 1876.

Come and Be Separate

Come out from among them and be separate, says the Lord. Do not touch what is unclean, and I will receive you. 2 Cor. 6:17.

Here is a promise to us on condition of obedience. If we will come out from the world and be separate, and touch not the unclean, He will receive us. Here are the conditions of our acceptance with God. We have something to do ourselves. Here is a work for us. We are to show our separation from the world. The friendship of the world is enmity with God. It is impossible for us to be friends of the world and yet be in union with Christ. But what does this mean, to be friends of the world? It is to unite hands with them, to enjoy what they enjoy, to love that which they love, to seek for pleasure, to seek for gratification, to follow our own inclinations. We do not in following inclination have our affections upon God; we are loving and serving ourselves. But here is a grand promise: "Come out from among them, and be ye separate." Separate from what? The inclinations of the world, their tastes, their habits; the fashions, the pride, and the customs of the world. . . . In making this move, in showing that we are not in harmony with the world, the promise of God is ours. He does not say perhaps I will receive you; but "I will receive you." It is a positive promise.

You have a surety that you will be accepted of God. Then in separating from the world you connect yourself with God; you become a member of the royal family; you become sons and daughters of the Lord Almighty; you are children of the heavenly King, adopted into His family, and have a hold from above, united with the infinite God whose arm moves the world.

What an exalted privilege is this to be thus favored, thus honored of God, to be called sons and daughters of the Lord Almighty. It is incomprehensible; but still, with all these promises and encouragements, there are many who question and hesitate. They are in an undecided position. They seem to think that if they were to become Christians, there would be a mountain of responsibilities to be borne in religious duties and Christian obligations. There is a mountain of responsibility, a lifetime of watchfulness, of battling with their own inclinations, with their own wills, with their own desires, with their own pleasures; and as they look at it, it seems like an impossibility for them to take the step, to decide that they will be children of God, servants of the Most High.—*Signs of the Times,* Jan. 31, 1878.

One Day at a Time

Walk worthy of the Lord, fully pleasing Him, being fruitful in every good work and increasing in the knowledge of God. Col. 1:10.

I am reminded of an incident I once read, of an aged gentleman who had been broken down by hard labor and yet was seeking some employment by which he could obtain means. A nobleman who had a hundred cords of wood to cut was informed of the wish of the old gentleman. He told him that if he would cut the wood he should have one hundred dollars for the job. But the old gentleman replied, No, he could never do that. It was impossible. He was an old man, and not able to undertake such a job. "Well," said the nobleman, "we will make a different bargain. Can you cut one cord today? If so, I will give you one dollar." The bargain was made, and the cord of wood was cut that day. "Now," said the nobleman, "you may cut another cord tomorrow," and another cord was cut the next day; and thus the whole job was accomplished. In one hundred days the work was completed, and the laborer was in just as good health as when he commenced the work. He could take it cord by cord, but when presented to him in one large job, the accomplishment of it seemed impossible.

This well represents the cases of many who are undecided. They have a desire to be Christians, yet the responsibilities of a Christian life seem so great to them that they fear they will make a failure, [and] are almost certain they can never reach the mark if they make the attempt. But when it is taken into consideration that it is not for them to see the end of the Christian's journey, it is not for them to comprehend and accomplish it at once. Only one day at a time with its burdens and responsibilities is presented to us.

Yes, dear friends, dear youth, tomorrow is not yours. It is the duties of today that you are to perform. If you resolve to be on the Lord's side, and come out from among the world and be separate, and choose to be sons and daughters of the Lord Almighty, to leave the ranks of the enemy, the service of sin and of Satan, make up your mind to always do present duty. Take hold of the duties of today, realizing that the Lord has claims upon you, that you are responsible to your Creator; these claims are to be met only a day at a time. In the strength of God take hold, believing that you can overcome for that one day.—*Signs of the Times,* Jan. 31, 1878.

May

17

Come Out From Among Them

*I will be a Father to you, and you shall be My sons and daughters,
says the Lord Almighty. 2 Cor. 6:18.*

There are only two roads; one leads to heaven, the other to death and hell. Every one has a work to do. Every one of us that has reasoning powers knows that there is a God. . . . We want an arm to lean upon in the hours of affliction that can sustain. We want such an arm to rely upon when the earth shall reel to and fro, and be removed as a cottage. We want to know then that God is our Father, that our life is hid with Christ in God. Every one of you needs this assurance. The students at our school need this assurance. Some will soon return to their homes. How many of them have come to this school without a hope in Christ? How many have given their hearts to Him since they have been attending our college? How many are still in a position of indecision, sometimes inclined to be wholly on the Lord's side, and then again draw back for the very reasons I have mentioned, the responsibilities and duties devolving upon the Christian? These seem so great that they hesitate and remain undecided. . . .

How long is the extent of your life? Who of you have the assurance that you will live until the next term of school? How many of you have any surety of your life? But if you had a lifetime before you, if you knew that you should live your three-score years and ten, what is that little span of life? Is it too much for you to give to God? . . . Does He require you to give anything that is for your interest or happiness to retain? Oh, no. . . .

How can any feel as though they were making a sacrifice, to be adopted into the family of the King of kings, the Lord who reigns in the heavens; know you not that it is the highest exaltation to become children of God, "sons and daughters of the Lord Almighty"?

Ever since I was 11 years old I have been in the service of this heavenly King. I can speak from experience. He has asked me to give Him nothing that was for my best interest to retain. Precious Jesus; precious Savior; I love Him; and I love His service.—*Signs of the Times,* Jan. 31, 1878.

[This discourse was followed by a large number coming forward for prayers. The interest continued till the camp meeting, when more than 130 were baptized, many of whom were students at Battle Creek College.]

The Two Ways

Enter by the narrow gate; for wide is the gate and broad is the way that leads to destruction, and there are many who go in by it. Because narrow is the gate and difficult is the way which leads to life, and there are few who find it. Matt. 7:13, 14.

These roads are distinct, separate, and in opposite directions. One leads to eternal life, the other to death, eternal death. There is a distinction between these roads, also between the companies traveling in them. One road is broad and smooth; the other is narrow and rugged. So the parties that travel in them are opposite in character, life, dress, and conversation.

Those traveling in the narrow way are talking of the joy and happiness at the end of the journey. Their countenances are often sad, yet beam with holy, sacred joy. A Man of sorrow and acquainted with grief opened that road for them, and traveled it Himself. His followers see His footsteps and are comforted. He went through safely; so can they if they follow Him.

In the broad road all are occupied with their dress and the pleasures in the way. They freely indulge in hilarity and glee, and think not of their journey's end, of the certain destruction that awaits them there. Every day they approach nearer their destination, yet they madly rush on, faster and faster.

Why is it so hard to lead a self-denying, humble life? Because professed Christians are not dead to the world. It is easier living for Christ after dying to the world. They desire to be as much like the world as possible and yet be considered Christians. Such seek to climb up some other way. . . . Earth attracts them. Its treasures seem of worth to them. They find enough to engross the mind, and have no time to prepare for heaven. . . .

Both young and old neglect the study of the Bible and do not make it their rule of life. That important book by which they are to be judged is scarcely studied at all. Idle stories have been attentively read, while the Bible has been passed by, neglected. A day is coming when all will wish to be thoroughly furnished by the plain truths of the Word of God. . . .

When Bible truths affect the heart, they cause a desire to be separate from the world, like the Master. Those who acquaint themselves with the meek and lowly Jesus will walk worthy of Him.—*Signs of the Times,* Apr. 1, 1880.

The Light of the World

For you were once darkness, but now you are light in the Lord. Walk as children of light. Eph. 5:8.

Christ said to His disciples, "Ye are the light of the world." As the sun goes forth in the heavens to fill the world with brightness, so must the followers of Jesus shed the light of truth upon those who are groping in the darkness of error and superstition. But Christ's followers have no light of themselves. It is the light of Heaven that falls upon them, which is to be reflected by them to the world. . . .

The light of life is freely proffered to all. Every one who will may be guided by the bright beams of the Sun of Righteousness. Christ is the great remedy for sin. None can plead their circumstances, their education, or their temperament as an excuse for living in rebellion against God. Sinners are such by their own deliberate choice. Said our Savior, "This is the condemnation, that light is come into the world, and men loved darkness rather than light, because their deeds were evil. For every one that doeth evil hateth the light, neither cometh to the light, lest his deeds should be reproved." . . .

When the claims of God are presented, those who love sin evince their true character by the satisfaction with which they point to the faults and errors of professed Christians. They are actuated by the same spirit as their master, Satan, whom the Bible declares to be the "accuser of the brethren." Let an evil report be started, and how rapidly it will be exaggerated and passed from lip to lip! How many will feast upon it, like vultures upon a heap of garbage. . . .

The true Christian, "he that doeth truth, cometh to the light, that his deeds may be made manifest, that they are wrought in God." His godly life and holy conversation are a daily testimony against sin and sinners. He is a living representative of the truth which he professes. Of these true-hearted followers, Jesus declares that He is not ashamed to call them brethren. Everyone who at last secures eternal life will here manifest zeal and devotion in the service of God. . . . To know their duty is to do it heartily and fearlessly. They follow the light as it shines upon their path, regardless of consequences. The God of truth is on their side and will never forsake them.—*Signs of the Times,* Mar. 9, 1882.

True Temperance Is Well-balanced Living

Do you not know that you are the temple of God and that the Spirit of God dwells in you? 1 Cor. 3:16.

Only one lease of life is granted us here; and the inquiry with everyone should be, How can I invest my life that it may yield the greatest profit? Life is valuable only as we improve it for the benefit of our fellow creatures and the glory of God. Careful cultivation of the abilities with which the Creator has endowed us will qualify us for elevated usefulness here and a higher life in the world to come.

That time is spent to good account which is directed to the establishment and preservation of sound physical and mental health. We cannot afford to dwarf or cripple a single function of the mind or body by overwork or abuse of any part of the living machinery. As surely as we do this, we must suffer the consequences. Our first duty to God and our fellow beings is that of self-development. Every faculty with which the Creator has endowed us should be cultivated to the highest degree of perfection, that we may be able to do the greatest amount of good of which we are capable. In order to purify and refine our characters, we need the grace given us of Christ that will enable us to see and correct our deficiencies and improve that which is excellent. This work, wrought for ourselves in the strength and name of Jesus, will be of more benefit to our fellow creatures than any sermon we might preach them. The example of a well-balanced, well-ordered life is of inestimable value.

Intemperance is at the foundation of the larger share of the ills of life. . . . We do not speak of intemperance as limited only to the use of intoxicating liquors; it has a broader meaning, including the hurtful indulgence of any appetite or passion. . . . If the appetites and passions were under the control of sanctified reason, society would present a widely different aspect. Many things that are usually made articles of diet are unfit for food; the taste for them is not natural, but has been cultivated. Stimulating food creates a desire for still stronger stimulants.

Indigestible food throws the entire system out of order, and unnatural cravings and inordinate appetites are the results. . . . True temperance teaches us to abstain entirely from that which is injurious and to use judiciously only such articles of food as are healthful and nutritious.—*Signs of the Times,* Apr. 20, 1882.

Work Is a Blessing

Look, this was the iniquity of your sister Sodom: . . . pride, fullness of food, and abundance of idleness. Eze. 16:49.

God gave labor to humanity as a blessing, to occupy our minds, to strengthen our bodies, and to develop our faculties. Adam and Eve labored in the Garden of Eden, and they found in mental and physical activity the highest pleasures of their holy existence. When they were driven from that beautiful home as the result of disobedience and were forced to struggle with a stubborn soil to gain their daily bread, that very labor was a relief to their sorrowing souls, a safeguard against temptation.

Judicious labor is indispensable both to the happiness and the prosperity of our race. It makes the feeble strong, the timid brave, the poor rich, and the wretched happy. Our varied trusts are proportioned to our various abilities, and God expects corresponding returns for the talents He has given to His servants. It is not the greatness of the talents possessed that determines the reward, but the manner in which they are used—the degree of faithfulness with which the duties of life are performed, be they great or small.

Idleness is one of the greatest curses that can fall upon us, for vice and crime follow in its train. Satan lies in ambush, ready to surprise and destroy those who are unguarded, whose leisure gives him opportunity to insinuate himself into their favor under some attractive disguise. He is never more successful than when he comes to men and women in their idle hours. . . .

The rich often consider themselves entitled to the preeminence among their fellow human beings and in the favor of God. Many feel above honest labor and look down with contempt upon their poorer neighbors. The children of the wealthy are taught that to be gentlemen and ladies they must dress fashionably, avoid all useful labor, and shun the society of the working classes. . . .

Such ideas are wholly at variance with the divine purpose in the creation of mankind. . . .

The Son of God honored labor. Though He was the Majesty of heaven, He chose His earthly home among the poor and lowly, and worked for His daily bread in the humble carpenter shop of Joseph. . . . The path of the Christian laborer may be hard and narrow, but it is honored by the footprints of the Redeemer, and they are safe who follow in that sacred way.—*Signs of the Times,* May 4, 1882.

The Eye of the Lord Is Upon You

The eyes of the Lord are on the righteous, and
His ears are open to their cry. Ps. 34:15.

The opinion is widely held that spirituality and devotion to God are detrimental to health. While this conclusion is radically false, it is not without apparent foundation. Many who profess to be Christians are ever walking under a cloud. They seem to think it a virtue to complain of depression of spirits, great trials, and severe conflicts.

But these persons do not correctly represent the religion of the Bible. So far from being antagonistic to health and happiness, the fear of the Lord lies at the foundation of all real prosperity. . . .

The consciousness of right-doing is the best medicine for diseased bodies and minds. Those who are at peace with God have secured the most important requisite to health. The blessing of the Lord is life to the receiver. The assurance that the eye of the Lord is upon us, and His ear open to our prayer, is a never-failing source of satisfaction. To know that we have an all-wise Friend, to whom we can confide all the secrets of the soul, is a privilege which words can never express.

The gloom and despondency supposed to be caused by obedience to God's moral law is often attributable to disregard of His physical laws. Those whose moral faculties are beclouded by disease are not the ones to rightly represent the Christian life, to show forth the joys of salvation or the beauties of holiness. They are too often in the fire of fanaticism or the water of cold indifference or stolid gloom. . . .

It is the duty of every Christian to follow closely the example of Christ— to cultivate peace and hope and joy, which will be manifested in unfeigned cheerfulness and habitual serenity. Thus may they shed light upon all around them, instead of casting the dark shadow of discouragement and gloom.

Many are constantly craving excitement and diversion. They are restless and dissatisfied when not absorbed in mirth, frivolity, and pleasure-seeking. These persons may make a profession of religion, but they are deceiving their own souls. They do not possess the genuine article. Their life is not hid with Christ in God. They do not find in Jesus their joy and peace.— *Signs of the Times,* June 15, 1882.

Science and Revelation

The fool has said in his heart, "There is no God." Ps. 14:1.

There are those who think they have made wonderful discoveries in science. They quote the opinions of learned people as though they considered them infallible, and teach the deductions of science as truths that cannot be controverted. And the Word of God, which is given as a lamp to the feet of the world-weary traveler, is judged by this standard, and pronounced wanting. The scientific research in which these individuals have indulged has proved a snare to them. It has clouded their minds, and they have drifted into skepticism. They have a consciousness of power, and instead of looking to the Source of all wisdom, they triumph in the smattering of knowledge they may have gained. They have exalted their human wisdom in opposition to the wisdom of the great and mighty God and have dared to enter into controversy with Him. The Word of Inspiration pronounces these persons "fools."

God has permitted a flood of light to be poured upon the world in discoveries in science and art, but when professed scientists lecture and write upon these subjects from a merely human standpoint, they will assuredly come to wrong conclusions. The greatest minds, if not guided by the Word of God in their research, become bewildered in their attempts to investigate the relations of science and revelation. The Creator and His works are beyond their comprehension; and because they cannot explain these by natural laws, Bible history is considered unreliable. Those who doubt the reliability of the records of the Old and New Testaments will be led to go a step farther and doubt the existence of God, and then, having let go their anchor, they are left to beat about upon the rocks of infidelity. Moses wrote under the guidance of the Spirit of God, and a correct theory of geology will never claim discoveries that cannot be reconciled with his statements. The idea that many stumble over, that God did not create matter when He brought the world into existence, limits the power of the Holy One of Israel.

Many, when they find themselves incapable of measuring the Creator and His works by their own imperfect knowledge in science, doubt the existence of God and attribute infinite power to nature. . . . The Bible is not to be tested by human ideas of science, but science is to be brought to the test of this unerring standard.—*Signs of the Times,* Mar. 13, 1884.

Cheerful Service

And we desire that each one of you show the same diligence to the full assurance of hope until the end. Heb. 6:11.

The Lord looks with approval upon the works of His faithful servants. . . . It has always been the duty of God's chosen people to labor unselfishly; but some neglect the work they ought to do, and others are overburdened to make up for their deficiencies. If all would cheerfully do their part, they would be sustained; but those who complain and murmur at every step will receive neither help nor reward.

God was displeased with the children of Israel because they murmured against Him and against Moses, whom He had sent to be their deliverer. In a marvelous manner He brought them out from their bondage in the land of Egypt, that He might elevate and ennoble them, and make them a praise in the earth. But there were difficulties to be encountered, and weariness and privations to be endured. It was necessary for them to bear these hardships. God was bringing them from a state of degradation and fitting them to occupy an honorable place among the nations, and to receive important and sacred trusts. . . .

They forgot their bitter service in Egypt. They forgot the goodness and power of God displayed in their behalf in their deliverance from bondage. They forgot how their children were spared when the destroying angel passed over Egypt. They forgot the grand exhibition of divine power at the Red Sea, when Jehovah proclaimed, "Here shall thy proud waves be stayed," and the waters were rolled together, forming a solid wall. They forgot that while they had crossed safely in the path that had been opened for them, the armies of their enemies, attempting to follow them, were overwhelmed by the waters of the sea. . . .

God does not bind upon anyone burdens so heavy that at every step he must complain of the load he is obliged to bear. It is the friction, and not the constant motion, that wears the machinery. It is the continual worry, and not the work they do, that is killing these persons. . . .

There is peace and contentment in the service of Christ. As He was about to leave His disciples, He made them this parting promise, . . . "Peace I leave with you, my peace I give unto you: not as the world giveth, give I unto you."—*Signs of the Times,* June 12, 1884.

Put God First

Command those who are rich in this present age not to be haughty,
nor to trust in uncertain riches but in the living God, who gives
us richly all things to enjoy. 1 Tim. 6:17.

It is dangerous to give time, thought, and strength to the pursuit of worldly gain, even if success follows persevering effort, for in thus doing there is danger of making God and His righteousness secondary. It is better far to be in poverty, to endure disappointment and have our earthly hopes shattered, than to have our eternal interests imperiled. Flattering inducements may be presented to us, and we may think to obtain wealth and honor, and so set our heart and soul on worldly enterprises. . . .

Money has become the measure of manhood in the world, and men are estimated, not by their integrity, but by the amount of wealth they possess. Thus it was in the days before the Flood. . . .

Let us not be determined to get rich. If we see that poverty will be our portion in abiding in the simple truth, let us abide by the truth and enter into life. Jesus said that "man shall not live by bread alone, but by every word of God." The devotees of the world may smile at this statement, but it is nevertheless the counsel of eternal wisdom. . . . Christians who are called into the world by their business, if they follow Christ, will bear their cross and meet their perplexities in the Spirit of Christ. They will not make the world their God, and give brain and bone and muscle to the service of mammon. They will realize that Heaven is looking upon them, and whatever success attends them, they will give glory to God. They will realize that God knows, as we do not, that a few more years will roll by and the treasures of earth be no more. . . .

It is the vision of the world to come that balances the mind so that the things which are seen do not obtain control over the affections, which have been bought with an infinite price by the world's Redeemer. Through the agency of the Holy Spirit the things unseen and eternal are brought before the soul, and the advantages of the eternal, imperishable treasure are made to appear before the mind's eye in their attractive beauty. In this way we learn to look to the unseen and the eternal, and to esteem the reproaches of Christ greater value than the treasures of the world.—*Signs of the Times,* June 26, 1893.

A Living Church

*We urge and exhort in the Lord Jesus that you should abound
more and more, just as you received from us how you ought
to walk and to please God. 1 Thess. 4:1.*

We long to see the true Christian character manifested in the church;
we long to see its members free from a light, irreverent spirit; and
we earnestly desire that they may realize their high calling in Christ Jesus.
Some who profess Christ are exerting themselves to the utmost to so live
and act that their religious faith may commend itself to people of moral
worth, that they may be induced to accept the truth. But there are many
who feel no responsibility even to keep their own souls in the love of God,
and who, instead of blessing others by their influence, are a burden to those
who would work and watch and pray. . . .

The present time calls for men and women who have a moral fixedness of
purpose, men and women who will not be molded or subdued by any unsanctified influences. Such persons will make a success in the work of perfecting Christian character through the grace of Christ so freely given. . . .

No one can succeed in the service of God whose whole soul is not in
the work and who does not count all things but loss for the excellency of
the knowledge of Christ. Those who make any reserve, who refuse to give
all that they have, cannot be disciples of Christ, much less His colaborers.
The consecration must be complete. Father, mother, wife and children,
houses and lands, everything which the servant of Christ possesses, must be
held subject to God's call—bound upon the sacred altar. . . .

Those who seek by earnest study of God's Word and fervent prayer the
guidance of His Spirit, will be led by Him. The pillar of cloud will guide
them by day, the pillar of fire by night; and with an abiding sense of God's
presence it will not be possible to disregard His holy law. . . .

Let us, as the peculiar people of God, elevate the standard of Christian
character, lest we come short of the reward that will be given to the good
and the faithful. . . . We must work out our own salvation with fear and
trembling. It is those who hold fast the beginning of their confidence steadfast unto the end that will receive the crown of immortal glory. . . .
Simplicity, purity, forbearance, benevolence, and love should characterize
our Christian experience.—*Review and Herald,* June 3, 1880.

Rest in Christ

You who are troubled rest with us. 2 Thess. 1:7.

L et us not forget that Christ is the way, the truth, and the life. The compassionate Savior invites all to come to Him. Let us believe the words
of our Lord and not make the way to Him so hard. Let us not travel the
precious road, cast up for the ransomed of the Lord to walk in, with murmuring, with doubts, with cloudy forebodings, groaning, as if forced to an
unpleasant, exacting task. The ways of Christ are ways of pleasantness, and
all His paths are peace. If we have made rough paths for our feet and taken
upon us heavy burdens of care in laying up for ourselves treasures upon the
earth, let us now change and follow the path Jesus has prepared for us.

We are not always willing to give our burdens to Jesus. We sometimes
pour our troubles into human ears and tell our afflictions to those who cannot help us, and neglect to confide all to Jesus, that He may change the sorrowful ways to paths of joy and peace. . . .

The shortness of time is urged as an incentive for us to seek righteousness
and to make Christ our friend. This is not the great motive. It savors of selfishness. Is it necessary that the terrors of the day of God be held before us
to compel us through fear to right action? This ought not to be. Jesus is attractive. He is full of love, mercy, compassion. He proposes to be our friend,
to walk with us through all the rough pathways of life. . . .

Christ's invitation to us all is a call to a life of peace and rest, a life of liberty
and love, and to a rich inheritance in the future immortal life. . . . We need
not be alarmed if this path of liberty is laid through conflicts and sufferings.
The liberty we shall enjoy will be the more valuable because we made sacrifices to obtain it. The peace which passeth knowledge will cost us battles with
the powers of darkness, struggles severe against selfishness and inward sins. . .
. In the face of temptation we should school ourselves to firm endurance,
which will not provoke one murmuring thought, although we may be weary
in toiling and in fighting the good fight of faith. . . .

We cannot appreciate our Redeemer in the highest sense until we can see
Him by the eye of faith reaching to the very depths of human wretchedness,
taking upon Himself the nature of humanity, the capacity to suffer, and by suffering putting forth His divine power to save and lift sinners up to companionship with Himself.—*Review and Herald,* Aug. 2, 1881.

Ordained to Bring Forth Fruit

I am the vine, you are the branches. He who abides in Me, and I in him,
bears much fruit; for without Me you can do nothing. John 15:5.

In the plan of restoring in men and women the divine image, it was provided that the Holy Spirit should move upon human minds and be as the
presence of Christ, a molding agency upon human character. Those who receive the truth become also recipients of the grace of Christ and devote their
sanctified human ability to the work in which Christ was engaged—men and
women become laborers together with God. It is to make them agents for
God that divine truth is brought home to their understanding. . . .

Through the mediumship of truth the character is transformed and fashioned after the divine similitude. Peter represents Christians as those who
have purified their souls through obedience to the truth through the operation of the Holy Spirit. . . .

It is the Christian's business to shine. The professed followers of Christ
are not fulfilling the requirements of the gospel unless they are ministering
to others. They are never to forget that they are to let their light so shine
before others that they, seeing their good works, may glorify their Father
which is in heaven. Their speech is to be always with grace and in harmony
with their profession of faith. Their work is to reveal Christ to the world.
Jesus Christ and Him crucified is their inexhaustible theme, of which they
are freely to speak, bringing out of the good treasure of their hearts the precious things of the gospel. The heart that is filled with the blessed hope, that
is big with immortality and full of glory, cannot be dumb. Those who have
a realization of the sacred presence of Christ cannot speak light and trifling
words, for their words are to be sober, a savor of life unto life. We are not
to be children tossed to and fro, but we are to be anchored in Jesus Christ
and to have something of solid worth of which to speak. . . . Christians are
to publish the good news of salvation, and they are never to weary of the
recital of God's goodness. . . .

You are to speak to sinners, for you know not but God is moving upon
their hearts. Never forget that great responsibility attaches to every word
you utter in their presence. Ask yourself the question, How many have I
spoken to with my heart filled with the love of Christ concerning the unspeakable gift of God's mercy and Christ's righteousness?—*Review and
Herald,* Feb. 12, 1895.

Be Separate From the World

I die daily. 1 Cor. 15:31.

Those who profess the name of Christ are to represent Christ as their pattern and example. They are to unfold to others the truth in its purity and make known to them what are the privileges and responsibilities of the Christian life; and this can be done by the professed followers of Christ only as they conform their characters to the sacred principles of truth. There must be no betrayal of sacred trusts on the part of anyone who professes to be a child of God. There must be no obliterating of the line of demarcation between Christians and the world. There must be no bringing down of the truth to a low, common level, for this will dishonor God, who has given an infinite sacrifice in the gift of His Son for the sins of the world. . . .

Many who claim to be the children of God do not seem to understand that the heart must be regenerated, for their practices ignore the words and works of Christ. By their actions they plainly say, "It is my privilege to act out myself. I should be perfectly miserable if I did not act out myself." This is the kind of religion that is current in the world, but it bears not the heavenly endorsement. . . .

Science so-called, human reasoning, and poetry cannot be passed on as of equal authority with revelation; but it is Satan's studied purpose to exalt human maxims, traditions, and inventions to an equal authority with the Word of God; and, having accomplished this, to exalt human words to the place of supremacy. . . .

There is no safety for any of us except as we daily receive a new experience in looking unto Jesus, the author and finisher of our faith. Day by day we are to behold Him and to become changed into His image. We are to represent the divine attributes and follow the footsteps of Jesus at whatever cost to ourselves. We are to place ourselves under divine guidance, consulting the Word of God, and daily inquiring, Is this the way of the Lord? . . . No deficiency of character will be immortalized and mar heaven with its imperfection. . . .

A profession of truth is of no value unless the soul grasps fast the principles, and appropriates and absorbs the rich nourishment of the truth, and thus becomes a partaker of the divine nature.—*Review and Herald,* Nov. 20, 1894.

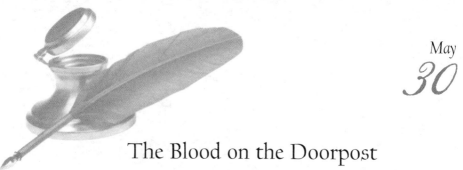

The Blood on the Doorpost

*And you shall take a bunch of hyssop, dip it in the blood that
is in the basin, and strike the lintel and the two doorposts with the blood.
Ex. 12:22.*

The directions that Moses gave concerning the Passover feast are full of significance, and have an application to parents and children in this age of the world. . . .

The father is to dedicate every inmate of his home to God and to do a work that is represented by the feast of the Passover. It is perilous to leave this solemn duty in the hands of others. This peril is well illustrated by an incident that is related concerning a Hebrew family on the night of the Passover.

The legend goes that the eldest daughter was sick, but that she was acquainted with the fact that a lamb was to be chosen for every family, and that its blood was to be sprinkled upon the lintel and side posts of the door so that the Lord might behold the mark of the blood and not suffer the destroyer to enter in to smite the firstborn. With what anxiety she saw the evening approach when the destroying angel was to pass by. She became very restless. She called her father to her side, and asked, "Have you marked the doorpost with blood?" He answered, "Yes, I have given directions in regard to the matter. Do not be troubled, for the destroying angel will not enter here."

The night came on, and again and again the child called her father, still asking, "Are you sure that the doorpost is marked with blood?" Again and again the father assured her that she need have no fear, that a command which involved such consequences would not be neglected by his trustworthy servants. As midnight approached, her pleading voice was heard saying, "Father, I am not sure. Take me in your arms, and let me see the mark for myself, so that I can rest."

The father conceded to the wishes of his child; he took her in his arms and carried her to the door; but there was no blood mark upon the lintel or the posts. He trembled with horror as he realized that his home might have become a house of mourning. With his own hands he seized the hyssop bough and sprinkled the doorpost with blood. He then showed the sick child that the mark was there.—*Review and Herald,* May 21, 1895.

There Is Work for Everyone

Each of us shall give account of himself to God. Rom. 14:12.

God has given to "every man his work." He has not left the spiritual interests of the church wholly in the hands of the minister. It is not for the good of the minister, nor for the good of the individual members of the church, that the minister should undertake exclusive charge of the Lord's heritage. Each member of the church has a part to act in order that the body may be preserved in a healthful condition. We are all members of the same body, and each member must act a part for the benefit of all the others. All members have not the same office. As the members of our natural body are directed by the head, so as members of the spiritual body we should submit ourselves to the direction of Christ, the living head of the church. . . .

The minister and the church members are to unite as one person in laboring for the upbuilding and prosperity of the church. Every one who is a true soldier in the army of the Lord will be an earnest, sincere, efficient worker, laboring to advance the interests of Christ's kingdom. . . .

Many members of the church have been deprived of the experience which they should have had, because the sentiment has prevailed that the minister should do all the work and bear all the burdens. Either the burdens have been crowded upon the minister, or he has assumed those duties that should have been performed by the members of the church. Ministers should take the officers and members of the church into their confidence, and teach them how to labor for the Master. Thus the minister will not have to perform all the labor himself, and at the same time the church will receive greater benefit than if he endeavored to do all the work and release the members of the church from acting the part which the Lord designed that they should. . . .

The burden of church work should be distributed among its individual members, so that each one may become an intelligent laborer for God. There is altogether too much unused force in our churches. . . . Many have willing hands and hearts, but they are discouraged from putting their energies into the work. . . . The wisdom to adapt ourselves to peculiar situations, the strength to act in time of emergency, are acquired by putting to use the talents the Lord has given us and by gaining an experience through personal work.—*Review and Herald,* July 9, 1895.

Jesus Is God

And the Word became flesh and dwelt among us, and we beheld His glory,
the glory as of the only begotten of the Father, full of grace and truth.
John 1:14.

Christ came to the world to reveal the character of the Father and to redeem the fallen race. The world's Redeemer was equal with God. His authority was as the authority of God. He declared that He had no existence separate from the Father. The authority by which He spoke and wrought miracles was expressly His own, yet He assures us that He and His Father are one....

As legislator, Jesus exercised the authority of God; His commands and decisions were supported by the Sovereignty of the eternal throne. The glory of the Father was revealed in the Son; Christ made manifest the character of the Father. He was so perfectly connected with God . . . that He who had seen the Son had seen the Father. His voice was as the voice of God....

Christ was misjudged by the Jews because He did not dwell constantly on the law as written in the tables of stone. He invited men and women to learn of Him, for He was a living representation of the law of God.... He knew that no one could point out any defect in His character or conduct. What power His spotless purity gave to His instructions, what force to His reproofs, what authority to His commands! Truth never languished on His lips, never lost any of its sacredness, because it was illustrated in the divine character of its Advocate....

When Jesus spoke, it was not with hesitating uncertainty, with repetition of words and familiar figures. The truth came from His lips clothed in new and interesting representations that gave it the freshness of a new revelation. His voice was never pitched to an unnatural key, and His words came with an earnestness and assurance appropriate to their importance and the momentous consequences involved in their reception or rejection. When His doctrines were opposed, He defended them with so great zeal and certainty as to impress His hearers that He would die, if need be, to sustain the authority of His teachings.

Jesus was the light of the world. He came forth from God with a message of hope and salvation to the fallen descendants of Adam. If men and women would but receive Him as their personal Savior, He promised to restore to them the image of God and to redeem all that had been lost through sin. He presented to them the truth without one thread of interwoven error.—
Review and Herald, Jan. 7, 1890.

Enmity, God's Gift

I will put enmity between you and the woman, and between your seed and her Seed; He shall bruise your head, and you shall bruise His heel.
Gen. 3:15.

In this first prophecy contained in the Scriptures is found an intimation of redemption. Though a part of the sentence pronounced upon the serpent, it was uttered in the hearing of our first parents, and hence must be regarded as a promise. While it announces war between Satan and mankind, it declares that the power of the great adversary will finally be broken.

Adam and Eve stood as criminals before their God, awaiting the sentence which transgression had incurred. But before they hear of the thorn and the thistle, the sorrow and anguish which should be their portion, and the dust to which they should return, they listen to words which must have inspired them with hope. Though they must suffer from the power of their adversary, they might look forward to ultimate victory.

God declares, "I will put enmity." This enmity is supernaturally put and not naturally entertained. When Adam and Eve sinned, their nature became evil, and they were in harmony, and not at variance, with Satan. The lofty usurper, having succeeded in seducing our first parents as he had seduced angels, counted on securing their allegiance and cooperation in all his enterprises against the government of heaven. There was no enmity between himself and the fallen angels. Whatever discord might exist between them, all were united, as by bands of steel, in their opposition and hatred against God. But when Satan heard that the Seed of the woman should bruise the serpent's head, he knew that though he had succeeded in depraving human nature and assimilating it to his own, yet by some mysterious process God would restore to humans their lost power and enable them to resist and overcome their conqueror.

It is the grace that Christ implants in the soul that creates the enmity against Satan. Without this grace we would continue to be the captives of Satan, servants ever ready to do his bidding. The new principle in the soul creates conflict where hitherto had been peace. The power which Christ imparts enables us to resist the tyrant and usurper. Whenever men and women are seen to abhor sin instead of loving it, when they resist and conquer those passions that have held sway within, there is seen the operation of a principle wholly from above.—*Review and Herald*, July 18, 1882.

Experiencing Forgiveness

Who is a God like You, pardoning iniquity and passing over the transgression of the remnant of His heritage? Micah 7:18.

We need greater faith in Jesus Christ. We need to bring Him into our everyday life. Then we shall have peace and joy, and we shall know by experience the meaning of His words, "If ye keep my commandments, ye shall abide in my love; even as I have kept my Father's commandments, and abide in his love." Our faith must claim the promise that we abide in the love of Jesus. . . .

Precious opportunities and privileges are granted to us to be a light and blessing to others, strengthening their faith and encouraging them through the heavenly sunshine in our own souls. We may gather for our own benefit precious rays of cheerful hope and peace and fullness of joy, and in so doing help everyone with whom we associate. Instead of strengthening unbelief and doubt, we shall inspire hope.

It is the privilege of all who comply with the conditions to have an experimental faith, to know for themselves that pardon is freely extended for every sin. God has pledged His word that when we confess our sins He will forgive them and cleanse from all unrighteousness. Put away unbelief. Put away the suspicion that these promises are not meant for you. They are for every repentant transgressor, and God is dishonored by your unbelief. Let those who have been filled with doubt only believe the words of Jesus fully, and thenceforward they will rejoice in blessedness of light. . . .

We keep the Savior too far apart from our everyday lives. We want Him abiding with us as an honored, trusted friend. We should consult Him on all subjects. We should tell Him every trial, and thus gain strength to meet temptation. . . .

What more can we ask of God than what He has already given us? Oh, the love, the infinite love of our blessed Lord, to be our sacrifice! What joy should fill the hearts of Christians, and what expressions of gratitude be heard from their lips, that through the blood of Jesus it is possible for us to gain the love of God, to be one with Him! . . . Believing on the Son, we shall be obedient to all of the Father's commandments and have life through Jesus Christ. . . .

Christ is our hope and our refuge. His righteousness is imputed only to the obedient. Let us accept it through faith, that the Father shall find in us no sin.—*Review and Herald,* Sept. 21, 1886.

Strong in Christ

That He would grant you, according to the riches of His glory, to be strengthened with might through His Spirit in the inner man. Eph. 3:16.

Our Savior represents His requirements as a yoke and the Christian life as one of burden-bearing. Yet, contrasting these with the cruel power of Satan and the burdens imposed by sin, He declares, "My yoke is easy, and my burden is light."

When we try to live the life of a Christian, to bear its responsibilities and perform its duties without Christ as a helper, the yoke is galling, the burden intolerably heavy. But Jesus does not desire us to do this. He bids the weary and heavy-laden, "Come unto me, . . . and I will give you rest." "Learn of me; for I am meek and lowly in heart; and ye shall find rest unto your souls." Here is revealed the secret of that rest which Christ promises to bestow. We must possess His meekness of spirit, and we shall find peace in Him.

Many profess to come to Christ while yet they cling to their own ways, which are as a painful yoke. Selfishness, love of the world, or other cherished sin destroys their peace and joy. My fellow Christian, . . . remember that you are in the service of Christ. Whatever your burden or cross, lift it in the name of Jesus; bear it in His strength. He pronounces the yoke easy and the burden light, and I believe Him. I have proved the truth of His words.

Those who are restless, impatient, dissatisfied under the weight of care and responsibility, are seeking to carry their burden without the aid of Jesus. If He were by their side, the sunshine of His presence would scatter every cloud, the help of His strong arm would lighten every burden. . . .

We cumber ourselves with needless cares and anxieties and weigh ourselves down with heavy burdens because we do not learn of Jesus. . . . Christ's true followers are unlike the world in words, in works, and in deportment. Oh, why will not all His professed children follow Him fully? Why will any bear burdens which He has not imposed? . . .

In every act of life Christians should seek to represent Christ—seek to make His service appear attractive. . . . Let the graces of the Spirit be manifested in kindness, meekness, forbearance, cheerfulness, and love. . . .

Love to Jesus will be seen, will be felt. It cannot be hidden. It exerts a wondrous power. It makes the timid bold, the slothful diligent, the ignorant wise. . . . Love to Christ will not be dismayed by tribulation nor turned aside from duty by reproaches.—*Review and Herald,* Nov. 29, 1887.

Sweet Thoughts

*I will sing praise to my God while I have my being. May my meditation
be sweet to Him; I will be glad in the Lord. Ps. 104:33, 34.*

If the mind is molded by the objects with which it has most to do, then
to think of Jesus, to talk of Him, will enable you to become like Him in
spirit and character. You will reflect His image in that which is great and
pure and spiritual. You will have the mind of Christ, and He will send you
forth to the world as His spiritual representative. . . .

The sun shining in the heavens pours its bright beams into all the highways and byways of life. It has sufficient light for thousands of worlds like
ours. And so it is with the Sun of Righteousness. His bright beams of healing and gladness are amply sufficient to save our little world, and are efficacious in establishing security in every world that has been created. . . .

It is growth in knowledge of the character of Christ that sanctifies the
soul. To discern and appreciate the wonderful work of the atonement transforms all who contemplate the plan of salvation. By beholding Christ, they
become changed into the same image, from glory to glory, as by the Spirit
of the Lord. The beholding of Jesus becomes an ennobling, refining process
to the actual Christian. . . .

What kind of faith is it that overcomes the world? It is that faith which
makes Christ your own personal Savior—that faith which, recognizing your
helplessness, your utter inability to save yourself, takes hold of the Helper who
is mighty to save as your only hope. It is faith that will not be discouraged,
that hears the voice of Christ saying, "Be of good cheer; I have overcome the
world, and my divine strength is yours." It is the faith that hears Him say, "Lo,
I am with you alway, even unto the end of the world." . . .

Every soul must have a realization that Christ is our personal Savior; then
love and zeal and steadfastness will be manifest in the Christian life. . . .

Christ should never be out of the mind. . . . He is the dispeller of all our
doubts, the earnest of all our hopes. How precious is the thought that we
may indeed become partakers of the divine nature, whereby we may overcome as Christ overcame! . . . He is the melody of our songs, the shadow of
a great rock in a weary land. He is living water to the thirsty soul. He is our
refuge in the storm. He is our righteousness, our sanctification, our redemption.—*Review and Herald,* Aug. 26, 1890.

Today's Assignment

Father, I desire that they also whom You gave Me may be with Me where I am, that they may behold My glory which You have given Me. John 17:24.

Christ was infinite in wisdom, and yet He thought best to accept of Judas, although He knew what were his imperfections of character. John was not perfect; Peter denied his Lord; and yet it was of men like these that the early Christian church was organized. Jesus accepted them that they might learn of Him what constitutes a perfect Christian character. The business of every Christian is to study the character of Christ. The lessons which Jesus gave His disciples did not always harmonize with their reasonings. . . . The Redeemer of the world ever sought to carry the mind from the earthly to the heavenly. Christ constantly taught the disciples, and His sacred lessons had a molding influence upon their characters. Judas alone did not respond to divine enlightenment. To all appearances he was righteous, and yet he cultivated his tendency to accuse and condemn others. . . .

Judas was selfish, covetous, and a thief, yet he was numbered with the disciples. He was defective in character, and he failed to practice the words of Christ. He braced his soul to resist the influence of the truth, and while he practiced criticizing and condemning others, he neglected his own soul, and cherished and strengthened his natural evil traits of character until he became so hardened that he could sell his Lord for thirty pieces of silver.

Oh, let us encourage our souls to look to Jesus! Tell everyone how dangerous it is to neglect the soul's eternal healthfulness by looking upon the diseased souls of others, by talking upon the uncomeliness of character found in those who profess the name of Christ. The soul does not become more and more like Christ by beholding evil, but like the evil which it beholds. . . .

Let us remember that our great High Priest is pleading before the mercy seat in behalf of His ransomed people. He ever liveth to make intercession for us. . . . The blood of Jesus is pleading with power and efficacy for those who are backslidden, for those who are rebellious, for those who sin against great light and love. . . . He will not forget His church in the world of temptation.—*Review and Herald,* Aug. 15, 1893.

Slow to Learn

In Him was life, and the life was the light of men. And the light shines in the darkness, and the darkness did not comprehend it. John 1:4, 5.

Christ was the foundation of the whole system of Jewish worship, and in it was shadowed forth the living reality—the manifestation of God in Christ. Through the sacrificial system all could see Christ's personality and look forward to their divine Savior. But when He stood before them representing the invisible God—for in Him dwelt "all the fulness of the Godhead bodily"—they were not able to discern His divine character because of their want of spirituality. Their own prophets had foretold Him as a Deliverer. . . . But though His character and mission had been so plainly delineated, though He came unto His own, His own received Him not. Occasionally divinity flashed through humanity—the glory escaped through the disguise of the flesh and brought forth an expression of homage from His disciples. But it was not until Christ ascended to His Father, not until the descent of the Holy Spirit, that the disciples fully appreciated the character and the mission of Christ. After the baptism of the Holy Spirit they began to realize that they had been in the very presence of the Lord of life and glory. As the Holy Spirit brought the sayings of Christ to their remembrance, their understanding was opened to comprehend the prophecies, to understand the mighty miracles which He had wrought. . . . They seemed of much less importance in their own eyes after their awakening to the fact that Christ had been among them than they did before they realized this. They never wearied of rehearsing every item which had come under their notice in connection with His words and works. They were often filled with remorse at their stupidity and unbelief and misapprehension as they recalled His lessons of instruction which they had but dimly understood when He had spoken them in their presence, and which now came to them as a fresh revelation. The Scriptures became a new book to them. . . .

The disciples remembered that Christ had said, "Sanctify them through thy truth: thy word is truth." The Word was to be their guide and director. As the disciples searched Moses and the prophets which testified of Christ, they were brought into fellowship with the Deity and learned anew of their great Teacher, who had ascended to heaven to complete the work which He had begun upon earth.—*Review and Herald,* Apr. 23, 1895.

The Great Source of Truth

Learn from Me, for I am gentle and lowly in heart, and you will find rest for your souls. Matt. 11:29.

Christ is the author of all truth. Every brilliant conception, every thought of wisdom, every human capacity and talent, is the gift of Christ. He borrowed no new ideas from humanity; for He originated all. But when He came to earth, He found the bright gems of truth which He had entrusted to the human race, all buried up in superstition and tradition. Truths of most vital importance were placed in the framework of error, to serve the purpose of the archdeceiver. Human opinions, the most popular sentiments of the people, were glossed over with the appearance of truth, and were presented as the genuine gems of heaven, worthy of attention and reverence. But Christ swept away erroneous theories of every grade. No one save the world's Redeemer had power to present the truth in its primitive purity, divested of the error that Satan had accumulated to hide its heavenly beauty.

Some of the truths that Christ spoke were familiar to the people. They had heard them from the lips of priests and rulers and from people of thought; but for all that, they were distinctively the thoughts of Christ. He had given them to people in trust, to be communicated to the world. On every occasion He proclaimed the particular truth He thought appropriate for the needs of His hearers, whether the ideas had been expressed before or not.

The work of Christ was to take the truth of which the people were in want, and separate it from error, and present it free from the superstitions of the world, that the people might accept it on its own intrinsic and eternal merit. He dispersed the mists of doubt, that the truth might be revealed, and shed distinct rays of light into the darkness of human hearts. He placed the truth in clear contrast with error, that it might appear as truth before the people. But how few appreciate the value of the work that Christ was doing! How few in our day have a just conception of the preciousness of the lessons which He gave to His disciples!

He proved Himself to be the way, the truth, the life. He sought to attract minds from the passing pleasures of this life to the unseen and eternal realities. Views of heavenly things do not incapacitate men and women for the duties of this life, but rather render them more efficient and faithful.—*Review and Herald,* Jan. 7, 1890.

Cleansing the Temple

"My house is a house of prayer," but you have made it a "den of thieves."
Luke 19:46.

Why was it that Christ's indignation was stirred as He came into the temple courts? His eye swept over the scene, and He saw in it the dishonor of God and the oppression of the people. He heard the lowing of the oxen, the bleating of the sheep, and the altercation between those who were buying and selling. In the courts of God even the priests and rulers were engaged in traffic. . . . When once their attention was called to Him, they could not withdraw their eyes from His face, for there was something in His countenance that awed and terrified them. Who was He? A humble Galilean, the son of a carpenter who had worked at His trade with His father, but as they gazed upon Him, they felt as though they were arraigned before the judgment bar. . . .

Christ saw the poor and the distressed and the afflicted in trouble and dismay because they had not sufficient to purchase even a dove for an offering. The blind, the lame, the deaf, the afflicted, were in suffering and distress because they longed to present an offering for their sins, but the prices were so exorbitant they could not compass it. It seemed that there was no chance for them to have their sins pardoned. . . .

When Christ had expelled those who had sold doves, He had said, "Take these things hence." He had not driven the doves out as He had the oxen and the sheep, and why? Because they were the only offering of the poor. He knew their necessities, and as the sellers were driven from the temple, the suffering and the afflicted were left in the courts. . . .

But the priests and the rulers, recovering from their dismay, said, "We will return and challenge Him, and ask Him by what authority He had presumed to expel us from the temple."

But what a scene met their eyes as they entered again the courts of the temple. Christ was ministering to the poor, the suffering, and the afflicted. . . . He gave the suffering tender comfort. He took the little ones in His arms and commanded freedom from disease and suffering. He gave sight to the blind, hearing to the deaf, health to the diseased, and comfort to the afflicted. . . .

He was doing the very work which had been prophesied that the Messiah would do.—*Review and Herald,* Aug. 27, 1895.

Jesus Loves You

But God demonstrates His own love toward us, in that while we were still sinners, Christ died for us. Rom. 5:8.

I love to speak of Jesus and His matchless love. I have not one doubt of the love of God. I know that He is able to save to the uttermost all that come unto Him. His precious love is a reality to me, and the doubts expressed by those who know not the Lord Jesus Christ have no effect upon me. . . . Take Jesus as your personal Savior. Come to Him just as you are, give yourself to Him, grasp His promise by living faith, and He will be to you all that you desire. . . .

Those who give their hearts to Christ will find rest in His love. We have a token of the magnitude of His love in His sufferings and death. . . . Jesus endured such agony . . . because He became the sinner's substitute and surety. He Himself bore the penalty of the law which sinners deserved in order that they might have . . . another chance to prove their loyalty to God. . . .

There are only two classes in the whole universe—those who believe in Christ and whose faith leads them to keep God's commandments, and those who do not believe in Him and are disobedient. . . .

You have every reason to believe that He can and will save you. Why? Because you are guiltless? No; because you are a sinner, and Jesus says, "I am not come to call the righteous, but sinners to repentance." The call is addressed to you, and when Satan says to you that there is no hope, tell him you know there is, "for God so loved the world, that he gave his only begotten Son, that whosoever believeth in him should not perish, but have everlasting life." . . .

The hand that was nailed to the cross for you is stretched out to save you. Believe that Jesus will hear your confession, receive your requests, forgive your sins, and make you a member of the royal family. You need the hope which Jesus will give to cheer you under every circumstance. . . .

Those who accept the truth will find their love for earthly things dislodged. They see the surpassing glory of heavenly things and appreciate the excellence of that which relates to everlasting life. They are charmed with the unseen and eternal. Their grasp loosens from earthly things; they fasten their eyes with admiration upon the invisible glories of the heavenly world. They realize that their trials are working out for them a far more exceeding and eternal weight of glory, and in comparison to the riches that are theirs to enjoy, they count them light afflictions which are for but a moment.— *Review and Herald,* June 23, 1896.

Jesus, the Fulfillment of Prophecy

For if you believed Moses, you would believe Me; for he wrote about Me.
John 5:46.

J esus] spoke with assurance and revealed a depth of knowledge far exceeding that of the most learned of the scribes and rabbis. It was evident
that He had a thorough knowledge of the Old Testament Scriptures and
that He presented truth that was unmingled with human sayings and maxims. The old truths fell upon their ears like a new revelation. . . .

Jesus presented His lessons to the people, but He did not make a practice of
asserting His high and authoritative claim. He had come to save the lost world,
and His words and works, His whole life in humanity, was to speak of His divinity. He left it to His own dignity, to His life, to His course of action, to witness to the people that He worked the works of God. He left it to them to draw
their own conclusion concerning His claims while He expounded to them the
prophecies concerning Himself. He directed them to search the Scriptures, for
it was essential that they should interpret correctly the mission and work of the
Son of God. He pointed out the fact to them that He was fulfilling the prophecies that had hitherto been given by holy men who were moved upon by the
Holy Spirit. He declared plainly that they wrote of Him, and brought the clear
rays of the light of prophecy to illuminate His words and works. . . . He stood
forth in His ministry as one distinguished from every other teacher. He Himself
had inspired the prophets to write of Him. His life work had been planned in
the eternal counsels of heaven before the foundation of the world. . . . His life
was the light of the world, and He presented His life before the people, that
their faith might lay hold upon it, and that they might become one with Him.

Though He presented infinite truth, He left many things unsaid that He
might have said, because even His disciples were not able to comprehend
them. He said, "I have yet many things to say unto you, but ye cannot bear
them now." The burden of His teaching was obedience to the commandments of God, that would work transformation of character and inculcate
moral excellence, shaping the soul after the divine similitude. Christ had been
sent to earth to represent God in character. Jesus was the Life-giver, the
Teacher sent of God to provide salvation for a lost world and to save us in spite
of all Satan's temptations and lying deceptions. He Himself was the gospel. In
His teachings He clearly presented the great plan devised for the redemption
of the race.—*Review and Herald*, July 7, 1896.

The Uplifted Savior

As Moses lifted up the serpent in the wilderness, even so must the Son of Man be lifted up, that whoever believes in Him should not perish but have eternal life. John 3:14, 15.

In humility Christ began His mighty work for the uplifting of the fallen race. Passing by the cities and the renowned seats of learning, He made His home in the humble and obscure village of Nazareth. In this place, from which it was commonly supposed that no good could come, the world's Redeemer passed the greater part of His life working at His trade as a carpenter. His home was among the poor; His family was not distinguished by learning, riches, or position. In the path which the poor, the neglected, the sorrowing, must tread, He walked while on earth, taking upon Him all the woes which the afflicted must bear.

It was the proud boast of the Jews that the Messiah was to come as a king, conquering His enemies and treading down the heathen in His wrath. But it was not the mission of Christ to exalt men and women by ministering to their pride. He, the humble Nazarene, might have poured contempt upon the world's pride, for He was commander in the heavenly courts; but He came in humility, showing that it is not riches or position or authority that the God of heaven respects, but that He honors a humble, contrite heart made noble by the power of the grace of Christ.

Christ closed His life of toil and denial in our behalf by a crowning sacrifice for us. . . . Christ is a living Savior. Today He sits at the right hand of God as our Advocate, making intercession for us; and He calls upon us to look unto Him and be saved. But it has ever been the tempter's determined purpose to eclipse Jesus from the view, that we may be led to lean upon the arm of humanity for help and strength; and he has so well accomplished his purpose that we, turning our eyes from Jesus, in whom all hope of eternal life is centered, look to our fellow men for aid and guidance. . . .

As the serpent was lifted up in the wilderness by Moses, that all who had been bitten by the fiery serpents might look and live, so must the Son of Man be lifted up before the world by His servants. Christ and Him crucified is the message God would have His servants sound through the length and breadth of the world.—*Review and Herald*, Sept. 29, 1896.

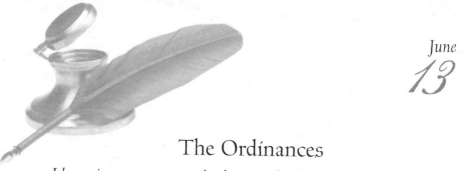

The Ordinances

I have given you an example, that you should do as I have done to you.
John 13:15.

The symbols of the Lord's house are simple and plainly understood, and the truths represented by them are of the deepest significance to us. In instituting the sacramental service to take the place of the Passover, Christ left for His church a memorial of His great sacrifice for sinners. "This do," He said, "in remembrance of me." This was the point of transition between two economies and their two great festivals. The one was to close forever; the other, which He had just established, was to take its place, and to continue through all time as the memorial of His death. . . .

With the rest of the disciples, Judas partook of the bread and wine symbolizing the body and blood of Christ. This was the last time that Judas would be present with the twelve; but that the scripture might be fulfilled, he left the sacramental table, Christ's last gift to His disciples, to complete his work of betrayal. . . .

The children of God are to bear in mind that God is brought sacredly near on every such occasion as the service of feet washing. . . .

The object of this service is to call to mind the humility of our Lord and the lessons He has given in washing the feet of His disciples. There is in us a disposition to esteem ourselves more highly than our brothers and sisters, to work for ourselves, to serve ourselves, to seek the highest places; and often evil surmisings and bitterness of spirit spring up over mere trifles. This ordinance, preceding the Lord's Supper, is to clear away these misunderstandings, to bring us out of our selfishness, down from our stilts of self-exaltation to the humility of spirit that will lead us to wash one another's feet. . . .

The ordinance of feet washing has been especially enjoined by Christ, and on these occasions the Holy Spirit is present to witness and put a seal to His ordinance. He is there to convict and soften the heart. He draws the believers together and makes them one in heart. They are made to feel that Christ indeed is present to clear away the rubbish that has accumulated to separate the hearts of the children of God from Him.—*Review and Herald,* June 22, 1897.

Principles in Business

What will it profit a man if he gains the whole world, and loses his own soul? Or what will a man give in exchange for his soul? Mark 8:36, 37.

It is the place of the followers of Christ to acknowledge their dependence upon God in everything and to carry out the principles of their faith in all the relations of life, including business transactions. They cannot otherwise correctly represent the religion of Christ. And they should be honest with God as well as with others. Can someone be dishonest with God? Read the prophet's answer: "Will a man rob God? Yet ye have robbed me." . . .

Tithes and offerings belong to God. The means in our possession should be regarded as a sacred trust, to be used to the glory of the Giver. Self-denial is the condition of salvation. The charity that seeketh not her own is the fruit of that disinterested love that characterized the life of our Redeemer. Those who for love to Christ deny themselves will find the happiness which the selfish seek in vain, but those who make their own pleasures and selfish interests the chief object of life will lose the happiness they think to enjoy.

The apostle Paul has something to say on the subject of system in giving: "Now concerning the collection for the saints, as I have given order to the churches of Galatia, even so do ye. Upon the first day of the week let every one of you lay by him in store, as God hath prospered him."

God's rule of giving, as expressed in His Word, excludes no one, and it presses heavily on no one. It touches the poor but lightly, and is not really felt by the rich. . . .

Said Christ, "Where your treasure is, there will your heart be also." If we lay up our treasure in heaven, our hearts will be in heaven; if our treasure is on the earth, our hearts will be set on things of the earth, worrying about losses, and anxious about gains and riches. . . .

As in the balances of the sanctuary the offering is estimated in accordance with the spirit of love and sacrifice that prompted it, the promises will just as surely be fulfilled to the liberal poor man or woman who has little to offer but gives that little freely, as to the wealthy who give largely of their abundance. . . .

Christ's kingdom should be superior to every other interest. . . . [God] feeds the sparrow and clothes the lily; will He be less mindful of the needs of His children?—*Bible Echo* (Australia), Dec. 9, 1895.

A Teacher Sent From God

If I cast out demons by the Spirit of God, surely the kingdom of God has come upon you. Matt. 12:28.

In Christ's mighty works there was sufficient evidence to convince anyone. But the Jewish rulers did not want the truth. They could not but acknowledge the reality of the works of Christ, but they cast condemnation upon them all. They were forced to acknowledge that supernatural power attended His work, but this power, they declared, was derived from Satan. Did they really believe this? No, but they were so determined that the truth should not lead to their conversion that they charged the work of the Spirit of God to the devil. . . .

All-compassionate Redeemer! What love, what matchless love, is Thine! Charged by the great men of Israel with doing His works of mercy by the power of the prince of devils, He was as one who saw and heard not. The work He came from heaven to do must not be left undone. Truth must be unfolded to humanity. The Light of the world must flash His beams into the darkness of sin and superstition. The truth found no place in the hearts of those who should have been foremost to receive it, because they were barricaded with prejudice and wicked unbelief. Among those who had not such exalted privileges, Christ prepared hearts to receive His message. He made new bottles for the new wine.

Every truth is invested by the God of heaven with an influence proportionate to its character and importance. The plan of redemption, which means everything to a lost and ruined world, was to be proclaimed, and the Spirit of God in Christ Jesus was brought into vital contact with the heart of the world. . . .

By Christ the truth was proclaimed. The hearts of those who professed to be the children of God were barricaded against it, but those who had not been so highly privileged, those who were not clothed with the garments of self-righteousness, were drawn to Christ. . . .

Today Satan endeavors to keep hidden from the world the great atoning sacrifice, which reveals the love of God and the binding claims of His law. He wars against the work of Christ. . . . But while he is carrying on this work, heavenly intelligences are combining with God's human instrumentalities in the work of restoration.—*Review and Herald*, Apr. 30, 1901.

Beholding Christ

*Therefore, if anyone is in Christ, he is a new creation; old things have
passed away; behold, all things have become new. 2 Cor. 5:17.*

Through the power that Jesus gives, we can be "more than conquerors."
But we cannot manufacture this power. Only through the Spirit of
God can we receive it. We need a deep insight into the nature of Christ and
into the mystery of His love, "which passeth knowledge." We are to live in
the warm, genial rays of the Sun of Righteousness. Nothing but Christ's
loving compassion, His divine grace, His almighty power, can enable us to
baffle the relentless foe and subdue the opposition of our own hearts. What
is our strength? The joy of the Lord. Let the love of Christ fill our hearts,
and then we shall be prepared to receive the power that He has for us.

Let us thank God every day for the blessings that are ours. If human
agents will humble themselves before God, realizing how inappropriate it
is for them to cherish self-sufficiency, realizing their utter inability to do the
work that needs to be done in order that their souls may be purified; if they
will cast away their own righteousness, Christ will abide in their hearts. He
will put His hand to the work of creating them anew and will continue the
work till they are complete in Him.

Christ will never neglect the work that has been placed in His hands. He
will inspire the resolute disciple with a sense of the perversity, the sin-
stained condition, the depravity, of the heart upon which He is working.
True penitents learn the uselessness of self-importance. Looking to Jesus,
comparing their own defective characters with the Savior's perfect character, they say only,

"In my hand no price I bring;
Simply to thy cross I cling."

With Isaiah they declare, "Lord, thou wilt ordain peace for us: for thou
also hast wrought all our works in us. O Lord our God, other lords beside
thee have had dominion over us: but by thee only will we make mention
of thy name."—*Review and Herald,* Mar. 31, 1904.

The Only Source of Truth

I am the bread of life. He who comes to Me shall never hunger, and he who believes in Me shall never thirst. John 6:35.

There are many in this age of the world who act as if they were at liberty to question the words of the Infinite, to review His decisions and statutes, endorsing, revising, reshaping, and annulling at their pleasure. We are never safe while we are guided by human opinions, but we are safe when we are guided by a "Thus saith the Lord." We cannot trust the salvation of our souls to any lower standard than the decisions of an infallible Judge. Those who make God their guide and His Word their counselor behold the lamp of life. God's living oracles guide their feet in straight paths. Those who are thus led do not dare to judge the Word of God, but ever hold that His Word judges them. They get their faith and religion from the Word of the living God. It is the guide and counselor that directs their path. The Word is indeed a light to their feet and a lamp to their path. They walk under the direction of the Father of light, with whom is no variableness, neither shadow of turning. He whose tender mercies are over all His works makes the path of the just as a shining light, which shineth more and more unto the perfect day. . . .

The world is perishing for want of pure, unadulterated truth. Christ is the truth. His words are truth, and they have a greater value and a deeper significance than appears on the surface. All the sayings of Christ have a value beyond their unpretending appearance. Minds that are quickened by the Holy Spirit will discern the value of these sayings. They will discern the precious gems of truth, though they may be buried treasure. . . .

The heart is the citadel of the being, and until that is wholly on the Lord's side, the enemy will gain constant victories over us through his subtle temptations.

If the life is given into its control, the power of the truth is unlimited. The thoughts are brought into captivity to Jesus Christ. From the treasure of the heart are brought forth appropriate and fitting words. Writing to Timothy, Paul says, "Hold fast the form of sound words, which thou hast heard of me, in faith and love which is in Christ Jesus."—*Review and Herald,* Mar. 29, 1906.

Secure in Jesus' Hands

*My sheep hear My voice, and I know them, and they follow Me. . . .
And they shall never perish; neither shall anyone snatch them out
of My hand. John 10:27, 28.*

When Satan heard the word, "I will put enmity between thee and the woman, and between thy seed and her seed," he knew that men and women would be given power to resist his temptations. He realized that his claim to the position of prince of the newly created world was to be contested, that One would come whose work would be fatal to his evil purposes, that he and his angels would be forever defeated. His assurance of certain power, his sense of security, was gone. Adam and Eve had yielded to his temptations, and their posterity would feel the strength of his assaults. But they would not be left without a helper. The Son of God was to come to the world, to be tempted in our behalf, and in our behalf to overcome.

There is enmity between fallen human beings and Satan only as they place themselves on God's side and yield obedience to the law of Jehovah. This brings to them power to withstand Satan's attacks. It is through Christ's sacrifice that they are enabled to obey. . . . The Son of God, bearing human nature, and tempted on all points as we are tempted, met and resisted the assaults of the enemy. And in His strength human beings can gain the victory, meeting the tempter, yet not overcome by his artifice and his presumptuous presentations. By accepting Christ as a personal Savior, men and women can stand firm against the temptations of the enemy. Human beings may have eternal life if they will accept the principles of heaven and allow Christ to bring the heart and mind into obedience to the law of Jehovah.

Christ saw the meaning of Satan's wiles, and till the end of His test and trial, He stood firm in His resistance, refusing to swerve from allegiance to God. . . .

The way in which Satan tempted Christ, he is today tempting every soul. He seeks to hold every person under his reasoning. The Savior warns us against entering into controversy with him or his agencies. We are not to meet them except on the Bible ground, "It is written." The less that we have to do with the arguments of those who are opposed to God, the firmer will be our foundation. We are to repeat as seldom as possible the sentiments of Satan's forming. Let every tempted soul keep looking at the principles that are wholly from above, remembering the promise, "I will put enmity between thee and the woman."—*Review and Herald,* May 3, 1906.

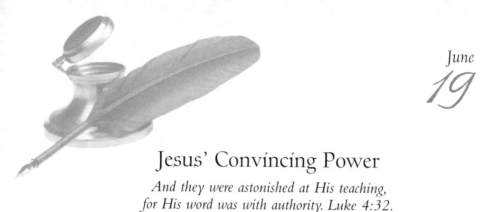

Jesus' Convincing Power

And they were astonished at His teaching,
for His word was with authority. Luke 4:32.

The mission of Jesus was demonstrated by convincing miracles. His doctrine astonished the people. It was not the contradictory jargon of the scribes, full of mysticism, burdened with absurd forms and meaningless exactions, but it was a system of truth that met the wants of the heart. His teaching was plain, clear, and comprehensive. The practical truths He uttered had a convincing power and arrested the attention of the people. Multitudes lingered at His side, marveling at His wisdom. His manner corresponded with the great truths He proclaimed. There was no apology, no hesitancy, not the shadow of a doubt or uncertainty that it might be other than He declared. He spoke of the earthly and the heavenly, of the human and the divine, with positive authority, and the people "were astonished at his doctrine: for his word was with power."

He had declared Himself to be the Messiah, but the people would not receive Him, though they saw His wonderful works and marveled at His wisdom. He did not meet their expectation of the Messiah. They had been instructed to look for earthly pomp and glory at the advent of their Deliverer, and they dreamed that under the power of "the Lion of the tribe of Judah" the Jewish nation would be exalted to preeminence among the nations of the world. With these ideas they were not prepared to receive the humble Teacher of Galilee, although He came just as the prophets had foretold that He would come. He was not recognized as "the truth," the "light of the world," although He spoke as never anyone spoke, for His appearance was humble and unpretending. He came without attendants of earthly pageant and glory. There was, however, a majesty in His very presence that bespoke His divine character. His manners, though gentle and winning, possessed an authority that inspired respect and awe. He commanded, and disease left the sufferer. The dead heard His voice and lived, the sorrowing rejoiced, and the weary and heavy-laden found rest in His compassionate love. . . .

The lame, the blind, the palsy-stricken, and leprous, and those afflicted with all manner of diseases came to Him, and He healed them all. . . . Heaven endorsed His claims with mighty manifestations.—*Review and Herald*, July 6, 1911.

As a Root Out of Dry Ground

For He shall grow up . . . as a root out of dry ground. He has no form or comeliness; and when we see Him, there is no beauty that we should desire Him. Isa. 53:2.

The people of Jesus' day could not see, beneath the disguise of humility, the glory of the Son of God. He was "despised and rejected of men; a man of sorrows, and acquainted with grief." He was to them as a root out of dry ground, with no form nor comeliness that they should desire Him. . . .

Christ reached the people where they were. He presented the plain truth to their minds in the most forcible and simple language. The humble poor, the most unlearned, could comprehend through faith in Him the most exalted truths of God. No one needed to consult the learned doctors as to His meaning. He did not perplex the ignorant with mysterious inferences nor use unaccustomed and learned words of which they had no knowledge. The greatest Teacher the world has ever known was the most definite, simple, and practical in His instruction.

While priests and rabbis were assuring themselves of their competency to teach the people and to cope even with the Son of God in expounding doctrine, He charged them with ignorance of the Scriptures or the power of God. It is not learning of the world's great persons that opens the mysteries of the plan of redemption. The priests and rabbis had studied the prophecies, but they failed to discover the precious proofs of the Messiah's advent, of the manner of His coming, of His mission and character. Those who claimed to be worthy of confidence because of their wisdom did not perceive that Christ was the Prince of life.

The rabbis looked with suspicion and contempt upon everything that did not bear the appearance of worldly wisdom, national exaltation, and religious exclusiveness; but the mission of Jesus was to oppose these very evils, to correct these erroneous views, and to work a reformation in faith and morals. He attracted attention to purity of life, to humility of spirit, and to devotion to God and His cause without hope of worldly honor or reward. . . .

He rejoiced in spirit as He beheld the poor of this world eagerly accepting the precious message which He brought. He looked up to heaven and said, "I thank thee, O Father, Lord of heaven and earth, because thou hast hid these things from the wise and prudent, and hast revealed them unto babes."—*Review and Herald,* Aug. 3, 1911.

True Riches

Foxes have holes and birds of the air have nests, but the Son of Man has nowhere to lay His head. Matt. 8:20.

Christ came to this world to live a life of perfect obedience to the laws of God's kingdom. He came to uplift and ennoble human beings, to work out an enduring righteousness for them. He came as a medium through which truth was to be imparted. In Him are found all the excellencies necessary to absolute perfection of character. . . .

Christ gave up His high command in the heavenly courts, and laying aside His royal robe and kingly crown, He clothed His divinity with humanity. For our sakes He became poor in earthly riches and advantages, that human beings might be rich in the eternal weight of glory. He took His place at the head of the human family and consented to endure in our behalf the trials and temptations that sin has brought. He might have come in power and great glory, escorted by a multitude of heavenly angels. But no, He came in humility, of lowly parentage. He was brought up in an obscure and despised village. He lived a life of poverty and suffered often with privation and hunger. This He did to show that earthly riches and high rank do not increase the value of souls in the sight of God. He has given us no encouragement to think that riches make anyone worthy of eternal life. Those church members who, when a brother becomes poor, treat him as if he were unworthy of their notice certainly did not learn this from Christ. . . .

It is submission to sin that brings the great unhappiness of the soul. It is not poverty but disobedience that lessens our hope of gaining eternal life, which the Savior came to bring us. True riches, true peace, true content, enduring happiness—these are found only in entire surrender to God, in perfect reconciliation to His will.

Christ came to our world to live a life of stainless purity, thus to show sinners that in His strength they, too, can obey God's holy precepts, the laws of His kingdom. He came to magnify the law and make it honorable by His perfect conformity to its principles. He united humanity and divinity, that fallen human beings might become partakers of the divine nature and thus escape the corruption that is in the world through lust.

It was from the Father that Christ constantly drew the power that enabled Him to keep His life free from spot or stain of sin.—*Review and Herald,* July 4, 1912.

Will a Man Rob God?

But you say, "In what way have we robbed You?" In tithes and offerings.
Mal. 3:8.

Would you do it? The Bible speaks of this as if it were an impossibility that anyone should venture to do such a thing. "Yet ye have robbed me.". . .

The Lord saw just how it would be when the world was filled with inhabitants, and therefore He makes a covenant with His people that they should give Him their tithes and offerings, according to the arrangement which He has made. This is His. It does not belong to any of you. God has made this arrangement with you, that you may show that you realize your dependence and accountability to God by returning to Him His portion. If you do this, His blessing will come upon you. All that we have is the Lord's, entrusted to us as His stewards. That which we hand back to Him He must first give to us. . . .

We breathe because God takes charge of the human machinery. Day by day He keeps it in working order, and He wants us to think of the infinite sacrifice He has made for us in suffering with One equal with Himself—His only begotten Son. He consented to let Him come to a world all seared and marred with the curse of sin, to stand at the head of humanity as a sin-bearing, sin-pardoning Savior. . . .

Christ declared that all power in heaven and earth has been given to Him. . . . He takes His position at the head of humanity, covering humanity with divinity. . . .

God forbid that any one of us should fail of gaining the precious boon of eternal life. Do not rob God. Walk honestly before Him. All is His. He has entrusted goods to His agents for the advancement of His work in the world. They are to bring to His treasury a faithful tithe, and besides this they are to bring gifts and offerings as the cause shall demand. . . . God desires us to realize that heaven has been brought near to earth. Ten thousand times ten thousand and thousands of thousands of angels minister to those who shall be heirs of salvation. . . .

God is in earnest with us. He expects us to help in planting His standard in places which have never heard the truth. . . . From all over the world, calls for help are coming. Lay out no money unnecessarily. Deny yourself, take up your cross, and follow the Master. You can never give Him as much as He has given you. He gave His life for you. What have you given for Him?—*General Conference Bulletin,* Apr. 8, 1901. (Taken from Ellen White's talk, Apr. 6, 1901.)

Remedy for Soul Poverty

Blessed are the poor in spirit, for theirs is the kingdom of heaven.
Matt. 5:3.

These comforting words of Christ are addressed not to the proud, not to the boastful and self-conceited, but to those who realize their own weakness and sinfulness. Those who mourn, the meek who feel themselves unworthy of the favor of God, and those who hunger and thirst after right-eousness are all included in "the poor in spirit." . . .

The poor in spirit feel their poverty, their want of the grace of Christ. They realize that they know little of God and His great love, and that they need light in order that they may know and keep the way of the Lord. They dare not face temptation in their own strength, for they realize that they have not moral force to resist evil. They have no pleasure in reviewing their past life and little confidence in looking to the future, for they are sick at heart. But it is to such that Christ says, "Blessed are the poor in spirit." Christ saw that those who feel their poverty may be made rich. . . .

What great privileges are within the reach of those who feel the poverty of their soul and submit to the will of God! The remedy for soul poverty is found alone in Christ. When the heart is sanctified by grace, when Christians have the mind of Christ, they have the love of Christ, which is spiritual riches more precious than the gold of Ophir. But before there can be an intense desire for the wealth contained in Christ, which is available to all who feel their poverty, there must be a sense of need. When the heart is full of self-sufficiency and preoccupied with the superficial things of earth, the Lord Jesus rebukes and chastens in order that men and women may awake to a realization of their true condition. . . .

You may come to Jesus in faith and without delay. His provision is rich and free, His love is abundant, and He will give you grace to wear His yoke and to lift His burden with cheerfulness. You may claim your right to His blessing by virtue of His promise. You may enter into His kingdom, which is His grace, His love, His righteousness, His peace and joy in the Holy Ghost. If you feel in deepest need, you may be supplied with all His fullness, for Christ says, "I came not to call the righteous, but sinners to repen-tance." Jesus calls you to come. "Blessed are the poor in spirit: for their's is the kingdom of heaven."—*The Signs of the Times,* Aug. 1, 1895.

Ministry of Comfort

Blessed are those who mourn, for they shall be comforted. Matt. 5:4.

The Lord works through human instrumentalities and has commissioned to His followers the duty of ministering to those who are desponding and distressed. There are hearts all around us that need to be uplifted, that need the bright beams of the Sun of Righteousness. The Lord looks to those whom He has comforted and blessed to enlighten those who are in darkness and to relieve those who are in sorrow. Those who have received light and peace and joy are not to pass by those who mourn, but are to come close to them in human sympathy and help them to see a sin-pardoning Savior, a merciful God.

Christ has borne our griefs and carried our sorrows, and He will give joy and gladness to those who mourn. Will you, my brother and sister who have felt the sorrows of earth, do service for Christ in helping the very ones who need your help? . . .

Those who love Jesus will have the mind of Christ and will comfort all who mourn; those who are poor, tempted, and discouraged they will help to walk in the light of the cross and not in the shadows and in the darkness. . . .

The Lord Jesus has given to His people the special work of comforting all that mourn. Christ is working for this class, and He calls upon human beings to become His instrumentalities in bringing light and hope to those who are mourning in the midst of apparently dark providences. . . . .

The furnace fire may kindle upon the servants of God, but it is for the purpose of purifying them from all dross, and not that they may be destroyed and consumed. . . .

We honor God by trusting in Him when all looks dark and forbidding. Let those who are afflicted look unto Him, and talk of His power, and sing of His mercy. . . .

There is a blessing pronounced upon all who mourn. Had there been no mourners in our world, Christ could not have revealed the parental character of God. Those oppressed by the conviction of sin are to know the blessedness of forgiveness and to have their transgressions blotted out. Had there been none who mourn, the sufficiency of Christ's expiation for sin would not have been understood.—*Signs of the Times,* Aug. 8, 1895.

Meekness, a Fruit of the Spirit

Blessed are the meek, for they shall inherit the earth. Matt. 5:5.

Those who have humbly sought God for comfort and peace in the midst of trial have had imparted to them the gentleness of Christ. Those who have learned of Him who is meek and lowly of heart express sympathy and manifest gentleness toward those who are in need of consolation, for they can comfort others with the consolation wherewith they are comforted of God. . . .

Meekness is a fruit of the Spirit and an evidence that we are branches of the living God. The abiding presence of meekness is an unmistakable evidence that we are branches of the True Vine and are bearing much fruit. It is an evidence that we are by faith beholding the King in His beauty and becoming changed into His likeness. Where meekness exists, the natural tendencies are under the control of the Holy Spirit. Meekness is not a species of cowardice. It is the spirit which Christ manifested when suffering injury, when enduring insult and abuse. To be meek is not to surrender our rights, but it is the preservation of self-control under provocation to give way to anger or to the spirit of retaliation. Meekness will not allow passion to take the lines.

When Christ was accused by the priests and Pharisees, He preserved His self-control, but He took His position decidedly that their charges were untrue. He said to them, "Which of you convinceth me of sin?" . . . He knew that His position was right. When Paul and Silas were beaten and thrust into prison without trial or sentence, they did not surrender their right to be treated as honest citizens. . . .

At all times and in all places Christians should be that which the Lord designs that they should be—free in Christ Jesus. Duty performed in the Spirit of Christ will be done with sanctified prudence. We shall be guided as with a light from heaven when we have a vital connection with God. . . . Those who have repented of their sins, who have cast their weary, heavy-burdened souls at the feet of Christ, who have submitted to His yoke and become His colaborers, will be partakers with Christ is His sufferings and partakers also of His divine nature. . . .

Jesus is our pattern, and it is from Him that we receive strength and grace to walk in humility and contrition before God.—*Signs of the Times,* Aug. 22, 1895.

Hungering for Righteousness

Blessed are those who hunger and thirst for righteousness,
for they shall be filled. Matt. 5:6.

The true bread of life is found only in Christ. Those who do not recognize that the bounties of rich grace, the heavenly banquet, have been prepared at an infinite cost to satisfy those who hunger and thirst after righteousness will not be refreshed. . . .

"Jesus said unto them, I am the bread of life: he that cometh to me shall never hunger." . . .

Those who hunger and thirst after righteousness are filled with a longing desire to become Christlike in character, to be assimilated to His image, to keep the way of the Lord, and to do justice and judgment. We should ever cultivate an earnest desire for the righteousness of Christ. No temporal wants should attract and divert the mind to such a degree that we should not experience this soul hunger to possess the attributes of Christ. . . . When in trouble and affliction, the soul longs for the love and power of God. There is an intense desire for assurance, for hope, for faith, for confidence. We should seek for pardon, for peace, for the righteousness of Christ. . . . Every soul who seeks the Lord with the whole heart is hungering and thirsting after righteousness. . . .

The soul hunger will be satisfied when our hearts are emptied of pride, vanity, and selfishness; for faith will then appropriate the promises of God, and Christ will supply the vacuum and abide in the heart. There will be a new song in the mouth, for the word will be fulfilled, "A new heart also will I give you." The testimony of the believer will be, "Of his fulness have all we received, and grace for grace." . . .

Without Christ the hunger and thirst of the soul would remain unsatisfied. The feeling of want, the craving after something not temporal, not tainted with earthliness and commonness, could never be appeased. The mind must grasp something higher and purer than anything that can be found in this world. . . .

Christ was crucified for the sin of the world, and after His resurrection and ascension all the world were invited to look to Him and live. We are enjoined to look at the things unseen, to keep before the mind's eye the most vivid images of eternal realities, that by beholding we may become changed into the image of Christ.—*Signs of the Times,* Aug. 29, 1895.

The Fruits of Mercy

Blessed are the merciful, for they shall obtain mercy. Matt. 5:7.

It is the duty of the children of God to be all light in the Lord and scatter blessings upon the path of others. They are not to say, "Be ye warmed, and be ye fed," and do nothing to relieve the necessities of those who are in want. . . .

We are the Lord's purchased possession, and as His human agents it is our positive duty to administer in temporal and spiritual things from the store which God has given us. Love must be kept in constant exercise to inspire faith in God, that praise may be called forth from human hearts to God and that the golden chain of love may bind the hearts of humanity together. Those who are recipients of the mercy, sympathy, and compassion of God should pass it along to others. . . .

The Son of the infinite God is our Pattern. Heaven is full of mercy, and it is constantly outflowing not only to a favored few, but for the blessing of those who need it most, for the benefit of those who have the least pleasantness and happiness brought into their lives. . . .

Those whom God has made stewards of capabilities and means, He commands, for their own interest, to lay up their treasure in heaven, and as He has given freely to them of His bountiful mercy, to give freely to others. Instead of living for themselves, Christ is to live in them, and His Holy Spirit is to lead them to dispense wisely their goods, being merciful to others even as He is merciful to all. No man or woman can be a follower of Christ and live for self. . . .

In proportion as goods are entrusted they should be dispensed to others. The humblest men and women are to trade upon the Lord's talents, realizing that what has been lent to them should be returned with usury to God. Though we have but one talent, if it be faithfully consecrated to God and employed in acts of mercy in temporal or spiritual things, we thus ministering to the wants of the needy, our talent will increase in value and be noted upon the heavenly record as exceeding our powers of computation. Every merciful action, every sacrifice, every self-denial, will bring a sure requital, a hundredfold in this time, and in the world to come everlasting life.—*Signs of the Times,* Sept. 12, 1895.

A Friend to the Pure in Heart

Blessed are the pure in heart, for they shall see God. Matt. 5:8.

The pure in heart shall see God. While all shall behold Christ as a judge, the pure in heart shall behold Him as a friend; for Jesus has said, "Henceforth I call you not servants; for the servant knoweth not what his lord doeth: but I have called you friends; for all things that I have heard of my Father I have made known unto you." The pure in heart shall see Christ as a friend and elder brother. Those who are constantly looking unto Christ for His counsel, who pray in sincerity for His Holy Spirit, will be grieved if a cloud hides Him from their sight. . . .

The Christian world in this age are inclined to accept the sophistries of Satan in the place of the words of God. Many have separated themselves from God by wicked works, and they love not to behold God or to retain Him in their knowledge. They do not want to see God any more than did Adam when he hid himself from the approach of his heavenly Father. . . .

We are to look unto Jesus as our only hope for the taking away of our sins, for in Him is no sin. He became sin for us that He might bear our guilt, standing before the Father as guilty in our place, while we who believe in Him as a personal Savior shall, because of His merits, be accounted as pure from the contaminating influence of sin. Through the imputed righteousness of Christ, we are accounted guiltless. Christ has given to every human being the evidence that He alone is able to bear human grief, sorrow, and sin. Those who claim Christ as their substitute and surety, hanging their helpless souls upon Christ, can endure as seeing Him who is invisible. The benediction, "Blessed are the pure in heart: for they shall see God" belongs to them.

When you are betrayed into sin, do not despair. Do not delay and mourn in hopeless unbelief, but take your case at once to Jesus. . . .

Christ passed over the ground where Adam failed, and redeemed his disgraceful failure. He was made perfect through suffering and is able to succor all who shall be tempted, and to make a way of escape that they may be able to endure temptation. . . . He knows how to sympathize with every human being, for He has identified His interest with the interests of those He came to save. What a wonderful high priest is Jesus! We may lay our very soul burden upon Him.—*Signs of the Times,* Oct. 3, 1895.

Harmony

Blessed are the peacemakers, for they shall be called sons of God.
Matt. 5:9.

Those who have glimpses of the perfection of Christ's character will be filled with a longing to become like Him. They will desire to be peacemakers and to receive the blessing He has promised to the peacemakers....

The enemy of all righteousness will be ready to lead you into a course that will be the very opposite of that which the peacemaker should take. He who loves discord and strife will tempt you to act a part in connection with himself to stir up strife. He will lead you to think that you see in some brother or sister something that is wrong, and Satan will urge you to go and tell it to others; but Christ has told you to go to your brother and "tell him his fault between thee and him alone." Which leader are you going to obey? It is not in accordance with the natural heart to deal frankly and faithfully one with another. It appears easier to tell your brother's fault to someone else than it does to tell it to him alone, but it is his ear alone that should hear your accusation.... They who are blessed are those who work in harmony with God, who are laborers together with Christ. The grace which the Spirit of God imparts is a wellspring of life to the soul and will refresh all who come in contact with the peacemaker....

It is important that we consider that the spirit we cherish now, the works that we now do, will testify to our fitness or unfitness for the future life. We are now upon trial, and it is to be seen whether or not we will fulfill the Lord's prayer and do the will of God on earth as it is done in heaven. Those who are carrying out Satan's plans and are hurting and bruising souls by their course of action prove that they are not the children of Christ....

It is best that every one of us should do right because it is right, and thus we may create about us an atmosphere of peace. We shall not then be found pressing to the side of Satan's human agents to catch their spirit and to repeat their words of accusation and reproach against those who are seeking to be obedient to the commandments of the Lord. We shall not link in with the adversary of souls and aid him in stirring up suspicion and strife and in causing souls who love God to be tempted to do evil.— *Signs of the Times,* Oct. 10, 1895.

Seek Peace

Blessed is the man whose strength is in You. Ps. 84:5.

B lessed are the peacemakers." . . . How many are there who are truly desirous of becoming blessed, who would not only hear but do the words
of Christ? Those who will not rely upon themselves, but who will put their
trust in a power out of and above themselves, will be enabled to become
doers of the words of Christ. . . .

"Blessed are they which are persecuted for righteousness' sake"(not for
their coarse, harsh spirit that leads them to stir up strife and dissension, but
"for righteousness' sake"). The righteous are those who desire peace and will
have peace at the cost of everything save the sacrifice of principle. Truth they
cannot sacrifice, though adherence to it costs them distress, reproach, suffering, and even death. "For their's is the kingdom of heaven." Those who are
persecuted for righteousness' sake place the commandments of God first in
their lives, and they allow no human policy, no promise of reward, no offer
of honor, to come between them and their God. They cannot be induced to
deny Christ and to betray His cause. The rich promises of God have a place
in their memory, and when the enemy comes in like a flood, the Spirit of
the Lord lifts up a standard against him. The Holy Spirit opens to the understanding the preciousness of the Scriptures. . . .

The church itself needs converting so that its members may be made
channels of light, may be blessed and made a blessing. A vague reliance
upon God's mercy will not obtain for us access to the throne of grace or
draw down the blessing from God the Father which He has provided for
those who do His will. Faith must center in the Word of God, which is
spirit and life. Every page of the Sacred Word is illumined with the beams
of the Sun of Righteousness.

The Word of God is to be the support of the afflicted, the comfort of the
persecuted. God Himself speaks to the believing, trusting soul, for God's
Spirit is in His Word, and a special blessing will be received by those who
accept the words of God when illuminated to their mind by the Holy
Spirit. It is thus that the believer eats of Christ, the Bread of Life. Truth is
seen in a new light, and the soul rejoices as in the visible presence of
Christ.—*Signs of the Times,* Oct. 10, 1895.

Salvation Promised

Look to Me, and be saved, all you ends of the earth! For I am God, and there is no other. Isa. 45:22.

When Adam and Eve were created and placed in their Eden home, they had a knowledge of the law that was to govern them....When they transgressed that law, fell from that state of happy innocence, and became sinners in the sight of God, the dark future of the fallen race was not relieved by a single ray of hope. Because of the transgression of the divine law, paradise was lost to the human family, the curse was pronounced upon the earth, and the reign of death commenced.

But Heaven pitied fallen men and women, and the plan of salvation was devised. When the curse was pronounced upon the race, in connection with the curse there was given the promise of pardon through a Savior who was to come. This promise was the star of hope that lighted up the gloom that, like the pall of death, hung over the future of Adam's descendants and of the world which was given them as their dominion. The gospel was first preached to Adam and Eve in Eden. They sincerely repented of their guilt, believed the promise of God, and were saved from utter ruin....

For three hundred years [Enoch] walked with God, giving to the world the example of a pure and spotless life, one which was in marked contrast with the lives of his contemporaries in that self-willed and perverse generation, who openly disregarded God's law and boasted of their freedom from its restraints. But his testimony and his example were alike unheeded, because men and women loved sin better than holiness. Enoch served God with singleness of heart; and the Lord communicated to him His will and through holy vision revealed to him the great events connected with Christ's second appearing. And then this favored servant of the Lord was borne to heaven by angels without seeing death.

At length the wickedness became so great that God could no longer bear with it; and He made known to Noah that because of the continual transgressions of His law, He would destroy those whom He had created by a flood of water which He would bring upon the earth. Noah and his family were obedient to the divine law, and for their loyalty to the God of heaven they were saved from the destruction that overwhelmed the ungodly world around them. Thus the Lord preserved to Himself a people in whose hearts was His law.—*Signs of the Times,* Apr. 22, 1886.

Cain and Abel Tested

It came to pass that Cain brought an offering of the fruit of the ground to the Lord. Abel also brought of the firstborn of his flock and of their fat. And the Lord respected Abel and his offering, but He did not respect Cain and his offering. Gen. 4:3-5.

Cain and Abel, the sons of Adam, were unlike in character. . . . These brothers were tested, as Adam had been tested before them, to see if they would be obedient to God's requirements. They had been instructed in regard to the provision made for the salvation of the human race. Through the system of sacrificial offerings, God designed to impress upon people's minds the offensive character of sin and to make known to them its sure penalty, death. The offerings were to be a constant reminder that it was only through the promised Redeemer that men and women could come into the presence of God. Cain and Abel understood the system of offerings which they were required to carry out. They knew that in presenting these offerings they showed humble and reverential obedience to the will of God and acknowledged faith in, and dependence upon, the Savior whom these offerings typified.

Cain and Abel erected their altars alike, and each brought an offering. Cain thought it unnecessary to be particular about fulfilling all the requirements of God; he therefore brought an offering without the shedding of blood. He brought of the fruits of the ground and presented his offering before the Lord; but there was no token from heaven to show that it was accepted. Abel entreated his brother to come into the presence of God only in the divinely prescribed way. But his remonstrances made Cain all the more determined to carry out his own purpose. As the eldest, he felt above being advised by his brother, and despised his counsel.

Abel brought of the firstlings of the flock, the very best, as God had commanded him. In the slain lamb he sees by faith the Son of God, appointed to death because of the transgression of His Father's law. God had respect to Abel's offering. Fire flashes from heaven and consumes the sacrifice of the penitent sinner.

Cain now has an opportunity to see and acknowledge his mistake. . . . And He who is no respecter of persons will have respect to the offering of faith and obedience. . . .

Abel's offering had been accepted, but this was because Abel had done in every particular as God required him to do.—*Signs of the Times,* Dec. 16, 1886.

The Anger of Cain

So the Lord said to Cain, "Why are you angry? And why has your countenance fallen? If you do well, will you not be accepted?" Gen. 4:6, 7.

The Lord was not ignorant of the feelings of resentment cherished by Cain, but He would have Cain reflect upon his course, and, becoming convinced of his sin, repent and set his feet in the path of obedience. There was no cause for his wrathful feelings toward either his brother or his God; it was his own disregard of the plainly expressed will of God that had led to the rejection of his offering. . . . Abel's offering had been accepted, but this was because Abel had done in every particular as God required him to do. This would not rob Cain of his birthright. . . . Thus the matter was plainly laid open before Cain; but his combativeness was aroused because his course was questioned and he was not permitted to follow his own independent ideas. He was angry with God and angry with his brother. He was angry with God because He would not accept the plans of a sinner in place of the divine requirements, and he was angry with his brother for disagreeing with him. . . .

Cain invites Abel to walk with him in the fields, and he there gives utterance to his unbelief and his murmuring against God. He claims that he was doing well in presenting his offering; and the more he talks against God and impeaches His justice and mercy in rejecting his own offering and accepting that of his brother Abel, the more bitter are his feelings of anger and resentment.

Abel defends the goodness and impartiality of God and places before Cain the simple reason why God did not accept his offering.

The fact that Abel ventured to disagree with him and even went so far as to point out his errors astonished Cain. . . . Cain's reason told him that Abel was right when he spoke of the necessity of presenting the blood of a slain victim if he would have his sacrifice accepted, but Satan presented the matter in a different light. He urged Cain on to a furious madness, till he slew his brother, and the sin of murder was laid upon his soul.—*Signs of the Times,* Dec. 16, 1886.

A More Excellent Sacrifice

By faith Abel offered to God a more excellent sacrifice than Cain, through which he obtained witness that he was righteous. Heb. 11:4.

These two brothers, Cain and Abel, represent the whole human family. They were both tested on the point of obedience, and all will be tested as they were. Abel bore the proving of God. He revealed the gold of a righteous character, the principles of true godliness. But Cain's religion had not a good foundation; it rested on human merit. He brought to God something in which he had a personal interest—the fruits of the ground, which had been cultivated by his toil; and he presented his offering as a favor done to God through which he expected to secure the divine approval. He obeyed in building an altar, obeyed in bringing a sacrifice, but it was only a partial obedience. The essential part, the recognition of the need of a Redeemer, was left out. . . .

Both were sinners, and both acknowledged the claims of God as an object of worship. To all outward appearance, their religion was the same up to a certain point of time; but the Bible history shows us that there was a time when the difference between the two became very great. This difference lay in the obedience of one and the disobedience of the other.

The apostle says that Abel offered unto God a more excellent sacrifice than Cain. Abel grasped the great principles of redemption. He saw himself a sinner, and he saw sin and its penalty, death, standing between his soul and communion with God. He brought the slain victim, the sacrificed life, thus acknowledging the claims of the law which had been transgressed. Through the shed blood he looked to the future Sacrifice, Christ dying on the cross of Calvary; and, trusting in the atonement that was there to be made, he had the witness that he was righteous and his offering accepted.

How did Abel know so well the plan of salvation? Adam taught it to his children and grandchildren. . . . After Adam had sinned, a feeling of terror seized him. A constant dread was upon him; shame and remorse tortured his soul. In this state of mind he wished to be as far removed as possible from the presence of God, whom he had so loved to meet in his Eden home. But the Lord followed this conscience-stricken man, and while He condemned the sin of which Adam had been guilty, gave him words of gracious promise.—*Signs of the Times,* Dec. 23, 1886.

The First Promise of the Gospel

For as in Adam all die, even so in Christ all shall be made alive.
1 Cor. 15:22.

"I will put enmity . . . between thy seed and her seed; it shall bruise thy head, and thou shalt bruise his heel."

This was the first gospel sermon every preached to sinners; this promise was the star of hope, illuminating the dark and dismal future of the race. Adam gladly received the welcome assurance of deliverance and diligently instructed his children in the way of the Lord. This promise was presented in close connection with the altar of sacrificial offerings. The altar and the promise stand side by side, and one casts clear beams of light upon the other, showing that the justice of an offended God could be appeased only by the death of His beloved Son. . . .

Abel heard these precious lessons, and to him they were like seed sown on good ground. Cain also heard them. He had the same privileges as his brother, but he did not improve them. He ventured to go contrary to the commands of God, and the result is strongly presented before us. Cain was not the victim of an arbitrary purpose; one was not elected to be chosen of God, and the other to be rejected. The whole matter rested upon doing or not doing as God had said.

In the case of Cain and Abel we have a type of two classes that will exist in the world till the close of time; and this type is worthy of close study. There is a marked difference in the characters of these two brothers, and the same difference is seen in the human family today. Cain represents those who carry out the principles and works of Satan, by worshipping God in a way of their own choosing. Like the leader whom they follow, they are willing to render partial obedience but not entire submission to God. . . .

The Cain class of worshippers includes by far the largest number, for every false religion that has been invented has been based on the Cain principle, that a sinner can depend upon his own merits and righteousness for salvation. . . .

The religion of Christ is for men and women to accept with all its inconveniences. They may invent an easier way, but it will not lead to the city of God, the saints' secure abode. Only those who "do his commandments" will have "right to the tree of life" and "enter in through the gates into the city."—*The Signs of the Times*, Dec. 23, 1886.

Enoch

After he begot Methuselah, Enoch walked with God three hundred years.
Gen. 5:22.

Enoch learned from the lips of Adam the painful story of the fall and the precious story of God's condescending grace in the gift of His Son as the world's Redeemer. He believed and relied upon the promise given. Enoch was a holy man. He served God with singleness of heart. He realized the corruptions of the human family and separated himself from the descendants of Cain and reproved them for their great wickedness. There were those upon the earth who acknowledged God, who feared and worshipped Him. Yet righteous Enoch was so distressed with the increasing wickedness of the ungodly that he would not daily associate with them, fearing that he should be affected by their infidelity and that he might not ever regard God with that holy reverence which was due His exalted character. His soul was vexed as he daily beheld them trampling upon the authority of God. He chose to be separate from them and spent much of his time in solitude, giving himself to reflection and prayer. He waited before God and prayed to know His will more perfectly, that he might perform it. God communed with Enoch through His angels and gave him divine instruction. He made known to him that He would not always bear with human beings in their rebellion—that it was His purpose to destroy the sinful race by bringing a flood of waters upon the earth.

The beautiful Garden of Eden, from which our first parents had been driven, remained until God determined to destroy the earth by a flood. The Lord had planted that garden and especially blessed it, and in His wonderful providence He withdrew it from the earth and will return it again, more gloriously adorned than before it was removed. God purposed to preserve a specimen of His perfect work of creation free from the curse which sin had brought upon the earth. . . .

Enoch continued to grow more heavenly while communing with God. His face was radiant with a holy light. . . . The Lord loved Enoch, because he steadfastly followed Him. . . . He yearned to unite himself still more closely to God, whom he feared, reverenced, and adored. The Lord would not permit Enoch to die like others, but sent His angels to take him to heaven without seeing death. In the presence of the righteous and the wicked, Enoch was removed from them.—*Signs of the Times,* Feb. 20, 1879.

Enoch and the Spirit of Prophecy

Now Enoch, the seventh from Adam, prophesied about these men also, saying, "Behold, the Lord comes with ten thousands of His saints." Jude 14.

The Lord opened . . . to Enoch the plan of salvation and by the Spirit of prophecy carried him down through the generations which should live after the Flood, and showed him the great events connected with the second coming of Christ and the end of the world.

Enoch was troubled in regard to the dead. It seemed to him that the righteous and the wicked would go to the dust together, and that would be their end. He could not see the life of the just beyond the grave. In prophetic vision he was instructed in regard to the Son of God, who was to die as a sacrifice, and was shown the coming of Christ in the clouds of heaven, attended by the angelic host, to give life to the righteous dead and ransom them from their graves. He also saw the corrupt state of the world at the time when Christ should appear the second time—that there would be a boastful, presumptuous, self-willed generation arrayed in rebellion against the law of God, denying the only Lord God and our Lord Jesus Christ, trampling upon His blood and despising His atonement. He saw the righteous crowned with glory and honor, while the wicked were separated from the presence of the Lord and consumed with fire. . . .

By the blessings and honors which He bestowed upon Enoch, the Lord teaches a lesson of the greatest importance, that all will be rewarded who by faith rely upon the promised Sacrifice and faithfully obey God's commandments. Here, again, two classes are represented which were to exist until the second coming of Christ—the righteous and the wicked, the loyal and the rebellious. God will remember the righteous, who fear Him. On account of His dear Son, He will respect and honor them and give them everlasting life. But the wicked, who trample upon His authority, He will destroy from the earth, and they will be as though they had not been.

After Adam's fall from a state of perfect happiness to a condition of sin and misery, there was danger that men and women would become discouraged. . . . But the instructions which God gave to Adam, and which were repeated by Seth and fully exemplified by Enoch, cleared away the gloom and darkness, and gave hope to all, that as through Adam came death, through Jesus, the promised Redeemer, would come life and immortality.—*Signs of the Times,* Feb. 20, 1879.

Modern-day Enochs

And Enoch walked with God; and he was not, for God took him.
Gen. 5:24.

A fter Adam's fall from a state of perfect happiness to a condition of sin and misery, there was danger that men and women would become discouraged. . . . But the instructions which God gave to Adam, and which were repeated by Seth and fully exemplified by Enoch, cleared away the gloom and darkness and gave hope to all that as through Adam came death, through Jesus, the promised Redeemer, would come life and immortality.

In the case of Enoch, the desponding faithful were taught that while living among a corrupt and sinful people who were in open and daring rebellion against their Creator, if they would obey Him and have faith in the promised Redeemer, they would work righteousness like the faithful Enoch, be accepted of God, and finally exalted to His heavenly throne.

Enoch, separating himself from the world and spending much of his time in prayer and communion with God, represents God's loyal people in the last days, who will be separate from the world. Unrighteousness will prevail to a dreadful extent upon the earth. People will give themselves up to follow every imagination of their corrupt hearts and carry out their deceptive philosophy and rebel against the authority of high heaven.

God's people will separate themselves from the unrighteous practices of those around them and will seek for purity of thought and holy conformity to His will until His divine image will be reflected in them. Like Enoch, they will be fitting for translation to heaven. While they endeavor to instruct and warn the world, they will not conform to the spirit and customs of unbelievers but will condemn them by their holy conversation and godly example. Enoch's translation to heaven just before the destruction of the world by a flood represents the translation of all the living righteous from the earth previous to its destruction by fire. The saints will be glorified in the presence of those who have hated them for their loyal obedience to God's righteous commandments.

Enoch instructed his family in regard to the Flood. Methuselah, the son of Enoch, listened to the preaching of his grandson Noah, who faithfully warned the inhabitants of the old world that a flood of waters was coming upon the earth. Methuselah and his sons and his grandsons lived in the time of the building of the ark. They, with some others, received instruction from Noah and assisted him in his work.—*Signs of the Times,* Feb. 20, 1879.

The Promise to Israel

In the Lord all the descendants of Israel shall be justified, and shall glory.
Isa. 45:25.

Abraham was called out from an idolatrous family and was appointed of God to preserve His truth amid the prevailing and increasing corruptions of that idolatrous age. The Lord appeared to Abraham and said, "I am the Almighty God; walk before me, and be thou perfect. And I will make my covenant between me and thee, and will multiply thee exceedingly." . . .

The Lord communicated His will to Abraham and gave him a distinct knowledge of the requirements of the moral law and of the salvation that would be accomplished through Himself. It was a high honor to which Abraham was called, that of being the father of the people who for centuries were the guardians and preservers of the truth of God for the world—of that people through whom all the nations of the earth should be blessed in the advent of the promised Messiah. . . .

God conferred upon His faithful servant special honor and blessings. Through vision and through the angels that walked and talked with him as friend with friend, he was made acquainted with the purposes as well as with the will of God. . . .

But the descendants of Abraham departed from the worship of the true God and transgressed His law. They mingled with the nations who had no knowledge or fear of God before their eyes, and gradually imitated their customs and manners until God's anger was kindled against them, and He permitted them to have their own way and follow the devices of their own corrupt hearts. . . .

But when they humbled themselves before God and acknowledged His dealings and cried unto Him earnestly for deliverance from the oppressive yoke of the Egyptians, their cries and their promises to be obedient reached heaven. Their prayers were answered in a most wonderful manner, and Israel was brought forth from Egypt, and the covenant made with their fathers was renewed to them.

Thus was the knowledge of the law of God preserved through successive generations from Adam to Noah, from Noah to Abraham, and from Abraham to Moses.—*Signs of the Times,* Apr. 22, 1886.

The Faith of Abraham, Part 1

Take now your son, your only son Isaac, whom you love, and go to the land of Moriah, and offer him there as a burnt offering on one of the mountains of which I shall tell you. Gen. 22:2.

A braham] was one hundred and twenty years old when this terrible and startling command came to him in a vision of the night. He was to travel three days' journey and would have ample time for reflection. Fifty years previous, at the divine command, he had left father and mother, relatives and friends, and had become a pilgrim and a stranger in a land not his own. He had obeyed the command of God to send away his son Ishmael to wander in the wilderness. His soul was bowed down with grief at this separation, and his faith was sorely tried, yet he submitted because God required it. . . .

Abraham was tempted to believe that after all, this might be a delusion. Stricken with grief, he bowed before God and prayed as never before for a confirmation of this strange command, for greater light if he must perform this terrible duty. He remembered the angels sent to tell him of God's purpose to destroy Sodom and those who bore to him the promise that he should have this same son Isaac. . . .

He finally awakened Isaac softly, informing him that he was commanded of God to offer sacrifice upon a distant mountain, and that he must accompany him. He called his servants and made every necessary preparation for his long journey. If he could unburden his mind to Sarah and they together bear the suffering and responsibility, it might bring him some relief; but he decided that this would not do, for her heart was bound up in her son, and she might hinder him. He went forth on his journey, with Satan by his side to suggest unbelief and impossibility. . . .

The journey of the third day is commenced. Abraham lifts his eyes to the mountains, and upon one he beholds the promised sign. He looks earnestly, and lo, a bright cloud hovered over the top of Mount Moriah. . . .

He was yet a great distance from the mountain, but he removed the burden from the shoulders of his servants and bade them remain behind while he placed the wood upon the shoulders of his son, and himself took the knife and fire.—*Signs of the Times,* Apr. 1, 1875.

The Faith of Abraham, Part 2

My son, God will provide for Himself the lamb for a burnt offering.
Gen. 22:8.

As they drew near the mountain, "Isaac spake unto Abraham his father, and said, My father: and he said, Here am I, my son. And he said, Behold the fire and the wood: but where is the lamb for a burnt offering?" These endearing words, "My father," pierced his affectionate heart, and again he thought, Oh! That I, in my old age, might die instead of Isaac. . . .

Isaac assisted his father in building the altar. Together they placed on the wood, and the last work preparatory to the sacrifice is done. With quivering lips and trembling voice, Abraham revealed to his son the message that God had sent him. . . . Isaac was the victim, the lamb to be slain. Had Isaac chosen to resist his father's command, he could have done so, for he was grown to manhood; but he had been so thoroughly instructed in the knowledge of God that he had perfect faith in His promises and requirements. . . .

He comforted his father by assuring him that God conferred honor upon him in accepting him as a sacrifice, that in this requirement he saw not the wrath and displeasure of God, but special tokens that God loved him, in that He required him to be consecrated to Himself in sacrifice.

He encouraged the almost nerveless hands of his father to bind the cords which confined him to the altar. The last words of endearing love were spoken by father and son, the last affectionate filial and parental tears were shed, the last embrace was given, and the father had pressed his beloved son to his aged breast for the last time. His hand is uplifted, grasping firmly the instrument of death which was to take the life of Isaac, when suddenly his arm is stayed. . . . "And Abraham lifted up his eyes, and looked, and behold behind him a ram caught in a thicket by his horns." . . . .

Our heavenly Father surrendered His beloved Son to the agonies of the crucifixion. Legions of angels witnessed the humiliation and soul anguish of the Son of God but were not permitted to interpose as in the case of Isaac. No voice was heard to stay the sacrifice. God's dear Son, the world's Redeemer, was insulted, mocked at, derided, and tortured until He bowed His head in death. What greater proof can the Infinite One give us of His divine love and pity?—*Signs of the Times,* Apr. 1, 1875.

Heaven's Ladder

This is none other than the house of God, and this is the gate of heaven!
Gen. 28:17.

Jacob was not perfect in character. He sinned against his father, his brother, his own soul, and against God. Inspiration faithfully records the faults of good men, those who were distinguished by the favor of God; indeed, their faults are much more fully transcribed than their virtues. . . . They were assaulted by temptations and were often overcome by them, but they were willing to learn in the school of Christ. Were these characters presented before us as faultless, it would tend to discourage us in our strivings after righteousness. . . . It shows that God will by no means clear the guilty. He sees sin in His most favored ones, and He punishes them even more decidedly than those who have less light and responsibility. But in contrast with the sins and errors of humanity there is presented one perfect character—that of the Son of God, who clothed His divinity with humanity, and walked a man among the children of men. . . .

Jacob obtained by fraud the blessing designed for his brother. God had promised him the birthright, and the promise would have been fulfilled in good time had he been willing to wait. But like many who now profess to be the children of God, he lacked faith and thought he must do something himself instead of submissively leaving the matter in the hands of the Lord. . . .

As he pursued his lonely way, he was greatly cast down and discouraged. . . . Yet God did not utterly forsake Jacob. His mercy was still extended to His erring, distrustful servant, although He would permit afflictions to come upon him until he should learn the lesson of patient submission. The Lord graciously and compassionately revealed just what Jacob needed, a Savior. . . .

Wearied with his journey, the wanderer lay down upon the ground with a stone for his pillow. And while he slept, the Lord gave him a vision. He beheld a ladder, bright and shining, whose base rested upon earth while the top reached to heaven. Upon this ladder angels were ascending and descending, and above it was the Lord of glory, who addressed Jacob in words of wonderful encouragement. He assured Jacob that he was under divine guardianship in his absence from home, and that the land whereon he lay as an exile and a fugitive would be given to him and his posterity.—*Signs of the Times,* July 31, 1884.

The Lord Is in This Place

Surely the Lord is in this place, and I did not know it. Gen. 28:16.

Jacob awoke with a solemn sense of the presence of God. . . . Through the Spirit of God, the plan of redemption was revealed to him, not fully, but such parts as it was essential for him to know. The time of Christ's first advent was yet far in the future, but God would not let His servant remain in ignorance of the fact that sinful men and women have been provided an Advocate with the Father.

Up to the time of Adam and Eve's rebellion against the government of God, there had been free communion with God. Heaven and earth had been connected by a path that the Lord loved to traverse. But the sin of Adam and Eve separated earth from heaven. The curse of sin was upon the human race and was so offensive to God that fallen humanity could have no communion with their Maker, however much they might desire it. They could not climb the battlements of heaven and enter the city of God, for there entereth into it nothing that defileth. The ladder represents Jesus, the appointed medium of communication. Had He not with His own merits bridged the gulf that sin had made, the ministering angels, ascending and descending on that ladder, would have held no communication with sinners.

All this was revealed to Jacob in his dream. Although his mind at once grasped a part of the revelation, its great and mysterious truths were the study of his lifetime and unfolded to his understanding more and more. In his conversation with Nathanael, Jesus referred to this mystic ladder on which Jacob gazed with pleased wonder. Said He, "Verily, verily, I say unto you, Hereafter ye shall see heaven open, and the angels of God ascending and descending upon the Son of man."

It is our lifework to commence at the lowest round of the ladder and step by step to ascend toward heaven. . . . We ascend by successive steps. When we let go of one round, it is to grasp another that is still higher. Thus the hand is constantly reaching upward for successive degrees of grace, and the feet are planted on one round after another, until finally an abundant entrance shall be administered to us into the kingdom of our Lord and Savior, Jesus Christ.—*Signs of the Times,* July 31, 1884.

An Example of Forgiveness

"I will provide for you and your little ones." And he comforted them and spoke kindly to them. Gen. 50:21.

The sons of Jacob returned to their father with the joyful tidings, "Joseph is yet alive, and he is governor over all the land of Egypt." At first the old man was overwhelmed; he could not believe what he heard, yet their words brought a faintness to his heart. But when he saw the carriages and the long line of loaded animals, and when Benjamin was at his side once more, he felt reassured and, in the fullness of his joy, exclaimed, "It is enough; Joseph my son is yet alive: I will go and see him before I die." The brothers then made their humiliating confession to their father and entreated his forgiveness for their wicked treatment of Joseph. Jacob had not suspected them of such cruelty, but he saw that God had overruled it all for good, and he forgave and blessed his erring children. . . .

In a vision of the night the divine words came to Jacob, "Fear not to go down into Egypt; for I will there make of thee a great nation. I will go down with thee into Egypt; and I will also surely bring thee up again: and Joseph shall put his hand upon thine eyes."

The meeting of Joseph and his father was very affective. Joseph left his chariot and ran to meet his father on foot and embraced him, and they wept over each other. "And Israel said unto Joseph, Now let me die, since I have seen thy face, because thou art yet alive." . . .

[Jacob's] last years were more peaceful. His sons had turned from their evil ways, Joseph had been restored to him, and, surrounded by every comfort which the prime minister of Egypt could bestow, and in the society of his children, he passed down gently and calmly toward the grave.

A short time before his death, his children gathered about him to receive his blessing and to listen to his last words of counsel. As he addressed them for the last time, the Spirit of God rested upon him, and he laid open before them their past lives and also uttered prophecies which reached far into the future. . . .

Jacob was an affectionate father. He had no resentful feelings toward his sorrowing children. He had forgiven them. He loved them to the last. But God, by the Spirit of prophecy, elevated the mind of Jacob above his natural feelings. In his last hours, angels were all around him, and the power of God rested upon him.—*Signs of the Times,* Feb. 5, 1880.

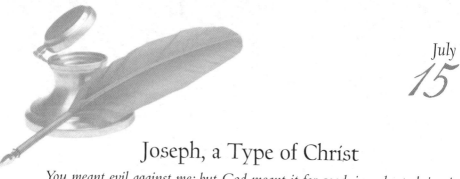

Joseph, a Type of Christ

You meant evil against me; but God meant it for good, in order to bring it about as it is this day, to save many people alive. Gen. 50:20.

Jacob predicted a cheerful future for most of his sons. Especially for Joseph he uttered words of eloquence of a happy character: "Joseph is a fruitful bough, even a fruitful bough by a well; whose branches run over the wall: the archers have sorely grieved him, and shot at him, and hated him: but his bow abode in strength, and the arms of his hands were made strong by the hands of the mighty God of Jacob." . . .

The life of Joseph illustrates the life of Christ. Joseph's brethren proposed to kill him but were finally content to sell him as a slave to prevent his becoming greater than themselves. They thought they had placed him where they would be no more troubled with his dreams and where there would not be a possibility of their fulfillment. But the very course which they pursued, God overruled to bring about that which they designed never should take place—that he should have dominion over them. . . .

Joseph walked with God. And when he was imprisoned and suffered because of his innocence, he meekly bore it without murmuring. His self-control, his patience in adversity, and his unwavering fidelity are left on record for the benefit of all who should afterward live on the earth. . . .

The life of Jesus, the Savior of the world, was a pattern of benevolence, goodness, and holiness. Yet He was despised and insulted, mocked and derided, for no other reason than because His righteous life was a constant rebuke to sin. His enemies would not be satisfied until He was given into their hands, that they might put Him to a shameful death. He died for the guilty race and, while suffering the most cruel torture, meekly forgave His murderers. He rose from the dead, ascended up to His Father, and received all power and authority, and returned to the earth again to impart it to His disciples. He "gave gifts unto men." And all who have ever come to Him repentant, confessing their sins, He has received into His favor and freely pardoned. And if they remain true to Him, He will exalt them to His throne and make them His heirs to the inheritance which He has purchased with His own blood.—*Signs of the Times,* Feb. 5, 1880.

Forty Years of Retraining

The children of Israel groaned because of the bondage, and they cried out; and their cry came up to God because of the bondage. Exodus 2:23.

Moses had become, in every sense, a great man. As a writer, as a military leader, and as a philosopher, he had no superior. Love of truth and righteousness had become the basis of his character and had produced a steadfastness of purpose which no fickleness of fashion, opinion, or pursuits could influence. Courtesy, diligence, and a firm trust in God marked his life. He was young and vigorous, overflowing with energy and manly strength. He had deeply sympathized with his brethren in their affliction, and his soul had kindled with a desire to deliver them. Surely, it would appear to human wisdom that he was in every way fitted for his work.

But God seeth not as man sees; His ways are not as ours. Moses is not yet prepared to accomplish this great work; neither are the people prepared for deliverance. He has been educated in the school of Egypt, but he has yet to pass through the stern school of discipline before he is qualified for his sacred mission. Before he can successfully govern the hosts of Israel, he must learn to obey, he must learn self-control. For forty long years he is sent into the retirement of the desert, that, in his life of obscurity, in the humble work of caring for the sheep and lambs of the flock, he may gain the victory over his own passions. He must learn entire submission to the will of God before he can teach that will to a great people.

Short-sighted mortals would have dispensed with that forty years of training amid the mountains of Midian, deeming it a great loss of time. But Infinite Wisdom placed him who was to be the mighty statesman, the deliverer of his people from slavery, in circumstances during this period to develop his honesty, his forethought, his faithfulness and caretaking, and his ability to identify himself with the necessities of his dumb charge. Those to whom God has entrusted important responsibilities have not been brought up in ease and luxury; the noble prophets, the leaders and judges of God's appointment, have been those whose characters were formed by the stern realities of life.

God does not select for His work persons of one mold and one temperament only, but individuals of varied temperaments.—*Signs of the Times*, Feb. 19, 1880.

The Unlearning Experience

*Then Moses was content to live with the man [the priest of Midian].
Ex. 2:21.*

The human element is seen in all who have been chosen to accomplish a work for God. . . . Connected with God, the source of all wisdom, individuals may reach any height of moral excellence. . . .

Moses had been learning much which he must unlearn. The influence which had surrounded him in Egypt—the love of his adopted mother, his own high position as the king's grandson, the enchantments of grandeur in art, the dissipation on every hand, the imposing display connected with the idolatrous worship, and the constant repetition, by the priests, of countless fables concerning the power of their gods—all had left deep impressions upon his developing mind and had molded, to some extent, his habits and character. These impressions, time, change of surroundings, and close connection with God could remove. Yet it must be by earnest, persevering effort, a struggle as for life, with himself, to uproot the seeds of error, and in their place have truth firmly implanted. At every point Satan would be prepared to strengthen error and dislodge truth, but while God designed that Moses should be self-trained by severe discipline, He Himself would be his ever-ready helper against Satan when the conflict should be too severe for human strength. . . .

The light of nature and that of revelation are from the same source, teaching grand truths and always agreeing with each other. As Moses saw that all God's created works act in sublime harmony with His laws, he realized how unreasonable it is for humans to array themselves in opposition to the law of God. The conflict was most trying, the effort long, to bring heart and mind on all points in harmony with truth and with heaven; but Moses was finally a victor. . . .

As year after year passed by and left the servant of God still in his humble position, it would have seemed to one of less faith than he as if God had forgotten him, as if his ability and experience were to be lost to the world. But as he wandered with his silent flocks in solitary places, the abject condition of his people was ever before him. He recounted all God's dealings with the faithful in ages past and His promises of future good, and his soul went out toward God in behalf of his brethren in bondage, and his fervent prayers echoed amid the mountain caverns by day and by night. He was never weary of presenting before God the promises made to His people, and pleading with Him for their deliverance.—*Signs of the Times,* Feb. 19, 1880.

The Call of Moses

Come now, therefore, and I will send you to Pharaoh that you may bring
My people, the children of Israel, out of Egypt. Ex. 3:10.

To the oppressed and suffering Hebrews the day of their deliverance
seemed to be long deferred, but in His own appointed time God designed to work for them in mighty power. Moses was not to stand, as he at
first anticipated, at the head of armies, with waving banners and glittering
armor. That people, so long abused and oppressed, were not to gain the victory for themselves by rising up and asserting their rights. God's purpose was
to be accomplished in a way to pour contempt on human pride and glory.
The deliverer was to go forth as a humble shepherd with only a rod in his
hand; but God would make that rod powerful in delivering His people from
oppression and in preserving them when pursued by their enemies.

Before Moses went forth, he received his high commission to his great
work in a way that filled him with awe and gave him a deep sense of his
own weakness and unworthiness. While engaged in his round of duties, he
saw a bush, branches, foliage, and trunk, all burning, yet not consumed. He
drew near to view the wonderful sight, when a voice addressed him from
out of the flame. It was the voice of God. It was He who, as an angel of the
covenant, had revealed Himself to the fathers in ages past. The frame of
Moses quivered, he was thrilled with terror, as the Lord called him by
name. With trembling lips he answered, "Here am I." He was warned not
to approach his Creator with undue familiarity: "Put off thy shoes from off
thy feet, for the place whereon thou standest is holy ground." . . .

Finite creatures may learn a lesson that should never be forgotten—to approach God with reverence. We may come boldly into His presence presenting the name of Jesus, our righteousness and substitute, but never with
the boldness of presumption as though He were on a level with ourselves.
We have heard some address the great and all-powerful and holy God, who
dwelleth in light unapproachable, as they would not address an equal or
even an inferior. . . . God is greatly to be reverenced; wherever His presence
is clearly realized, sinners will bow in the most humble attitude.—*Signs of
the Times,* Feb. 26, 1880.

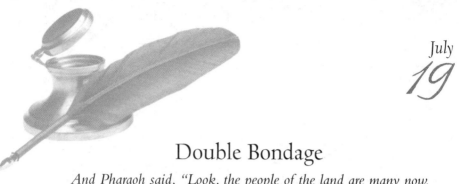

Double Bondage

And Pharaoh said, "Look, the people of the land are many now, and you make them rest from their labor!" Ex. 5:5.

Aaron, being instructed by angels, went forth to meet his brother, from whom he had been separated for many years, and they met amid the desert solitudes in the mount of God. . . . Together they journeyed over the Arabian wastes, toward Egypt; and having reached the land of Goshen, they proceeded to assemble together the elders of Israel. Aaron, the eloquent spokesman, communicated to them all the dealings of God with Moses, and then they gave the signs before the people. "The people believed: and when they heard that the Lord had visited the children of Israel, and that he had looked upon their affliction, then they bowed their heads and worshiped."

The next work of the two brothers was to communicate with the king himself. They entered the great palace of the Pharaohs as commissioners from Jehovah; they felt that God was with them there, and they spoke with authority: "Thus saith the Lord God of Israel, Let my people go, that they may hold a feast unto me in the wilderness." . . .

The king had heard of them before, and of the excitement among the people. He became very angry. . . .

The same day the king issued orders to all the officers superintending the work of the Israelites, to do that which made their slavery doubly severe and cruel. The buildings of that country were and still are made of sundried bricks, with cut straw intermixed to hold the earth together, even their finest edifices being so constructed, and then faced with stone. The king now commanded that no more straw should be issued to the workmen, but the same amount of brick was rigidly required. . . .

When the unfeeling requirement of the king was put in force, the people scattered themselves throughout the land to gather stubble instead of straw, but they found it impossible to accomplish the usual amount of labor. For this failure, the Hebrew officers, as well as the people, were cruelly beaten. . . .

The Hebrews had expected to be released from bondage without any particular trial of faith or any suffering on their part. But they were not yet prepared to be delivered. They had but little faith and were unwilling patiently to suffer their afflictions until God should work for them a glorious deliverance.—*Signs of the Times,* Mar. 4, 1880.

God Will Surely Visit You

Joseph said to his brethren, "I am dying; but God will surely visit you, and bring you out of this land to the land of which he swore to Abraham, to Isaac, and to Jacob." Gen. 50:24.

Only a few families went down into Egypt, but they had become a great multitude. And being surrounded with idolatry, many had lost the knowledge of the true God and had forgotten His law. Yet there were some among them who still worshipped . . . the maker of the heavens and the earth. They were grieved to see their children daily witnessing, and even engaging in, the abominations of the idolatrous people around them. . . . In their distress the faithful cried unto the Lord for deliverance from the Egyptian yoke. . . .

They did not conceal their faith but openly acknowledged before the Egyptians that they served the only true and living God. They rehearsed the evidences of His existence and power, from Creation down. The Egyptians thus had an opportunity to become acquainted with the faith of the Hebrews, and their God. . . .

The elders of Israel endeavored to encourage the sinking faith of their brethren by referring to the promise made to Abraham and the prophetic words of Joseph before his death, foretelling their deliverance from Egypt. Some would listen and believe. Others looked at their own sad condition and would not hope. When the Egyptians learned the expectations of the children of Israel, they derided their hopes of deliverance and spoke scornfully of the power of their God. . . .

The faithful servants of God understood that it was because of their unfaithfulness to Him as a people and their disposition to intermarry with other nations, thus being led into idolatry, that the Lord had suffered them to go into Egypt. . . .

But many of the Hebrews were content to remain in bondage rather than to go to a new country and meet the difficulties attending such a journey; and the habits of some had become so much like those of the Egyptians that they preferred to dwell in Egypt. Therefore the Lord did not deliver them by the first display of His signs and wonders before Pharaoh. He overruled events to more fully develop the tyrannical spirit of the Egyptian king, and also by manifestations of almighty power to give the Israelites more exalted views of the divine character, that they might be anxious to leave Egypt and choose the service of the true and merciful God.—*Signs of the Times*, Mar. 4, 1880.

God's Superior Power

*You shall speak all that I command you. And Aaron your brother shall tell
Pharaoh to send the children of Israel out of his land. Ex. 7:2.*

The Lord directed Moses to go again to the children of Israel and repeat
the promise of deliverance, with a fresh assurance of divine favor. Moses
went as he was commanded, but the people were in no mood to receive
him; their hearts were full of bitterness, the lash was still sounding in their
ears, the cry of anguish and distress drowned all other sounds, and they
would not listen. Moses bowed his head in humiliation and disappointment,
and again God's voice was heard by him—"Go in, speak unto Pharaoh king
of Egypt, that he let the children of Israel go out of his land." . . .

He was informed that the monarch would not give his consent until God
should lay His hand in judgment upon Egypt and bring Israel out by His
almighty power. . . . He would show them by His servant Moses that the
Maker of the heavens and the earth is the living and all-powerful God,
above all gods; that His strength is mightier than the strongest—that
Omnipotence could bring forth His people with a high hand and with an
outstretched arm. . . .

Obedient to the command of God, Moses and Aaron again entered the
lordly halls of the king of Egypt. There, surrounded by the massive and
richly sculptured columns and the gorgeousness of rich hangings and
adornments of silver and gold and gems, before the monarch of the most
powerful kingdom then in existence stood these two men of the despised
race, one with a rod in his hand, come once more to deliver their request
that he would let their people go.

The king demanded a miracle. Moses and Aaron had been previously directed of God how to act in case such a demand should be made, and Aaron
now took the rod and cast it down before the king. It became a serpent.
The monarch sent for his "wise men and the sorcerers," who, at his command "cast down every man his rod, and they became serpents: but Aaron's
rod swallowed up their rods." . . . The magicians did not really cause their
rods to become serpents, but by magic, aided by the great deceiver, made
them appear like serpents, to counterfeit the work of God. . . .

The work of God was thus shown to be superior to the power of
Satan.—*Signs of the Times,* Mar. 11, 1880.

Let the Plagues Begin

Go to Pharaoh in the morning, . . . and you shall stand by the river's bank to meet him; and the rod which was turned to a serpent you shall take in your hand. Ex. 7:15.

Moses and his brother were next directed to meet the king as he visited the river in the morning, and standing upon its bank they were again to repeat their message to him, and as proof that God had indeed sent them, they were to stretch out the rod over the waters in all directions, thus changing them into blood. It was done, and the river ran blood, and all the water in their houses was changed to blood, the fish died, and the water became offensive to the smell. But "the magicians of Egypt did so with their enchantments," changing in the same way the water drawn from wells. Still the king hardened his heart and refused to yield. For seven days the plague continued, the inhabitants being obliged to dig wells to supply themselves with water.

Another effort at moving the king was now made. The rod was again stretched out over the waters, and frogs came up from the river and spread over the country—into the houses and bedchambers and ovens and kneading troughs. The magicians with their enchantments appeared to bring up similar animals. The general nuisance soon became so intolerable that the king was earnest to have it removed. But although the magicians had succeeded in producing frogs, they could not remove them. When Pharaoh saw this, he was somewhat humbled and desired Moses and Aaron to entreat the Lord for him that the plague might be stayed. They reminded the haughty king of his former boasting and asked where was now the vaunted power of his magicians; then they requested him to appoint a time for their prayers, and at the hour specified the living cause was removed, though the effect remained; for the frogs, perishing, polluted the atmosphere.

The work of the magicians had led Pharaoh to believe that these miracles were performed by magic, but he had abundant evidence that this was not the case when the plague of frogs was removed. The Lord could have caused them to disappear and return to dust in a moment, but He did not do this, lest, after they should be removed, the king and the Egyptians should say that it was the result of magic, like the work of the magicians. . . . Here the king and all Egypt had evidence which their vain philosophy could not dispose of, that this work was not accomplished by magic, but was a judgment from the God of heaven.—*Signs of the Times,* Mar. 11, 1880.

Now Lice and Flies

So the Lord said to Moses, "Say to Aaron, 'Stretch out your rod, and strike the dust of the land, so that it may become lice throughout all the land of Egypt.'" Ex. 8:16.

The frogs died and were then gathered together in heaps. Here the king and all Egypt had evidence which their vain philosophy could not dispose of, that this work was not accomplished by magic, but was a judgment from the God of heaven.

When the king was relieved of his immediate distress, he again stubbornly refused to let Israel go. Aaron, at the command of God, stretched out his hand and caused the dust of the earth to become lice throughout all the land of Egypt. Pharaoh called upon the magicians to do the same with their enchantments, but they could not. . . . The magicians themselves acknowledged that their imitative power was at an end, saying, "This is the finger of God." But the king was still unmoved.

Still another trial was made, after another appeal to "let my people go." Flies filled the houses and swarmed upon the ground, so that "the land was corrupted by reason of the swarm of flies." These were not such flies as harmlessly annoy us at some seasons of the year, but they were large and venomous. Their sting was very painful to man and beast. It had been previously stated that the land of Goshen would be exempt from this visitation, which was accordingly found to be true.

Pharaoh now sent for the two brothers and told them that he would allow the Israelites to offer sacrifices in Egypt itself; but this offer was refused. Certain animals were regarded as objects of worship by the Egyptians, and such was the reverence in which these creatures were held that to slay one, even accidentally, was a crime punishable with death. Moses assured the king that it was impossible for them to sacrifice to God in the land of Egypt, for they might select for their offering some one of the animals which the Egyptians considered sacred.

Moses again proposed to go three days' journey into the wilderness. The king consented and begged the servants of God to entreat that the plague might be removed. They promised to do this but cautioned him against dealing deceitfully with them. The plague ceased at their prayer. But the king's heart had become hardened by his persistent rebellion, and he still refused to let the people go.—*Signs of the Times,* Mar. 11, 1880.

Then Pestilence, Boils, and Hail

Behold, the hand of the Lord will be on your cattle in the field, . . .
a very severe pestilence. Ex. 9:3.

Pharaoh was now forewarned of a still more terrible visitation, that of murrain [pestilence] upon all the Egyptian cattle which were out in the field. It was distinctly stated that the Hebrews should be exempted from this evil. The plague came, as predicted, and Pharaoh, on sending messengers to the homes of the Israelites, found that they had entirely escaped. Still the king was obstinate, and he was encouraged in his persistency by the priests and magicians.

But they also were to feel the judgments of God. Moses and Aaron were commanded to take ashes of the furnace and sprinkle them in the air before Pharaoh. As they did so, the fine particles spread as dust over all the land of Egypt, and where it settled became a "boil breaking forth with blains upon man, and upon beast." The magicians could not by any of their enchantments shield themselves from the grievous plague. They could no longer stand before Moses and Aaron, because of this affliction. The Egyptians were thus permitted to see how useless it would be for them to put their trust in the boasted power of the magicians, when they could not protect even their own persons.

Still there was no yielding on the part of the monarch. . . . Then a plague of hail was threatened which would destroy the cattle and every man and woman found in the field. Here was an opportunity to test the pride of the Egyptians and to show how many were really affected by the wonderful dealings of God with His people. All who regarded the word of the Lord gathered their cattle into barns and houses, while those who disbelieved the warning left their animals in the field. In thus providing a way of escape for all who chose to act upon the warning given, we see the mercy of God in the midst of judgment.

The storm came on the morrow as predicted—thunder and hail, and fire mingled with it, destroying every herb, shattering trees, and smiting man and beast. Hitherto none of the lives of the Egyptians had been taken, but now death and desolation followed in the track of the destroying angel. The land of Goshen alone was spared. Here the Lord demonstrated to the Egyptians that the whole earth is under the command of the God of the Hebrews, that even the elements obey His voice.—*Signs of the Times,* Mar. 18, 1880.

A False Confession and Promise

I have sinned this time. The Lord is righteous,
and my people and I are wicked. Ex. 9:27.

My people shall dwell in a peaceable habitation, and in sure dwellings, and in quiet resting places." . . .

The only true safety of nations and individuals is to be obedient to the voice of God and to ever stand on the side of truth and righteousness. Pharaoh now humbled himself and said, "I have sinned this time: the Lord is righteous, and I and my people are wicked." He entreated the servants of God to intercede with Him, that the terrific thunder and lightning might cease.

Moses knew that the contest was not ended, for he understood the workings of the human heart that is set in proud defiance against God. Pharaoh's confessions and promises were not made because there was any change in his mind or heart; but terror and anguish compelled him, for the time being, to yield the controversy with God. Moses, however, promised to grant his request as though his confession was genuine and his repentance sincere, for he would not give him any occasion for future exhibitions of stubbornness. . . .

On going out of the city he "spread abroad his hands unto the Lord: and the thunders and hail ceased, and the rain was not poured upon the earth." But as soon as the awful exhibitions of divine power had passed, the heart of the king returned to its stubbornness and rebellion.

The Lord was manifesting His power to confirm the faith of His people Israel in Him as the only true and living God. He would give them unmistakable evidences of the difference He placed between the Egyptians and His people. He would cause all nations to know that although they had been bound down by hard labor and had been despised, yet He had chosen them as His peculiar people, and that He would work for their deliverance in a wonderful manner.

By long association with the Egyptians and continually beholding the imposing worship of idols, the Hebrews' idea of the true and living God had become degraded. . . . They saw the idolatrous Egyptians enjoying an abundant prosperity, while they were continually taunted with the remark, "Your God has forsaken you." But by His mighty works, the Lord would now teach His people in regard to His character and divine authority and show them the utter worthlessness of false gods.—*Signs of the Times,* Mar. 18, 1880.

Locusts

Then the Lord said to Moses, "Stretch out your hand over the land of Egypt for the locusts, that they may come upon the land of Egypt, and eat every herb of the land—all that the hail has left." Ex. 10:12.

M oses . . . warned the monarch that . . . a plague of locusts would be sent, which would cover the face of the earth and eat up every green thing. . . .

The counselors of Pharaoh were appalled at this new danger. They had sustained great loss in the death of their cattle. Many of their people had been killed by the hail. . . .

Then Moses and Aaron were again summoned, and the monarch said to them, "Go, serve the Lord your God: but who are they that shall go?"

The answer was, "We will go with our young and with our old, with our sons and with our daughters, with our flocks and with our herds will we go; for we must hold a feast unto the Lord."

The king was filled with rage. . . .

Does your God think that I will let you go, with your wives and children, upon so dangerous an expedition? I will not do this; only you that are men shall go to serve the Lord. This hard-hearted, oppressive king, who had sought to destroy the Israelites by hard labor, would now pretend that he had a deep interest in their welfare and a tender care for their little ones, when he only designed to keep them as a pledge of their return. . . .

Moses was commanded to stretch out his hand over the land, and an east wind blew and brought locusts: "very grievous were they; before them there were no such locusts as they, neither after them shall be such." They filled the sky till the land was darkened, and devoured every green thing on the ground and among the trees.

The king sent for Moses and Aaron in haste, and said to them, "I have sinned against the Lord your God, and against you. Now therefore forgive, I pray thee, my sin only this once, and intreat the Lord your God, that he may take away from me this death only."

They did so, and a strong west wind arose, which carried away the locusts toward the Red Sea so that not one was left behind. But notwithstanding the king's humility while death threatened him, as soon as the plague was removed he hardened his heart and again refused to let Israel go.—*Signs of the Times,* Mar. 18, 1880.

Darkness Over the Land

*Then the Lord said to Moses, "Stretch out your hand toward heaven,
that there may be darkness over the land of Egypt, darkness which
may even be felt." Ex. 10:21.*

The people of Egypt were in despair. The scourges which had already fallen upon them seemed almost beyond endurance, and they were filled with fears for the future. The people had worshipped Pharaoh as being a representative of their god and carrying out his purposes. But notwithstanding, many were convinced that he was opposing his will to a superior Power who held all nations under His control. Suddenly a darkness settled over the land, so thick and black that it seemed a darkness which could be felt. Not only were the people deprived of light, but the atmosphere was very oppressive, so that breathing was difficult. . . . But all the children of Israel had light and a pure atmosphere in their dwellings. . . .

The Hebrew slaves were continually favored of God and were becoming confident that they would be delivered. The taskmasters dared not exercise their cruelty as heretofore, fearing lest the vast Hebrew host would rise up and be revenged for the abuse they had already suffered.

This terrible darkness lasted three days, and during this time the busy activities of life could not be carried on. This was God's plan. He would give them time for reflection and repentance before bringing upon them the last and most dreadful scourge, the death of the firstborn. He would remove everything which would divert their attention and give them time for meditation, thus giving new evidence of His compassion and unwillingness to destroy.

At the end of the three days of darkness, Pharaoh sent for Moses and said, "Go ye, serve the Lord; only let your flocks and your herds be stayed: let your little ones also go with you." The answer was, "Thou must give us also sacrifices and burnt offerings, that we may sacrifice unto the Lord our God. Our cattle also shall go with us; there shall not an hoof be left behind; for thereof must we take to serve the Lord our God; and we know not with what we must serve the Lord, until we come thither."

The king was stern and determined. "Get thee from me," he cried, "take heed to thyself, see my face no more; for in that day thou seest my face thou shalt die." The answer was, "Thou hast spoken well, I will see thy face again no more."—*Signs of the Times,* Mar. 18, 1880.

Death of the Firstborn

And all the firstborn in the land of Egypt shall die, from the firstborn of Pharaoh who sits on his throne, even to the firstborn of the female servant who is behind the handmill, and all the firstborn of the animals. Ex. 11:5.

As Moses had witnessed the wonderful works of God, his faith had been strengthened and his confidence established. God had been qualifying him, by manifestations of divine power, to stand at the head of the armies of Israel and, as a shepherd of His people, to lead them from Egypt. He was elevated above fear by his firm trust in God. This courage in the presence of the king annoyed his haughty pride, and he uttered the threat of killing the servant of God. In his blindness, he did not realize that he was contending not only against Moses and Aaron, but against the mighty Jehovah, the maker of the heavens and the earth. If Pharaoh had not been blinded by his rebellion, he would have known that He who could perform such mighty miracles as had been wrought would preserve the lives of His chosen servants, even though He should have to slay the king of Egypt. Moses had obtained the favor of the people. He was regarded as a wonderful personage, and the king would not dare to harm him.

Moses had still another message for the rebellious king, and before leaving his presence he fearlessly declared the word of the Lord. "About midnight will I go out into the midst of Egypt: and all the firstborn in the land of Egypt shall die, from the firstborn of Pharaoh that sitteth upon his throne, even unto the firstborn of the maidservant that is behind the mill; and all the firstborn of beasts. And there shall be a great cry throughout all the land of Egypt, such as there was none like it, nor shall be like it any more. But against any of the children of Israel shall not a dog move his tongue, against man or beast: that ye may know how that the Lord doth put a difference between the Egyptians and Israel." . . .

As Moses faithfully portrayed the nature and effects of the last dreadful plague, the king became exceedingly angry. He was enraged because he could not intimidate Moses and make him tremble before the royal authority. But the servant of God leaned for support upon a mightier arm than that of any earthly monarch.—*Signs of the Times,* Mar. 18, 1880.

The Passover

And they shall take some of the blood and put it on the two doorposts and on the lintel of the houses. Ex. 12:7.

The Lord gave Moses special directions for the children of Israel in regard to what they must do to preserve themselves and their families from the fearful plague that He was about to send upon the Egyptians. Moses was also to give his people instructions in regard to their leaving Egypt. On that night, so terrible to the Egyptians and so glorious to the people of God, the solemn ordinance of the Passover was instituted. By the divine command, each family, alone or in connection with others, was to slay a lamb or a goat "without blemish," and with a bunch of hyssop sprinkle its blood on "the two side posts, and on the upper door post" of their houses, as a token, that the destroying angel, coming at midnight, might not enter that dwelling. They were to eat the flesh roasted, with bitter herbs, at night, as Moses said, "with your loins girded, your shoes on your feet, and your staff in your hand; and ye shall eat it in haste: it is the Lord's passover." This name was given in memory of the angel's passing by their dwellings; and such a feast was to be observed as a memorial by the people of Israel in all future generations.

Leaven works secretly and is a fit emblem of hypocrisy and deceit. And on this occasion the children of Israel were to abstain from leavened bread, that their minds might be impressed with the fact that God requires truth and sincerity in His worship. The bitter herbs represented their long and bitter servitude in Egypt, also the bondage of sin. It was not enough to simply slay the lamb and sprinkle its blood upon the doorposts, but it was to be eaten, thus representing the close union which must exist between Christ and His followers.

A work was required of the children of Israel to prove them and to show their faith in the great deliverance which God had been bringing about for them. In order to escape the terrible judgment about to fall upon Egypt, the token of blood must be seen upon their houses. And they were required to separate themselves and their children from the Egyptians and gather them into their own houses; for if any of the Israelites were found in the dwellings of the Egyptians, they would fall by the hand of the destroying angel. They were also directed to keep the feast of the Passover for an ordinance, that when their children should inquire what such service meant, they should relate to them their wonderful preservation in Egypt.—*Signs of the Times,* Mar. 25, 1880.

Christ, the Passover Lamb

And you shall observe this thing as an ordinance for you and your sons forever.
Ex. 12:24.

There were quite a number of the Egyptians who were led to acknowledge, by the manifestations of the signs and wonders shown in Egypt, that the gods whom they had worshipped were without knowledge and had no power to save or to destroy, and that the God of the Hebrews was the only true God. They begged to be permitted to come to the houses of the Israelites with their families upon that fearful night when the angel of God should slay the firstborn of the Egyptians. The Hebrews welcomed these believing Egyptians to their homes, and the latter pledged themselves henceforth to choose the God of Israel as their God and to leave Egypt and go with the Israelites to worship the Lord.

The Passover pointed backward to the deliverance of the children of Israel and was also typical, pointing forward to Christ, the Lamb of God, slain for the redemption of fallen humanity. The blood sprinkled upon the doorposts prefigured the atoning blood of Christ and also the continual dependence of sinners upon the merits of that blood for safety from the power of Satan and for final redemption. Christ ate the Passover supper with His disciples just before His crucifixion, and the same night instituted the ordinance of the Lord's Supper, to be observed in commemoration of His death. . . . After partaking of the passover with His disciples, Christ arose from the table and said unto them, "With desire I have desired to eat this passover with you before I suffer." He then performed the humiliating office of washing the feet of His disciples. Christ gave His followers the ordinance of washing feet for them to practice, which would teach them lessons of humility. . . .

The example of washing the feet of His disciples was given for the benefit of all who should believe in Him. . . .

The salvation of men and women depends upon a continual application to their hearts of the cleansing blood of Christ. Therefore, the Lord's Supper was to be observed more frequently than the annual Passover. This solemn ordinance commemorates a far greater event than the deliverance of the children of Israel from Egypt. That deliverance was typical of the great atonement which Christ made by the sacrifice of His own life for the final redemption of His people.—*Signs of the Times,* Mar. 25, 1880.

The Repairer of the Breach

You shall be called the Repairer of the Breach, the Restorer of Streets to Dwell in. Isa. 58:12.

We have reason to rejoice that the world has not been left in solitary hopelessness. Jesus left the royal throne and His high command in heaven and became poor, that we through His poverty might be made rich. He took upon Himself our nature, that He might teach us how to live. In the steps which the sinner must take in conversion—repentance, faith, and baptism—He led the way. He did not repent for Himself, for He was sinless, but in behalf of sinners.

Jesus became "the repairer of the breach, the restorer of paths to dwell in." He became an exile to earth to bring back the one lost, straying sheep, the one world ruined by sin. In Him were combined the earthly and the heavenly, the human and the divine; otherwise, He could not be a Mediator whom the sinful could approach, and through whom they could be reconciled to their Maker. But now He encircles the race in arms of sympathy and love while He grasps the throne of the Infinite, thus uniting us in our weakness and helplessness with the Source of strength and power. . . .

We are indebted to Jesus for all the blessings we enjoy. We should be deeply grateful that we are the subjects of His intercession. But Satan deceives men and women by presenting the service of Christ before them in a false light and making them think that it is a condescension on their part to accept Jesus as their Redeemer. If we viewed the Christian privilege in the right light, we should consider it the highest exaltation to be accounted a child of God, an heir of heaven, and we should rejoice that we can walk with Jesus in His humiliation. . . .

Will you leave the dark abodes of sin and woe, and seek the mansions Jesus has gone to prepare for His followers? In His name we beseech you to plant your feet firmly on the ladder and climb upward. Forsake your sins, overcome your defects of character, and cling with all your powers to Jesus, the way, the truth, and the life. We may every one of us succeed. None who shall persevere will fail of everlasting life. Those who believe on Christ shall never perish; neither shall any pluck them out of His hand.—*Signs of the Times,* July 31, 1884.

God Fulfilled His Promises

But when the fullness of the time had come, God sent forth His Son.
Gal. 4:4.

Christ came to this world to reveal the Father, to give to humanity a true knowledge of God. He came to manifest the love of God. Without a knowledge of God, humanity would be eternally lost. . . . Life and power must be imparted by Him who made the world.

The promise made in Eden—the seed of the woman shall bruise the serpent's head—was the promise of the Son of God, through whose power alone could the counsel of God be fulfilled and the knowledge of God be imparted.

God made the promise to Abraham, "In thee shall all families of the earth be blessed." To Abraham was unfolded God's purpose for the redemption of the race. . . . Christ declared, "Your father Abraham rejoiced to see my day: and he saw it, and was glad."

Jacob declared, "The sceptre shall not depart from Judah, nor a lawgiver from between his feet, until Shiloh come; and unto him shall the gathering of the people be."

To Moses God talked face to face, as one talks with a friend. On him shone the light regarding the Savior. He said to the people, "The Lord thy God will raise up unto thee a Prophet from the midst of thee, of thy brethren, like unto me; unto him ye shall hearken."

The sacrifices and offerings told their story of the coming Savior, who was to be offered up for the sins of the world. They pointed forward to a better service than theirs, when God would be worshipped in spirit and truth and in the beauty of holiness.

In the Jewish service was typified the atonement demanded by the broken law. The victim, a lamb without spot or blemish, represented the world's Redeemer, who is so holy and so efficient that He can take away the sin of the world.

To David was given the promise that Christ should reign forever and ever, and that of His kingdom there should be no end.

The Hebrews lived in an attitude of expectancy, looking for the promised Messiah. Many died in faith, not having received the promises; but having seen them afar off, they believed and confessed that they were strangers and pilgrims on the earth.—*Youth's Instructor,* Sept. 13, 1900.

One Equal With God

Who, being in the form of God, did not consider it robbery to be equal with God. Phil. 2:6.

The divine Son of God was the only sacrifice of sufficient value to fully satisfy the claims of God's perfect law. The angels were sinless but of less value than the law of God. They were amenable to law. . . . They were created beings and probationers. Upon Christ no requirements were laid. He had power to lay down His life and to take it again. No obligation was laid upon Him to undertake the work of atonement. It was a voluntary sacrifice that He made. His life was of sufficient value to rescue sinners from their fallen condition. . . .

The sacrificial offerings and the priesthood of the Jewish system were instituted to represent the death and mediatorial work of Christ. All those ceremonies had no meaning and no virtue, only as they related to Christ, who was Himself the foundation of, and who brought into existence, the entire system. The Lord had made known to Adam, Abel, Seth, Enoch, Noah, Abraham, and the ancient worthies, especially Moses, that the ceremonial system of sacrifices and the priesthood, of themselves, were not sufficient to secure the salvation of one soul.

The system of sacrificial offerings pointed to Christ. Through these, the ancient worthies saw Christ and believed in Him. These were ordained of Heaven to keep before the people the fearful separation which sin had made between God and the human family, requiring a mediating ministry. Through Christ the communication which was cut off because of Adam's transgression was opened between God and the ruined sinner. . . .

The Jewish system was symbolical and was to continue until the perfect Offering should take the place of the figurative. . . . The people of God, from Adam's day down to the time when the Jewish nation became a separate and distinct people from the world, had been instructed in regard to the Redeemer to come, which their sacrificial offerings represented. This Savior was to be a mediator, to stand between the Most High and His people. Through this provision, a way was opened whereby the guilty sinner might find access to God through the mediation of another. . . . Christ alone could open the way by making an offering equal to the demands of the divine law. He was perfect and undefiled by sin. He was without spot or blemish.—*Review and Herald*, Dec. 17, 1872.

An Unprepared People

And she will bring forth a Son, and you shall call His name Jesus, for He will save His people from their sins. Matt. 1:21.

The Jewish nation had corrupted their religion by useless ceremonies and customs. . . . They were also under bondage to the Romans and required to pay tribute to them. The Jews were unreconciled to their bondage and looked forward to the triumph of their nation through the Messiah, the powerful deliverer foretold in prophecy. . . . They thought the Coming One would, at His appearing, assume kingly honors and by force of arms subdue their oppressors and take the throne of David. Had they, with humble minds and spiritual discernment, studied the prophecies, they would not have been found in so great error as to overlook the prophecies which pointed to His first advent in humility, and misapply those which spoke of His second coming with power and great glory. . . . They could not distinguish between those prophecies which pointed to the first advent of Christ and those that described His second, glorious appearing. The power and glory described by the prophets as attending His second advent, they looked for at His first advent. . . .

When the time was fulfilled, Christ was born in a stable and cradled in a manger, surrounded by the beasts of the stall. . . . His divine glory and majesty were veiled by humanity, and angels heralded His advent. The tidings of His birth were borne with joy to the heavenly courts, while the great men of the earth knew it not. . . . They looked for a mighty prince who should reign upon David's throne and whose kingdom should endure forever. Their proud and lofty ideas of the coming of the Messiah were not in accordance with the prophecies which they professed to be able to expound to the people. . . .

In heaven it was understood that the time had come for the advent of Christ to the world, and angels leave glory to witness His reception by those He came to bless and save. They had witnessed His glory in heaven, and they anticipate that He will be received with honor in accordance with His character and the dignity of His mission. . . . The angels from heaven behold with astonishment the indifference of the people and their ignorance in regard to the advent of the Prince of life.—*Review and Herald*, Dec. 17, 1872.

The Joyful News

Now there were in the same country shepherds living out in the fields, keeping watch over their flock by night. And behold, an angel of the Lord stood before them. . . . Then the angel said to them, "Do not be afraid, for behold, I bring you good tidings of great joy which will be to all people." Luke 2:8-10.

Angels behold the weary travelers, Joseph and Mary, making their way to the city of David to be taxed, according to the decree of Caesar Augustus. Here, in the providence of God, Joseph and Mary had been brought, for this was the place prophecy had predicted that Christ should be born. They seek a place of rest at the inn, but are turned away because there is no room. The wealthy and honorable have been welcomed and find refreshment and room, while these weary travelers are compelled to seek refuge in a coarse building which shelters the dumb beasts.

Here the Savior of the world is born. The Majesty of glory, who filled all heaven with admiration and splendor, is humiliated to a bed in a manger. In heaven He was surrounded by holy angels, but now His companions are the beasts of the stall. What humiliation is this! . . .

As there are none among the children of humanity to herald the advent of the Messiah, angels must now do that work which it was the honored privilege of human beings to do. . . .

Humble shepherds, who are guarding their flocks by night, are the ones who joyfully receive their testimony. . . . They do not at first discern the myriads of angels that are congregated in the heavens. The brightness and glory from the heavenly host illuminate and glorify the entire plain. . . .

The shepherds are filled with joy, and as the bright glory disappears and the angels return to heaven, they are all aglow with the glad tidings and hasten in search of the Savior. They find the infant Redeemer, as the celestial messengers had testified, wrapped in swaddling clothes and lying in the narrow confines of a manger.

The events which had but just transpired have made indelible impressions upon their minds and hearts, and they are filled with amazement, love, and gratitude for the great condescension of God to the human family in sending His Son into the world.—*Review and Herald,* Dec. 17, 1872.

Where His Voice Was Heard

He will not cry out, nor raise His voice, nor cause His voice to be heard in the street. . . . He will bring forth justice for truth. Isa. 42:2, 3.

From His childhood Jesus conformed His life strictly to the Jewish laws. He manifested great wisdom in His youth. The grace and power of God were upon Him. The word of the Lord, by the mouth of the prophet Isaiah, describes the office and work of Christ and shows the sheltering care of God over His Son in His mission to earth, that the relentless hatred of men and women, inspired by Satan, should not be permitted to thwart the design of the great plan of salvation. . . .

The voice of Christ was not heard in the street in noisy contention with those who were opposed to His doctrine. Neither was His voice heard in the street in prayer to His Father. . . . His voice was not heard in joyful mirth. His voice was not raised to exalt Himself and to gain the applause and flattery of sinners. When engaged in teaching, He withdrew His disciples away from the noise and confusion of the busy city to some retired place more in harmony with the lessons of humility, piety, and virtue which He would impress upon their minds. He shunned human praise and preferred solitude and peaceful retirement to the noise and confusion of mortal life. His voice was often heard in earnest, prevailing intercessions to His Father, yet for these exercises He chose the lonely mountain and frequently spent whole nights in prayer for strength to sustain Him under the temptations He should meet and to accomplish the important work He came to do for the salvation of humanity. His petitions were earnest and mingled with strong cries and tears. And notwithstanding the labor of soul during the night, He ceased not His labor through the day. . . .

The chief priests and scribes and elders loved to pray in the most public places—not only in the crowded synagogues, but in the corners of the streets, that they might be seen by all and praised for their devotion and piety. Their acts of charity were done in the most public manner and for the purpose of calling the attention of the people to themselves. Their voices were indeed heard in the streets, not only in exalting themselves but in contention with those who differed with them in doctrine. . . . The Lord, through His faithful prophet, shows the life of Christ in marked contrast to the hypocritical chief priests, scribes, and Pharisees.—*Review and Herald,* Dec. 31, 1872.

Christ as a Child

He was in the world, and the world was made through Him,
and the world did not know Him. John 1:10.

The apocrypha of the New Testament attempts to supply the silence of the Scriptures in reference to the early life of Christ by giving a fancy [fanciful] sketch of His childhood years. These writers relate wonderful incidents and miracles which characterized His childhood and distinguished Him from other children. They relate fictitious tales and frivolous miracles which they say He wrought, attributing to Christ the senseless and needless display of His divine power and falsifying His character by attributing to Him acts of revenge and deeds of mischief which were cruel and ridiculous.

In what marked contrast is the history of Christ as recorded by the evangelists, which is beautiful in its natural simplicity, with these unmeaning stories and fictitious tales. They are not at all in harmony with His character. They are more after the order of the novels that are written, which have no foundation in truth, but the characters delineated are of fancy creating.

The life of Christ was distinguished from the generality of children. His strength of moral character and His firmness ever led Him to be true to His sense of duty and to adhere to the principles of right, from which no motive, however powerful, could move Him. Money or pleasure, applause or censure, could not purchase or flatter Him to consent to a wrong action. He was strong to resist temptation, wise to discover evil, and firm to abide faithful to His convictions. . . .

His wisdom was great, but it was childlike, and increased with His years. His childhood possessed peculiar gentleness and marked loveliness. His character was full of beauty and unsullied perfection. . . .

The path of obedience is exalted by the Majesty of heaven coming to the earth and condescending Himself to become a little child and living simply and naturally as children should live, submitting to restraint and privation, giving youth an example of faithful industry, showing them by His own life that body and soul are in harmony with natural laws. . . .

Although children live in a fallen world, they need not be corrupted by vice. They may be happy and through the merits of Christ attain heaven at last.—*Youth's Instructor,* April 1872.

The Father's Business

Why did you seek Me? Did you not know that I must be about My Father's business? Luke 2:49.

The parents of Jesus yearly visited Jerusalem, in accordance with the Jewish law. Their son Jesus, then twelve years old, accompanied them. In returning to their home, after they had gone a day's journey, their anxiety was aroused as they missed Jesus. . . . They hastened back to Jerusalem, their hearts heavy with sorrow. . . .

While the parents of Christ were in search of Him, they saw large numbers flocking to the temple, and as they entered it, the well-known voice of their Son arrested their attention. They could not get sight of Him for the crowd, but they knew that they were not mistaken, for no voice was like His, marked with solemn melody. The parents gazed in astonishment at the scene. Their Son, in the midst of the grave and learned doctors and scribes, was giving evidence of superior knowledge by His discreet questions and answers. His parents were gratified to see Him thus honored. But the mother could not forget the grief and anxiety she had suffered because of His tarry at Jerusalem, and she, in a reproving manner, inquired why He had thus dealt with them, relating her fears and sorrow on His account.

Said Jesus, "How is it that ye sought me?" This pointed question was to lead them to see that if they had been mindful of their duty, they would not have left Jerusalem without Him. He then adds, "Wist ye not that I must be about my father's business?" While they had been unmindful of the responsible charge intrusted to them, Jesus was engaged in the work of His Father. Mary knew that Christ did not refer to His earthly father, Joseph, but to Jehovah. . . .

It was His choice to return from Jerusalem with His parents alone, for in being retired, His father and mother would have more time for reflection and for meditation upon the prophecies which referred to His future sufferings and death. . . . After the celebration of the Passover, they sought Him sorrowing for three days. When He should be slain for the sins of the world, He would be separated from them, lost to them, for three days. But after that, He would reveal Himself to them, and be found of them, and their faith rely upon Him as the Redeemer of the fallen race, the advocate with the Father in their behalf.—*Review and Herald,* Dec. 31, 1872.

An Example of Love

My mother and My brothers are these who hear the word of God and do it. Luke 8:21.

Jesus loved children and ever influenced them for good. He cared for the poor and needy even in His childhood. In every gentle, tender, and submissive way He sought to please those with whom He came in contact; but though so gentle and submissive, no one could lead Him to do anything that was contrary to the Word of God. Some admired His perfection of character and often sought to be with Him, but others who regarded human sayings more than the Word of God turned away from Him and avoided His company. . . .

As Jesus looked upon the offerings that were brought as a sacrifice to the temple, the Holy Spirit taught Him that His life was to be sacrificed for the life of the world. . . . From His earliest years He was guarded by heavenly angels, yet His life was one long struggle against the powers of darkness. Satan sought in every way to tempt and try Him. He caused people to misunderstand His words so that they might not receive the salvation He came to bring them. . . .

He was faithful in obeying the commands of God, and this made Him very different from those around Him, who disregarded the Word of God. His stainless life was a rebuke, and many avoided His presence, but there were some who sought to be with Him because they felt at peace where He was. . . .

He did not fail nor become discouraged. He lived above the difficulties of His life, as if in the light of God's countenance. He bore insult patiently and in His human nature became an example for all children and youth.

Christ showed the greatest respect and love for His mother. Though she often talked with Him and sought to have Him do as His brethren desired Him to do, He never showed her the least lack of devotion. . . .

Mary had felt greatly troubled when the priests and rulers came to her to complain about Jesus, but peace and confidence came to her troubled heart as her Son showed her what the Scriptures said about His practices. At times she wavered between Jesus and His brethren, who did not believe that He was sent of God; but she saw enough to show her that His was a divine character.—*Youth's Instructor,* Dec. 12, 1895.

The Youthful Jesus

And Jesus increased in wisdom and stature, and in favor with God and men. Luke 2:52.

Before He came to this earth, Jesus was a great king in heaven. He was as great as God, and yet He loved the poor people of this earth so much that He was willing to lay aside His kingly crown, His beautiful robe, and come to this earth as one of the human family. . . . He could have come to earth in such beauty that He would have been unlike the children of humanity. . . . He could have come in such a way as to charm those who looked upon Him; but this was not the way that God planned He should come among us. He was to be like those who belonged to the human family and to the Jewish race. His features were to be like those of other human beings, and He was not to have such beauty of person as to make people point Him out as different from others. . . . He had come to take our place, to pledge Himself in our behalf, to pay the debt that sinners owed. He was to live a pure life on the earth and show that Satan had told a falsehood when he claimed that the human family belonged to him forever, and that God could not take them out of his hands.

Mankind first beheld Christ as a babe, as a child. His parents were very poor, and He had nothing in this earth save that which the poor have. He passed through all the trials that the poor and lowly pass through from babyhood to childhood, from youth to adulthood. . . .

In His youth He worked with His father at the carpenter's trade and thus showed that there is nothing of which to be ashamed in work. Though He was the king of heaven, He yet worked at a humble trade and thus rebuked all idleness in human beings. . . . Those who are idle do not follow the example that Christ has given, for from His childhood He was a pattern of obedience and industry. He was as a pleasant sunbeam in the home circle. Faithfully and cheerfully He acted His part, doing the humble duties that He was called to do in His lowly life. Christ became one with us in order that He might do us good. . . . The world's Redeemer did not live a life of selfish ease and pleasure. He did not choose to be the son of a rich man or to be in a position where people would praise and flatter Him. He passed through the hardships of those who toil for a living, and He could comfort all those who have to work at some humble trade. The story of His life of toil is written so that we may receive comfort out of it.—*Youth's Instructor,* Nov. 21, 1895.

A Model for the Young

And the Child grew and became strong in spirit, filled with wisdom.
Luke 2:40.

The Jewish people had wrong ideas about the Messiah and His work. . . .
They were looking for the glory that will be seen when Christ comes
the second time, and did not study the Bible so that they could know that
He was to come the first time in a very lowly way. But Jesus asked questions
about the scriptures that pointed to His first appearing, that flashed light into
the minds of those who were willing to receive the truth. Before He had
come to the earth, He had given these prophecies to His servants who had
written them down, and now as He studied the Bible, the Holy Spirit
brought these things to His mind and showed Him the great work that He
was to do in the earth. As He grew in knowledge, He imparted knowledge
to others. But though He was wiser than the learned men, He did not become proud or feel that He was above doing the most humble toil. He took
His share of the burden, with His father, mother, and brethren, and toiled to
help support the family. Though the doctors had been amazed at His wisdom,
He obeyed His parents and worked with His own hands as any toiler would
work. It is stated of Jesus that as He grew older He "increased in wisdom and
stature, and in favour with God and man."

The understanding that He obtained from day to day, that showed Him
how wonderful should be His mission in the world, did not lead Him to
neglect the humblest duties. He cheerfully took up the work that children
and youth who dwell in humble households are called upon to do, for He
knew what it was to be pressed by poverty. He understands the temptations
of children, for He bore their sorrows and trials. Firm and steadfast was His
purpose to do the right; though others tried to lead Him to do evil, He yet
never did wrong and would not turn away in the least from the path of
truth and right. He always obeyed His parents and did every duty that lay
in His path. But His childhood and youth were anything but smooth and
joyous. His spotless life aroused the envy and jealousy of His brethren, for
they did not believe on Him. They were annoyed because He did not act
in all things as they did and would not become one with them in doing
evil. In His home life He was cheerful but never boisterous. He ever seemed
like one who was seeking to learn. He took great delight in nature, and
God was His teacher.—*Youth's Instuctor,* Nov. 28, 1895.

Living the Truth

The grace of God was upon Him. Luke 2:40.

Even in His childhood Jesus saw that the people did not live in the way that the Bible pointed out as the way for them to live. He studied the Bible and followed the simple habits and ways that the Word of God directs; and when people found fault with Him because He was so lowly and simple, He pointed them to the Word of God. His brothers told Him that He thought Himself much better than they were, and reproved Him for setting Himself up above the priests and rulers of the people. Jesus knew that if He obeyed the Word of God, He would not find rest and peace in the home circle.

As He grew in knowledge, He knew that great errors were increasing among His people and that because they followed human commands instead of obeying the commands of God, simplicity and truth and true piety were becoming lost in the earth. He saw the people going through forms and ceremonies in their worship of God and passing by the sacred truths that made their service of value. He knew that their faithless services could not do them any good and would not bring them peace or rest. They could not know what it was to have freedom of spirit when they did not serve God in truth.

Jesus did not always silently look upon these worthless services but sometimes told the people where they were going wrong. Because He was so quick to see what was false and what was true, His brethren were greatly annoyed at Him, for they said that whatever the priest taught ought to be considered as sacred as a command of God. But Jesus taught both by His words and by His example that men and women ought to worship God just as He has directed them to worship Him and not follow the ceremonies that human teachers have said ought to be followed. . . .

The priests and the Pharisees also were annoyed because this child would not accept their human inventions, maxims, and traditions. They thought that He showed great disrespect to their religion and to the rabbis who had commanded these services. He told them that He would heed every word that came from the mouth of God and that they must show Him from the Bible where He was in error. He pointed out to them the fact that they were placing the word of human beings above the Word of God and causing people to show disrespect to God through obeying these human commandments.—*Youth's Instructor,* Dec. 5, 1895.

Scripture Was Jesus' Guide

And all who heard Him were astonished at His
understanding and answers. Luke 2:47.

They [the rabbis] knew that He was far in advance of them in spiritual understanding and that He lived a blameless life, yet they were angry with Him because He would not violate His conscience by obeying their dictates. Failing to convince Him that He ought to look upon human tradition as sacred, they came to Joseph and Mary and complained that Jesus was taking a wrong course in regard to their customs and traditions. Jesus knew what it was to have His family divided against Him on account of His religious faith. He loved peace; He craved the love and confidence of the members of His family; but He knew what it was to have them withdraw their affection from Him. He suffered rebuke and censure because He took a straightforward course and would not do evil because others did evil, but was true to the commandments of Jehovah. His brethren rebuked Him because He stood aloof from the ceremonies that were taught by the rabbis, for they regarded the word of human beings more highly than the word of God because they loved the praise of men more than the praise of God.

Jesus made the Scriptures His constant study; and when the scribes and Pharisees tried to make Him accept their doctrines, they found Him ready to meet them with the Word of God, and they could do nothing to convince Him that they were right. He seemed to know the Scriptures from beginning to end and repeated them in such a way that their true meaning shone out. . . . They were angry that this child should dare to question their word, when it was their calling to study and explain the Scriptures. . . .

His brethren threatened Him and sought to compel Him to take a wrong course, but He passed on, making the Scriptures His guide. From the time His parents found Him in the temple asking and answering questions among the doctors, they could not understand His course of action. Quiet and gentle, He seemed as one who was set apart. Whenever He could, He went out alone into the fields and on the mountainsides to commune with the God of nature. When His work was done, He wandered by the lakeside, among the trees of the forest, and in the green valleys where He could think about God and lift His soul to heaven in prayer. After a season thus spent, He would return to His home to take up again the humble duties of His life and to give to all an example of patient labor.—*Youth's Instructor,* Dec. 5, 1895.

Jesus Was From Nazareth

Can anything good come out of Nazareth? John 1:46.

The first thirty years of the life of Christ were passed in the obscure village of Nazareth. The inhabitants of this village were proverbial for
their wickedness, hence the inquiry of Nathanael, "Can there any good
thing come out of Nazareth?" The evangelists say but very little in regard
to the early life of Christ. With the exception of a brief account of His ac-
companying His parents to Jerusalem, we have the simple statement only,
"And the child grew, and waxed strong in spirit, filled with wisdom: and
the grace of God was upon him." . . .

Children and youth are frequently situated where their surroundings are
not favorable to a Christian life, and they quite readily yield to temptations
and plead as an excuse for pursuing a course of sin that their surroundings
are unfavorable. . . .

Christ placed His feet in the most uneven path that children and youth will
ever be called to travel. He did not have allotted to Him a life of affluence
and indolence. His parents were poor and dependent upon their daily toil for
sustenance; therefore the life of Christ was one of poverty, self-denial, and privation. He shared with His parents their life of diligent industry.

None will ever be called to perfect Christian character under more unfavorable circumstances than that of our Savior. The fact that Christ lived
thirty years in Nazareth, from which many thought it a wonder if any good
thing could come, is a rebuke to the youth who consider that their religious
character must conform to circumstances. If the surroundings of youth are
unpleasant and positively bad, many make this an excuse for not perfecting
Christian character. The example of Christ would rebuke the idea that His
followers are dependent upon place, fortune, or prosperity in order to live
blameless lives. Christ would teach them that their faithfulness would make
any place, or position, where the providence of God called them, honorable, however humble. . . .

The trials and privations of which so many youth complain, Christ endured without murmuring. And this discipline is the very experience the
youth need, which will give firmness to their character and make them like
Christ, strong in spirit to resist temptation. . . . Through daily prayer to God
they will have wisdom and grace from Him to bear the conflicts and stern
realities of life and come off victorious.—*Youth's Instructor,* March 1872.

By Words and by Example

And the common people heard Him gladly. Mark 12:37.

Christ passed no human being by as worthless and hopeless, but sought to apply the saving remedy to every soul who needed help. Wherever He was found, He had a lesson to present that was the right one for the time and circumstance. He sought to inspire with hope the most rough and unpromising, setting before them the idea that they might become blameless and harmless and attain a character that would be Christlike. They could be the children of God and shine as lights in the world, even though they lived among evil people. This was the reason that so many heard Him gladly. From His very childhood He worked for others, letting His light shine amid the moral darkness of the world. In bearing burdens in His home life and in laboring in more public fields, He showed everyone what the character of God is. He encouraged everything that had a bearing on the real interests of life, but He did not encourage the youth in dreaming of what would be in the future. He taught them by His words and by His example that the future would be decided by the way in which they spent the present. Our destiny is marked out by our own course of action. Those who cherish that which is right, who work out God's plan though it be in a narrow sphere of action, and who do right because it is right will find wider fields of usefulness. . . .

It is our privilege now to act a part in the work and mission of Christ. We may be laborers together with Him. In whatever work we are called to engage, we may work with Christ. He is doing all that He can to set us free, to make our lives that seem so cramped and narrow reach out to bless and help others. He would have us understand that we are held responsible to do good, and have us realize that in shunning our work we are bringing loss upon ourselves. . . .

Jesus carried the burden of the salvation of the human family upon His heart. He knew that unless men and women would receive Him and become changed in purpose and life, they would be eternally lost. This was the burden of His soul, and He was alone in carrying this load. No one knew how heavy was the weight that rested upon His heart; but from His youth He was filled with a deep longing to be a lamp in the world, and He purposed that His life should be "the light of the world." This He was, and that light still shines to all who are in darkness. Let us walk in the light which He has given.—*Youth's Instructor,* Jan. 2, 1896.

Overcoming As Christ Overcame

For we do not have a High Priest who cannot sympathize with our weaknesses, but was in all points tempted as we are, yet without sin. Heb. 4:15.

As Christ's ministry was about to begin, He received baptism at the hands of John. Coming up out of the water, He bowed on the banks of the Jordan and offered to the Father such a prayer as heaven had never before listened to. . . . The heavens were opened, and a dove, in appearance like burnished gold, rested upon Jesus; and from the lips of the infinite God were heard the words, "This is my beloved Son, in whom I am well pleased."

This visible answer to the prayer of God's Son is of deep significance to us. . . .

All may find rest and peace and assurance in sending their prayers to God in the name of His dear Son. As the heavens were open to Christ's prayer, so they will be opened to our prayers. . . .

From the Jordan, Jesus was led into the wilderness of temptation. "And when he had fasted forty days and forty nights, he was afterward an hungered. And when the tempter came to him, he said, If thou be the Son of God, command that these stones be made bread." . . .

Adam had failed on the point of appetite, and Christ must conquer here. The power that rested upon Him came directly from the Father, and He must not exercise it in His own behalf. . . . He met and resisted the enemy in the strength of a "Thus saith the Lord." "Man shall not live by bread alone," He said, "but by every word that proceedeth out of the mouth of God." . . . .

Christ's experience is for our benefit. His example in overcoming appetite points out the way for those to overcome who would be His followers.

Christ was suffering as the members of the human family suffer under temptation, but it was not the will of God that He should exercise His divine power in His own behalf. Had He not stood as our representative, Christ's innocence would have exempted Him from all this anguish; but it was because of His innocence that He felt so keenly the assaults of Satan. All the suffering that is the result of sin was poured into the bosom of the sinless Son of God. Satan was bruising the heel of Christ, but every pang endured by Christ, every grief, every disquietude, was fulfilling the great plan of our redemption. Every blow inflicted by the enemy was rebounding on himself. Christ was bruising the serpent's head.—*Youth's Instructor,* Dec. 21, 1899.

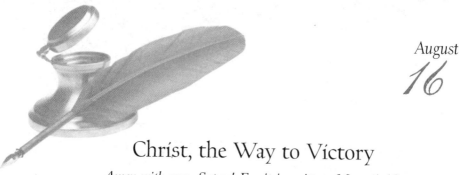

Christ, the Way to Victory

Away with you, Satan! For it is written. Matt. 4:10.

S atan had been defeated in the first temptation. He next took Christ to the pinnacle of the temple at Jerusalem and asked Him to prove His Sonship to God by throwing Himself down from the dizzy height. "If thou be the Son of God," he said, "cast thyself down: for it is written, He shall give his angels charge concerning thee: and in their hands they shall bear thee up, lest at any time thou dash thy foot against a stone." But to do this would be presumption on the part of Christ, and He would not yield. "It is written again," He replied, "thou shalt not tempt the Lord thy God." Again the tempter was baffled. Christ was victor still.

Presumption is a common temptation, and when Satan assails us with this, he gains the victory almost every time. Those who claim to be enlisted in the warfare against evil frequently plunge without thought into temptation from which it would require a miracle to bring them forth unsullied. God's precious promises are not given to strengthen us in a presumptuous course or to rely upon when we rush needlessly into danger. The Lord requires us to move with a humble dependence upon His guidance. "It is not in man that walketh to direct his steps." In God is our prosperity and our life. . . . "Commit thy way unto the Lord; trust also in him; and he shall bring it to pass." As children of God, we are to maintain a consistent Christian character.

While you pray . . . that you may not be led into temptation, remember that your work does not end with prayer. As far as possible you must answer your own prayers by resisting temptation. Ask Jesus to do for you that which you cannot do for yourself. With God's Word for our guide and Jesus for our teacher, we need not be ignorant of God's requirements or of Satan's devices.

"Again, the devil taketh him up into an exceeding high mountain, and sheweth him all the kingdoms of the world, and the glory of them; and saith unto him, All these things will I give thee, if thou wilt fall down and worship me." Then divinity flashed through humanity. "Get thee hence, Satan," Christ said, "for it is written, Thou shalt worship the Lord thy God, and him only shalt thou serve." Satan did not then present another temptation. He left the presence of Christ a conquered foe.—*Youth's Instructor,* Dec. 21, 1899.

Rejected

He came to His own, and His own did not receive Him. John 1:11.

At the first advent of Christ, which was in apparent obscurity, the angels of heaven could scarcely be restrained from pouring forth their glories to grace the birth of the Son of God. The glorious manifestations of heaven were not entirely restrained. The wonderful event was not without some attestations of a divine character. That birth, so little prepared for on earth, was celebrated in the heavenly courts with praise and thanksgiving in behalf of sinners. . . .

He who came in human flesh and submitted to a life of humiliation was the Majesty of heaven, the Prince of life, and yet the wise men of the earth, the princes and rulers, and even His own nation, knew Him not. They did not recognize Him as the long-looked-for Messiah. Notwithstanding mighty miracles did show forth themselves in Him, notwithstanding He opened the eyes of the blind and raised the dead to life, Christ suffered the hatred and abuse of the people He came to bless. They regarded Him as a sinner and accused Him of casting out devils through the prince of devils. The circumstances of His birth were mysterious and were remarked upon by the rulers. They charged Him with being born in sin. The Prince of heaven was insulted because of the corrupt minds and the sinful, blasphemous unbelief of His people. What a baleful thing is unbelief! It originated with the first great apostate, and to what fearful lengths it will lead all who enter upon its path is seen in the Jews' rejection of their Messiah. . . .

The leaders in Israel professed to understand the prophecies, but they had received false ideas in regard to the manner of Christ's coming. . . .

The very One who died for sinners is to judge them in the last day; for the Father "hath committed all judgment unto the Son" and "hath given him authority to execute judgment also, because he is the Son of man."

What a day that will be, when those who rejected Christ will look upon Him whom their sins have pierced. They will then know that He proffered them all heaven if they would but stand by His side as obedient children; that He paid an infinite price for their redemption; but that they would not accept freedom from the galling slavery of sin. They chose to stand under the black banner of rebellion to the close of mercy's hour.—*Review and Herald*, Sept. 5, 1899.

Revealing the Father

He who has seen Me has seen the Father. John 14:9.

The fact that the people were more interested in Christ's teaching than they were in the dry, tedious arguments of the Jewish teachers maddened the scribes and Pharisees. These teachers spoke with uncertainty, interpreting the Scriptures to mean one thing and then another. This left the people in great confusion. But as they listened to Jesus, their hearts were warmed and comforted. He presented God as a loving Father, not as an avenging judge. He drew all, high and low, rich and poor, to see God in His true character, leading them to call Him by the endearing name, "Our Father."

By loving words and by works of mercy, Christ bore down old traditions and man-made commandments and presented the love of the Father in its exhaustless fullness. His calm, earnest, musical voice fell like balm on the wounded spirit. He was revealing the image of God mirrored in Himself. He presented to His hearers the truths of the prophecies, separating them from the obscure interpretations which the scribes and Pharisees had attached to them. He scattered the heavenly grains of truth wherever He went.

Determined to hear what Christ said to His disciples, the scribes and Pharisees kept spies on His track. These spies noted His words and reported them to the Jewish authorities, who, when they heard them, were almost beside themselves with ill-concealed rage, which they interpreted to be zeal for God.

As the members of the Sanhedrin counseled together, there were not wanting men with strong, determined prejudices who advised that this man who claimed so much be at once put down. . . .

They saw that Christ's influence over the people was fast becoming greater than theirs. They longed to crush Him for daring to make their traditions of none effect, but they feared to move openly because of the people. They thought that if they worked secretly, watching His words and actions, they would soon find such accusations against Him that He could be put on trial for His life. . . .

Christ was giving the rulers of Israel light which would make them inexcusable. Nothing was left undone that could be done to convince them of their error.—*Review and Herald,* Mar. 5, 1901.

Blinded by Prejudice

But you do not have His word abiding in you, because whom He sent, Him you do not believe. John 5:38.

As at different times during Christ's work divinity flashed through humanity and He stood transfigured before the people, the Jewish leaders were deeply impressed. But as they talked it over with one another, their unbelief strengthened, and the evidence that should have convinced them was rejected. The strongest evidence was no evidence to them, while the weakest, most superficial arguments, if against the truth which the Savior brought, were sound in their estimation. They had started upon a path leading to eternal ruin. . . .

Christ saw that the Jewish teachers misinterpreted the Word of God, and He urged upon them a more diligent study of its precepts. In Him were fast being fulfilled the types and shadows of the Jewish economy. If they searched the Scriptures as they should, they would find that He claimed nothing which was not rightfully His.

Had the Jews searched God's Word as they should, they would have seen that Jesus of Nazareth is the Messiah. But they searched with proud, selfish ambition as a guide, and they found a Messiah of their own imagination. Therefore when the Savior came, a humble man, bringing to naught by His teaching long-established theories and traditions, presenting truth entirely opposite to their practices, they said, Who is this invader that dares to set aside our authority? Christ did not come as they had expected; therefore they refused to receive Him and called Him a deceiver and an impostor. Instead of listening to Him that they might learn the truth, they listened with evil intent, that they might find something over which to cavil. And when once they had set their feet in the path of the great leader in rebellion, it was an easy matter for Satan to strengthen them in opposition. Christ's wonderful works, which God meant to be heaven-sent evidence to them, Satan caused them to interpret against Him. The more marked the way in which God spoke to them by His works of mercy and love, the more confirmed did they become in their resistance. Blinded by prejudice, they refused to acknowledge that Jesus is divine. . . .

He was God in human flesh, and He could not but work the works of God.—*Review and Herald,* Mar. 26, 1901.

August

20

Act When Opportunity Knocks

Do you want to be made well? John 5:6.

The healing of the sick man at Bethesda has a lesson of priceless worth to every Christian, a lesson of solemn and fearful import to the unbelieving and the skeptical. As the paralytic lay beside the pool, helpless and well-nigh hopeless, Jesus drew near and asked, in tones of pity, "Wilt thou be made whole?" Be made whole! This had been the burden of his desire and prayers for long, weary years. With trembling eagerness he told the story of his efforts and disappointments. No friend was at hand to bear him with sturdy arm into the healing fountain. His agonizing appeals for help fell unheeded; all around him were those who sought for their own loved ones the coveted boon. When at the troubling of the waters he painfully sought to reach the pool, another would be hurried down before him.

Jesus looked upon the sufferer and said, "Rise, take up thy bed, and walk." There was no assurance of divine help, no manifestation of miraculous power. What marvel, had the man made answer, "It is impossible! How can I be expected now to use my limbs that have not obeyed my will for thirty-eight years?" From a merely human standpoint, such reasoning would appear consistent. The sufferer might have given place to doubt and thus have permitted that God-given opportunity to pass unimproved. But no; without a question he seized his only chance. As he attempted to do what Christ had commanded, strength and vigor came; he was made whole.

Would you, doubting reader, receive the blessing of the Lord? Cease to question His word and distrust His promises. Obey the Savior's bidding, and you will receive strength. If you hesitate, to enter into a discussion with Satan or to consider the difficulties and improbabilities, your opportunity will pass, perhaps never to return.

The miracle at Bethesda should have convinced all beholders that Jesus is the Son of God. . . .

At Christ's command, the paralytic had borne away the simple mat on which he had lain; and now Satan, ever ready with his insinuations, suggested that this act might be construed into a violation of the Sabbath. . . . It was hoped that a controversy on this point would destroy the faith inspired in some hearts by our Savior's act of healing.— *Signs of the Times,* June 8, 1882.

244

Abundant Evidence for Faith

The man . . . told the Jews that it was Jesus who had made him well.
John 5:15.

As the restored one went on his way with quick, elastic step, his pulses bounding with the vigor of renewed health, his countenance glowing with hope and joy, he was met by the Pharisees, who told him, with an air of great sanctity, that it was not lawful to carry his bed on the Sabbath day. There was no rejoicing at the deliverance of that long-imprisoned captive, no grateful praise that One was among them who could heal all manner of disease. Their traditions had been disregarded, and this closed their eyes to all the evidence of divine power.

Bigoted and self-righteous, they would not admit that they could have misapprehended the true design of the Sabbath. Instead of criticizing themselves, they chose to condemn Christ. We meet with people of the same spirit today, who are blinded by error and yet flatter themselves that they are right, and all who differ from them are in the wrong.

The man on whom the miracle had been wrought entered into no controversy with his accusers. He simply answered, "He that made me whole, the same said unto me, Take up thy bed, and walk." . . .

When the Jews were informed that it was Jesus of Nazareth who had performed the miracle of healing, they openly sought to put Him to death, "because he had done these things on the sabbath day." These pretentious formalists were so full of zeal for their own traditions that to sustain them they were ready to violate the law of God!

To their charges, Jesus replied calmly, . . . "I am working in perfect harmony with my Father." This answer furnished another pretext to condemn Him. Murder was in their hearts, and they waited only for a plausible excuse to take His life. But Jesus steadily continues to assert His true position. "The Son can do nothing of himself, but what he seeth the Father do: for what things soever he doeth, these also doeth the Son likewise." . . .

God works through whom He will by ways and means of His own choosing, but there are ever some to act the part of the criticizing Pharisees. . . .

God designs that all shall believe, not because there is no possibility of doubt, but because there is abundant evidence for faith.—*Signs of the Times,* June 8, 1882.

The Blind Man Healed

Neither this man nor his parents sinned, but that the works of God should be revealed in him. John 9:3.

A nd as Jesus passed by, he saw a man which was blind from his birth. And his disciples asked him, saying, Master, who did sin, this man, or his parents, that he was born blind?" . . .

In the question the disciples asked Jesus, they showed that they thought all disease and suffering the result of sin. This is indeed truth, but Jesus showed that it was an error to suppose that everyone who was a great sufferer was also a great sinner. While He corrected their errors, He spat upon the ground and made clay of the spittle, and anointed the eyes of the blind man with the clay and said unto him, "Go, wash in the pool of Siloam, (which is by interpretation, Sent)," and he went his way, and came seeing. Jesus answered the question the disciples put to Him in a practical way, and in the way He usually answered questions put to Him from curiosity. The disciples were not called upon to discuss the question of who had sinned or not sinned but to understand the power of God, His mercy and compassion, in giving sight to the blind. It was that all might be convinced that there was no healing virtue in the clay or in the pool wherein he was sent to wash, but that virtue was in Christ. . . .

The friends and neighbors of the young man who had been healed looked upon him with doubt, for when his eyes were opened, his countenance had been changed and brightened, and made him appear like another man. From one to another the question was passed, "Is it he?" And some said, "It is like him," but he who had received the great blessing settled the controversy by saying, "I am he." He then told them of Jesus and by what means Jesus had healed him, and they inquired, "Where is he? He said, I know not. They brought to the Pharisees him that aforetime was blind. And it was the sabbath day when Jesus made the clay, and opened his eyes. . . . Therefore said some of the Pharisees, This man is not of God, because he keepeth not the sabbath day. Others said, How can a man that is a sinner do such miracles? And there was a division among them." . . .

They knew not that it was He who had made the Sabbath, who knew all its obligations, who had healed the man.—*Signs of the Times,* Oct. 23, 1893.

The Water of Life

A woman of Samaria came to draw water. Jesus said to her,
"Give Me a drink." John 4:7.

As the world's Redeemer, the Son of God took upon Him our human nature. . . . Hungry and thirsty, He tarried to rest at Jacob's well, near the city of Sychar, while His disciples went to buy food in the city. . . .

As Jesus sat by the well side, the cool, refreshing water, so near and yet so inaccessible to Him, only increased His thirst. He had neither rope nor bucket with which to draw, and He waited until someone should come to the well. He might have performed a miracle and thus have obtained a draft from the well, had He wished, but this was not God's plan. . . .

"There cometh a woman of Samaria to draw water: Jesus saith unto her, Give me to drink." The woman answered, "How is it that thou, being a Jew, askest drink of me, which am a woman of Samaria? for the Jews have no dealings with the Samaritans." Christ was near to the woman of Samaria, and she knew Him not. She was thirsting for the truth, yet knew not that He, the Truth, was beside her and was able to enlighten her. And today there are thirsting souls sitting close by the living fountain. But they are looking far away from the well that contains the refreshing water, and, though told that the water is close by, they will not believe.

Jesus answered the woman, saying, "If thou knewest the gift of God, and who it is that saith to thee, Give me to drink; thou wouldest have asked of him, and he would have given thee living water. The woman saith unto him, Sir, thou hast nothing to draw with, and the well is deep: from whence then hast thou that living water? Art thou greater than our father Jacob, which gave us the well, and drank thereof himself, and his children, and his cattle?" Yes, Jesus could have answered, the One who is speaking to you is the only begotten Son of God; I am greater than your father Jacob, for before Abraham was, I am. But He made answer, "Whosoever drinketh of this water shall thirst again: but whosoever drinketh of the water that I shall give him shall never thirst; but the water that I shall give him shall be in him a well of water springing up into everlasting life." . . .

Christ was just as truly the water of life to Abel, Seth, Enoch, Noah, and all who received His instruction then as He is at the present time to those who ask of Him the refreshing draft.—*Signs of the Times,* Apr. 22, 1897.

Quenching the Soul's Thirst

Sir, give me this water, that I may not thirst, nor come here to draw. John 4:15.

The woman was so astonished at His words that she rested her pitcher on the well, and, forgetting the thirst of the stranger and His request to give Him to drink, forgetting her errand to the well, she was lost in her earnest desire to hear every word. . . .

Jesus now abruptly changed the subject of conversation and bade the woman call her husband. She frankly replied, "I have no husband. Jesus said unto her, Thou hast well said, I have no husband: for thou hast had five husbands; and he whom thou now hast is not thy husband: in that saidst thou truly."

As the past of her life was spread out before her, the listener trembled. Conviction of sin was awakened. She said, "Sir, I perceive that thou art a prophet." And then, in order to change the conversation to some other subject, she endeavored to lead Christ into a controversy upon their religious differences. . . .

The conviction of the Spirit of God had come to the heart of the Samaritan woman. . . . No teaching that she had hitherto heard had aroused her moral nature and awakened her to a sense of her higher need.

Christ reads beneath the surface, and He revealed to the woman of Samaria her soul thirst, which the water from the well of Sychar could never satisfy. . . .

The natural thirst of the woman of Samaria had led her to a thirst of soul for the water of life. . . .

Forgetting the errand that had brought her to the well, the woman left her water pot and went into the city, saying to all whom she met, "Come, see a man, which told me all things that ever I did: is not this the Christ?" . . .

Earth's cisterns will often be emptied, its pools become dry; but in Christ there is a living spring from which we may continually draw. . . . There is no danger of exhausting the supply; for Christ is the inexhaustible wellspring of truth. He has been the fountain of living water ever since the fall of Adam. He says, "If any man thirst, let him come unto me, and drink." And "whosoever drinketh of the water that I shall give him shall never thirst; but the water that I shall give him shall be in him a well of water springing up into everlasting life."—*Signs of the Times,* Apr. 22, 1897.

Feeding the 5,000

You give them something to eat. Matt. 14:16.

The disciples thought they had withdrawn where they would not be discovered, but as soon as the multitude missed the divine Teacher, they inquired, "Where is he?" Some among them had noticed the direction in which Christ and His disciples had gone, and soon an immense crowd was looking for Christ. Fresh additions were made to this number until the congregation was composed of no less than five thousand men, besides women and children.

From the hillside Jesus looked upon the moving multitude, and His great heart of love and compassion was stirred with sympathy. Interrupted as He was and robbed of His rest, He was not impatient. . . . Leaving His mountain retreat, He found a convenient place where He could minister to their spiritual destitution. . . .

The people listened to the words of mercy flowing so freely from the lips of the Son of God. They heard the gracious words, so simple and so plain that they were as the balm of Gilead to their souls. The healing of His divine hand brought gladness and life to the dying and ease and health to those suffering with disease. The day seemed to them like heaven upon earth, and they were utterly unconscious of how long it was since they had eaten anything.

"And when the day was now far spent, his disciples came unto him, and said, This is a desert place, and now the time is far passed: send them away, that they may go into the country round about, and into the villages, and buy themselves bread: for they have nothing to eat. He answered and said unto them, Give ye them to eat." Surprised and astonished, they say unto Him, "Shall we go and buy two hundred pennyworth of bread, and give them to eat? He saith unto them, How many loaves have ye? go and see. And when they knew, they say, Five, and two fishes. And he commanded them to make all sit down by companies upon the green grass. . . . And when he had taken the five loaves and the two fishes, he looked up to heaven, and blessed, and brake the loaves, and gave them to his disciples to set before them; and the two fishes divided he among them all. And they did all eat, and were filled. And they took up twelve baskets full of the fragments, and of the fishes."

He who taught the people the way to secure peace and happiness was just as thoughtful of their temporal necessities as of their spiritual need.—*Signs of the Times,* Aug. 12, 1897.

Receive to Give

*I planted, Apollos watered, but God gave the increase.
So then neither he who plants is anything, nor he who waters,
but God who gives the increase. 1 Cor. 3:6, 7.*

The work of building up the kingdom of Christ will go forward, though to all appearances it moves slowly, and means are so limited that impossibilities seem to testify against advance. . . .

The disciples were bidden to feed the hungry multitude before eating themselves. After the wants of all had been supplied, the command was given, "Gather up the fragments that remain, that nothing be lost." Twelve baskets full were gathered up, and then Christ and His disciples ate of the precious, heaven-supplied food. . . .

In the place of shifting your responsibility upon someone whom you think more richly endowed than you are, work according to your ability, even though you have but one talent. . . .

Christ received from the Father; He imparted to the disciples; and they imparted to the multitude. All who are united to Christ will be doers of His word, receiving the bread of life . . . and imparting it to others. . . .

Our Savior placed in the hands of His disciples the food for the people, and as they emptied their hands, they were again filled with the food, which multiplied in Christ's hands as fast as it was called for. . . . This should be a great encouragement to the disciples of Christ today. Christ is the great center, the source of all strength. . . .

A Paul may plant, and an Apollos water, but God only giveth the increase. This is so that no one may boast. The most intelligent, the most spiritually-minded, can bestow only as they receive. Of themselves they can manufacture nothing for the needs of the soul. We can impart only that which we receive from the hands of Christ, and we can receive only as we impart to others. As we continue imparting, we continue to receive, and the more we impart, the more we shall receive. Thus we may be constantly believing, trusting, receiving, and imparting. . . .

In the hand of Christ the small supply of food remained undiminished until the famished multitude were satisfied. . . . If we go to the Source of all strength with our hands of faith outstretched to receive, we shall be sustained in our work, even under the most forbidding circumstances, and shall be enabled to give to others the Bread of Life.—*Signs of the Times,* Aug. 19, 1897.

The Joy of Christ's Fellowship in Heaven

There is laid up for me the crown of righteousness, which the Lord, the righteous Judge, will give me on that Day, and not to me only but also to all who have loved His appearing. 2 Tim. 4:8.

While sitting round the Communion table, Christ spoke words of intense interest to His disciples. He was soon to pass through scenes that would be to them the severest test. Not only did He see distinctly His own humiliation and suffering, but He saw also the effect that this would have upon the disciples. He would not leave them in darkness regarding His future work. . . . He knew that in their sorrow they would be assailed by the enemy, for Satan's craft is most successful when carried on against those who are depressed by difficulties. . . .

During these last sorrowful hours, Christ told His disciples that on the night of His trial, they would all be offended because of Him, and that He would be left alone. He told them that for a little while after His death they would be sorrowful, but that their sorrow would be turned into joy. He told them that the time was coming when they would be put out of the synagogues, and that those who killed them would think that they were doing God service. He stated plainly why He told them these things while He was yet with them—that when His words were fulfilled, they would remember that He had told them of them before they came to pass, and thus be strengthened to believe in Him as their Redeemer. . . .

Christ's statements saddened and amazed the disciples. But they were followed by the comforting assurance, "Let not your heart be troubled: ye believe in God, believe also in me. In my Father's house are many mansions: if it were not so, I would have told you. I go to prepare a place for you. And if I go and prepare a place for you, I will come again, and receive you unto myself; that where I am, there ye may be also." . . .

Not only to the disciples, but to us, are these words of comfort spoken. In the last scenes of this earth's history, war will rage. There will be pestilence, plague, and famine. The waters of the deep will overflow their boundaries. Property and life will be destroyed by fire and flood. We should be preparing for the mansions that Christ has gone to prepare for them that love Him. There is a rest from earth's conflict. Where is it? "That where I am, there ye may be also." Heaven is where Christ is. Heaven would not be heaven to those who love Christ if He were not there.—*Review and Herald*, Oct. 19, 1897.

Coworkers With Christ

Greater works than these he will do, because I go to My Father.
John 14:12.

Christ's work was largely confined to Judea. But though His personal ministry did not extend to other lands, people from all nations listened to His teaching and carried the message to all parts of the world. Many heard of Jesus by hearing of the wonderful miracles that He performed. And the knowledge of His suffering and death, which were to be witnessed by the large number in attendance at the Passover, would be spread from Jerusalem to all parts of the world.

Used as Christ's representatives, the apostles would make a decided impression on all minds. The fact that they were humble men would not diminish their influence but increase it. The minds of their hearers would be carried from them to the Majesty of heaven. . . . Their words of trust would assure all that it was not by their own power they worked, but that they were only continuing the same work carried forward by the Lord Jesus when He was with them. Humbling themselves, they would declare that He whom the Jews had crucified was the Prince of life, the Son of the living God, and that in His name they did the works that He had done. . . .

The whole universe is under the control of the Prince of life. . . . He paid the ransom money for the whole world. All may be saved through Him. He calls upon us to obey, believe, receive, and live. He would gather together a church embracing the whole human family, if all would leave the black banner of rebellion and place themselves under His banner. Those who believe on Him, He will present to God as loyal subjects. He is our Mediator as well as our Redeemer. He will defend His chosen followers against Satan's power and subdue all their enemies. . . .

Christ desired His disciples to understand that He would not leave them orphans. . . . He was about to die, but He desired them to realize that He would live again. And although after His ascension He would be absent from them, yet by faith they might see and know Him, and He would have the same loving interest in them that He had while with them.

Christ assured His disciples that after His resurrection He would show Himself alive to them. . . . They would then understand that which they had not in the past understood—that there is a complete union between Christ and His Father, a union that will always exist.—*Review and Herald,* Oct. 26, 1897.

Gethsemane

Then they came to a place which was named Gethsemane; and He said to His disciples, "Sit here while I pray." Mark 14:32.

As Christ left the disciples, bidding them pray for themselves and for Him, He selected three, Peter, James, and John, and went still farther into the seclusion of the garden. These three disciples had been with Him at His transfiguration; they had seen the heavenly visitors, Moses and Elias, talking with Jesus, and Christ desired their presence on this occasion also. . . .

Christ expressed His desire for human sympathy and then withdrew Himself from them about a stone's cast. Falling upon His face He prayed, saying, "O my Father, if it be possible, let this cup pass from me: nevertheless not as I will, but as thou wilt."

At the end of an hour, Jesus, feeling the need of human sympathy, rose from the ground and staggered to the place where He had left His three disciples. . . . He longed to hear from them words that would bring Him some relief in His suffering. But He was disappointed. They did not bring to Him the help He craved. Instead, He "findeth them sleeping."

Just before He bent His footsteps to the garden, Jesus had said to His disciples, "All ye shall be offended because of me this night"; and they had given Christ the strongest assurances that they would never forsake their Lord, that they would go to prison with Him, and if need be would suffer and die with Him. And poor, self-sufficient Peter had added, "Although all shall be offended, yet will not I." But the disciples trusted in their own strength; they did not look to the mighty Helper, as Christ had counseled them to do. . . . Even the ardent Peter, who only a few hours before had declared that he would die with his Lord, was sleeping. . . .

Again the Son of God was seized with superhuman agony, and, fainting and exhausted, He staggered back to the place of His former struggle. . . . Only a short time before, Christ had poured out His soul in songs of praise in unfaltering accents, as one who was conscious of His Sonship to God. . . . Now His voice came to them on the still evening air, not in tones of triumph but full of human anguish. So lately He had been serene in His majesty; He had been like a mighty cedar. Now He was as a broken reed. . . .

Although sin was the awful thing that had opened the floodgates of woe upon the world, He would become the propitiation of a race that had willed to sin.—*Signs of the Times,* Dec. 2, 1897.

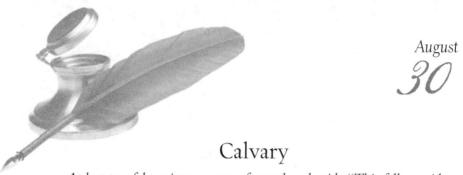

Calvary

At last two false witnesses came forward and said, "This fellow said,
'I am able to destroy the temple of God and to build it in three days.'"
Matt. 26:60, 61.

This was the only charge that could be brought against Christ. But these words had been misstated and misapplied. Christ had said, "Destroy this temple, and in three days I will raise it up.... But he spake of the temple of his body."

Priests and rulers, with many others, taunted Him with this false statement. While He hung upon the cross, it was repeated in mockery by the scribes and Pharisees and echoed by the multitude. "They that passed by reviled him, wagging their heads, and saying, Thou that destroyest the temple, and buildest it in three days, save thyself." But though misstated, Christ's words were being fulfilled. Publicity was given to them, and they were made more impressive by the proclamations of His enemies....

Those who in derision uttered the words, "He trusted in God; let him deliver him now, if he will have him: for he said, I am the Son of God," little thought that their testimony would sound down the ages. But although spoken in mockery, never were words more true. They led people to search the Scriptures for themselves. Wise men heard, searched, pondered, and prayed. There were those who never rested until, by searching the Scriptures and comparing passage with passage, they saw the meaning of Christ's mission. They saw that free forgiveness was provided by Him whose tender mercy embraces the whole world....

Never before was there such a general knowledge of Jesus as when He hung upon the cross. He was lifted up from the earth to draw all unto Him. Into the hearts of many who beheld the crucifixion scene and who heard Christ's words was the light of truth to shine. With John they would proclaim, "Behold the Lamb of God, which taketh away the sin of the world."...

This scene was transacted in the sight of heaven and earth. Angels beheld the pitiless scorn and contempt shown to Jesus by those who should have acknowledged Him as the Messiah....

Again came the cry, as of one in mortal agony, "It is finished." "Father, into thy hands I commend my spirit: and having said thus, he gave up the ghost." Christ, the Majesty of heaven, the King of glory, was dead.—*Review and Herald*, Dec. 28, 1897.

A Job Well Done

*I have glorified You on the earth. I have finished the work
which You have given Me to do. John 17:4.*

When Christ expired on the cross, crying with a loud voice, "It is finished," His work was completed. The way was laid open, the veil
was rent in twain. Humanity could approach God without sacrificial offerings, without the service of earthly priests. Christ Himself was a priest forever after the order of Melchizedek. Heaven was His home. He came to this
world to reveal the Father. His work on the field of His humiliation and
conflict was now done. He ascended up into the heavens and is forever set
down on the right hand of God.

Christ's life on this earth had been a life of toil, a busy, earnest life. He
rose from the dead and for forty days remained with His disciples, instructing them preparatory to His departure from them. He was ready for the
leave-taking. He had demonstrated the fact that He was a living Savior; His
disciples need no longer associate Him with the tomb of Joseph. They
could think of Him as glorified amid the heavenly host. . . .

All heaven waited with eager earnestness for the end of the tarrying of
the Son of God in a world all seared and marred with the curse. In proportion to Christ's humiliation and suffering was to be His exaltation. He became the Savior, the Redeemer, only by first becoming the Sacrifice. . . .

Christ came to earth as God in the guise of humanity. He ascended to
heaven as the King of saints. His ascension was worthy of His exalted character. He ascended from the Mount of Olives in a cloud of angels, who tri-
umphantly escorted Him to the city of God. Not in His own interest did
He go, but as the covenant-making Redeemer of His believing sons and
daughters, who are made thus through faith in His name. He went as one
mighty in battle, a conqueror, leading captivity captive, amid acclamations
of praise and celestial song. . . .

What a contrast between Christ's reception on His return to heaven and
His reception on this earth! In heaven all was loyalty. There was no sorrow,
no suffering, to meet Him at every turn. . . .

The time had come for the universe of heaven to accept their King.—
Signs of the Times, Aug. 16, 1899.

Representative Men and Women

Just as Christ was raised from the dead by the glory of the Father,
even so we also should walk in newness of life. Rom. 6:4.

Those who would be His disciples He invites to take His yoke upon them and to learn of Him who is meek and lowly of heart; and He promises those who do this that they shall find rest unto their souls. The meekness and humility that characterized the life of Christ will be made manifest in the life and character of those who "walk, even as he walked." . . .

Blessed is the soul who can say, "I am guilty before God, but Jesus is my Advocate. I have transgressed His law. I cannot save myself, but I make the precious blood that was shed on Calvary all my plea." . . .

Christ came to magnify the law and to make it honorable; He came to extol the old commandment which ye had from the beginning. Then we need the law and the prophets. We need the Old Testament to bring us down along the line to the New Testament, which does not take the place of the Old Testament but more distinctly reveals to us the plan of salvation, giving significance to the whole system of sacrifices and offerings and to the word which we had from the beginning. Perfect obedience is enjoined upon every soul, and obedience to the expressed will of God will make you one with Christ. You will be enabled to live nobly, for the life of Christ as a servant of Jehovah was noble. . . . Self-reliance and an unsanctified independence hold many away from the richest gifts in Christ. . . .

It was the same Jesus who commanded that love should be the ruling principle in the old dispensation, that commanded that love should be the ruling principle in the hearts of His followers in the New Testament. The working out of the principle of love is true sanctification. Those who walk in the light will be the children of the light and will diffuse light to those who are around them in kindness, in affection, in unmistakable love. . . .

Pure doctrine will blend with works of righteousness; heavenly precepts will mingle with holy practices. The heart that is filled with the grace of Christ will be made manifest by its peace and joy; and where Christ abides, the character will become purified, elevated, ennobled, and glorified.—
Youth's Instructor, Nov. 8, 1894.

The Wise Men

Now after Jesus was born in Bethlehem of Judea in the days of Herod the king, behold, wise men from the East came to Jerusalem, saying, "Where is He who has been born King of the Jews? For we have seen His star in the East and have come to worship Him." Matt. 2:1, 2.

While the magi were studying the heavens, a luminous star, entirely new to them, made its appearance. As they stood gazing at it, they were impressed that it was the herald of some great event. They decided to investigate the matter, hoping that they would be rewarded by a knowledge of the promised Messiah. The Lord encouraged them to go forward; and as the pillar of cloud moved before the children of Israel through the wilderness, so the star guided the wise men as they journeyed toward Jerusalem. . . . Entering Jerusalem, the magi made the eager inquiry, "Where is he that is born King of the Jews? for we have seen his star in the east, and are come to worship him." . . .

The Jewish rulers were in ignorance of the coming of the Just One because they had not been making ready for Him. . . . They had not heard the angel's message, "Behold, I bring you good tidings of great joy." . . .

The shepherds had borne witness regarding the visit of the angels; now men from the Far East bore the tidings, "We have seen his star in the east, and are come to worship him." Men of another nation and faith were the first to herald the advent of the Messiah. . . .

Herod was surprised that the Jewish rabbis—men looking upon themselves as favored above all other people—should apparently be in darkness, while those they termed heathen had received a sign from heaven that the King had been born. . . .

Calling the wise men to him, Herod "enquired of them diligently what time the star appeared. . . . When they had heard the king, they departed; and, lo, the star, which they saw in the east, went before them, till it came and stood over where the young child was. . . . And when they were come into the house, they saw the young child with Mary his mother, and fell down, and worshipped him: and when they had opened their treasures, they presented unto him gifts; gold, and frankincense, and myrrh. And being warned of God in a dream that they should not return to Herod, they departed into their own country another way."—*Youth's Instructor,* Oct. 19, 1899.

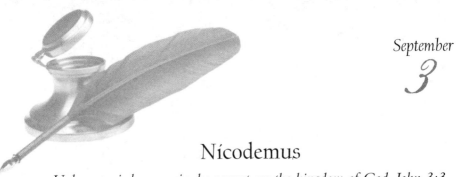

Nicodemus

Unless one is born again, he cannot see the kingdom of God. John 3:3.

Nicodemus held a high position of trust in the Jewish nation. He was highly educated and possessed talents of no ordinary character. With others, he had been stirred by the teaching of Jesus of Galilee. Though rich, learned, and honored, he had been strangely attracted by the humble Nazarene. The lessons, so new and strange, which had fallen from the lips of this Teacher had greatly impressed him, and he resolved to seek Jesus, that he might learn more of these wonderful truths.

But he did not visit Jesus by day; it would have been too humiliating for a ruler of the Jews to acknowledge himself in sympathy with a teacher as yet so little known. Learning by special inquiry where Jesus would be likely to retire for the night, he waited till the city was hushed in slumber and then sought Him.

"Rabbi," he said, "we know that thou art a teacher come from God: for no man can do these miracles that thou doest, except God be with him." By speaking of Christ's rare gifts as a teacher and also of His wonderful power to perform miracles, he hoped to pave the way for his interview. But in His infinite wisdom, Christ saw before Him a seeker after truth. He knew the real object of the visit, and with a desire to deepen the conviction already resting upon His listener's mind, He came directly to the point, saying solemnly yet kindly, "Verily, verily, I say unto thee, Except a man be born again, he cannot see the kingdom of God."

This was a very humiliating statement to Nicodemus, and with a feeling of irritation he took up the words of Christ, saying, "How can a man be born when he is old?" But the Savior did not meet argument with argument. Raising His hand with solemn, quiet dignity, He pressed the truth home with greater assurance, "Verily, verily, I say unto thee, Except a man be born of water and of the Spirit, he cannot enter into the kingdom of God." . . .

In this memorable interview, Christ laid down principles of the greatest importance to everyone. He defined the terms of salvation in clear terms and emphasized the necessity for a new life. . . . To everyone who names the name of Christ, who has decided to follow the meek and lowly Jesus, just as truly as to the Jewish ruler, these words are addressed, "Ye must be born again."—*Youth's Instructor,* Sept. 2, 1897.

Full Surrender

Do not marvel that I said to you, "You must be born again." John 3:7.

As God's purchased possession, we are under contract to work as Christ worked in His divine service, not in accordance with our natural inclinations but in harmony with the Spirit of God. But the lives of all people, as the gospel finds them, are full of sin. By yielding to temptation they have weakened their power to obey. Their hearts are "deceitful above all things, and desperately wicked." They are dead in trespasses and sins, and in their own strength they can do no good.

In order to serve God acceptably, we must be "born again." Our natural dispositions, which are in opposition to the Spirit of God, must be put away. We must be made new men and women in Christ Jesus. Our old, unrenewed lives must give place to a new life—a life full of love, of trust, of willing obedience. . . . Unless the change takes place, we cannot serve God aright. Our work will be defective. Earthly plans will be brought in; strange fire, dishonoring to God, will be offered. Our lives will be unholy and unhappy, full of unrest and trouble. . . .

Christ came to our world because He saw that we had lost the image and nature of God. He saw that we had wandered far from the path of peace and purity, and that, if left to ourselves, we would never find our way back. He came with a full and complete salvation, to change our stony hearts to hearts of flesh, to change our sinful natures into His similitude, that, by being partakers of the divine nature, we might be fitted for the heavenly courts. . . .

To all who, anxious for the salvation of their souls, come to Christ for aid, He says, as He said to Nicodemus, "Except a man be born again, he cannot see the kingdom of God." He is knocking at the door of your heart, asking for admittance. He longs to renew your heart, filling it with a love for all that is pure and true. He longs to crucify self for you, raising you to newness of life in Him. Nicodemus was converted as a result of his interview with Christ. . . . Fear not to make a full surrender of yourself to Christ. Place yourself, without reserve, under His control. Learn what it means to cease from sin, what it means to have a new heart, to bear the divine similitude. As you behold Christ, self will sink into insignificance, and you will be changed into His image, "from glory to glory even as by the Spirit of the Lord."—*Youth's Instructor,* Sept. 9, 1897.

The Call of Elisha

Then Elijah passed by him and threw his mantle on him. 1 Kings 19:19.

We would do well to consider the case of Elisha when chosen for his work. The prophet Elijah was about to close his earthly labors. Another was to be called to carry forward the work for that time. In his course of travel, Elijah was directed northward. How changed the scene before him now from that which the country had presented a little while before. Then the farming districts were unworked; the ground was parched, for neither dew nor rain had fallen for three years. Now everything seems to be springing up as if to redeem the time of famine and dearth. The plenteous rains had done more for the earth than for the hearts of humanity; the fields were better prepared for labor than were the hearts of apostate Israel.

Wherever Elijah looked, the land he saw was owned by one man—a man who had not bowed the knee to Baal, whose heart had remained undivided in the service of God. Even during the captivity there were souls who had not gone into apostasy, and this family was included in the seven thousand who had not bowed the knee to Baal. The owner of the land was Shaphat. Busy activity was seen among the workers. While the flocks were enjoying the green pastures, the busy hands of his servants were sowing the seed for a harvest.

The attention of Elijah was attracted to Elisha, the son of Shaphat, who with the servants was plowing with twelve yoke of oxen. . . . Far from city and court dissipation, Elisha had received his education. He had been trained in habits of simplicity, of obedience to his parents and to God. . . .

Elisha waited contentedly, doing his work with fidelity. Day by day, through practical obedience and the divine grace in which he trusted, he obtained rectitude and strength of purpose. While doing all that he possibly could in cooperating with his father in the home firm, he was doing God's service. He was learning how to cooperate with God.—*Youth's Instructor,* Apr. 14, 1898.

When the prophet saw Elisha with his servants plowing with twelve yoke of oxen, he came to the field of labor, and while passing by, he unfastened his mantle and threw it upon the shoulders of Elisha. He then passed on as if that were the end of the matter. But he knew that Elisha understood the significance of the action; and he left him, without speaking a word, to decide whether he would accept or reject the call.—*Youth's Instructor,* Apr. 21, 1898.

Answering God's Call

Then he arose and followed Elijah, and became his servant. 1 Kings 19:21.

During the three years and a half of barrenness and famine, the family of Shaphat had become familiar with the mission of Elijah the prophet, and the Spirit of God impressed the heart of Elisha in regard to the meaning of this action [Elijah's placing his mantle on him]. This was the signal that God had called him to be the successor of Elijah. He hastened after the prophet and, overtaking him, asked permission to take leave of his parents and bid farewell to his family.

The answer of Elijah was, "Go back again: for what have I done to thee?" This was not a repulse, but a test. If Elisha's heart clung to his home and its advantages, he was at liberty to remain there. But Elisha was prepared to hear the call of God. . . .

Had Elisha asked Elijah what was expected of him, what would be his work, he would have been answered, God knows; He will make it known to you. If you wait upon the Lord, He will answer your every question. You may come with me if you have evidence that God has called you; if not, forbear. Come not simply because I have called you. Know for yourself that God stands back of you, and that it is His voice you hear. If you can count everything but dross that you may win Christ, come. . . .

The call of Elijah [to Elisha] was similar to the commission of Christ to the young ruler. The ruler was commanded to leave all—houses, lands, friends, riches, comforts, and ease—and follow Jesus. . . . But with the call of Christ comes the question, Are we ready to advance? Are we willing? Shall we, like Moses, cheerfully deem the reproach of Christ greater riches than the treasures in Egypt?

The Lord will not accept halfhearted service. Those alone who love to do the will of God can do perfect service. . . . If we follow on to know the Lord, willingly, gladly, we shall know that "his going forth is prepared as the morning." If we have decided to obey Christ, we shall respond to His call, "If any man will come after me, let him deny himself, and take up his cross, and follow me." . . .

The work of God is a perfect whole, . . . and it is important that the worker for Christ shall take his Master with him in every department of labor. Whatever is done should be done with an exactness and dispatch that will bear inspection. The heart should be in the work.—*Youth's Instructor,* Apr. 21, 1898.

Never Look Back

I press toward the goal for the prize of the upward call of God. Phil. 3:14.

Elisha immediately left all to begin his ministry. His leave-taking was not with mourning and bitter regrets. They made a feast in his home in commemoration of the honor conferred upon one of the family. And what was the first work of Elisha? It was to take up the little things and do them with heartiness. He was the prophet's personal attendant. He is spoken of as pouring water on the hands of Elijah his master.

After Elisha had been some time in the service of the prophet, he was called to take his place in the first rank. No one in that time was to be greater than he. He had worked under Elijah as a learner, and the time came when the head manager was removed, and the one under him came to the front. And as Elijah was prepared to be translated, so Elisha was prepared to become his successor as a prophet. . . .

There was a school of the prophets at Gilgal, and also at Bethel and at Jericho. Elijah wished to visit these important places before he was parted from them. His spirit was cheered as, by the direction of God, he was permitted to see the schools of the prophets and the work that was going on in those institutions—an education which was to keep the wonderful works of God continually before the students, and which magnified the law of God and made it honorable. . . .

At every place where Elisha tarried with Elijah, he was given opportunity to separate from him. "Tarry here, I pray thee," said Elijah. Thus Elisha's faith was tried at every point. But by plowing in the field, Elisha had learned not to yield to discouragement. He had now set his hand to the plow in another work, and he would not fail nor be discouraged. Every time the invitation to turn back was given, he declared, "As the Lord liveth, and as thy soul liveth, I will not leave thee." . . .

Henceforth Elisha stood in the place of Elijah. . . . The greatest qualification for anyone in a position of trust is to obey implicitly the word of the Lord. . . . Elisha had put his hand to the plow, and he would not look back. He revealed his determination and firm reliance upon God.

This lesson is for us to study carefully. We are in no case to swerve from our allegiance. . . . The Word of God is to be our counselor. It is only those who render perfect and thorough obedience to God that He will choose.—*Youth's Instructor,* Apr. 28, 1898.

Timothy

Let no one despise your youth, but be an example to the believers in word, in conduct, in love, in spirit, in faith, in purity. 1 Tim. 4:12.

The Word of God was the rule which guided Timothy. . . . His home instructors cooperated with God in educating this young man to bear the burdens that were to come upon him at an early age.

Timothy was a mere youth when he was chosen by God as a teacher. But his principles had been so established by a correct education that he was fitted to be placed as a religious teacher in connection with Paul, the great apostle to the Gentiles. And though young, he bore his great responsibilities with Christian meekness. He was faithful, steadfast, and true; and Paul made him his companion in labor and travel, that he might have the benefit of the apostle's experience in preaching the gospel and establishing churches.

Paul loved Timothy because Timothy loved God. The great apostle often drew him out and questioned him in regard to Scripture history. He taught him the necessity of shunning every evil way and told him that blessing would surely attend all who were faithful and true, giving them a noble manhood. . . .

The words of the apostle Paul just prior to his death were, "Continue thou in the things which thou hast learned and hast been assured of, knowing of whom thou hast learned them; and that from a child thou hast known the holy scriptures, which are able to make thee wise unto salvation through faith which is in Christ Jesus." . . .

Paul could safely write this, for Timothy did not go forward in a self-sufficient spirit. He worked in connection with Paul, seeking his advice and instruction. He did not move from impulse. He exercised consideration and calm thought, inquiring at every step, "Is this the way of the Lord?" . . .

"Take heed unto thyself, and unto the doctrine; continue in them: for in doing this thou shalt both save thyself, and them that hear thee."

The charge given to Timothy should be heeded in every household and become an educating power in every family and in every school.—*Youth's Instructor,* May 5, 1898.

Joseph, God's Unwavering Witness

The Lord was with Joseph, and he was a successful man; and he was in the house of his master the Egyptian. Gen. 39:2.

It was God's design that through Joseph, Bible religion should be introduced among the Egyptians. This faithful witness was to represent Christ in the court of kings. Through dreams God communicated with Joseph in his youth, giving him an intimation of the high position he would be called to fill. The brothers of Joseph, to prevent the fulfillment of his dreams, sold him as a slave, but their cruel act resulted in bringing about the very thing the dreams had foretold.

Those who seek to turn aside the purpose of God and oppose His will may appear for a time to prosper; but God is at work to fulfill His own purposes, and He will make manifest who is the ruler of the heavens and the earth.

Joseph regarded his being sold into Egypt as the greatest calamity that could have befallen him, but he saw the necessity of trusting in God as he had never done when protected by his father's love. Joseph brought God with him into Egypt, and the fact was made apparent by his cheerful demeanor amid his sorrow. . . . It is God's purpose that those who love and honor His name shall be honored also themselves, and that the glory given to God through them shall be reflected upon themselves.

Joseph's character did not change when he was exalted to a position of trust. He was brought where his virtue would shine in distinct light to good works. The blessing of God rested upon him in the house and in the field. All the responsibilities of Potiphar's house were placed upon him. And in all this he manifested steadfast integrity, for he loved and feared God.

Placed as he was in the society of learned men, he gained a knowledge of science and language. This was his training school, that in early manhood he might become qualified to be prime minister of Egypt. He learned those things that would be essential in his future position of trust. He gathered all the wisdom and knowledge and tact that his opportunities presented, and these were not few. Yet his heart was steadfast with God. Human knowledge and divine wisdom were combined, that he should be a shining light, reflecting the bright beams of the Sun of Righteousness amid the gross darkness of heathenism. Here the religion of the Hebrew was seen to be of an altogether different character from the religious rites and customs of the idolatrous Egyptians.—*Youth's Instructor,* Mar. 11, 1897.

Victorious Over Temptation

How then can I do this great wickedness, and sin against God?
Gen. 39:9.

When trial came, when the arts of woman were exercised to draw him into iniquity, Joseph preserved his integrity. Fair words and guileful entreaties did not cause him to swerve one hair from the right. All fell on ears that heard not. The law of the Lord garrisoned his soul. He said to the bold enchantress, "How then can I do this great wickedness, and sin against God?"

The woman signally failed to lead Joseph into sin. Satan was defeated. And then Joseph found that the lips which could praise could also lie. The wife of Potiphar revenged herself upon him by her accusations against him. Because Joseph would not sin against one who had trusted him, he was deprived of the honor which, through the grace of God, he had justly earned and which had brought him into relation with the great men of Egypt.

This sudden humiliation from the position of a trusted, honored servant to that of a condemned criminal would have overwhelmed him had not the hand of the Lord upheld him. But his confidence in God was unshaken. The love of God kept his soul in perfect peace. Heaven was very near the fertile valley of Egypt, for there was a youth who kept the ways of the Lord. The presence of Jesus was with him in prison, instructing, strengthening, and sustaining his mind and soul, that the light of heaven might shine forth.

Joseph had been tried by parental fondness and partiality; by the enmity, envy, and hatred of his brothers; by the esteem and confidence of his master; and by his high position of honor. He was tried by the seduction of woman's charms, by the flattery of her lips and her lawless love. But the steadfast virtue of Joseph would not permit him to listen to the voice of the tempter. The law of the Lord was his delight, and he would not depart from its precepts. . . .

Even while in prison, Joseph was allowed to be at liberty and had opportunity to give the light to his fellow prisoners. This prison was to him an educating school. . . . He saw in every phase of its management the superiority of the law of God, and by his experience and observation was learning to be just and merciful, thus representing the character of God.

Power was to be put into the hands of Joseph, and through him God was to be revealed as the ruler of the heavens and the earth. But he was to be trained in adversity—the school in which God designs that His children shall learn.—*Youth's Instructor,* Mar. 11, 1897.

Interpreter of Dreams

I have had a dream, and there is no one who can interpret it. But I have heard it said of you that you can understand a dream, to interpret it.
Gen. 41:15.

When Joseph interpreted the dreams of the butler and the cupbearer, he begged to be remembered when the chief butler should be reinstated in his position; but he was forgotten, and remained two years longer in the prison.

But a more exalted person than the butler had a dream, and when there could be found no one able to interpret it, Joseph was called to the remembrance of the butler. "Then Pharaoh sent and called Joseph, and they brought him hastily out of the dungeon: and he shaved himself, and changed his raiment, and came in unto Pharaoh. And Pharaoh said unto Joseph, I have dreamed a dream, and there is none that can interpret it: and I have heard say of thee, that thou canst understand a dream to interpret it." Joseph did not take the glory to himself. He pointed Pharaoh to God, saying, "It is not in me: God shall give Pharaoh an answer of peace."

Through the wisdom given him of God, Joseph could see the true meaning of the dream. He saw the wonderful workings of God, and he laid the whole matter distinctly before Pharaoh. He revealed to him the long famine that was to visit the land, and the plans to be pursued in order to save the nation from destruction. . . . His words were received as gold, and the answer was returned to him, "Forasmuch as God hath shewed thee all this, there is none so discreet and wise as thou art: thou shalt be over my house, and according unto thy word shall all my people be ruled: only in the throne will I be greater than thou." . . .

Joseph represented Christ. He stood for many years as the honored ruler of Egypt. In his life and character was manifested that which was lovely, and pure, and noble. In bearing his sorrows under trying circumstances and in enduring temptation, Joseph was one in character with Christ. . . .

The example of Joseph, shining with heaven's brightness, did not shine in vain among this people for whom Christ had pledged Himself to become an offering—a people whom God had taken under His guardianship, and upon whom He was bestowing not only temporal but spiritual blessings, in order to attract them to Himself.—*Youth's Instructor,* Mar. 11, 1897.

September

12

The Call of Gideon

So Israel was greatly impoverished because of the Midianites, and the children of Israel cried out to the Lord. Judges 6:6.

Alas, that in the history of God's chosen people the sorrowful story of apostasy and its punishment must be so oft repeated! . . .

Because of their sins, the protecting hand of God was withdrawn from Israel, and they were left to the mercies of their enemies. The wild, fierce inhabitants of the desert [the Midianites and Amalekites], "as grasshoppers for multitude," came swarming into the land with their flocks and herds and pitched their tents in plain and valley. They came as soon as the harvests began to ripen and remained until the last fruits of the earth had been gathered. They stripped the fields of their increase and robbed and maltreated the inhabitants, and then returned to the deserts. . . .

For seven years this oppression continued, and then in their distress the people remembered Him who had so often delivered them; and they cried unto the Lord for help. . . .

Their prayers were heard, and again the Lord sent forth the man of His choice to act as deliverer for Israel. The one thus selected was Gideon, of the tribe of Manasseh. . . . It was only with the greatest difficulty that the Hebrews could secrete sufficient food to save them from actual starvation. Gideon had, however, retained possession of a small quantity of wheat, and fearing to beat it out in the threshing floor, he had taken it to the vineyard, near the winepress. The time of ripe grapes being far off, the attention of the Midianites would not be directed to that place. . . . Gideon almost despaired of inspiring the people with faith or courage, but he knew that the Lord would work mightily for Israel as He had done in the past. . . .

While Gideon's mind was absorbed in meditations like these, suddenly an angel of the Lord appeared to him and addressed him with the words, "The Lord is with thee, thou mighty man of valour."

The melancholy nature of Gideon's thoughts is revealed by his answer, "Oh my Lord, if the Lord be with us, why then is all this befallen us?" . . . With a sense of his own unfitness for so important a work, Gideon exclaimed, "Oh my Lord, wherewith shall I save Israel? behold, my family is poor in Manasseh, and I am the least in my father's house." . . . Then the angel gave him the gracious assurance, "Surely I will be with thee, and thou shalt smite the Midianites as one man."—*Signs of the Times,* June 23, 1881.

Growing Confidence

If now I have found favor in Your sight, then show me a sign that it is You who talk with me. Judges 6:17.

Gideon desired some token that the One now addressing him was the same that spoke to Moses in the burning bush. The angel had veiled the divine glory of His presence, but it was none other than Christ, the Son of God. When a prophet or an angel delivered a divine message, his words were, "The Lord saith, I will do this," but it is stated of the Person who talked with Gideon, "The Lord said unto him, Surely I will be with thee."

Desiring to show special honor to his illustrious Visitor, and having obtained the assurance that the Angel would tarry, Gideon hastened to his tent, and out of his scanty store prepared a kid and unleavened cakes, which he brought forth to set before Him. Gideon was poor, yet he was ready to use hospitality without grudging.

As the gift was presented, the Angel said, "Take the flesh and unleavened cakes, and lay them upon this rock, and pour out the broth." Gideon did so, and then the Lord gave him the sign which he desired. With the staff in His hand, the Angel touched the flesh and the unleavened cakes, and a fire rose up out of the rock and consumed the whole as a sacrifice, and not as a hospitable meal; for He was God, and not man. After this token of His divine character, the Angel disappeared.

When convinced that he had looked upon the Son of God, Gideon was filled with fear, and exclaimed, "Alas, O Lord God! for because I have seen an angel of the Lord face to face." Then the Lord graciously appeared to Gideon a second time and said, "Peace be unto thee; fear not: thou shalt not die." . . .

The family to which Gideon belonged was grievously infected with idolatry. His father erected at Ophrah, where he dwelt, a large altar to Baal, at which the people of the towns worshipped. Gideon was commanded to destroy this altar, to cut down the groves that surrounded it, and in its stead to erect an altar to Jehovah, over the rock on which the offering had been consumed, and then to offer a sacrifice unto the Lord. Gideon faithfully carried out these directions, performing the work by night, lest he should be compelled to desist if he attempted it by day.—*Signs of the Times,* June 23, 1881.

Righteousness Gains the Victory

The Lord said to him, ". . . tear down the altar of Baal that your father has, and cut down the wooden image that is beside it." Judges 6:25.

The deliverer of Israel must declare war upon idolatry before he went to battle with the enemies of his people. He must esteem the honor of God above the credit of his father and regard the divine commands as more obligatory than parental authority.

The offering of sacrifice unto the Lord had been committed to the priests and Levites and had been restricted to the altar at Shiloh, but He who had established the Jewish economy, and to whom all its services pointed, had power to change its requirements. In this instance He saw fit to depart from the ritual appointment. It was of great importance that the deliverance of Israel should be preceded by a solemn protest against the worship of Baal and an acknowledgment of Jehovah as the only true and living God.

When the men of the city, early in the morning, came to pay their devotions to Baal, they were greatly surprised and enraged at what had taken place. Soon it was known that Gideon had done this, and then nothing but his blood could satisfy those deluded idolaters. . . .

Gideon had told his father, Joash, of the Angel's visit and the promise that Israel should be delivered. He also related to him the divine command to destroy the altar of Baal. The Spirit of God moved upon the heart of Joash. He saw that the gods whom he had worshipped had no power even to save themselves from utter destruction, and hence they could not protect their worshippers. When the idolatrous multitude clamored for the death of Gideon, Joash fearlessly stood in his defense and endeavored to show the people how powerless and unworthy of trust or adoration were their gods: "Will ye plead for Baal? will ye save him? he that will plead for him, let him be put to death whilst it is yet morning: if he be a god, let him plead for himself, because one hath cast down his altar." . . .

All thoughts of violence were dismissed, and when, moved by the Spirit of the Lord, Gideon sounded the trumpet of war, they were among the first to gather to him. He then sent messengers throughout his own tribe of Manasseh, and also to Asher, Zebulon, and Naphtali, and all cheerfully obeyed the call. . . .

Evil may seem for a time to prevail, but in the end righteousness will gain the victory. —*Signs of the Times,* June 23, 1881.

The Need for More Trust

It was dry on the fleece only, but there was dew on all the ground.
Judges 6:40.

Gideon deeply felt his own insufficiency for the great work before him. He dared not place himself at the head of the army without positive evidence that God had called him to this work and that He would be with him. He prayed, "If thou wilt save Israel by mine hand, as thou hast said, behold, I will put a fleece of wool in the floor; and if the dew be on the fleece only, and it be dry upon all the earth beside, then shall I know that thou wilt save Israel by mine hand, as thou hast said."

The Lord granted the prayer of His servant. In the morning the fleece was wet while the ground was dry. But now unbelief suggested that wool naturally absorbs moisture when there is any in the air, and that the test was not decisive. Hence, he asked a renewal of the sign, humbly pleading that unbelief might not move the Lord to anger. His request was granted.

The Lord does not always choose for His work people of the greatest talents, but He selects those whom He can best use. . . .

God will accept the services of all who will work in obedience to His will, who will not for any consideration bring a stain upon the conscience, who will not permit any influence to lead them from the path of duty. If we choose, we may make the record of our lives such as we shall not be ashamed to own when the secrets of all hearts shall stand revealed, and everyone's work shall be weighed in the balances of truth. The Lord employs men and women as His colaborers, but let none imagine that they are essential to the work of God, that they cannot be dispensed with.

The teachable and trusting ones, having a right purpose and a pure heart, need not wait for great occasions or for extraordinary abilities before they employ their powers. They should not stand irresolute, questioning, and fearing what the world will say or think of them. We are not to weary ourselves with anxious care, but to go on, quietly performing with faithfulness the work which God assigns us, and leaving the result wholly with Him. . . .

Let the daily life be a reflection of the life of Christ, and the testimony thus borne to the world will have a powerful influence. . . . The great contest of truth against error must be carried forward by men and women who kindle their taper at the divine altar.—*Signs of the Times,* June 23, 1881.

Qualifications of the Chosen

The people who are with you are too many for Me to give the Midianites into
their hands, lest Israel claim glory for itself against Me, saying,
"My own hand has saved me." Judges 7:2.

Gideon's courage was greatly strengthened by the tokens of divine favor
vouchsafed to him. Without delay he went out with his forces to give
battle to the Midianites. But now another severe trial of faith awaited him.
With the immense host of invaders spread out before him—the thirty-two
thousand of the Hebrews seeming, in contrast, like a mere handful—the
word of the Lord came to him, "The people that are with thee are too
many for me to give the Midianites into their hands, lest Israel vaunt themselves against me, saying, Mine own hand hath saved me. Now therefore go
to, proclaim in the ears of the people, saying, Whosoever is fearful and
afraid, let him return and depart early from mount Gilead." . . .

Because of the weak condition of the armies of Israel in contrast with the
numbers of the enemy, Gideon had refrained from making the usual proclamation. He was filled with astonishment at the declaration that his force was
too large. But the Lord saw the pride and unbelief existing in the hearts of this
people. Aroused by the stirring appeals of Gideon, they had readily enlisted;
but when they saw the multitudes of the Midianites, their courage failed. . . .

Instead of being too many, the Israelites felt that their numbers were too
few; but Gideon made the proclamation as the Lord had directed. With
sinking heart he saw . . . more than two thirds of his entire force, depart. . . .

Again the word of the Lord came to His servant, "The people are yet too
many; bring them down unto the water, and I will try them for thee there:
and it shall be, that of whom I say unto thee, This shall go with thee, the
same shall go with thee; and of whomsoever I say unto thee, This shall not
go with thee, the same shall not go." . . .

A few hastily took a little water in the hand and sucked it up as they went
on, but nearly all bowed upon their knees and leisurely drank from the surface of the water. Those who took of the water in their hands were but
three hundred out of the ten thousand; yet these were selected, and the
great body of the army were permitted to return to their homes.

Here we see the simple means by which character is often tested. . . . The
men of God's choice were the few who would not permit their own wants
to hinder them in the discharge of duty.—*Signs of the Times,* June 30, 1881.

Eavesdropping

Go down to the camp with Purah your servant, and you shall hear what they say. Judges 7:10, 11.

When Gideon stood at the head of thirty thousand men to make war against the Midianites, he felt that unless God should work for Israel, their cause would be hopeless. At the divine command the Hebrew force had been reduced by successive tests until there remained with him only three hundred men to oppose that countless multitude. What wonder that his heart sank within him as he thought of the conflict of the morrow.

But the Lord did not leave His faithful servant to despair. He spoke to Gideon in the night season, and bade him, with Phurah, his trusty attendant, go down to the camp of the Midianites, intimating that he would there hear matter for his encouragement. He went, and waiting there in darkness and silence, he heard one soldier, just awakened, relate a dream to his companion, "Lo, a cake of barley bread tumbled into the host of Midian, and came unto a tent, and smote it that it fell, and overturned it, that the tent lay along."

The other answered in words that stirred the heart of that unseen listener, "This is nothing else save the sword of Gideon the son of Joash, a man of Israel: for into his hand hath God delivered Midian, and all the host."

Gideon recognized the voice of God speaking to him through the words of these Midianitish strangers. His faith and courage were greatly strengthened, and he rejoiced that Israel's God could work through the humblest means to abase human pride. With confidence and hope he returned to the few men under his command, saying, "Arise; for the Lord hath delivered into your hand the host of Midian." . . .

As that loaf overthrew the tent upon which it fell, so would the handful of Israelites destroy their numerous and powerful enemies.

The Lord Himself directed Gideon's mind in the adoption of a plan which the latter immediately set out to execute. . . .

What lessons of humility and faith may we not learn as we trace the dealings of God with His creatures.—*Signs of the Times,* July 14, 1881.

God's Overarching Love

The sword of the Lord and of Gideon! Judges 7:18.

The Lord Himself directed Gideon's mind in the adoption of a plan. . . . [Gideon] divided his three hundred men into three companies. To every man was given a trumpet, and a pitcher containing a lighted lamp. He then stationed his men in such a manner that they surrounded the entire camp of Midian. They had been previously instructed how to proceed, and at midnight, at a signal from Gideon, all the three companies blew their trumpets, uncovered their lamps, and broke the pitchers, at the same time shouting, "The sword of the Lord, and of Gideon!." The light of three hundred lamps piercing the midnight darkness and that mighty shout from three hundred voices suddenly aroused the sleeping army. Believing themselves at the mercy of an overwhelming force, the Midianites were panic-stricken. A terrible scene of confusion ensued. In their fright they fled in all directions, and mistaking their own companions for enemies, they slew one another.

As the news of Israel's victory spread, many who had been sent to their homes returned and joined in the pursuit of their fleeing enemies. Gideon also sent messengers to the Ephraimites, requesting them to seize the fords of the Jordan that the fugitives might not escape eastward.

In this terrible overthrow, not less than one hundred and twenty thousand of the invaders were slain, and so completely were the Midianites subdued that they were never again able to make war upon Israel. A remnant of fifteen thousand who managed to escape across the river were pursued by Gideon and his faithful three hundred and utterly defeated, and Zebah and Zalmunna, two Midianite princes, were slain. . . .

Because of the pride and ambition of the human race, God has chosen to perform His mighty works by the most simple and humble means. . . .

His care for the works of His creation is unwearied and incessant. When men and women go forth to their daily toil, as when they engage in prayer; when they lie down at night, and when they rise in the morning; when the rich feast in their palaces, when the poor gather their children about the scanty board, all are tenderly watched by their heavenly Father. . . .

With humble prayer and trusting faith, we would seek counsel from God. . . . Then all our acts would be governed by discretion, our energies would be rightly directed.—*Signs of the Times,* July 14, 1881.

God's Victory

*Then the Lord said to Gideon, "By the three hundred men
who lapped I will save you." Judges 7:7.*

After the overthrow of the Midianites, the tidings spread swiftly far and
wide that Israel's God had again fought for His people. No words can
describe the terror of the surrounding nations when they learned what simple means had prevailed against all the power and skill of a bold, warlike race.

Wherever the news spread, all felt that the victory must be ascribed to
God alone. Thus the Lord's name was glorified, the faith of Israel strengthened, and their enemies were brought to shame and confusion.

It is not safe for God's people to adopt the maxims and customs of the
ungodly. The divine principles and modes of working are widely different
from those of the world. The history of nations presents no such victories
as the conquest of Jericho or the overthrow of the Midianites. No general
of heathen armies had ever conducted warfare as Joshua and Gideon had
done. These victories teach the great lesson that the only sure ground of
success is the help of God, working with human effort. Those who trust to
their own wisdom and their own skill will surely be disappointed. The only
safe course in all the plans and purposes of life is to preserve the simplicity
of faith. Humble trust in God and faithful obedience to His will are as essential to the Christian in waging spiritual warfare as they were to Gideon
and his brave associates in fighting the battles of the Lord.

God's commands must be implicitly obeyed, irrespective of the world's
opinion. This lesson should not be disregarded by those who occupy positions of responsibility among their fellow men. . . . All should earnestly improve every religious privilege and inquire of God daily to learn His will.
The life and words of Christ must be diligently studied and His instructions
cheerfully obeyed. Those who will thus gird on the armor of righteousness
need not fear the enemies of God. They may be assured of the presence and
protection of the Captain of the Lord's host. . . .

The Lord is willing to give His people a precious experience. . . . He
would teach them to submit their judgment and their will implicitly to
Him. Then will they see and know that of themselves they can do nothing;
that God is all and in all.—*Signs of the Times,* July 21, 1881.

God Provides

Nevertheless at Your word I will let down the net. Luke 5:5.

John was one of the first to acknowledge Jesus as the Messiah. He had lis- tened to the preaching of John the Baptist and knew that he was sent as the forerunner of Him who was the Hope of Israel. To John and Andrew the Baptist pointed out Jesus as "the Lamb of God." ... Jesus saw them fol- lowing Him and welcomed them to His humble abode. They remained with Him that night, and when they left His presence, it was with their faith in His divine character and mission fully confirmed.

Andrew went in search of his own brother, Simon, and brought him to Jesus with the welcome announcement, "We have found the Messias." The next day Jesus called Philip to follow Him. ...

Andrew, Peter, James, and John were henceforth known as disciples of Jesus. ...

Though they attended upon the preaching of Jesus and were much in His society, they still pursued their humble calling; but the time came when they were to leave their nets and their fishing boats and be more closely as- sociated with Jesus. Crowds now attended upon His ministry, and as He taught by the lake of Gennesaret, they so "pressed upon him to hear the word of God." that He entered into Peter's boat, and from it taught the people on the shore. When He had ceased speaking, He said unto Peter, "Launch out into the deep, and let down your nets for a draught."

Peter answered that they had toiled all night and had taken nothing. Their labors had been fruitless in the usual time for fishing, and there was no human probability of success now; "nevertheless," said Peter, "at thy word I will let down the net." It was done, and the draft of fishes was so great that the net could not contain them, and James and John, the partners of Andrew and Peter, were called to their assistance. ...

An important and solemn work was before them. They were to give up their only means of support and spend their lives in unselfish efforts to save perishing sinners, but before He called them to this life of self-denial and dependence upon God, the loving Savior showed them that, as Lord of heaven and earth, He was abundantly able to provide for all their wants.— *Signs of the Times,* Jan. 8, 1885.

Simple Faith

And the Philistine said, "I defy the armies of Israel this day; give me a man, that we may fight together." 1 Sam. 17:10.

For forty days the host of Israel had trembled before the haughty challenge of Goliath, the Philistine giant. Their hearts failed within them as they looked upon his massive form, measuring six cubits and a span, or ten and a half feet [nearly 3.2 meters] in height. Upon his head was a helmet of brass; he was clothed with a coat of mail that weighed five thousand shekels, or about a hundred and fifty-seven pounds [more than 70 kilograms]; and he had greaves of brass upon his legs. The coat was made of plates of brass that overlaid one another like the scales of a fish, and they were so closely joined that no dart or arrow could possibly penetrate the armor. . . .

For forty days, morning and evening, Goliath had approached the camp of Israel, saying with a loud voice, "Why are ye come out to set your battle in array? am not I a Philistine, and ye servants to Saul? choose you a man for you, and let him come down to me. If he be able to fight with me, and to kill me, then will we be your servants: but if I prevail against him, and kill him, then shall ye be our servants, and serve us. . . . When Saul and all Israel heard those words of the Philistine, they were dismayed, and greatly afraid." No one had dared to go against this boaster until David, stirred with indignation at the proud words of the idolater, offered himself to Saul as one who was willing to fight for the glory of God and the honor of Israel.

Saul decided to permit the shepherd to make the venture, but he had small hope that David would be successful in his courageous undertaking. Command was given to clothe the youth in the king's own armor. The heavy helmet of brass was put upon his head, and the coat of mail was placed upon his body, while he was girded with the monarch's sword. Thus equipped, he started upon his errand; but erelong he turned back and began to retrace his steps. . . . The first thought in the minds of the anxious spectators was that David had decided not to risk his life in meeting an antagonist in so unequal an encounter. But this was far from the thought of the brave young man.

When he returned to Saul, he begged permission to lay aside the heavy armor, and he said, "I cannot go with these; for I have not proved them." . . .

What an inspiration of courage and lofty faith was displayed by the simple shepherd before the armies of the Israelites and the Philistines.—*Signs of the Times,* Aug. 10, 1888.

Acting on Faith

You come to me with a sword, with a spear, and with a javelin. But I come to you in the name of the Lord of hosts, the God of the armies of Israel, whom you have defied. 1 Sam. 17:45.

He [David] laid off the king's armor and in its stead took only his staff in his hand, with his shepherd's pouch, and a simple sling. Choosing five smooth stones out of the brook, he put them in his bag, and with his sling in his hand he drew near to the Philistine. The champion strode boldly and proudly forward, expecting to meet with the mightiest of the warriors of Israel. His armor-bearer walked before him, and he looked as if nothing could stand before him. As he came nearer to David, he saw but a stripling, called a boy because of his youth. His countenance was ruddy with health; and his slender form, unprotected by armor, displayed all its youthful outline in marked contrast to the massive proportions of the Philistine.

Goliath was filled with amazement and anger. His indignation burst forth in words that were calculated to terrify and overwhelm the daring youth before him. "Am I a dog," exclaimed the giant, "that thou comest to me with staves?" Then the Philistine poured upon David the most terrible curses by all the gods of his knowledge. He cried in derision, "Come to me, and I will give thy flesh unto the fowls of the air, and to the beasts of the field." This haughty threat only served to inspire the youth with loftier courage and to kindle in his breast a greater zeal to silence the enemy of his people. He did not weaken before the champion of the Philistines. He knew that he was about to fight for the honor of his God and the deliverance of Israel, and his heart was full of calm faith and hope.

David stepped forward and addressed his antagonist in language that was both modest and eloquent. And he said to the Philistine, "Thou comest to me with a sword, and with a spear, and with a shield: but I come to thee in the name of the Lord of hosts, the God of the armies of Israel, whom thou hast defied. This day will the Lord deliver thee into mine hand; and I will smite thee, and take thine head from thee; and I will give the carcases of the host of the Philistines this day unto the fowls of the air, and to the wild beasts of the earth; that all the earth may know that there is a God in Israel."—*Signs of the Times,* Aug. 10, 1888.

Simple Faith Rewarded

All this assembly shall know that the Lord does not save with sword and spear; for the battle is the Lord's, and He will give you into our hands.
1 Sam. 17:47.

What an inspiration of courage and lofty faith was displayed by the simple shepherd before the armies of the Israelites and the Philistines. There was a ring of fearlessness in his tone, a look of triumph and rejoicing upon his fair countenance. . . .

As David's rich voice uttered the words of trust and triumph, the anger of Goliath was roused to the very highest heat. In his rage, he pushed up the helmet that protected his forehead and rushed with determined hatred to wreak vengeance upon his opponent. The son of Jesse was preparing for his foe. Both armies were watching with the most intense interest. "And it came to pass, when the Philistine arose, and came and drew nigh to meet David, that David hasted, and ran toward the army to meet the Philistine. And David put his hand in his bag, and took thence a stone, and slang it, and smote the Philistine in his forehead, that the stone sunk into his forehead; and he fell upon his face to the earth."

Amazement spread along the lines of the two armies. They had been confident that David would be slain; but when the stone went whizzing through the air, straight to the mark, they saw the mighty warrior tremble and reach forth his hands as if he were struck with sudden blindness. The giant reeled, and staggered, and fell prostrate to the ground. David did not wait an instant. He knew not that life was extinct. He sprang upon the prostrate form of the Philistine, and with both hands he laid hold of Goliath's heavy sword. A moment before, the giant had flourished it before the face of David with the boast that he would sever the youth's head from his shoulders and give his body to the fowls of the air. Now it served to work the will of the servant of God. It was lifted in the air, and then the head of the boaster rolled from his trunk, and a shout of exultation went up from the camp of Israel.

The Philistines were smitten with terror. They knew that the day was lost. In horror and confusion they began an irregular retreat. . . . The triumphant Hebrews . . . rushed after their retreating enemies, and they "pursued the Philistines, until thou come to the valley, and to the gates of Ekron. . . . And David took the head of the Philistine, and brought it to Jerusalem; but he put his armour in his tent."—*Signs of the Times,* Aug. 10, 1888.

Daniel's Commitment to God

He was faithful; nor was there any error or fault found in him. Dan. 6:4.

When Darius set over the provinces of his kingdom a hundred and twenty princes, and over these, three presidents to whom the princes were to give account, we read that "Daniel was preferred above the presidents and princes, because an excellent spirit was in him; and the king thought to set him over the whole realm." But evil angels, fearing the influence of this good man over the king and in the affairs of the kingdom, stirred up the presidents and princes to envy. These wicked men watched Daniel closely, that they might find some fault in him which they could report to the king; but they failed. "He was faithful, neither was there any error or fault found in him."

Then Satan sought to make Daniel's faithfulness to God the cause of his destruction. The presidents and princes came tumultuously together unto the king, and said, "All the presidents of the kingdom, the governors, and the princes, the counsellors, and the captains, have consulted together to establish a royal statute, and to make a firm decree, that whosoever shall ask a petition of any God or man for thirty days, save of thee, O king, he shall be cast into the den of lions." The king's pride was flattered. He was ignorant of the mischief purposed against Daniel, and he granted their request. The decree was signed and became one of the unalterable laws of the Medes and Persians.

These envious men did not believe that Daniel would be untrue to his God or that he would falter in his firm adherence to principle, and they were not mistaken in their estimate of his character. Daniel knew the value of communion with God. With full knowledge of the king's decree, he still bowed in prayer three times a day, "his windows being open in his chamber toward Jerusalem." He did not seek to conceal his act, although he knew full well the consequences of his fidelity to God. He saw the dangers that beset his path, but his steps faltered not. Before those who were plotting his ruin, he would not allow even the appearance that his connection with Heaven was severed. . . .

He knew that no man, not even his king, had a right to come between his conscience and his God and interfere with the worship due to his Maker.—*Signs of the Times,* Nov. 4, 1886.

An Example of Trust and Prayer

But the king spoke, saying to Daniel, "Your God, whom you serve continually, He will deliver you." Dan. 6:16.

On account of his praying to God, Daniel was cast into the lions' den. . . . But Daniel continued to pray, even among the lions. Did God forget His faithful servant and suffer him to be destroyed? Oh, no; Jesus, the mighty Commander of the hosts of heaven, sent His angels to close the mouths of those hungry lions, that they should not hurt the praying man of God; and all was peace in that terrible den. The king witnessed the miraculous preservation of Daniel and brought him out with honors, while those who had plotted his destruction were utterly destroyed, with their wives and children, in the terrible manner in which they had planned to destroy Daniel.

Through the moral courage of this one man who chose, even in the face of death, to take a right course rather than a politic one, Satan was defeated and God honored. . . .

Daniel was a moral and intellectual giant; yet he did not reach this preeminence all at once and without effort. He was continually seeking for greater knowledge, for higher attainments. Other young men had the same advantages, but they did not, like him, bend all their energies to seek wisdom—the knowledge of God as revealed in His Word and in His works. Daniel was but a youth when he was brought into a heathen court in service to the king of Babylon; and because of his extreme youth when he was exposed to all the temptations of an Eastern court, his noble resistance of wrong and his steadfast adherence to the right throughout his long career are the more admirable. His example should be a source of strength to the tried and tempted, even at the present day. . . .

From the history of Daniel we may learn that a strict compliance with the requirements of God will prove a blessing, not only in the future, immortal life, but also in the present life. Through religious principles, we may triumph over the temptations of Satan and the devices of evildoers, even though it costs us a great sacrifice. . . .

We are living in the most solemn period of this world's history, when the last conflict between truth and error is raging; and we need courage and firmness for the right and a prayerful trust in God no less than Daniel did.—*Signs of the Times,* Nov. 4, 1886.

Miraculous Transformation

The Son of Man did not come to destroy men's lives but to save them.
Luke 9:56.

John was the disciple whom Jesus loved, because he was believing and trustful and loved his Master with devotion. His love for Christ was characterized by simplicity and ardor. There are many who think that this love for Christ was something natural to the character of John, and the disciple is frequently represented by the artist as of a soft, languid, feminine appearance, but such representations are incorrect. John and his brother were called the "sons of thunder." John was a man of decided character, but he had learned lessons from the great Teacher. He had defects of character, and any slight shown to Jesus aroused his indignation and combativeness. His love for Christ was the love of a soul saved through the merits of Jesus, but with this love there were natural evil traits that had to be overcome. At one time he and his brother claimed the right to the highest position in the kingdom of heaven, and at another he forbade a man to cast out devils and heal diseases because he followed not with the disciples. At another time, when he saw his Lord slighted by the Samaritans, he wanted to call down fire from heaven to consume them. But Christ rebuked him, saying, "The Son of man is not come to destroy men's lives, but to save them."

In the character and teaching of Christ, the disciples had both precept and example, and the grace of Christ was a transforming power, working marvelous changes in the life of the disciples. The natural traits of character, the spirit of criticism, revenge, ambition, evil temper, were all in the beloved disciple and had to be overcome in order that he might be a representative of Christ. He was not only a hearer but a doer of the words of his Lord. He learned of Jesus to be meek and lowly of heart. . . . This was the result of companionship with his Master. . . .

We have need of constant watchfulness, for we are nearing the coming of Christ, nearing the time when Satan is to work "with all power and signs and lying wonders, and with all deceivableness of unrighteousness in them that perish; because they received not the love of the truth, that they might be saved." We must study the Pattern and become like Jesus, who was meek and lowly of heart, pure and undefiled. We should ever remember that God is near us, and all things great and small are under His control.—*Signs of the Times,* Apr. 20, 1891.

Judas and John Contrasted

Most assuredly, I say to you, one of you will betray Me. John 13:21.

The opportunities and advantages offered to John were given to Judas also. The same principles of truth were set before his understanding; the same example in the character of Christ was his to contemplate and imitate. But Judas failed to become a doer of the words of Christ. Evil temper, revengeful passions, dark and sullen thoughts, were cherished until Satan had full control of the man. John walked in the light and improved the opportunities given him to overcome; but Judas chose his defects and refused to be transformed into the image of Christ, and therefore became a representative of the enemy of Christ and manifested the attributes of the evil one. When Judas came into association with Christ, he had some precious traits of character that might have been used of God and made a blessing to the church. If he had been willing to wear the yoke of Christ, to become meek and lowly of heart, he might have been among the chief of the apostles; but he hardened his heart when his defects were pointed out, and in pride and rebellion chose his own selfish ambitions, and so unfitted himself for the work God might have given him. John and Peter, though imperfect, became sanctified through the truth.

It is the same today as it was in the days of Christ. As the disciples were brought together, each with different faults, some inherited or cultivated tendency to evil, so in our church relations we find men and women whose characters are defective; not one of us is perfect. But in Christ, and through Christ, we are to dwell in the family of God, learning to become one in faith, in doctrine, in spirit, that at last we may be received into our eternal habitation. We shall have our tests, our grievances, our differences of opinion; but if Christ is abiding in the heart of each, there can be no dissension. The love of Christ will lead to love of one another, and the lessons of the Master will harmonize all differences, bringing us into unity, till we shall be of one mind and one judgment. Strife for supremacy will cease, and no one will be disposed to glory over another, but we shall esteem others better than ourselves and so be built up into a spiritual temple for the Lord. . . .

The lessons given to Peter, Judas, and the other disciples are profitable to us and have a special importance at this time.—*Signs of the Times,* Apr. 20, 1891.

Mary's Offering

Why do you trouble her? She has done a good work for Me. Mark 14:6.

The feast at Simon's house brought together many of the Jews, for they knew that Christ was there. They came not only to see Jesus, but many were curious to see one who had been raised from the dead. They thought that Lazarus would have some wonderful experience to relate, and were surprised that he told them nothing. . . . Lazarus had a wonderful testimony to bear, however, in regard to the work of Christ. He had been raised from the dead for this purpose. He was a living testimony to the divine power. With assurance and power he declared that Jesus was the Son of God. . . .

At the feast the Savior sat at the table with Simon, whom He had cured of a loathsome disease, on one side, and Lazarus, whom He had raised from the dead, on the other. Martha served at the table, but Mary was listening earnestly to every word that fell from the lips of Jesus. In His mercy Christ had pardoned Mary's sins, which had been many and grievous. Lazarus, her beloved brother, had been called from the grave and restored to his family by the power of the Savior; and Mary's heart was filled with gratitude. She longed to do Him honor. At great personal sacrifice she had purchased an alabaster box of precious ointment with which to anoint the body of Jesus at His death. Now, taking the box in her hands, she quietly broke it and poured the contents upon the head and feet of her Master.

Her movements might have passed unnoticed had not the ointment made its presence known by its rich fragrance and published her act to all present. "When his disciples saw it, they had indignation, saying, To what purpose is this waste?" Judas was the first to make this suggestion, and others were ready to echo his words. . . .

Jesus saw Mary shrink away abashed, expecting to hear reproof from the One she loved and worshipped. But instead of this she heard words of commendation. "Why trouble ye the woman?" Christ said. "For she hath wrought a good work upon me." . . . "Verily I say unto you, Wheresoever this gospel shall be preached in the whole world, there shall also this, that this woman hath done, be told for a memorial of her." . . .

Christ delighted in Mary's earnest desire to do the will of her Lord. . . . The desire that Mary had to do this service was of more value to Christ than all the precious ointment in the world, because it expressed her appreciation of her Redeemer.—*Youth's Instructor,* July 12, 1900.

Learning From Peter's Experience

If I have to die with You, I will not deny You! Mark 14:31.

The reason so many of Christ's professed disciples fall into grievous temptation is that they have not a correct knowledge of themselves. Here is where Peter was so thoroughly sifted by the enemy. If we could understand our own weakness, we should see so much to do for ourselves that we would humble our hearts under the mighty hand of God. Hanging our helpless souls upon Christ, we would supplement our ignorance with His wisdom, our weakness with His strength, our frailty with His enduring might. . . .

Mark the course pursued by Peter. His fall was not instantaneous, but gradual. Step after step was taken until the poor, sinful one denied his Lord with cursing and swearing. . . .

The crowing of the cock reminded Peter of the words of Christ, and, surprised and shocked, he turned and looked at his Master. At that moment Christ looked at Peter, and beholding that grieved look, in which compassion and love for him were blended, Peter understood himself. With startling vividness his self-confident words flashed upon his mind, "Although all shall be offended, yet will not I." "I am ready to go with thee, both into prison, and to death." And yet he had denied his Lord with cursing and swearing!

But Peter was not left in hopelessness. The look that Christ had given him brought a ray of hope to the erring disciple. He read there the words, "Peter, I am sorry for you. Because you are sorry and repent, I forgive you." While Peter's soul was passing through such deep humiliation, through the awful struggle with satanic agencies, he remembered the words of Christ, "I have prayed for thee," and they were to him a precious assurance. . . .

In Peter's fall we have before us our own individual cases. Just as verily as did Peter, many of the professedly commandment-keeping people of God dishonor and bring reproach upon their best Friend—the One who can save them to the uttermost. But the Lord would restore to Himself all who have put Him to shame by their unscriptural course of action.

Peter sinned against light and knowledge and against great and exalted privileges. It was self-confidence that caused him to fail, and it is this same evil that is now working in human hearts. It may be our purpose to be right and to do right, but we shall most surely err unless we are constant learners in the school of Christ. Our only safety is in walking humbly with God.— *Youth's Instructor,* Dec. 15, 1898.

September

30

Peter's Restoration

Simon, son of Jonah, do you love Me more than these? John 21:15.

Peter never forgot the painful scene of his humiliation. He did not forget his denial of Christ and think that, after all, it was not a very great sin. . . .

No restoration can be complete unless it reaches to the very depth of the soul by the transforming power of the Holy Spirit. Under the Holy Spirit's influence, Peter stood before a congregation of thousands and in holy boldness charged the wicked priests and rulers with the very sin of which he himself had been guilty. . . .

Three times after His resurrection, Christ tested Peter. "Simon, son of Jonas," He said, "lovest thou me more than these? He saith unto him, Yea, Lord; thou knowest that I love thee. He saith unto him, Feed my lambs. He saith to him again the second time, Simon, son of Jonas, lovest thou me? He saith unto him, Yea, Lord; thou knowest that I love thee. He saith unto him, Feed my sheep." . . .

When the third time Christ said to Peter, "Lovest thou me?" the probe reached the soul center. Self-judged, Peter fell upon the Rock, saying, "Lord, thou knowest all things; thou knowest that I love thee." . . .

Some assert that if a soul stumbles and falls, he can never regain his position; but the case before us contradicts this. Before his denial, Christ said to Peter, "When thou art converted, strengthen thy brethren." In committing to his stewardship the souls for whom He had given His life, Christ gave to Peter the strongest evidence of His confidence in his restoration. . . .

Peter was now humble enough to understand the words of Christ, and without further questioning, the once restless, boastful, self-confident disciple became subdued and contrite. He followed his Lord indeed—the Lord he had denied. The thought that Christ had not denied and rejected him was to Peter a light and comfort and blessing. He felt that he could be crucified from choice, but it must be with his head downward. . . .

Christ is our tower of strength, and Satan can have no power over the soul who walks with God in humility of mind. . . . If we lean to our own wisdom, our wisdom will prove to be foolishness. But if we will give ourselves unselfishly to the work, never swerving in the least from principle, the Lord will throw about us the everlasting arms and will prove a mighty helper.—*Youth's Instructor,* Dec. 22, 1898.

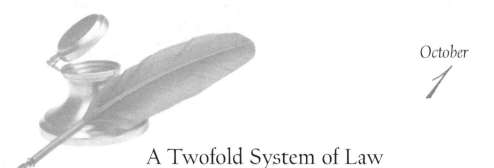

A Twofold System of Law

For He made Him who knew no sin to be sin for us, that we might become the righteousness of God in Him. 2 Cor. 5:21.

The fact that the holy pair, in disregarding the prohibition of God in one particular, thus transgressed His law, and as the result suffered the consequences of the Fall, should impress all with a just sense of the sacred character of the law of God. . . .

God's people, whom He calls His peculiar treasure, were privileged with a twofold system of law, the moral and the ceremonial. The one, pointing back to Creation to keep in remembrance the living God who made the world, whose claims are binding upon all in every dispensation, and which will exist through all time and eternity. The other, given because of Adam's transgression of the moral law, the obedience to which consisted in sacrifices and offerings pointing to the future redemption. . . .

The love that God bore to humanity, whom He had created in His own image, led Him to give His Son to die for their transgression, and lest the increase of sin should lead them to forget God and the promised redemption, the system of sacrificial offerings was established to typify the perfect offering of the Son of God. . . .

Christ became sin for the fallen race in taking upon Himself the condemnation resting upon the sinner for his transgression of the law of God. Christ stood at the head of the human family as their representative. He had taken upon Himself the sins of the world. In the likeness of sinful flesh He condemned sin in the flesh. . . .

The law of Jehovah, dating back to Creation, was comprised in the two great principles, "Thou shalt love the Lord thy God with all thy heart, and with all thy soul, and with all thy mind, and with all thy strength: this is the first commandment. And the second is like, namely this, Thou shalt love thy neighbour as thyself. There is none other commandment greater than these." . . .

What is the will of the Father? That we keep His commandments. . . .

The death of Jesus Christ for the redemption of mankind lifts the veil and reflects a flood of light back hundreds of years upon the whole institution of the Jewish system of religion. Without the death of Christ, all this system was meaningless.—*Review and Herald,* May 6, 1875.

God's Eternal Law

So shall I keep Your law continually, forever and ever. Ps. 119:44.

How wonderful in its simplicity, its comprehensiveness and perfection, is the law of Jehovah! . . .

There is no mystery in the law of God. The feeblest intellect can grasp these rules to regulate the life and form the character after the divine Model. . . .

The infinite sacrifice which Christ has made to magnify and exalt the law testifies that not one jot or tittle of that law will relinquish its claims upon the transgressor. Christ came to pay the debt which the sinner had incurred by transgression, and by His own example to teach us how to keep the law of God. Said Christ, "I have kept my Father's commandments." In consideration of all the facts so clearly establishing the claims of God's law, with heaven and eternal life in view to inspire hope and induce effort, it is inconceivable how so many professing to be servants of God can set aside His law and teach sinners that they are not amenable to its precepts. What a fatal delusion! Satan first devised this heresy, and by it he enticed Eve into sin. The sad results of that transgression are before us. . . .

Christ came to teach us the way of salvation. And when the shadowy services of the former dispensation were no longer of any value—when type had met antitype in the death of Christ—then we might expect that if the law of ten commandments were no longer binding, Christ would declare its abrogation. If the Old Testament Scriptures were no longer to be regarded as a guide for Christians, He would make known the fact. . . .

Holy prophets have foretold the manner of Christ's birth, the events of His life, His mission, and His death and resurrection. In the Old Testament we find the gospel of a coming Savior. In the New Testament we have the gospel of a Savior revealed as prophecy had foretold. . . .

There is no discord between the teachings of Christ in the Old Testament and His teachings in the New. . . .

In the very last message to His church, by way of Patmos, the risen Savior pronounces a benediction upon those who keep His Father's law: "Blessed are they that do his commandments, that they may have right to the tree of life, and may enter in through the gates into the city."—*Review and Herald,* Sept. 14, 1886.

October

3

Glorifying God

That you may with one mind and one mouth glorify the God and Father of our Lord Jesus Christ. Rom. 15:6.

Supreme love to God will be shown by every man or woman who is a true follower of Jesus Christ. . . . We are His creatures, the work of His hands, and He is justly entitled to reverence, honor, and love. . . .

In love, with a desire to elevate and ennoble us, God provided for us a standard of obedience. In awful majesty, amid thundering and lightning, He proclaimed from Mount Sinai His ten holy precepts. . . .

God saw the sinner's hopeless condition. He looked with sorrow upon the world, which was steadily growing more and more degraded and sinful. He could not change His law to meet our deficiencies; for He says, "My covenant will I not break, nor alter the thing that is gone out of my lips." But in His great love for the human race, in His desire that we should not be left to meet the penalty of our transgression, but that we should be elevated and ennobled, He "gave his only begotten Son, that whosoever believeth in him should not perish, but have everlasting lif." Christ laid aside His royal robes and came to this earth, bringing with Him a power sufficient to overcome sin. He came to live the law of God in humanity, that by partaking of His divine nature, we also might live that law. . . .

Before the universe of heaven, before the fallen angels, and before those whom He had come to save, Christ lived the law of God. By His supreme obedience to its requirements, He exalted and enforced it. By His purity, goodness, beneficence, devotion, and zeal for the glory of God, by His unsurpassed love for others, He made known the perfection of the law. By His blameless life He illustrated its excellence. . . .

Obedience must come from the heart. It was heart work with Christ. . . . If we draw near to God, the unfailing source of strength, we shall realize the fulfillment of the promise, "Ask, and ye shall receive." . . .

As Christ lived the law in humanity, so we may do if we will take hold of the Strong for strength. As we realize that we can do nothing of ourselves, we shall receive wisdom from on high to honor and glorify God. And as we behold "the glory of the Lord," we shall be changed into the same image, "from glory to glory."—*Signs of the Times,* Mar. 4, 1897.

The Dynamic Duo

Is the law then against the promises of God? Certainly not! Gal. 3:21.

The law and the gospel cannot be separated. In Christ mercy and truth are met together; righteousness and peace have kissed each other. The gospel has not ignored the obligations due to God by men and women. The gospel is the law unfolded, nothing more nor less. It gives no more latitude to sin than does the law. The law points to Christ; Christ points to the law. The gospel calls us to repentance. Repentance of what? Of sin. And what is sin? It is the transgression of the law. Therefore the gospel calls sinners from their transgression back to obedience to the law of God. Jesus in His life and death taught the strictest obedience. He died, the just for the unjust, the innocent for the guilty, that the honor of God's law might be preserved, and yet humanity not utterly perish.

The work of salvation in both the Old and New Testament dispensation is the same. . . .

Satan is working with all his deceptive power to ensnare the world. He would have them believe that this great sacrifice was made in order to abolish God's law. He represents Christ as opposed to the law of God's government in heaven and in earth. But the Sovereign of the world has a law by which to govern His heavenly intelligences and His human family, and the death of His Son fixes the immutability of that law beyond any question. God has no intention of doing away with His great standard of righteousness. By this standard He can define what a correct character is. . . .

It is necessary that every intelligent being shall understand the principles of the law of God. Christ through the apostle James declares, "Whosoever shall keep the whole law, and yet offend in one point, he is guilty of all." These words were spoken this side of the death of Christ; therefore the law was binding upon all at that time. . . .

People may talk of freedom, of gospel liberty. They may assert that they are not in bondage to the law. But the influence of a gospel hope will not lead sinners to look upon the salvation of Christ as a matter of free grace while they continue to live in transgression of the law of God. When the light of truth dawns upon their minds, and they fully understand the requirements of God and realize the extent of their transgressions, they will reform their ways, become loyal to God through the strength obtained from their Savior, and lead a new and purer life.— *Signs of the Times,* Feb. 25, 1897.

Rest in Christ

Therefore, since a promise remains of entering His rest, let us fear lest any of you seem to have come short of it. Heb. 4:1.

Jesus, our compassionate Savior, is the way, the truth, and the life. Why will we not accept His gracious offer of mercy, believe His words of promise, and not make the way of life so hard? As we travel the precious road cast up for the ransomed of the Lord to walk in, let us not overcast it with doubts and gloomy forebodings and pursue our way murmuring and groaning, as though forced to an unpleasant, exacting task. The ways of Christ are ways of pleasantness, and all His paths are peace. If we have made rough paths for our feet and taken heavy burdens of care in laying up for ourselves treasures upon the earth, let us now change and follow the path Jesus has prepared for us.

We are not always willing to come to Jesus with our trials and difficulties. Sometimes we pour our troubles into human ears and tell our afflictions to those who cannot help us, and neglect to confide all to Jesus, who is able to change the sorrowful way to paths of joy and peace. Self-denying, self-sacrificing, gives glory and victory to the cross. The promises of God are very precious. We must study His Word if we would know His will. The words of inspiration, carefully studied and practically obeyed, will lead our feet in a plain path where we may walk without stumbling. Oh, that all, ministers and people, would take their burdens and perplexities to Jesus, who is waiting to receive them and to give them peace and rest! He will never forsake those who put their trust in Him. . . .

It is our duty to love Jesus as our Redeemer. He has a right to command our love, but He invites us to give Him our heart. He calls us to walk with Him in the path of humble, truthful obedience. His invitation to us is a call to a pure, holy, and happy life—a life of peace and rest, of liberty and love—and to a rich inheritance in the future, immortal life. Which will we choose—liberty in Christ, or bondage and tyranny in the service of Satan? Why should we reject the invitation of mercy and refuse the proffers of divine love? If we choose to live with Christ through the ceaseless ages of eternity, why not choose Him now as our most loved and trusted Friend, our best and wisest Counselor?—*Signs of the Times,* Mar. 17, 1887.

Onward and Upward

I also count all things loss for the excellence of the knowledge of Christ Jesus my Lord. Phil. 3:8.

To love God supremely and our neighbor as ourselves is to keep the first four and the last six commandments. God has given to us a large field in which we may work; and in doing the work appointed us of God, we will not lift up ourselves but will exalt Christ. We will cherish love for God and love for our brethren and for all people. Love will soon die out of the heart if it is left without cultivation; we can only keep divine love in the soul by doing the words of the Master. Are there not many claiming to keep the commandments who are living in transgression of the sacred precepts? We cannot keep the law of God unless we give to our Creator and Redeemer our undivided affection. It is impossible to keep the last six commandments unless we keep the first four. . . .

When we come into close sympathy with Jesus, He will impart His love, and this will flow out in loving acts, in tender compassion to others. When we fail to love God supremely, we surely fail to love our neighbor as ourselves. When you love God with all your heart, might, mind, soul, and strength, you will be as a living stream in the desert to all around you. There will be no expressed doubts, no sowing of tares in your suggestions. You will not rest satisfied with a meager experience. . . .

There is no standing still in the Christian life. The followers of Jesus see ever before them higher things to be attained, and they will not be satisfied with a low standard. There is great danger in being satisfied, in not pressing forward for the prize of the high calling of God in Christ Jesus. . . .

In the truth, Jesus is unfolded in all His matchless loveliness; but of what advantage will be our knowledge of truth if it does not lead us to Jesus, if it does not increase our knowledge of Him and our love for Him? As soon as you surrender your whole heart to God, you will render self-denying, cheerful obedience. God requires that we shall be found in Him, not having our own righteousness, but the righteousness of Christ. When, with grateful appreciation of His love, we open the door of our heart to Jesus, saying, "Come in," the heavenly Guest is with us. When we love Jesus, we love all whom Jesus loves.—*Signs of the Times,* Sept. 22, 1890.

Like Christ

By which have been given to us exceedingly great and precious promises, that through these you may be partakers of the divine nature. 2 Peter 1:4.

Christ is an open fountain, an inexhaustible fountain, from which all may drink and drink again, and ever find a fresh supply. But none will ever come to Him save those who will respond to the drawing of His love. None will feed on the bread of life which came down from heaven, none will drink of the water of life flowing down from the throne of God, save those who yield to the pleadings of the Spirit. Since God has given the treasures of heaven in the gift of His only begotten Son, how shall the sinner escape who neglects so great salvation and sets at naught the great provision of God? The justice of God is manifested in the condemnation of all who are finally impenitent and unbelieving. There will be no excuse for the sinner who willfully rejects and neglects so great salvation.

The gift of life has been freely, graciously, joyously offered to fallen humanity. Through Christ we may become partakers of the divine nature and obtain the gift of eternal life; for it has been abundantly provided for all who will come and receive it through God's appointed means. When Paul beheld the wonders of redemption and the foolishness of those who did not comprehend its nature, he exclaimed, "O foolish Galatians, who hath bewitched you, that ye should not obey the truth, before whose eyes Jesus Christ hath been evidently set forth, crucified among you?" . . .

Those who go on to know the Lord know that His goings forth are prepared as the morning, and all who receive the precious jewels of truth will hasten to impart the knowledge of their riches in Christ to those who are around them. When people respond to the drawing of Christ and view Jesus as the royal Sufferer on the cross of Calvary, they enter into oneness with Christ, they become the elect of God, not by works of their own, but through the grace of Christ; for all their good works are wrought through the power of the Spirit of God. All is of God, and not of themselves. . . .

The fruit we are to bring forth is the fruit of the Spirit. . . . Your fruit is to remain, to be of such a character that it shall not perish but reproduce after its kind a harvest of a precious order.—*Signs of the Times,* May 2, 1892.

A New Creation

For in Christ Jesus neither circumcision nor uncircumcision avails anything, but a new creation. Gal. 6:15.

The grace of Jesus Christ alone can change the heart of stone to a heart of flesh and make it alive unto God. Men and women may perform great deeds in the eyes of the world; their achievements may be many and of a high order in the sight of others, but all the talent, all the skill, all the ability of the world, will fail to transform the character and make a degraded child of sin a child of God, an heir of heaven. We have no power to justify the soul, to sanctify the heart. . . .

How the wondrous provision of the plan of God for the salvation of mankind widens and exalts our ideas of the love of God! How it binds our hearts to the great heart of Infinite Love! How it makes us delight in His service, as our hearts respond to the drawing of His loving kindness and tender mercy! . . .

This is the work that is before us. We are to have the faith that works by love and purifies the soul. Through faith our lives are to be hid with Christ in God. We shall then be God's hidden ones; for the value of Christian character is not discerned by the world. The world admire honesty, and the manifestations of the virtues and graces of Christian character; but at the same time they make a jest of true Christian conscientiousness because it is a rebuke to their own lives of sin. The living stones that shine in the spiritual temple of the Lord are a great annoyance to Satan, and he ever seeks to cut off the light and eclipse the Sun of Righteousness by interposing his shadow between the soul and God. . . .

Before human beings and angels, Christians are required to show by precept and example the value of Christian character. Those who receive Christ as their personal Savior will be able to do this, and for them Christ has gone to prepare mansions in heaven. There are some who declare that all are entitled to a place in heaven, and in the same breath they acknowledge that all are not fitted for that heavenly abode. If all . . . would but accept the truth as it is in Jesus and give it a place in the inner sanctuary of the soul, that they might become sanctified through it, they would be fitted for heaven. . . .

Those whose lives are hid with Christ in God, who have been clothed upon with His righteousness, will have a right to the inheritance, incorruptible, undefiled, and that fadeth not away.—*Signs of the Times,* May 2, 1892.

The Purpose of Grace

For by grace you have been saved through faith, and that not of yourselves;
it is the gift of God. Eph. 2:8.

The purpose and plan of grace existed from all eternity. Before the foundation of the world it was according to the determinate counsel of God that humanity should be created, endowed with power to do the divine will. But the defection of the human race, with all its consequences, was not hidden from the Omnipotent, and yet it did not deter Him from carrying out His eternal purpose, for the Lord would establish His throne in righteousness. God knows the end from the beginning: "Known unto God are all his works from the beginning of the world." Therefore redemption was not an afterthought—a plan formulated after the fall of Adam—but an eternal purpose to be wrought out for the blessing not only of this atom of a world but for the good of all the worlds which God has created.

The creation of the worlds, the mystery of the gospel, are for one purpose, to make manifest to all created intelligences, through nature and through Christ, the glories of the divine character. By the marvelous display of His love in giving "his only begotten Son, that whosoever believeth in him should not perish, but have everlasting life," the glory of God is revealed to lost humanity and to the intelligences of other worlds. The Lord of heaven and earth revealed His glory to Moses when he offered his prayer to Jehovah in behalf of idolatrous Israel and pleaded, "Shew me thy glory." . . .

It is the privilege of every follower of Christ to behold the glory of God, to understand His goodness, and know that He is a God of infinite mercy and love. . . . Jesus came to reveal the Father, to make His glory known before humanity. No one was excluded from the privileges of the gospel. . . .

The mystery of the gospel had been spoken in Eden when the lost pair were first in the guilt of transgression, for God said to the serpent, "I will put enmity between thee and the woman, and between thy seed and her seed; it shall bruise thy head, and thou shalt bruise his heel." If Satan could have touched the head with his specious temptations, the human family would have been lost, but the Lord had made known the purpose and plan of the mystery of grace, for "God so loved the world, that he gave his only begotten Son, that whosoever believeth in him should not perish, but have everlasting life."—*Signs of the Times,* Apr. 25, 1892.

The Impact of Truth

Now may the God of peace Himself sanctify you completely.
1 Thess. 5:23.

Christ represents the truth as a treasure that is hid in the field, for which, if men and women would possess it, they must search diligently. In the field of revelation are hid the unsearchable riches of Christ. . . . Every part of the field of revelation is to be diligently explored and searched with persevering effort, in order that precious jewels of truth may reward the diligent seeker and may be restored to their proper framework in the plan of redemption. Let the shaft sink deep into the mines of truth. If you come to the searching of the Scriptures with contrition of soul, with a humble, teachable spirit, rich and precious treasures will reward your search. . . .

In the teachings of Christ, the doctrine of the Holy Spirit is made prominent. What a vast theme is this for contemplation and encouragement! What treasures of truth did He add to the knowledge of His disciples in His instruction concerning the Holy Spirit, the Comforter! He dwelt upon this theme in order to console His disciples in the great trial they were soon to experience, that they might be cheered in their great disappointment. . . .

And yet, though Christ made much of this theme concerning the Holy Spirit, how little is it dwelt upon in the churches! The name and presence of the Holy Spirit are almost ignored, yet the divine influence is essential in the work of perfecting the Christian character. . . .

The Lord has given us a divine directory by which we may know His will. . . . Those who are guided by the Holy Spirit have cast their anchors within the veil wherein Jesus has entered for us. They search the Scriptures with eager earnestness and seek for light and knowledge to guide them amid the perplexities and perils which at every step compass their path. . . .

To the sincere, contrite heart, truth is truth; and if it is allowed, it will sanctify the soul and transform the character into the divine image. . . . Those who realize what is the character of the work that they must do in order to represent Christ will walk softly and tremblingly before God, looking unto Jesus, who is the Author and Finisher of their faith. They dare not trust themselves, they dare not kindle a fire of their own and walk in sparks of their own kindling, for the Lord has said that all such shall lie down in sorrow. The Lord has entrusted to His people the treasures of sacred truth.—*Signs of the Times,* Aug. 14, 1893.

Christ in Light of the Law

Therefore the law is holy, and the commandment holy and just and good.
Rom. 7:12.

Those who desire salvation should fix their mind upon the cross of Calvary. It is there that sinners may behold what sin has done. There they can see the infinite sacrifice that has been made to redeem them from the penalty of the broken law of God. As transgressors realize their lost condition, they see in Christ their only hope of salvation. From the cross they learn precious lessons of the life... of the Son of God, who gave Himself for us. Calvary portrays the matchless attributes of the divine character. As they look to the cross, they will hate sin, for they will understand that it was sin that rejected, reproached, denied, scourged, and crucified the Majesty of heaven. . . .

The cross of Calvary tells how Christ has magnified the law and made it honorable. It required the infinite merits of His blood to make an atonement for those who receive His love and follow in His footsteps. Sinners may obtain pardon and peace only through Him who has loved us and who will wash us from our sins in His own blood. Those who have been convinced of sin before the law and have exercised repentance toward God and faith toward our Lord Jesus Christ cease to make void the law of God. . . .

We could never have known the value of Christ except through an understanding of the exalted claims of the law of Jehovah. We could never have appreciated the depth of the pit from which Christ has rescued us except through a comprehension of the excellence of the precepts of truth. Never could we have understood the depth of the love of God which is in Christ Jesus unless we could have beheld the marvelous character of the law of heaven and earth. In the light of that holy law, sinners see the Redeemer as He is—full of mercy, compassion, goodness, and love; and by looking to Jesus and by contemplating His matchless love to such sinners as themselves, their hearts are filled with gratitude and heavenly peace. . . .

Although the law of God is of a holy and unchangeable character, the adversary of God and humanity, the first great rebel who transgressed its precepts in heaven, has led men and women in all ages to war against God. . . . As sinners see that sin is the transgression of the law and that the law is the foundation of God's government in heaven and in earth, they make haste to place their feet in the path of righteousness, that they may be without offense.—*Signs of the Times,* July 6, 1888.

Walk in Christ

As you therefore have received Christ Jesus the Lord, so walk in Him.
Col. 2:6.

W alk in love, as Christ also hath loved us, and hath given himself for us an offering and a sacrifice to God for a sweetsmelling savour." . . .
Obedience to the law of God is sanctification. There are many who have erroneous ideas in regard to this work in the soul, but Jesus prayed that His disciples might be sanctified through the truth, and added, "Thy word is truth." Sanctification is not an instantaneous but a progressive work, as obedience is continuous. Just as long as Satan urges his temptations upon us, the battle for self-conquest will have to be fought over and over again; but by obedience, the truth will sanctify the soul. Those who are loyal to the truth will, through the merits of Christ, overcome all weakness of character which has led them to be molded by every varying circumstance of life.

Many have taken the position that they cannot sin because they are sanctified, but this is a delusive snare of the evil one. There is constant danger of falling into sin, for Christ has warned us to watch and pray lest we enter into temptation. If we are conscious of the weakness of self, we shall not be self-confident and reckless of danger, but we shall feel the necessity of seeking to the Source of our strength, Jesus our righteousness. We shall come in repentance and contrition, with a despairing sense of our own finite weakness, and learn that we must daily apply to the merits of the blood of Christ, that we may become vessels fit for the Master's use.

While thus depending upon God, we shall not be found warring against the truth, but we shall always be enabled to take our stand for the right. We should cling to the teaching of the Bible and not follow the customs and traditions of the world, the sayings and doings of humanity. When errors arise and are taught as Bible truth, those who have a connection with Christ will not trust to what the minister says, but, like the noble Bereans, they will search the Scriptures daily to see if these things are so. When they discover what is the word of the Lord, they will take their stand on the side of truth. They will hear the voice of the true Shepherd saying, "This is the way, walk ye in it." Thus you will be educated to make the Bible the man of your counsel, and the voice of a stranger you will neither hear nor follow.—*Signs of the Times,* May 19, 1890.

Two Vital Lessons

Gather my saints together to Me, those who have made a covenant with Me by sacrifice. Ps. 50:5.

If the soul is to be purified and ennobled and made fit for the heavenly courts, there are two lessons to be learned—self-sacrifice and self-control. Some learn these important lessons more easily than do others, for they are exercised by the simple discipline the Lord gives them in gentleness and love. Others require the slow discipline of suffering, that the cleansing fire may purify their hearts of pride and self-reliance, of earthly passion and self-love, that the true gold of character may appear, and that they may become victors through the grace of Christ. The love of God will strengthen the soul, and through the virtue of the merits of the blood of Christ we may stand unscathed amid the fire of temptation and trial; but no other help can avail to save but Christ, our righteousness, who is made unto us wisdom and sanctification and redemption.

True sanctification is nothing more or less than to love God with all the heart, to walk in His commandments and ordinances blameless. Sanctification is not an emotion, but a heaven-born principle that brings all the passions and desires under the control of the Spirit of God; and this work is done through our Lord and Savior.

Spurious sanctification does not glorify God, but leads those who claim it to exalt and glorify themselves. Whatever comes in our experience, whether of joy or sorrow, that does not reflect Christ and point to Him as its author, . . . is not true Christian experience.

When the grace of Christ is implanted in the soul by the Holy Spirit, its possessor will become humble in spirit and will seek for the society of those whose conversation is upon heavenly things. Then the Spirit will take the things of Christ and show them unto us, and will glorify, not the receiver, but the Giver. If, therefore, you have the sacred peace of Christ in your heart, your lips will be filled with praise and thanksgiving to God. Your prayers, the discharge of your duty, your benevolence, your self-denial, will not be the theme of your thought or conversation, but you will magnify Him who gave Himself for you when you were yet a sinner. You will say, "I give myself to Jesus. I have found Him of whom Moses in the law, and the prophets, did write." As you praise Him, you will have a precious blessing, and all the praise and glory for that which is done through your instrumentality will be given back to God.—*Signs of the Times,* May 19, 1890.

Would You Have Peace?

Mark the blameless man, and observe the upright; for the future of that man is peace. Ps. 37:37.

The peace of Christ is not a boisterous, untamable element made manifest in loud voices and bodily exercises. The peace of Christ is an intelligent peace, and it does not make those who possess it bear the marks of fanaticism and extravagance. It is not a rambling impulse, but an emanation from God. When the Savior imparts His peace to the soul, the heart will be in perfect harmony with the Word of God, for the Spirit and the Word agree. The Lord honors His Word in all His dealings with humanity. It is His own will, His own voice, that is revealed to them, and He has no new will, no new truth, aside from His Word to unfold to His children. If you have a wonderful experience that is not in harmony with the expressed directions of God's Word, you may well doubt it; for its origin is not from above. The peace of Christ comes through the knowledge of Jesus whom the Bible reveals.

If happiness is drawn from outside sources and not from the Divine Fount, it will be as changeable as varying circumstances can make it; but the peace of Christ is a constant and abiding peace. It does not depend on any circumstance in life, on the amount of worldly goods, or the number of earthly friends. Christ is the fountain of living waters, and happiness and peace drawn from Him will never fail, for He is a wellspring of life. Those who trust in Him can say, "God is our refuge and strength, a very present help in trouble." . . .

We have reason for ceaseless gratitude to God that Christ, by His perfect obedience, has won back the heaven that Adam lost through disobedience. Adam sinned, and the children of Adam share his guilt and its consequences; but Jesus bore the guilt of Adam, and all the children of Adam that will flee to Christ, the second Adam, may escape the penalty of transgression. Jesus regained heaven for us by bearing the test that Adam failed to endure, for He obeyed the law perfectly, and all who have a right conception of the plan of redemption will see that they cannot be saved while in transgression of God's holy precepts. They must cease to transgress the law, and lay hold on the promises of God that are available for us through the merits of Christ.

Our faith is not to stand in human ability but in the power of God. . . . Christ must be our strength and our refuge. . . . Pure, living religion is found in obedience to every word that proceedeth out of the mouth of God.—*Signs of the Times,* May 19, 1890.

How Faith Works

But without faith it is impossible to please Him, for he who comes to God must believe that He is, and that He is a rewarder of those who diligently seek Him. Heb. 11:6.

When through repentance and faith we accept Christ as our Savior, the Lord pardons our sins and remits the penalty prescribed for the transgression of the law. The sinner then stands before God as a just person, is taken into favor with heaven, and through the Spirit has fellowship with the Father and the Son. Then there is yet another work to be accomplished, and this is of a progressive nature. The soul is to be sanctified through the truth. And this also is accomplished through faith. For it is only by the grace of Christ, which we receive through faith, that the character can be transformed.

It is important that we understand clearly the nature of faith. There are many who believe that Christ is the Savior of the world, that the gospel is true and reveals the plan of salvation, yet they do not possess saving faith. They are intellectually convinced of the truth, but this is not enough; in order to be justified, sinners must have that faith that appropriates the merits of Christ to their own soul. We read that the devils "believe, and tremble"; but their belief does not bring them justification, neither will the belief of those who give a merely intellectual assent to the truths of the Bible bring them the benefits of salvation. This belief fails of reaching the vital point, for the truth does not engage the heart or transform the character.

In genuine, saving faith, there is trust in God through the belief in the great atoning sacrifice made by the Son of God on Calvary. In Christ, the justified believers behold their only hope and deliverer. Belief may exist without trust, but confidence born of trust cannot exist without faith. All sinners brought to a knowledge of the saving power of Christ will make manifest this trust in greater degree as they advance in experience.

The words of the apostle shed light upon what constitutes genuine faith. He says, "If thou shalt confess with thy mouth the Lord Jesus, and shalt believe in thine heart that God hath raised him from the dead, thou shalt be saved. For with the heart man believeth unto righteousness; and with the mouth confession is made unto salvation." To believe with the heart is more than conviction, more than assent to the truth. This faith is sincere, earnest, and engages the affections of the soul; it is the faith that works by love and purifies the heart.—*Signs of the Times, Nov. 3, 1890.*

Be Honest With God

For God will bring every work into judgment, including every secret thing, whether good or evil. Eccl. 12:14.

God reveals Christ to sinners, and they behold Him dying upon Calvary for the sin of His creatures. They then understand how they are condemned by the law of God, for the Spirit works upon their consciences, enforcing the claim of the broken law. They are then given the opportunity of defying the law, of rejecting the Savior, or of yielding to its claims and receiving Christ as their Redeemer. God will not compel the service of sinners, but He reveals to them their obligation, unfolds to them the requirements of His holy law, and sets before them the result of their choice—to obey and live, or to disobey and perish.

The command from heaven is, "Thou shalt love the Lord thy God with all thy heart, and with all thy soul, and with all thy strength, and with all thy mind; and thy neighbor as thyself." When the force of this requirement is understood, the conscience is convicted, the sinner is condemned. The carnal mind, which is not subject to the law of God, neither indeed can be, rises up in rebellion against the holy claims of the law. But as sinners behold Christ hanging upon the cross of Calvary, suffering for their transgression, deeper conviction takes hold upon them, and they see something of the offensive nature of sin.

Where there is a true conception of the spirituality and holiness of the divine law, sinners are under condemnation, and their sins stand arrayed before them in their true character. By the law is the knowledge of sin, and in its light they understand the evil of secret thoughts and deeds of darkness. . . .

Character is tested and registered by Heaven more by the inward spirit, the hidden motives, than by that which appears to others. People may have a pleasing exterior and be outwardly excellent, while they are but whited sepulchers, full of corruption and uncleanness. Their works are registered as unsanctified, unholy. Their prayers and works, devoid of the righteousness of Christ, do not ascend before God as sweet fragrance, but they are abomination in the eyes of the Lord. To those who will open their eyes, the law presents a perfect likeness of the soul, a complete photograph of the inner being; and as this picture is unveiled before sinners, they are constrained to acknowledge that they are sold under sin, but that the law is holy, and just, and good.—*Signs of the Times,* Nov. 3, 1890.

Guided by the Holy Spirit

The Spirit of the Lord shall rest upon Him, the Spirit of wisdom and understanding, the Spirit of counsel and might, the Spirit of knowledge and of the fear of the Lord. Isa. 11:2.

If we live in the Spirit, let us also walk in the Spirit." ...We cannot spiritually discern the character of God or accept of Jesus Christ by faith unless our life and character are marked by purity, by the casting down of imaginations and of every high thing that exalts itself against the knowledge of God, and by bringing into captivity every thought to the obedience of Christ. . . .

The Lord is more willing to give the Holy Spirit to them that earnestly desire it than are earthly parents to give good gifts to their children. Christ has promised the Holy Spirit to guide us unto all truth and righteousness and holiness. The Holy Spirit is not given by measure to those who earnestly seek for it, who by faith stand upon the promises of God. They plead the pledged word of God, saying, "Thou hast said it. I take thee at thy word."

The Comforter is given that He may take of the things of Christ and show them unto us, that He may present in their rich assurance the words that fell from His lips and convey them with living power to the soul who is obedient, who is emptied of self. It is then that the soul receives the image and superscription of the divine. Then Jesus Christ is formed within, the hope of glory. . . .

Food is the substance of which we partake, that our bodies may be strengthened and built up. In like manner we are to feed upon that which will build up our spiritual nature. Jesus said, "It is the spirit that quickeneth; the flesh profiteth nothing: the words that I speak unto you, they are spirit, and they are life." Our bodies are composed of that upon which we feed; so our spiritual life will be composed of that upon which we feed. If we feed on Christ, by thinking of Him, by obeying His words, we are built up in Him and grow in grace and in the knowledge of the truth unto the full stature of men and women in Christ Jesus. . . .

As God works in us to will, we are to cooperate with God, manifesting a determination like that of Daniel to do the will of God, working in harmony with the divine Agent. Then we shall have rest in God.—*Signs of the Times,* Dec. 25, 1893.

Evidence of the Spirit's Work

Create in me a clean heart, O God, and renew a steadfast spirit within me. Ps. 51:10.

The Holy Spirit is a free, working, independent agency. The God of heaven uses His Spirit as it pleases Him; and human minds, human judgment, and human methods can no more set boundaries to its working . . . than they can say to the wind, "I bid you to blow in a certain direction and to conduct yourself in such and such a manner." As the wind moves in its force, bending and breaking the lofty trees in its path, so the Holy Spirit influences human hearts, and no finite human can circumscribe its work. . . .

The fountain of the heart must be purified before the streams can become pure. There is no safety for one who has merely a legal religion, a form of godliness. The Christian's life is not a modification or improvement of the old life, but a transformation of the nature. There is a death to sin and self, and a new life altogether. This change can be brought about only by the effectual working of the Holy Spirit. . . .

The Spirit of God is manifested in different ways upon different individuals. Some, under the movings of this Power, will tremble before the Word of God. Their convictions are so deep that a tumult of feeling seems to rage in their heart, and their whole being is prostrated under the convicting power of the truth. . . .

Others are brought to Christ in a more gentle way. Men and women who have been dead in trespasses and sins become convicted and converted under the operations of the Spirit. The thoughtless and wayward become serious. The hardened repent of their sins, and the faithless believe. The gambler, the drunkard, the licentious, become steady, sober, and pure. The rebellious and obstinate become meek and Christlike. . . .

The Holy Spirit moves upon the inner self until it becomes conscious of the divine power of God, and every spiritual faculty is quickened to decided action. A deep and thorough work is wrought in the soul, which the world cannot see. . . .

Those who truly love God have the internal evidence that they are beloved of God. They have communion with Christ, and their hearts are warmed with fervent love toward Him. God claims them for Himself and will impart to them special favors, enabling them to be complete in Christ, more than conquerors through Him who has loved them.—*Signs of the Times,* Mar. 8, 1910.

Lights Shining in Darkness

You are all sons of light and sons of the day. 1 Thess. 5:5.

Ye shall receive power, after that the Holy Ghost is come upon you." . . . God has left nothing undone that could in any way work for the recovering of sinners from the toils of the enemy. He poured upon the disciples the Holy Spirit in order that they might be enabled to cooperate with divine agencies in reshaping and remodeling human character. . . .

There is more joy in heaven over one sinner that repents than over the ninety and nine who suppose they need no repentance. When we hear of the success of the truth in any locality, let the whole church join in songs of rejoicing, let praises ascend to God. Let the name of the Lord be glorified by us. . . .

Entire consecration to the service of God will reveal the molding influence of the Holy Spirit at every step along the way. When apparent impossibilities arise in your path, present the ever ready, complete efficiency of the Holy Spirit before your unbelieving heart, that it may shame away your overcautious spirit. When your faith is weak, your efforts feeble, talk of the great Comforter, the Strength of heaven. When you are inclined to doubt that God is working by His Holy Spirit through human agents, remember that God has used the church and is using it to the glory of His own name. If we will not obstruct the way, God will move upon the minds of many more to engage in active service for Him. . . .

The end of all things is at hand. God is moving upon every mind that is open to receive the impressions of His Holy Spirit. He is sending out messengers, that they may give the warning in every locality. God is testing the devotion of His churches and their willingness to render obedience to the Spirit's guidance. Knowledge is to be increased. The messengers of heaven are to be seen running to and fro, seeking in every possible way to warn the people of the coming judgments, and presenting the glad tidings of salvation through our Lord Jesus Christ. The standard of righteousness is to be exalted. The Spirit of God is moving upon sinful hearts, and those who respond to its influence will become lights in the world. Everywhere they are seen going forth to communicate to others the light they have received, as they did after the descent of the Holy Spirit on the day of Pentecost. And as they let their light shine, they receive more and more of the Spirit's power. The earth is lighted with the glory of God.—*Review and Herald,* July 16, 1895.

Gifts of the Spirit

Now concerning spiritual gifts, brethren, I do not want you to be ignorant.
1 Cor. 12:1.

Before He left His disciples, Christ breathed on them and said, "Receive ye the Holy Ghost." Again He said, "Behold, I send the promise of my Father upon you." But not until after the Ascension was this gift received in its fullness. Not until through faith and prayer the disciples had surrendered themselves fully for His working was the outpouring of the Spirit bestowed. . . .

"When he ascended up on high, he led captivity captive, and gave gifts unto men." . . . The gifts are already ours in Christ, but their actual possession depends upon our reception of the Spirit of God.

The talents that Christ entrusts to His church represent especially the gifts and blessings imparted by the Holy Spirit. . . . Not all the gifts are imparted to each believer, but to every servant of the Master some gift of the Spirit is promised, according to that one's need for the Lord's work.

In all the Lord's arrangements, there is nothing more beautiful than His plan of giving to men and women a diversity of gifts. . . . Many have received but a limited religious and intellectual training, but God has a work for this class to do if they will labor in humility, trusting in Him. . . .

Different gifts are imparted to different ones, that the workers may feel their need of one another. God bestows these gifts, and they are employed in His service, not to glorify the possessor, not to uplift human beings, but to uplift the world's Redeemer. . . .

It may seem to some that the contrast between their gifts and the gifts of a fellow laborer is too great to allow them to unite in harmonious effort; but when they remember that there are varied minds to be reached and that some will reject the truth as it is presented by one laborer, only to open their hearts to the same truth as presented in a different manner by another, they will hopefully endeavor to labor together in unity. Their talents, however diverse, may all be under the control of the same Spirit. In every word and act, kindness and love will be revealed; and as the workers fill their appointed places faithfully, the prayer of Christ for the unity of His followers will be answered, and the world will know that these are His disciples.— *Signs of the Times,* Mar. 15, 1910.

Pentecost

When the Day of Pentecost had fully come, they were all with one accord in one place. . . . And they were all filled with the Holy Spirit. Acts 2:1-4.

During the Jewish economy, the influence of God's Spirit had been seen in a marked manner, but not in full. For ages prayers had been offered for the fulfillment of God's promise to impart His Spirit, and not one of these earnest supplications had been forgotten.

Christ determined that when He ascended from this earth He would bestow a gift on those who had believed on Him and those who should believe on Him. What gift could He bestow rich enough to signalize and grace His ascension to the mediatorial throne? It must be worthy of His greatness and His royalty. He determined to give His representative, the third Person of the Godhead. This gift could not be excelled. . . .

The Spirit had been waiting for the crucifixion, resurrection, and ascension of Christ. For ten day the disciples offered their petitions for the outpouring of the Spirit, and Christ in heaven added His intercession. . . .

The Spirit was given as Christ had promised, and like a rushing mighty wind it fell upon those assembled, filling the whole house. It came with a fullness and power, as if for ages it had been restrained. . . .

On the day of Pentecost, Christ's witnesses proclaimed the truth, telling others the wonderful news of salvation through Christ. And as a flaming two-edged sword the truth flashed conviction into human hearts. People were brought under Christ's control. The glad tidings were carried to the uttermost bounds of the inhabited world. The church beheld converts flocking to her from all directions. The altar of the cross, which sanctifies the gift, was rebuilt. Believers were reconverted. Sinners united with Christians in seeking the pearl of great price. The prophecy was fulfilled: the weak "shall be as David," and David "as the angel of the Lord." Every Christian saw in his brother the divine similitude of benevolence and love. One interest prevailed. One object swallowed up all others. Every pulse beat in healthy concert. The only ambition of the believers was to see who could reveal most perfectly the likeness of Christ's character, who could do the most for the enlargement of His kingdom. . . . The Spirit of Christ animated the whole congregation, for they had found the pearl of great price.—*Signs of the Times,* Dec. 1, 1898.

The Fruits of Pentecost

Now when they saw the boldness of Peter and John, . . . they realized that they had been with Jesus. Acts 4:13.

After the crucifixion of Christ, the disciples were a helpless, discouraged company—as sheep without a shepherd. Their Master had been rejected, condemned, and nailed to the ignominious cross. Scornfully the Jewish priests and rulers had declared, "He saved others; himself he cannot save." . . .

But the cross, that instrument of shame and torture, brought hope and salvation to the world. The disciples rallied; their hopelessness and helplessness left them. They were transformed in character, and united in bonds of Christian love. They were but humble men, without wealth and with no weapon but the Word and Spirit of God, counted by the Jews as mere fishermen. Yet in Christ's strength they went forth to witness for the truth and to triumph over all opposition. Clothed with the divine panoply, they went forth to tell the wonderful story of the manger and the cross. Without earthly honor or recognition, they were heroes of faith. From their lips came words of divine eloquence that shook the world.

Those who had rejected and crucified the Savior expected to find the disciples discouraged and crestfallen, ready to disown their Lord. They heard with amazement the clear, bold testimony of the apostles given under the power of the Holy Spirit. The disciples worked and spoke as their Master had worked and spoken, and all who heard them said, "They have been with Jesus, and learned of Him."

As the apostles went forth, preaching Jesus everywhere, they did many things that the Jewish rulers did not approve. The people brought their sick and those vexed with unclean spirits into the streets; crowds collected round them, and those who had been healed shouted the praises of God and glorified the name of Him whom the Jews had condemned, crowned with thorns, and caused to be scourged and crucified. Jesus was now extolled above priest and ruler, and there was danger that the doctrines of the rabbis would be brought into disrepute, for the apostles were even declaring that Christ had risen from the dead. . . .

"Daily in the temple, and in every house, they ceased not to teach and preach Jesus Christ." "And the Lord added to the church daily such as should be saved."—*Signs of the Times,* Sept. 20, 1899.

Pray for God's Spirit

How much more will your heavenly Father give the Holy Spirit to those who ask Him? Luke 11:13.

The promise of the Holy Spirit was the brightest hope and the strongest consolation that Christ could leave His disciples when He ascended to heaven. The truths of God's Word had been buried beneath the rubbish of misinterpretation; human maxims, the sayings of finite beings, had been exalted above the Word of the living God. Under the enlightening power of the Holy Spirit, the apostles separated truth from false theories and gave to the people the Word of life. . . .

The Spirit of God inspired His servants, who, irrespective of the fear or the favor of others, declared the truths which had been committed to them. And under the demonstration of the Spirit's power the Jews could not but see their guilt in refusing the evidences God had sent. But they would not yield their wicked resistance. . . .

We need to pray for the impartation of the divine Spirit as the remedy for sin-sick souls. The surface truths of revelation, made plain and easy to be understood, are accepted by many as supplying all that is essential; but the Holy Spirit, working upon the mind, awakens an earnest desire for truth uncorrupted by error. Those who are really desirous to know what is truth cannot remain in ignorance; for precious truth rewards the diligent seeker. We need to feel the converting power of God's grace, and I urge all who have closed their heart against God's Spirit to unlock the door, and plead earnestly, Abide with me. . . .

The Lord would have every one of His children rich in faith, and this faith is the fruit of the working of the Holy Spirit upon the mind. It dwells with each soul who will receive it. . . .

The Holy Spirit never leaves unassisted a soul who is looking to Jesus. It takes of the things of Christ, and shows them to the seeker. And if the eye is kept fixed upon Jesus, the work of the Spirit ceases not until the soul is conformed to His image. Through the gracious influence of the Spirit sinners are changed in spirit and purpose till they become one with Christ. Their affection for God increases; they hunger and thirst for righteousness, and by beholding Christ they are changed from glory to glory, from character to character, and become more and more like their Master.—*Signs of the Times,* Sept. 27, 1899.

The Coming Test

Stand therefore, having girded your waist with truth. Eph. 6:14.

God has made full provision in the Scriptures for our equipment against deception, and we shall be without excuse if, through neglect of God's Word, we are unable to resist the errors of the evil one. We need to watch unto prayer. We need daily to search the Scriptures diligently, that we may not be ensnared by some delusive error that seems like truth. . . .

John writes concerning scenes that have to do with our own time. He says, "The temple of God was opened in heaven, and there was seen in his temple the ark of his testament." That ark contains the tables whereon is engraven the law of God. On the Isle of Patmos, John beheld in prophetic vision the people of God, and saw that at this time the attention of the loyal and true followers of Christ would be attracted to the open door of the most holy place in the heavenly sanctuary. He saw that by faith they would follow Jesus within the veil where He ministers above the ark of God containing His immutable law. The prophet described the faithful ones, saying, "Here are they that keep the commandments of God, and the faith of Jesus." This is the class that excite the wrath of the dragon because they obey God. . . .

The winds of doctrine will blow fiercely about us, but we should not be moved by them. God has given us a correct standard of righteousness and truth—the law and the testimony. There are many who profess to love God, but when the Scriptures are opened before them and evidences are presented showing the binding claims of God's law, they manifest the spirit of the dragon. They hate the light and will not come to it, lest their deeds should be reproved. They will not compare their faith and doctrine with the law and the testimony. They turn away their ears from hearing the truth, and impatiently declare that all they want to hear about is faith in Christ. . . . They refuse to acknowledge the fourth commandment, which requires us to keep holy the Sabbath day. They declare that the Lord has instructed them that they need not keep the Sabbath of His law.

The Word of God declares, "He that saith, I know him, and keepeth not his commandments, is a liar, and the truth is not in him." . . . Our work is to hold up the law of God; for Christ has said, . . . "Blessed are they that do his commandments, that they may have right to the tree of life, and may enter in through the gates into the city."—*Signs of the Times,* Apr. 22, 1889.

25

Last-day Delusions

Now the Spirit expressly says that in latter times some will depart from the faith, giving heed to deceiving spirits and doctrines of demons. 1 Tim. 4:1.

Before the last developments of the work of apostasy there will be a confusion of faith. There will not be clear and definite ideas concerning the mystery of God. One truth after another will be corrupted. . . . There are many who deny the preexistence of Christ and therefore deny His divinity; they do not accept Him as a personal Savior. This is a total denial of Christ. He was the only begotten Son of God, who was one with the Father from the beginning. By Him the worlds were made.

In denying the miraculous incarnation of Christ, many turn from other truths of heavenly origin and accept fables of Satan's invention. They lose spiritual discernment and practice that which is brought to them and impressed upon their minds through the agency of Satan. . . .

Spiritualism is about to take the world captive. There are many who think that spiritualism is upheld through trickery and imposture; but this is far from the truth. Superhuman power is working in a variety of ways, and few have any idea as to what will be the manifestations of spiritualism in the future. The foundation for the success of spiritualism has been laid in the assertions that have been made from the pulpits of our land. The ministers have proclaimed, as Bible doctrines, falsehoods that have originated from the archdeceiver. The doctrine of consciousness after death, of the spirits of the dead being in communion with the living, has no foundation in the Scriptures, and yet this theory is affirmed as truth. Through this false doctrine the way has been opened for the spirits of devils to deceive the people in representing themselves as the dead. Satanic agencies personate the dead and thus bring souls into captivity. Satan has a religion; he has a synagogue and devout worshippers. . . .

The signs and wonders of spiritualism will become more and more pronounced as the professed Christian world rejects the plainly revealed truth of the Word of God and refuses to be guided by a plain "Thus saith the Lord," accepting instead the doctrines and the commandments of men. . . .

The confederacy of evil will not stand. The Lord says: . . . "Sanctify the Lord of hosts himself; and let him be your fear, and let him be your dread. And he shall be for a sanctuary."—*Signs of the Times,* May 28, 1894.

October

26

Spiritualism and Its End

For they are spirits of demons, performing signs, which go out to the kings of the earth and of the whole world. Rev. 16:14.

The great power that attends spiritualism has its origin in the great leading rebel, Satan, the prince of devils. It is through his artifice that evil angels have been able to substitute themselves for the dead, and through lying hypocrisy they have led men and women to have communion with devils. Those who commune with the supposed spirits of the dead are communing with those who will have a corrupting, demoralizing power upon the mind. Christ commanded that we should have no communion with sorcerers and with those who have familiar spirits. . . .

For years spiritualism has been growing in strength and gaining in popularity by advocating a certain kind of faith in Christ, and thus many Protestants are becoming infatuated with this mystery of iniquity. It is little wonder that they are deluded when they persistently retain the error that, as soon as the breath leaves the body, the spirit goes immediately to heaven or hell. Through the hold this doctrine has upon them, the way is prepared for the delusive working of the prince of the power of the air. . . .

As the Spirit of God shall be withdrawn from the earth, Satan's power will be more and more manifest. The knowledge that he had through being in connection with God as a covering cherub, he will now use to subordinate his subjects who fell from their high estate. He will use every power of his exalted intellect to misrepresent God and to instigate rebellion against Jesus Christ, the Commander of heaven. In the synagogue of Satan he brings under his scepter and into his counsels those agents whom he can use to promote his worship. It is not a strange matter to find a species of refinement and a manifestation of intellectual greatness in the lives and characters of those who are inspired by fallen angels. Satan can impart scientific knowledge and give people chapters upon philosophy. He is conversant with history and versed in worldly wisdom. . . .

Satan will use his agencies to carry out diabolical devices to overpower the saints of God, . . . yet the people of God can look calmly at the whole array of evil and come to the triumphant conclusion that because Christ lives, we shall live also. . . . The confederacy of evil will finally be destroyed.—*Signs of the Times,* May 28, 1894.

Be on Guard

Watch therefore, for you do not know what hour your Lord is coming.
Matt. 24:42.

The condition of society today is the same as when God presented before Israel the abominations of the heathen, and the same warnings are necessary to the remnant people. Spiritualism is advancing through the land in triumph. "The spirits of devils, working miracles" are going "forth unto the kings of the earth and of the whole world, to gather them to the battle of that great day of God Almighty." Men and women are seeking unto them that have familiar spirits, but the people of God cannot in any sense follow the practices of the world. They must keep the commandments of the Lord. The line of separation must be distinctly marked between the obedient and the disobedient. There must be open and avowed enmity between the church and the serpent, between her seed and his seed.

Satan was determined to keep his hold on the land of Canaan, and when it was made the habitation of the children of Israel and the law of God was made the law of the land, he hated Israel with a cruel and malignant hatred and plotted their destruction. Strange gods were introduced through the agency of evil spirits, and because of transgression the chosen people were finally scattered from the land of promise.

The same experience is repeating in the history of God's people. . . .

It is time to heed the Savior's injunction as never before, "Watch ye and pray, lest ye enter into temptation." Trust in God, however perplexing may be your situation. Seek His counsel, and turn not after them that have familiar spirits to be defiled by them. He who has died to redeem you has promised to guide you and clothe you with His own righteousness, if you will but loathe sin and purge yourself from evil by washing your robes of character and making them white in the blood of the Lamb.

What love, what wonderful love, that God bears with the perversity of His people and sends help to every soul that desires to do His will and forsake sin! If we will but cooperate with the agencies of heaven, we may come off more than conquerors. Fallen creatures as we are, capable of the most revolting crimes, yet we may become victors through the power of the grace of Christ and have a place in His everlasting kingdom, to reign with Him forevermore.—*Signs of the Times,* Aug. 26, 1889.

Final Preparation

Therefore you also be ready, for the Son of Man is coming at an hour you do not expect. Matt. 24:44.

To us has been given the message of Christ's soon coming. At the ascension of our Lord, angels stood beside the disciples and with them watched the Savior as He passed into the heavens. Then they turned to the disciples with the words, "This same Jesus, which is taken up from you into heaven, shall so come in like manner as ye have seen him go into heaven." . . .

Only the covering which Christ Himself has provided can make us meet [fit] to appear in God's presence. This covering, the robe of His own righteousness, Christ will put upon every repenting, believing soul. . . .

This robe, woven in the loom of heaven, has in it not one thread of human devising. Christ in His humanity wrought out a perfect character, and this character He offers to impart to us. "All our righteousnesses are as filthy rags." Everything that we of ourselves can do is defiled by sin. . . .

By His perfect obedience, He has made it possible for every human being to obey God's commandments. When we submit ourselves to Christ, the heart is united with His heart; the will is merged in His will; the mind becomes one with His mind; the thoughts are brought into captivity to Him; we live His life. This is what it means to be clothed with the garment of His righteousness. Then, as the Lord looks upon us, He sees, not the fig-leaf garment, not the nakedness and deformity of sin, but His own robe of righteousness, which is perfect obedience to the law of Jehovah. . . .

There will be no second probation in which to prepare for eternity. It is in this life that we are to put on the robe of Christ's righteousness. This is our only opportunity to form characters for the home which Christ has made ready for those who obey His commandments.

The days of our probation are fast closing. The end is near. Solemnly there come down to us through the centuries the warning words of our Lord from the Mount of Olives, "Take heed to yourselves, lest . . . that day come upon you unawares." . . . "Watch ye therefore, and pray always, that ye may be accounted worthy to escape all these things that shall come to pass, and to stand before the Son of man."—*Signs of the Times,* Nov. 22, 1905.

Nearness of the End

At that time Michael shall stand up, . . . and there shall be a time of trouble, such as never was since there was a nation, even to that time. Dan. 12:1.

Troublous times are right upon us. The fulfilling of the signs of the times gives evidence that the day of the Lord is near at hand. The daily papers are full of indications of a terrible conflict in the future. Bold robberies are of frequent occurrence. Strikes are common. Thefts and murders are committed on every hand. Men possessed of demons are taking the lives of men and women and little children. All these things testify that the coming of Christ is near at hand.

The doctrine that men and women are released from obedience to God's requirements has weakened the force of moral obligation and opened the floodgates of iniquity upon the world. . . .

Courts of justice are corrupt. Rulers are actuated by a desire for gain and love of sensual pleasure. Intemperance has beclouded the faculties of many, so that Satan has almost complete control of them. Jurists are perverted, bribed, deluded. Drunkenness and revelry, passion, envy, dishonesty of every sort, are represented among those who administer the laws. "Justice standeth afar off: for truth is fallen in the street, and equity cannot enter." People are rushing on in the mad race for gain and selfish indulgence as if there were no God, no heaven, and no hereafter. . . .

The "time of trouble, such as never was," is soon to open upon us, and we shall need an experience which many are too indolent to obtain. It is often the case that trouble is greater in anticipation than in reality, but this is not true of the crisis before us. The most vivid presentation cannot reach the magnitude of the ordeal. In that trial all must stand for themselves before God. . . .

Now, while our great High Priest is making the atonement for us, we should seek to become perfect in Christ. Not even by a thought could our Savior be brought to yield to the power of temptation. Satan finds in human hearts some point where he can gain a foothold; some sinful desire is cherished, by means of which his temptations assert their power. But Christ declared of Himself, "The prince of this world cometh, and hath nothing in me." Satan could find nothing in the Son of God that would enable him to gain the victory. He had kept His Father's commandments, and there was no sin in Him that Satan could use to his advantage. This is the condition in which those must be found who shall stand in the time of trouble.—*Review and Herald,* Mar. 14, 1912.

Fasten Your Eyes on the Future

And God will wipe away every tear from their eyes; there shall be no more death, nor sorrow, nor crying. There shall be no more pain, for the former things have passed away. Rev. 21:4.

In the darkest days of her long conflict with evil, the church of the living God has been given revelations of the eternal purpose of Jehovah. His people have been permitted to look beyond the trials of the present to the triumphs of the future, when, the warfare having been accomplished, the redeemed will enter into possession of the Promised Land. These visions of future glory, scenes pictured by the hand of God, should be dear to His church today, when the controversy of the ages is rapidly closing and the promised blessings are soon to be realized in all their fullness. . . .

Often the church militant is called upon to suffer trial and affliction, for not without severe conflict is the church to triumph. "The bread of adversity, and the water of affliction." are the common lot of all; but none who put their trust in the One mighty to deliver will be utterly overwhelmed. . . .

Clad in the armor of Christ's righteousness, the church is to enter upon her final conflict. "Fair as the moon, clear as the sun, and terrible as an army with banners," she is to go forth into all the world, conquering and to conquer.

The darkest hour of the church's struggle with the powers of evil is that which immediately precedes the day of her final deliverance. But none who trust in God need fear. . . .

To us who are standing on the very verge of their fulfillment, of what deep moment, what living interest, are these delineations of the things to come—events for which, since our first parents turned their steps from Eden, God's children have watched and waited, longed and prayed! . . .

The nations of the saved will know no other law than the law of heaven. All will be a happy, united family, clothed with the garments of praise and thanksgiving. Over the scene the morning stars will sing together and the sons of God will shout for joy, while God and Christ will unite in proclaiming, There shall be no more sin; neither shall there be any more death.—*Review and Herald,* July 1, 1915.

A Divine Command

Watch therefore, and pray always. Luke 21:36.

In the solemn language of this scripture, a duty is pointed out which lies in the daily pathway of everyone, whether old or young. This is the duty of watchfulness, and upon our faithfulness here our destiny for time and for eternity depends.

We are living in an important time. When in 1844 the message was proclaimed, "Fear God, and give glory to him; for the hour of his judgment is come," that announcement stirred every soul to its very depths. A deep solemnity rested upon all who heard it. How earnest we were to show our faith by our works and to have our words and actions make a favorable impression on the world. . . .

Today angels are watching the development of character, and soon our lives will have to pass in review before God. Soon we shall be weighed in the balances of the sanctuary, and over against our names will be recorded the judgment rendered. And we shall receive the crowning gift of eternal life or be punished with everlasting destruction from the presence of the Lord. We may be unwilling to examine ourselves closely now to see what our spiritual condition is and whether our hearts are being suitably impressed by the testing message of truth; but that will not make any difference with the work of the judgment. Its decisions will be rendered just the same. . . .

"Watch ye therefore, and pray always." There is great need of watchfulness, not for our own sakes only, but also for the sake of our influence upon others. Our influence is far-reaching. We may think that it is confined to our own households; that only the members of our own families know what we are and what we are doing. In some cases this may seem to be true; but in some way the influence of the home life goes out beyond the home. . . .

If we would share in the glorious reward promised to the overcomer, we must fight the good fight of faith. This is what the apostle Paul did, and he says, "Henceforth there is laid up for me a crown of righteousness, which the Lord, the righteous judge, shall give me at that day." Let us be of the number of those that are "rich in good works," "laying up in store for themselves a good foundation against the time to come, that they may lay hold on eternal life."—*Signs of the Times*, Jan. 7, 1886.

The Chosen of God

For you are a holy people to the Lord your God; the Lord your God has chosen you to be a people for Himself, a special treasure above all the peoples on the face of the earth. Deut. 7:6.

These words were spoken by Christ when enshrouded in the pillar of cloud and were given to Moses for the chosen people of God. The Lord has not left the world without witness. He has His loyal, chosen people. They do not make this world their home, but they are here to witness for God, and as long as probation lasts, a living witness will be borne by these faithful messengers. . . .

By the mighty cleaver of truth, God has separated a people from the quarry of the world and brought them into His workshop. Here the Master Worker can successfully hew them with ax and chisel, and polish them for a place in His kingdom. No longer are they like the mass from which they were taken. They stand like noble pillars, to be used for God's glory.

The future glory of the adopted sons and daughters of God is not now discerned. By the world God's people are scorned and despised. But they have the sympathies of a better world than this, even a heavenly. . . .

The Word of God, just as it reads, is the ground of our faith. That Word is the sure word of prophecy, and it demands implicit faith from all who claim to believe it. It is authoritative, containing in itself the proof of its divine origin. . . .

What are we who claim to be one with Christ? "We are labourers together with God." Between the true believer and the unbeliever there will ever be the same conflict that there was between Christ and those who rejected Him. Those who are partakers with Christ in His sufferings will also be partakers with Him in His glory. But those who evade the cross here deny Him who has bought them at an infinite price, and in the day of judgment they will be denied. Many, many, are misrepresenting and denying Christ by their low standard of Christianity. Those who truly believe in Christ will show their faith by a well-ordered life and godly conversation. By working in Christ's lines, they will show that they have been adopted into the family of heaven. Of all such God says, "I will dwell in the high and holy place, with him also that is of a contrite and humble spirit, to revive the spirit of the humble, and to revive the heart of the contrite ones."—*Signs of the Times,* June 2, 1898.

A Peculiar People

Who gave Himself for us, that He might . . . purify for Himself His own special people, zealous for good works. Titus 2:14.

The Lord hath set apart them that are godly for Himself, and this consecration to God and separation from the world are plainly declared and positively enjoined in both the Old and New Testaments. There is a wall of separation which the Lord Himself has established between the things of the world and the things He has chosen out of the world and sanctified unto Himself. The calling and the character of God's people are peculiar. Their prospects are peculiar, and these peculiarities distinguish them from all people. All of God's people upon the earth are one body, from the beginning to the end of time. They have one Head that directs and governs the body. The same injunctions rest upon God's people now, to be separate from the world, as rested upon ancient Israel. The great Head of the church has not changed. The experience of Christians in these days is much like the travels of ancient Israel. . . .

As we read the Word of God, how plain that God's people are peculiar and distinct from the unbelieving world around them. Our position is interesting and fearful; living in the last days, how important that we imitate the example of Christ and walk even as He walked. . . .

The servants of Christ have not their home or their treasure here. Would that all of them could understand that it is only because the Lord reigns that we are even permitted to dwell in peace and safety among our enemies. It is not our privilege to claim special favors of the world. We must consent to be poor and despised in this world until the warfare is finished and the victory won. The members of Christ are called to come out and be separate from the friendship and spirit of the world, and their strength and power consist in their being chosen and accepted of God. . . .

Even so the members of Christ are as He was in this world. They are the sons and daughters of God and joint heirs with Christ, and the kingdom and dominion belong to them. The world understand not their character and holy calling. They perceive not their adoption into the family of God. Their union and fellowship with the Father and the Son are not manifest to the world, and while they behold their humiliation and reproach, it does not appear what they shall be. They are strangers. The world knows them not and appreciates not the motives which actuate them.—*Review and Herald,* July 5, 1875.

Separation From the World

You shall be My sons and daughters, says the Lord Almighty. 2 Cor. 6:18.

I have been bidden to call the attention of our people to the instruction given by the Lord to Israel regarding the importance of separation from the world. . . .

Under David's rule, the people of Israel gained strength and uprightness through obedience to God's law. But the kings that followed strove for self-exaltation. . . .

God bore long with them, calling them often to repentance. But they refused to hear, and at last God spoke in judgment, showing them how weak they were without Him. He saw that they were determined to have their own way, and He gave them into the hands of their enemies. . . .

The alliances made by the Israelites with their heathen neighbors resulted in the loss of their identity as God's peculiar people. They became leavened by the evil practices of those with whom they formed forbidden alliances. Affiliation with worldlings caused them to lose their first love and their zeal for God's service. The advantages they sold themselves to gain brought only disappointment and caused the loss of many souls.

The experience of Israel will be the experience of all who go to the world for strength, turning away from the living God. Those who forsake the mighty One, the source of all strength, and affiliate with worldlings, placing on them their dependence, become weak in moral power, as are those in whom they trust.

God comes with entreaties and assurances to those who are making mistakes. He seeks to show them their error and lead them to repentance. But if they refuse to humble their hearts before Him, if they strive to exalt themselves above Him, He must speak to them in judgment. No semblance of nearness to God, no assertion of connection with Him, will be accepted from those who persist in dishonoring Him by leaning upon the arm of worldly power.

Today God's word to His people is: "Come out from among them, and be ye separate, . . . and touch not the unclean thing; and I will receive you, and will be a Father unto you, and ye shall be my sons and daughters." . . .

God's people are to be distinguished as a people who serve Him fully, wholeheartedly, taking no honor to themselves, and remembering that by a most solemn covenant they have bound themselves to serve the Lord, and Him only.—*Review and Herald*, Aug. 4, 1904.

God's People Identified

Hallow My Sabbaths, and they will be a sign between Me and you, that you may know that I am the Lord your God. Eze. 20:20.

The Lord spake unto Moses, saying, Speak thou also unto the children of Israel, saying, Verily my sabbaths ye shall keep: for it is a sign between me and you throughout your generations; that ye may know that I am the Lord that doth sanctify you." . . .

Do not these words point us out as God's denominated people? And do they not declare to us that so long as time shall last we are to cherish the sacred, denominational distinction placed on us? . . . The Sabbath has lost none of its meaning. It is still the sign between God and His people, and it will be so forever. . . .

God is testing His people to see who will be loyal to the principles of His truth. Our work is to proclaim to the world the first, second, and third angels' messages. In the discharge of our duty, we are neither to despise nor fear our enemies. To bind ourselves up by contracts or in partnerships or business associations with those not of our faith is not in the order of God. We are to treat with kindness and courtesy those who refuse to be loyal to God, but we are never, never to unite with them in counsel regarding the vital interests of His work. . . .

Putting our trust in God, we are to move steadily forward, doing His work with unselfishness, . . . committing ourselves and our present and future to His wise providence, holding the beginning of our confidence firm unto the end, remembering that it is not because of our worthiness that we receive the blessings of heaven, but because of the worthiness of Christ and our acceptance, through faith in Him, of God's abounding grace.

I pray that my brethren may realize that the third angel's message means much to us, and that the observance of the true Sabbath is to be the sign that distinguishes those who serve God from those who serve Him not. . . . We are called to be holy, and we should carefully avoid giving the impression that it is of little consequence whether or not we retain the peculiar features of our faith. Upon us rests the solemn obligation of taking a more decided stand for truth and righteousness than we have taken in the past. The line of demarcation between those who keep the commandments of God and those who do not is to be revealed with unmistakable clearness.—*Review and Herald,* Aug. 4, 1904.

Christ's Representatives

And we are His witnesses to these things, and so also is the Holy Spirit whom God has given to those who obey Him. Acts 5:32.

True Christians will be Christlike. The Redeemer clothed His divinity with humanity and came to our world—a world seared and marred by the curse of sin, a vale of darkness and woe—to accomplish a great work, as He announced in the synagogue of Nazareth: "The Spirit of the Lord is upon me, because he hath anointed me to preach the gospel to the poor." . . .

Each church member is to be a representative of the character and spirit of Christ. By precept and example the essential elements of a true, healthy, influential Christianity are to be revealed. Christ should be constantly set forth as the fountain of life, mercy, and love. . . .

By beholding we become changed. Through close study and earnest contemplation of the character of Christ, His image is reflected in our own lives, and a higher tone is imparted to the spirituality of the church. If the truth of God has not transformed our characters into the likeness of Christ, all our professed knowledge of Him and the truth is but as sounding brass and a tinkling cymbal. . . .

Let all who claim to keep the commandments of God look well to this matter and see if there are not reasons why they do not have more of the outpouring of the Holy Spirit. How many have lifted up their souls unto vanity! They think themselves exalted in the favor of God, but they neglect the needy, they turn a deaf ear to the calls of the oppressed, and speak sharp, cutting words to those who need altogether different treatment. Thus they offend God daily by their hardness of heart. These afflicted ones have claims upon the sympathies and the interest of their fellow human beings. They have a right to expect help, comfort, and Christlike love. But this is not what they receive. Every neglect of God's suffering ones is written in the books of heaven as if shown to Christ Himself. Let all members of the church closely examine their heart and investigate their course of action to see if these are in harmony with the spirit and work of Jesus; for if not, what can they say when they stand before the Judge of all the earth? Can the Lord say to them, "Come, ye blessed of my Father, inherit the kingdom prepared for you from the foundation of the world?"—*Review and Herald,* Apr. 24, 1913.

Working With Christ

For God is not unjust to forget your work and labor of love which you have shown toward His name, in that you have ministered to the saints, and do minister. Heb. 6:10.

Christ has identified His interest with that of suffering humanity; and while He is neglected in the person of His afflicted ones, all our assemblies, all our appointed meetings, all the machinery that is set in operation to advance the cause of God, will be of little avail. . . .

All who are to be saints in heaven will first be saints upon the earth. They will not follow the sparks of their own kindling, they will not work for praise nor speak words of vanity, nor put forth the finger in condemnation and oppression; but they will follow the light of Life, diffuse light, comfort, hope, and courage to the very ones who need help, and not censure and reproach. . . .

The rich, clear light that has been shining upon our pathway has placed us on vantage ground, and we should improve every opportunity to do good. Christ came from the royal courts of heaven to seek and save the lost, and this is to be our work. The zeal which we manifest in this direction will show the measure of our love for Jesus and for others, [the measure] of our efficiency and missionary spirit.

To every member of the church is committed a work, and their sanctification will be seen in the efficiency, the unselfishness, the zeal and purity and intelligence, with which they do the work. The cause of humanity and religion must not retrograde. Progress is expected of those who have received great light and have many advantages.

The church must be a working church if it would be a living church. It should not be content merely to hold its own against the opposing forces of sin and error, not be content to advance with dilatory step, but it should bear the yoke of Christ and keep step with the Leader, gaining new recruits along the way.

When we are truly Christ's, our hearts will be full of meekness, gentleness, and kindness, because Jesus has forgiven our sins. As obedient children we shall receive and cherish the precepts He has given and shall attend to the ordinances He has instituted. We shall be seeking constantly to obtain a knowledge of Him.—*Review and Herald,* May 1, 1913.

The Church to Advance God's Work

Do the work of an evangelist, fulfill your ministry. 2 Tim. 4:5.

Those who are Christ's disciples will take the work where He left it and carry it forward in His name. They will copy the words, the spirit, the practices, of none but Him. Their eye is upon the Captain of their salvation. His will is their law. And as they advance, they catch more and clearer views of His countenance, of His character, of His glory. They do not cling to self, but hold fast His word, which is spirit and life. "If ye continue in my word, then are ye my disciples indeed; and ye shall know the truth, and the truth shall make you free." They reduce their knowledge of His will to practice. They hear and do the things that Jesus teaches.

In the church is work for all who love God and keep His commandments. The profession people may make is not certain evidence that they are Christians. The words they may speak give no surety that they are converted. Hear the words of Christ, "Why call ye me, Lord, Lord, and do not the things which I say?" Unless the daily life conforms to the will and works of Christ, no one can establish a claim to be a child of God, an heir of heaven. There is a legal religion, which the Pharisees had, but such a religion does not give to the world a Christlike example; it does not represent Christ's character. Those who have Christ abiding in the heart will work the works of Christ. Such are entitled to all the promises of His Word. Becoming one with Christ, they do the will of God and exhibit the riches of His grace. "Then shalt thou call, and the Lord shall answer; thou shalt cry, and he shall say, Here I am." Oh, precious promise! "And if thou draw out thy soul to the hungry, and satisfy the afflicted soul; then shall thy light rise in obscurity, and thy darkness be as the noon day: and the Lord shall guide thee continually, and satisfy thy soul in drought, and make fat thy bones: and thou shalt be like a watered garden, and like a spring of water, whose waters fail not."

In marked contrast to the murmuring and complaining of the wicked, the servants of God will sing: "I will praise thee with my whole heart. . . . Though the Lord be high, yet hath he respect unto the lowly: but the proud he knoweth afar off." Then let not a semblance of pride or self-importance be cherished, for it will crowd Jesus out of the heart, and the vacuum will be filled with the attributes of Satan.—*Review and Herald, May 1, 1913.*

An Enlightened Church

And that from childhood you have known the Holy Scriptures, which are able to make you wise for salvation through faith which is in Christ Jesus. 2 Tim. 3:15.

The Lord cannot use men and women in His service, in any branch of His work, unless they possess a meek and teachable spirit. Those whom God employs in His service must be true to principle, but, while they must not swerve from the plain path of duty for any selfish interest, they are not to be bigoted and puffed up with self-esteem. Unless the heart is in connection with the Source of all wisdom, there will not be an abiding sense of the sacredness of the work. Workers for Christ must derive all their life and inspiration from God. They must seek to be conformed to His will and His ways and not seek to have their own will and way. Those who would become a living channel of light must be governed by something more than habit or opinion. They must live hourly in conscious communion with God. Their lives must be brought into contact with the principles of truth and righteousness. They must become partakers of divine nature.

The servant of God must be continually seeking for intellectual power, and every acquisition of the mind must be devoted to glorifying God. We must have enlarged conceptions of what the requirement of God is of His people. . . .

We must not be content with anything short of the divine illumination from the central Light of the universe. When we have this illumination, we shall see the necessity of pressing onward and upward, of elevating the standard, of cultivating the loftiest ambition, and of reaching the highest attainments. We shall constantly draw from the Source of all wisdom and live as in the sight of the Lord. . . .

Your talent has been entrusted to you by the Lord, and you will be held responsible for its employment and improvement. . . . We must manifest the glory of God. This is the high aim of our existence. We must be in such a condition that we can appreciate the light that God has brought into the experience of others. Our lives and characters are influenced by the physical, intellectual, and moral acquirements of past generations. If we remain in ignorance, we have no one to blame but ourselves. If we put to the stretch every power, and task every ability to the utmost, with an eye single to the glory of God, we shall not fail of doing a valuable work for God.— *Signs of the Times,* Nov. 30, 1888.

Someone Is at the Door

Behold, I stand at the door and knock. Rev. 3:20.

The time in which we live is full of the most solemn importance. There is nothing that can be more acceptable to God than to have the youth dedicate their lives to His service in the bloom and freshness of their years. Their talents may become a power for God when they are properly culti-vated. Their characters may be characters that will be acceptable to Heaven, but they must be shaped by line upon line and precept upon precept. They must be modeled after the divine pattern. . . .

In the work of saving souls, we are to know whereof we speak. The words of John are full of significance when he says, "That which we have seen and heard declare we unto you." . . .

When your soul is the temple for the indwelling Spirit of the Savior, the gross elements of your nature will be consumed, and the whole being will become a living purpose. Whoever is truly Christ's will have an experience like that of Daniel, and the fruits of the Spirit will appear in the life. There are powers within us that are paralyzed through sin, that need the vivifying influence of the grace of Christ, that they may be restored. A mighty power from the Life Giver must quicken them to life and rouse them to action. When this is your experience, you can work as Jesus has given you an ex-ample. Divine light and love will be reflected upon those who feel that they are sick in both soul and body. Jesus invites His own presence to your soul. He says, "Behold, I stand at the door, and knock: if any man hear my voice, and open the door, I will come in to him, and sup with him, and he with me." Shall we not open the door of our hearts to the divine Guest?

Those who engage in the work of God must be pure in heart and cir-cumspect in deportment. The souls of God's people should not be like a barren waste, as are so many souls at this time. God has given to everyone some ability to use in His service, and it is God's design that it should be employed to His glory and the good of others. Many are losing much, sim-ply because they will not learn in the school of Christ. They might gain eternal treasure, but, in turning away from the divine Teacher, their con-sciences are violated and seared, and the admonitions of God's Word lose all power to stir their hearts. But there is no need of making such a failure. Christ will come into the heart and abide there if you will but cleanse the soul temple of every defilement.—*Signs of the Times,* Nov. 30, 1888.

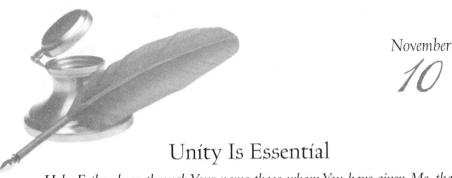

Unity Is Essential

Holy Father, keep through Your name those whom You have given Me, that they may be one as We are. John 17:11.

The Holy Spirit will work with the consecrated human instrument, for this is God's purpose. God has opened a door between heaven and earth which no power can close. . . . When God's people place themselves in proper relation to Him and to one another, there will be a full impartation of the Holy Spirit for the harmonious combination of the whole body.

Nothing so manifestly weakens a church as disunion and strife. Nothing so wars against Christ and the truth as this spirit. . . .

We can be united with one another only as we are united with Christ. . . . Many who have dwelt much upon doctrinal subjects, but who have not learned of Christ, have been found unable to control themselves. They need the Holy Spirit's power. We should seek to understand what it means to be in complete union with Christ, who is the propitiation for our sins and for the sins of the whole world. Our life should be bound up with His life. . . .

When God's chosen people are of one mind, barriers of selfishness will disappear as by magic, and many, many more souls will be converted because of the unity which exists among believers. There is one body and one spirit. Those who have been building territorial lines of distinction, barriers of color and caste, might better take these down much faster than they put them up.

Those in whose hearts Christ abides recognize Christ abiding in the hearts of others. Christ never wars against Christ. Christ never exerts an influence against Christ. Christians are to do their work, whatever it may be, in the unity of the Spirit, for the perfecting of the whole body. The church is to be purified, refined, ennobled. The members are to cast from their hearts the idols which have hindered their advancement in spirituality. By the influence of the Spirit, the most discordant may be brought into harmony. Unselfishness is to bind God's people together with firm, tender bonds. There is a vast power in the church when the energies of the members are under the control of the Spirit, gathering good from every source, educating, training, and disciplining self. Thus is presented to God a powerful organization through which He can work for the conversion of sinners. Thus heaven and earth are connected, and all the divine agencies cooperate with human instrumentalities.—*Signs of the Times,* Feb. 7, 1900.

A Challenge to God's Church

Then I saw another beast coming up out of the earth, and he had two horns like a lamb and spoke like a dragon. Rev. 13:11.

To the apostle John on the Isle of Patmos were opened scenes of deep and thrilling interest in the experience of the church. Subjects of intense interest and vast importance were presented to him in figures and symbols, that the people of God might become intelligent concerning the perils and conflicts before them. . . .

Under the symbols of a great red dragon, a leopardlike beast, and a beast with lamblike horns, the earthly governments which would especially engage in trampling upon God's law and persecuting His people were presented to John. The war is carried on till the close of time. The people of God, symbolized by a holy woman and her children, were represented as greatly in the minority. In the last days only a remnant still existed. . . .

Through paganism, and then through the Papacy, Satan exerted his power for many centuries in an effort to blot from the earth God's faithful witnesses. Pagans and papists were actuated by the same dragon spirit. They differed only in that the Papacy, making a pretense of serving God, was the more dangerous and cruel foe. Through the agency of Romanism, Satan took the world captive. The professed church of God was swept into the ranks of this delusion, and for more than a thousand years the people of God suffered under the dragon's ire.

And when the Papacy, robbed of its strength, was forced to desist from persecution, John beheld a new power coming up to echo the dragon's voice and carry forward the same cruel and blasphemous work. This power, the last that is to wage war against the church and the law of God, was symbolized by a beast with lamblike horns. The beasts preceding it had risen from the sea, but this came up out of the earth, representing the peaceful rise of the nation which is symbolized. The "two horns like a lamb" well represent the character of the United States Government as expressed in its two fundamental principles, Republicanism and Protestantism. These principles are the secret of our power and prosperity as a nation. Those who first found asylum on the shores of America rejoiced that they had reached a country free from the arrogant claims of popery and the tyranny of kingly rule. They determined to establish a government upon the broad foundation of civil and religious liberty.— *Signs of the Times,* Nov. 1, 1899.

God's Final Warning

If anyone worships the beast and his image, . . . he himself shall also drink of the wine of the wrath of God. Rev. 14:9, 10.

But the stern tracing of the prophetic pencil reveals a change in this peaceful scene [civil and religious liberty]. The beast with lamblike horns speaks with the voice of a dragon, and "exerciseth all the power of the first beast before him." Prophecy declares that he will say to them that dwell on the earth that they should make an image to the beast, and that "he causeth all, both small and great, rich and poor, free and bond, to receive a mark in their right hand, or in their foreheads: and that no man might buy or sell, save he that had the mark, or the name of the beast, or the number of his name." Thus Protestantism follows in the steps of the Papacy.

It is at this time that the third angel is seen flying in the midst of heaven, proclaiming: "If any man worship the beast and his image, and receive his mark in his forehead, or in his hand, the same shall drink of the wine of the wrath of God, which is poured out without mixture into the cup of his indignation." "Here are they that keep the commandments of God, and the faith of Jesus." In marked contrast to the world stands the little company who will not swerve from their allegiance to God. . . .

The most solemn warning and the most awful threatening ever addressed to mortals is that contained in the third angel's message. The sin that calls down the wrath of God unmixed with mercy must be of the most heinous character. Is the world to be left in darkness as to the nature of this sin? Most assuredly not. God does not deal thus with His creatures. His wrath is never visited upon sins of ignorance. Before His judgments are brought upon the earth, the light in regard to this sin must be presented to the world, that all may know why these judgments are to be inflicted and may have opportunity to escape them.

The message containing this warning is the last to be proclaimed before the revelation of the Son of man. The signs which He Himself has given declare His coming to be near at hand. For well-nigh forty years [as of 1899] has the message of the third angel been sounding. . . . The time has come when all who have an interest in their soul's salvation should earnestly and solemnly inquire, What is the seal of God? and what is the mark of the beast? How can we avoid receiving it?—*Signs of the Times*, Nov. 1, 1899.

Seal of God and Mark of the Beast

Do not harm the earth, the sea, or the trees till we have sealed the servants of our God on their foreheads. Rev. 7:3.

The seal of God, the token or sign of His authority, is found in the fourth commandment. This is the only precept of the Decalogue that points to God as the Creator of the heavens and the earth, and clearly distinguishes the true God from all false gods. Throughout the Scriptures the fact of God's creative power is cited as proof that He is above all heathen deities.

The Sabbath enjoined by the fourth commandment was instituted to commemorate the work of Creation, thus to keep the minds of all ever directed to the true and living God. Had the Sabbath always been kept, there would never have been an idolater, an atheist, or an infidel. The sacred observance of God's holy day would have led the minds of men and women to their Creator. The things of nature would have brought Him to their remembrance, and they would have borne witness to His power and His love. The Sabbath of the fourth commandment is the seal of the living God. It points to God as the Creator and is the sign of His rightful authority over the beings He has made.

What, then, is the mark of the beast, if it is not the spurious sabbath which the world has accepted in the place of the true?

The prophetic declaration that the Papacy was to exalt itself above all that is called God, or that is worshipped, has been strikingly fulfilled in the changing of the Sabbath from the seventh to the first day of the week. Wherever the papal sabbath is honored in preference of the Sabbath of God, there the man of sin is exalted above the Creator of heaven and earth.

Those who assert that Christ changed the sabbath are directly contradicting His own words. In the Sermon on the Mount He declared, "Think not that I am come to destroy the law, or the prophets: I am not come to destroy, but to fulfil." . . .

Roman Catholics acknowledge that the change in the Sabbath was made by their church, and they cite this very change as evidence of the supreme authority of this church. They declare that by observing the first day of the week as the Sabbath, Protestants are recognizing her power to legislate in divine things. . . . As the Sunday institution gains favor, he [the papist] rejoices, feeling assured that it will eventually bring the whole Protestant world under the banner of Rome.—*Signs of the Times,* Nov. 1, 1899.

Image to the Beast

Telling those who dwell on the earth to make an image to the beast who was wounded by the sword and lived. Rev. 13:14.

The change of the Sabbath is a sign or mark of the authority of the Romish Church. Those who, understanding the claims of the fourth commandment, choose to observe the false sabbath in the place of the true are thereby paying homage to that power by which alone it is commanded. . . .

There are true Christians in every church, not excepting the Roman Catholic communion. None are condemned until they have had the light and have seen the obligation of the fourth commandment. But when the decree shall go forth enforcing the counterfeit sabbath, and the loud cry of "the third angel" shall warn the world against the worship of the beast and his image, the line will be clearly drawn between the false and the true. Then those who still continue in transgression will receive the mark of the beast.

With rapid steps we are approaching this period. When Protestant churches shall unite with the secular power in sustaining a false religion, for opposing which their ancestors endured the fiercest persecution, then will the papal sabbath be enforced by the combined authority of church and state. There will be a national apostasy which will end only in national ruin. . . .

By compromises and concessions, Protestants have tampered with and patronized popery, giving her vantage ground which papists themselves are surprised to see and fail to understand. The Protestant world needs to be aroused to resist the advances of this most dangerous foe to civil and religious liberty.

When the state shall enforce the decrees and sustain the institutions of the church, then will Protestant America have formed an image of the Papacy. Then the true church will be assailed by persecution as were God's people in ancient times. Almost every century furnishes instances of what human hearts, controlled by rage and malice, can do under a plea of serving God by protecting the rights of the church and state. The Protestant churches that have followed in the steps of Rome by forming alliances with worldly powers have manifested a similar desire to restrict liberty of conscience. How many nonconformist ministers have suffered under the power of the Church of England! Persecution always follows a restriction of religious liberty on the part of secular governments.—*Signs of the Times,* Nov. 8, 1899.

History Repeats Itself

For the time will come when they will not endure sound doctrine, but according to their own desires, because they have itching ears, they will heap up for themselves teachers. 2 Tim. 4:3.

It is urged by many that the intellectual and moral darkness prevailing during the Middle Ages favored the spread of dogma, superstition, and the oppression of popery, and that the general diffusion of knowledge and the well-nigh universal acceptance of the principles of religious liberty forbid a revival of superstition and tyranny. It is true that great light, intellectual, moral, and religious, is shining upon this generation. Since 1844 light from the heaven of heavens has beamed from the open door of the temple of God. But it is to be remembered that the greater the light bestowed, the greater the delusion and darkness of those who reject the Word of God and accept fables, teaching for doctrine the commandments of men.

Satan will excite the indignation of apostate Christendom against the humble remnant who conscientiously refuse to accept false customs and traditions. Blinded by the prince of darkness, popular religionists will see only as he sees and feel as he feels. . . . Liberty of conscience, which has cost so great a sacrifice, will no longer be respected. The church and the world will unite, and the world will lend to the church power to crush out the right of the people to worship God according to His Word.

The decree which is to go forth against the people of God in the near future is in some respects similar to that issued by Ahasuerus against the Jews in the time of Esther. The Persian edict sprang from the malice of Haman against Mordecai. Not that Mordecai had done Haman harm, but he had refused to flatter his vanity by showing him the reverence which is due only to God. . . .

History repeats itself. The same masterful mind that plotted against the faithful in ages past is now at work to gain control of the Protestant churches, that through them he may condemn and put to death all who will not worship the idol sabbath. We have not to battle with mere mortals, as it may appear. We wrestle not against flesh and blood, but against principalities, against powers, against the rulers of the darkness of this world, against spiritual wickedness in high places. But if the people of God will put their trust in Him, and by faith rely upon His power, the devices of Satan will be defeated in our time as signally as in the days of Mordecai.— *Signs of the Times,* Nov. 8, 1899.

Victory at Last!

Then I looked, and behold, a Lamb standing on Mount Zion, and with Him one hundred and forty-four thousand, having His Father's name written on their foreheads. Rev. 14:1.

The decree is to go forth that all who will not receive the mark of the beast shall neither buy nor sell and, finally, that they shall be put to death. But the saints of God do not receive this mark. The prophet of Patmos beheld those that had gotten the victory over the beast and over his image and over his mark and over the number of his name, standing on the sea of glass, having the harps of God, and singing the song of Moses and the Lamb.

To every soul will come the searching test, Shall I obey God rather than men? The decisive hour is even now at hand. Satan is putting forth his utmost efforts in the rage of a last despairing struggle against Christ and His followers. False teachers are employing every device possible to stimulate the hardened sinner in his rebellious daring, to confirm the questioning, the doubting, the unbelieving, and, by misrepresentation and falsehood, to deceive, if it were possible, the very elect. Who are prepared to stand firmly under the banner on which is inscribed, "The commandments of God, and the faith of Jesus"?

Christ never purchased peace and friendship by compromise with evil. Though His heart overflowed with love toward the human race, He could not be indulgent to their sins. Because He loved men and women, He was a stern reprover of their vices. His life of suffering, the humiliation to which He was subjected by a perverse nation, show His followers that there must be no sacrifice of principle. God's tried people must maintain watchfulness, with fervent prayer, lest, in their eagerness to prevent discord, they surrender truth and thus dishonor the God of truth. Peace is too dearly obtained if purchased by the smallest concession to Satan's agencies. The least surrender of principle entangles us in the snare of the enemy.

Paul writes to the Romans, "If it be possible, as much as lieth in you, live peaceably with all men." But there is a point beyond which it is impossible to maintain union and harmony without the sacrifice of principle. Separation then becomes an absolute duty. The laws of nations should be respected when they do not conflict with the laws of God. But when there is collision between them, every true disciple of Christ will say, as did the apostle Peter when commanded to speak no more in the name of Jesus, "We ought to obey God rather than men."—*Signs of the Times,* Nov. 8, 1899.

Channels for the Sun of Righteousness

Now then, we are ambassadors for Christ. 2 Cor. 5:20.

The professed church of God may be possessed of wealth, education, and knowledge of doctrine, and may say by her attitude, "I am rich, and increased with goods, and have need of nothing"; but if its members are devoid of inward holiness, they cannot be the light of the world. The church is to reflect light into the moral darkness of the world as the stars reflect light into the darkness of the night. These who have a form of godliness but deny the power thereof do not reflect light into the world and will not have power to reach the hearts of the unsaved. Without vital connection with Christ the value of truth cannot be made to appear in good fruit in the world; but if Christ is formed within, the hope of glory, His saving grace will be manifested in sympathy and love for perishing souls.

Every soul truly converted to God will be a light in the world. Bright, clear rays from the Sun of Righteousness will shine forth through human agents who use their entrusted ability to do good; for they will cooperate with heavenly agencies and labor with Christ for the conversion of souls. They will diffuse the light which Christ sheds upon them. The Sun of Righteousness shining in their hearts will shine forth, enlightening and blessing others.

The rays of heaven shining from human agents will exert a subduing influence upon those whom Christ is drawing to Himself. The church is weak before the angels of heaven unless power is revealed through its members for the conversion of those who are perishing. Unless the church is the light of the world, it is darkness. But of the true followers of Christ it is written, "We are labourers together with God: ye are God's husbandry, ye are God's building."

The church may be composed of those who are poor and uneducated; but if they have learned of Christ the science of prayer, the church will have power to move the arm of Omnipotence. The true people of God will have an influence that will tell upon hearts. It is not the wealth or the educated ability which the members of the church may possess that constitutes their efficiency. . . . It is when the Sun of Righteousness shines forth from the people of God that Christ is glorified and His kingdom advanced. It is then that they are chosen vessels of salvation and are fitted for the Master's use.—*Signs of the Times,* Sept. 11, 1893.

Source of All Truth

I am the way, the truth, and the life. John 14:6.

If the churches established in our world would follow Christ, they would pray as Christ prayed, and the result of their prayers would be seen in the conversion of souls; for when communication is opened up between souls and God, a divine influence is shed upon the world. When the members of the church abide in Christ, they deliver an effective testimony in their lives. They fulfill the words of Christ, "Ye are my witnesses." By their influence all the day long, by precept and example, they say, "Come," "behold the Lamb of God, which taketh away the sin of the world." . . .

Jesus is the fountainhead of knowledge, the treasure-house of truth, and He longed to open before His disciples treasures of infinite value, that they in turn might open them to others. But because of their blindness He could not unfold to them the mysteries of the kingdom of heaven. He said to them, "I have yet many things to say unto you, but ye cannot bear them now." The minds of the disciples were to a great degree influenced by the traditions and maxims of the Pharisees, who placed the commandments of God on a level with their own inventions and doctrines. The scribes and Pharisees did not receive or teach the Scriptures in their original purity, but interpreted the language of the Bible in such a way as to make it express sentiments and injunctions that God had never given. They put a mystical construction upon the writing of the Old Testament and made indistinct that which the infinite God had made clear and plain. These learned men placed before the people their own ideas and made patriarchs and prophets responsible for things they never uttered. These false teachers buried the precious jewels of truth beneath the rubbish of their own interpretations and maxims, and covered up the plainest specifications of prophecy regarding Christ. . . .

When the Author of truth came to our world and was the living interpreter of His own laws, the Scriptures were opened to His hearers like a new revelation; for He taught as one having authority, as one who knew whereof He was speaking. The minds of people were confused with false teaching to such an extent that they could not fully grasp the meaning of divine truth, and yet they were attracted to the great Teacher and said, "Never man spake like this man."—*Signs of the Times,* Sept. 11, 1893.

The Proclamation of God's Remnant

Then I saw another angel flying in the midst of heaven, having the everlasting gospel to preach to those who dwell on the earth. Rev. 14:6.

The fourteenth chapter of Revelation outlines the work that is to be done by the people of God just before the second advent of our Savior. Three messages are there represented, which must go to all the inhabitants of the world.

John writes of an angel which he saw flying "in the midst of heaven, having the everlasting gospel to preach unto them that dwell on the earth, and to every nation, and kindred, and tongue, and people. . . . And there followed another angel, saying, Babylon is fallen, is fallen. . . . And the third angel followed them, saying with a loud voice, If any man worship the beast and his image, and receive his mark in his forehead, or in his hand, the same shall drink of the wine of the wrath of God. . . ."

These three angels represent the people who accept the light of God's messages and go forth as His agents to sound the warning throughout the length and breadth of the earth. Christ declared to His followers, "Ye are the light of the world." To every soul that accepts Jesus, the cross of Calvary speaks: "Behold the worth of the soul. 'Go ye into all the world, and preach the gospel to every creature.' " Nothing is to be permitted to hinder this work. It is the all-important work for this time, and it is to be far-reaching as eternity. . . .

In this day, God has called His church, as He called ancient Israel, to stand as a light in the earth. By the mighty cleaver of truth—the messages of the first, second, and third angels—He has separated a people from the churches and from the world, to bring them into a sacred nearness to Himself. He has made them the depositaries of His law and has committed to them the great truths of prophecy for this time. Like the holy oracles committed to ancient Israel, these are a sacred trust to be communicated to the world. . . .

In the issue of the contest, all Christendom will be divided into two great classes—those who keep the commandments of God and the faith of Jesus, and those who worship the beast and his image and receive his mark. . . . The prophet of Patmos beholds "them that had gotten the victory over the beast, . . . having the harps of God" and singing the "song of Moses the servant of God, and the song of the Lamb."—*Signs of the Times,* Jan. 25, 1910.

The Closing Work

Behold, I am coming quickly, and My reward is with Me. Rev. 22:12.

Look upon the world today. Is the voice of prayer heard amidst the din of confusion? Altars are erected, but it is not to God that the sacrifices are offered. Deceivers, robbers, and murderers are many. Pride of ancestry and pride of wealth minister to the work of soul destruction. Avarice, sensuality, malice—these are the attributes that bear sway. Thousands are standing on the brink of perdition. Do you not see them, many of them lost, eternally lost, whilst professing Christians sleep the sleep of indifference?

Earnest, self-sacrificing men and women are needed, men and women who will go to God, and with strong crying and tears plead for the precious souls that are going to ruin. . . . Christ gave His life to save sinners, and He says to His followers, "Go ye into all the world, and preach the gospel to every creature." "Lo, I am with you alway, even unto the end." He has laid out before us the work to be done and has declared that He will give power for the accomplishment of this work. . . .

The work is fast closing up, and on every side wickedness is increasing. We have but a short time in which to work. God is not willing that any should perish. He has provided abundantly for the salvation of all. If His people had gone forth as they should, giving the invitation of mercy, many souls would have been won to Christ. Let us awake from spiritual slumber and consecrate all that we have and are to the Lord. His Spirit will abide with true missionaries, furnishing them with power for service. God is an overflowing fountain of efficiency and strength. The gospel is the power of God unto salvation to everyone that believes. When this power is utilized, it will be found to be more than sufficient to meet the power of the enemy.

It is impossible for those of us who believe in Christ to see the work that needs to be done and not do anything. Daily the church is to receive from heaven the healing balm of God's grace to impart to the needy and suffering. The church of God is weighted with the most sacred responsibilities and the most glorious privileges. All who believe the message of Christ's soon coming will go forth to do something for the Master. . . . In practical obedience to the divine command, their confidence will increase and their talents will multiply.—*Signs of the Times,* Nov. 28, 1906.

Forgiveness Is Not Impossible

For if you forgive men their trespasses, your heavenly Father
will also forgive you. Matt. 6:14.

Forgive us our debts, as we forgive our debtors," Christ taught us to pray. But it is most difficult even for those who claim to be followers of Jesus to forgive as He forgave us. The true spirit of forgiveness is so little practiced, and so many interpretations are placed upon Christ's requirement, that its force and beauty are lost sight of. We have very uncertain views of the great mercy and loving-kindness of God. He is full of compassion and forgiveness and freely pardons when we truly repent and confess our sins. . . . We must bring into our characters the love and sympathy expressed in Christ's life. . . .

If we have received the gift of God and have a knowledge of Jesus Christ, we have a work to do for others. We must imitate the long-suffering of God toward us. The Lord requires of us the same treatment toward His followers that we receive of Him. We are to exercise patience and to be kind, even though they do not meet our expectations. The Lord expects us to be piti-ful and loving, to have sympathetic hearts. He desires us to show the fruits of the grace of God in our deportment one to another. Christ did not say, You may tolerate your neighbor, but, "Thou shalt love thy neighbour as thyself." This means a great deal more than professing Christians carry out in their daily life. . . .

Christ proceeds to teach that the principles of God's law reach even to the intents and purposes of the mind. And He plainly states that if we faith-fully keep the ten precepts, we shall love our neighbor as ourselves. . . .

A consistent religious life, holy conversation, a godly example, true-hearted benevolence, mark the representatives of Christ. They will labor to pluck sinners as brands from the burning; they will perform every duty faithfully. Thus they will become a beacon light.

Reader, we are nearing the judgment. Talents have been lent us on trust. Let none of us be at last condemned as slothful servants. Send forth the words of life to those in darkness. Let the church be true to her trust. Her earnest, humble prayers will make the presentation of truth effectual, and Christ will be glorified.—*Review and Herald,* May 19, 1910.

Work in the Cities

*On the next Sabbath almost the whole city came together
to hear the word of God. Acts 13:44.*

The message of the third angel of Revelation 14 is now to be proclaimed not only in lands far off, but in neglected places close by, where multitudes dwell unwarned and unsaved. God is calling His people at this time to a long-delayed work. Decided efforts are to be made to enlighten those who have never yet been warned. The work in the cities is now to be regarded as of special importance. Let workers be carefully selected to labor two and two in the cities in harmony with the counsel of experienced leaders and under the direction and commission of Jesus Christ.

God desires His people to labor in perfect harmony in an effort to carry the truth into the cities. I am bidden to keep this matter before the attention of the believers until they shall be aroused to a realization of its importance. Let not ill-advised lips utter words of discouragement, but let everyone in responsibility unite in planning for the accomplishment of this work, knowing that He who has led His servants hitherto will not fail them in this time of special need. Angels of God will go before the workers and will be their sufficiency. Angels will be in the assemblies to make an impression upon the hearts of the hearers. . . .

The labors of the apostles in the early Christian church were characterized by wonderful manifestations of the power of God in the lives of the believers. Through the inspiration of the Holy Spirit, multitudes were brought to a knowledge of the truth as it is in Christ Jesus. The needs of the world today are no less than they were in the days of the apostles. Those who labor for souls in these times of impenitence and unbelief must yield themselves wholly to God, and work in unison with heavenly intelligences. The power of the Holy Spirit will accompany the labors of those who dedicate their energies and their all unreservedly to the completion of the work that must be done in the last days. Angels from heaven will cooperate with them, and many will be brought to a knowledge of the truth and will gladly cast in their lot with God's commandment-keeping people. Means will flow into the treasury, strong laborers will be raised up, the unwarned fields of the great regions beyond will be entered, and the work will soon close in triumph.—*Review and Herald,* Apr. 7, 1910.

Reject Speculation

Preach the word! Be ready in season and out of season. 2 Tim. 4:2.

The experience of the past will be repeated. In the future, Satan's superstitions will assume new forms. Errors will be presented in a pleasing and flattering manner. False theories, clothed with garments of light, will be presented to God's people. Thus Satan will try to deceive, if possible, the very elect. Most seducing influences will be exerted; minds will be hypnotized.

Corruptions of every type, similar to those existing among the antediluvians, will be brought in to take minds captive. The exaltation of nature as God, the unrestrained license of the human will, the counsel of the ungodly—these Satan uses as agencies to bring about certain ends. He will employ the power of mind on mind to carry out his designs. The most sorrowful thought of all is that under his deceptive influence men and women will have a form of godliness without having a real connection with God. Like Adam and Eve, who ate the fruit from the tree of the knowledge of good and evil, many are even now feeding upon the deceptive morsels of error.

Satanic agencies are clothing false theories in an attractive garb, even as Satan in the Garden of Eden concealed his identity from our first parents by speaking through the serpent. These agencies are instilling into human minds that which in reality is deadly error. The hypnotic influence of Satan will rest upon those who turn from the plain Word of God to pleasing fables.

It is those who have had the most light that Satan most assiduously seeks to ensnare. He knows that if he can deceive them, they will, under his control, clothe sin with garments of righteousness and lead many astray.

I say to all, Be on your guard; for as an angel of light Satan is walking in every assembly of Christian workers and in every church, trying to win the members to his side. I am bidden to give the people of God the warning, "Be not deceived; God is not mocked." . . .

Walk firmly, decidedly, your feet shod with the preparation of the gospel of peace. You may be sure that pure and undefiled religion is not a sensational religion. God has not laid upon anyone the burden of encouraging an appetite for speculative doctrines and theories. My brethren, keep these things out of your teaching. Do not allow them to enter into your experience. Let not your lifework be marred by them.—*Review and Herald,* Mar. 3, 1904.

The Holy Spirit and the Remnant

After these things I saw another angel coming down from heaven, having great authority, and the earth was illuminated with his glory. Rev. 18:1.

We see before us a special work to be done. We are now to pray as never before for the Holy Spirit's guidance. Let us seek the Lord with the whole heart, that we may find Him. We have received the light of the three angels' messages; and we need now to come decidedly to the front and take our position on the side of truth. . . .

The saving knowledge of God will accomplish its purifying work on the mind and heart of every believer. The Word declares: "Then will I sprinkle clean water upon you, and ye shall be clean. . ." This is the descent of the Holy Spirit, sent from God to do its office work. The house of Israel is to be imbued with the Holy Spirit and baptized with the grace of salvation.

Amid the confusing cries, "Lo, here is Christ! Lo, there is Christ!" will be borne a special testimony, a special message of truth appropriate for this time, which message is to be received, believed, and acted upon. . . . The eternal truth of the Word will stand forth free from all seductive errors and spiritualistic interpretations, free from all fancifully drawn, alluring pictures. Falsehoods will be urged upon the attention of God's people, but the truth is to stand clothed in its beautiful, pure garments. The Word, precious in its holy, uplifting influence, is not to be degraded to a level with common, ordinary matters. It is always to remain uncontaminated by the fallacies by which Satan seeks to deceive, if possible, the very elect.

The proclamation of the gospel is the only means in which God can employ human beings as His instrumentalities for the salvation of souls. As men, women, and children proclaim the gospel, the Lord will open the eyes of the blind to see His statutes and will write upon the hearts of the truly penitent His law. The animating Spirit of God, working through human agencies, leads the believers to be of one mind, one soul, unitedly loving God and keeping His commandments—preparing here below for translation. . . .

Let the work of proclaiming the gospel of Christ be made efficient by the agency of the Holy Spirit. Let not one believer, in the day of trial and proving that has already begun, listen to the devising of the enemy. The living Word is the sword of the Spirit. Mercies and judgments will be sent from heaven. The working of providence will be revealed both in mercies and in judgments.—*Review and Herald,* Oct. 13, 1904.

A Holy People

The righteous shall be glad in the Lord, and trust in Him.
And all the upright in heart shall glory. Ps. 64:10.

This scripture will be literally fulfilled. Everything is to be shaken that can be shaken, that those things that cannot be shaken may remain. I am amazed as I consider the past, present, and future of the people of God. The Lord will have a pure, holy people—a people who will stand the test. All believers need now to search their hearts as with a lighted candle....

Before us is held out the wonderful possibility of being like Christ—obedient to all the principles of the law of God. But of ourselves we are utterly powerless to attain to this condition. All that is good in us comes to us through Christ. The holiness that God's Word declares we must have before we can be saved is the result of the working of divine grace as we bow in submission to the discipline and restraining influence of the Spirit of truth....

The work of transformation from unholiness to holiness is a continuous work. Day by day God labors for our sanctification, and we are to cooperate with Him by putting forth persevering efforts in the cultivation of right habits. The way in which we are to work out our own salvation is plainly specified in the first chapter of Second Peter. Constantly we are to add grace to grace, and as we do this, God will work for us upon the plan of multiplication. He is always ready to hear and answer the prayer of the contrite heart, and grace and peace are multiplied to His faithful ones. Gladly He grants them the blessings that they need in their struggle against the evils that beset them. Those who listen to the counsels of His Word shall not want any good thing....

God will more than fulfill the highest expectations of those who put their trust in Him. He desires us to remember that when we are humble and contrite, we stand where He can and will manifest Himself to us. He is well pleased when we urge past mercies and blessings as a reason why He should bestow on us higher and greater blessings. He is honored when we love Him and bear testimony to the genuineness of our love by keeping His commandments. He is honored when we set apart the seventh day as sacred and holy. To those who do this, the Sabbath is a sign, "that they might know," God declares, "that I am the Lord that sanctify them." Sanctification means habitual communion with God. There is nothing so great and powerful as God's love for those who are His children.—*Review and Herald,* Mar. 15, 1906.

A Perfected Church

And He is the head of the body, the church, who is the beginning, the firstborn from the dead, that in all things He might have the preeminence. Col. 1:18.

Christ "loved the church, and gave himself for it; that he might sanctify and cleanse it with the washing of water by the word, that he might present it to himself a glorious church, not having spot, or wrinkle, or any such thing; but that it should be holy and without blemish."

When God gave His Son to the world, He made it possible for men and women to be perfect by the use of every capability of their beings to the glory of God. In Christ He gave to them the riches of His grace and a knowledge of His will. . . .

The church is yet militant in a world that is apparently in midnight darkness, and growing worse and worse. While the requirements of a plain "Thus saith the Lord" remain unheeded by the worldly element in the church, the voices of God's faithful servants are to be strengthened to give the solemn message of warning. The works that should characterize the church militant and the works of the church that has had the light of truth for this time do not correspond. The Lord calls upon church members to clothe themselves with the beautiful garments of Christ's righteousness. . . .

God needs men and women who will work in the simplicity of Christ to bring the knowledge of truth before those who need its converting power. The message of Christ's righteousness must be proclaimed from one end of the earth to the other. Our people are to be aroused to prepare the way of the Lord. The third angel's message—the last message of mercy to a perishing world—is so sacred, so glorious. Let the truth go forth as a lamp that burneth. Mysteries into which angels desired to look, which prophets and kings and the righteous desired to know, the church of God is to make known.

Christ's wonderful sacrifice for the world testifies to the fact that men and women may be rescued from iniquity. If they will break with Satan and confess their sins, there is hope for them. People—sinful, blinded, wretched—may repent and be converted and day by day be forming a character like the character of Christ. Human beings may be reclaimed, re-generated, and may learn to live before the world precious, Christlike lives.—*Review and Herald*, Apr. 22, 1909.

A Reflection of Christ

*Put on the new man which was created according to God, in true
righteousness and holiness. Eph. 4:24.*

God is waiting to see revealed in His people a faith that works by love
and purifies the soul; for this alone will fit them for the future, immortal life. There is a great work to be accomplished and little time in which
to do it. The cause needs converted, devoted men and women who will
make the Lord their dependence. Through such workers the Lord will reveal the power of His grace. . . .

My brethren and sisters, let the truth of God abide in your heart by a living, holy faith. Bible truth must be comprehended before it can convict the
conscience and convert the life. The remnant people of God must be a converted people. The presentation of this message is to result in the conversion
and sanctification of souls. We are to feel the power of the Spirit of God in
this movement. This is a wonderful, definite message; it means everything
to the receiver, and it is to be proclaimed with a loud cry. We must have
true, eternal faith that this message will go forth with increasing importance
to the close of time.

Christ desires to see His likeness reflected in every renewed soul. Those
who continue meek and lowly in heart, He will make laborers together
with God. Our spiritual conflicts might often be called our spiritual rebellions. It is the heart's lack of submission to the will of God that so often
brings us into difficulty. We want our own way, and this often means rebellion against God's way. We need to do as Christ did—wrestle with the
Father in prayer for strength and for power to make Him known in our
words and actions. . . .

To do the Master's bidding and to promote His work in the earth should
be the one aim and purpose of our lives. Then there would be an upward
growth, and the Holy Spirit would work upon the heart to transform the
character. A generous spirit would be revealed in kindness and tender regard
for others. Self would be hid with Christ in God. Beholding the character
of Christ, we would become changed into His likeness.

Let us forsake self and accept Jesus Christ as the way, the truth, and the life.
Faith in Him is the only valuable science. He is the living representative of
perfect obedience to the eternal Word.—*Review and Herald,* Aug. 26, 1909.

Separate From the World

Keep yourselves in the love of God, looking for the mercy of our Lord Jesus Christ unto eternal life. Jude 21.

Those who hear from the lips of Christ the words, "Well done, thou good and faithful servant," will be heroic ministers of righteousness. They may never preach a discourse from the pulpit, but loyal to a sense of God's claims upon them and jealous of His honor, they will minister to the souls who are the purchase of Christ's blood. They will see the necessity of carrying into their work a willing mind, an earnest spirit, and a hearty, unselfish zeal. They will not study how best they can preserve their own dignity, but by care and thoughtfulness will seek to win the hearts of those whom they serve. . . .

The apostle Paul urges upon us the advantages placed within our reach. "Having therefore these promises, dearly beloved," he says, "let us cleanse ourselves from all filthiness of the flesh and spirit, perfecting holiness in the fear of God." We are to separate from the world in spirit and practice if we would become sons and daughters of God. In His prayer for His followers, Christ asked, "I pray not that thou shouldest take them out of the world, but that thou shouldest keep them from the evil. They are not of the world, even as I am not of the world. Sanctify them through thy truth: thy word is truth."

There is earnest work before each one of us. Right thoughts, pure and holy purposes, do not come to us naturally. We shall have to strive for them. . . . Those who are under the control of the Spirit of God will not seek their own pleasure or amusement. If Christ presides in the hearts of the members of His church, they will answer to the call, "Come out from among them, and be ye separate." Partake not of her sin.

God has a work for His faithful sentinels to do in standing in defense of the truth. They are to warn and entreat, showing their faith by their works. They are to stand as did Noah, in noble, whole-souled fidelity, their characters untarnished by the evil around them. They are to be saviors of humanity, as Christ was. Workers who thus stand true to their trust will be exposed to hatred and reproach. False accusations will be brought against them to drag them from their high position. But they have their foundation upon the Rock, and they remain unmoved, warning, entreating, rebuking sin and pleasure-loving by their own moral rectitude and circumspect lives.—*Review and Herald,* Nov. 28, 1899.

God's Temple

The temple of God is holy, which temple you are. 1 Cor. 3:17.

The church on earth is God's temple, and it is to assume divine proportions before the world. This building is to be the light of the world. It
is to be composed of living stones laid close together, stone fitting to stone,
making a solid building. All these stones are not of the same shape or di-
mension. Some are large and some are small, but each one has it own place
to fill. In the whole building there is not to be one misshapen stone. Each
one is perfect. And each stone is a living stone, a stone that emits light. The
value of the stones is determined by the light they reflect to the world.

Now is the time for the stones to be taken from the quarry of the world and
brought into God's workshop to be hewed, squared, and polished, that they
may shine. This is God's plan, and He desires all who profess to believe the truth
to fill their respective places in the great, grand work for this time. . . .

It is God's design that His church shall ever advance in purity and knowledge, from light to light, from glory to glory. . . . His church is the court of
holy life, filled with varied gifts and endowed with the Holy Spirit.
Appropriate duties are assigned by Heaven to the church on earth, and the
members are to find their happiness in the happiness of those whom they
help and bless.

Through the ages of moral darkness, through centuries of strife and persecution, the church of Christ has been as a city set on a hill. From age to
age, through successive generations, to the present time, the pure doctrines
of the Bible have been unfolding within her borders. The church of Christ,
enfeebled and defective as she may appear, is the one object on earth on
which He bestows in a special sense His love and regard. The church is the
theater of His grace, in which He delights to make experiments of mercy
on human hearts.

The church is God's fortress, His city of refuge, which He holds in a re-
volted world. Any betrayal of her sacred trust is treachery to Him who has
bought her with the precious blood of His only begotten Son. In the past,
faithful souls have constituted the church on earth, and God has taken them
into covenant relation with Himself, uniting the church on earth with the
church in heaven. He has sent forth His holy angels to minister to His
church, and the gates of hell have not been able to prevail against it.—
Review and Herald, Dec. 4, 1900.

Coworkers With the Church in Heaven

Looking unto Jesus, the author and finisher of our faith. Heb. 12:2.

Today, as in the past, all heaven is watching to see the church develop in the true science of salvation. Christ has bought the church with His blood, and He longs to clothe her with salvation. He has made her the depositary of sacred truth, and He wishes her to partake of His glory. But in order that the church may be an educating power in the world, she must cooperate with the church in heaven. Her members must represent Christ. Their hearts must be open to receive every ray of light that God may see fit to impart. As they receive this light, they will be enabled to receive and impart more and more of the rays of the Sun of Righteousness.

There is need of a higher grade of spirituality in the church. There is need of heart purification. God calls His people to their posts of duty. He calls upon them to purge themselves from that which has been revealed as the bane of the churches—an exalting of those who are placed in positions of trust. There is earnest work to be done. Upon their knees men and women are to seek God in faith and then go forth to speak the word with power sent down from on high. Such believers come before the people direct from the audience-chamber of the Most High, and their words and works promote spirituality. When they come in contact with wrong principles, they plant their feet firmly upon the words, "It is written." . . .

The church today needs laborers who, like Enoch, walk with God, revealing Christ to the world. Church members need to reach a higher standard. . . . Our views of the Sun of Righteousness are clouded by self-seeking. Christ is crucified afresh by many who through self-indulgence allow Satan to gain control over them. The church needs men and women of devotion to bear to the world the message of salvation, pointing sinners to the Lamb of God—workers who, by their works of righteousness and their pure, true words, can lift those around them out of the pit of degradation.

With pity and compassion, with tender yearning and love, the Lord is looking upon His tempted and tried people. . . . It is God's purpose that all shall be tested and tried, that He may see whether they are loyal or disloyal to the laws that govern the kingdom of heaven. To the last, God permits Satan to reveal himself as a liar, an accuser, and a murderer. Thus the final triumph of His people is made more marked, more glorious, more full and complete.—*Review and Herald,* Dec. 4, 1900.

A Colorado Sunset

They desire a better, that is, a heavenly country. Therefore God is
not ashamed to be called their God, for He has prepared a city for them.
Heb. 11:16.

As the [railroad] cars bore our company into the city of Denver, we were charmed in beholding one of the beautiful sunsets of Colorado. The sun was passing behind the snowcapped mountains, leaving its softened beams of golden light to tint the heavens. As the blending tints were deepening and extending athwart the skies, with indescribable beauty, it seemed the gates of heaven were ajar to let the gleamings of its glory through. The golden hues were every moment more and more entrancing, as if to invite our imagination to picture the greater glory within. . . . If this so charms our senses, what must be the fullness of the glory in heaven itself. . . .

Heaven seemed very near. . . . As the eye was turned from the dazzling glories of the closing day, we could but reflect that should we see more of heaven by the eye of faith, greater light, more peace and joy, would be all along life's pathway. . . . If the eye of faith were uplifted to see through the veil of the future and discern the tokens of God's love and glory in the promised life beyond, we should be more spiritually minded, and the beauties and joys of heaven would mingle with our daily life. We should be fitting up for the faithful performance of our work in this life, and for the higher life beyond. . . .

Our heavenly Father has hung out glories in the firmament of the heavens, that we may have an expression of His love in the revealing of His wondrous works. God would not have us indifferent to the symbols of the glories of His infinite power in the heavens. David delighted to dwell upon these glories. He composed psalms which the Hebrew singers chanted to the praise of God. "The heavens declare the glory of God; and the firmament sheweth His handywork. . . . In them hath he set a tabernacle for the sun, which is as a bridegroom coming out of his chamber, and rejoiceth as a strong man to run a race." . . .

All the powers of our being, every means of our existence and happiness, all the blessings of the warm sunshine and the refreshing showers, causing vegetation to flourish, every comfort and every blessing of this life, come from God. He sendeth rain on the just and on the unjust. The treasures of heaven are poured out to all.—*Signs of the Times,* Dec. 12, 1878.

John the Baptist's Example

There was a man sent from God, whose name was John. John 1:6.

The birth of John the Baptist had been foretold by prophets, and an angel was sent to notify Zacharias of the event. The heavenly messenger expressly enjoined upon the father to bring up the child with strictly temperate habits. . . .

John did not feel strong enough to stand the great pressure of temptation he would meet in mingling with society. He feared his character would be molded according to the prevailing customs of the Jews, and he chose to separate himself from the world and make the wilderness his home. . . . So far from being lonely, gloomy, or morose, he enjoyed his life of simplicity and retirement, and his temperate habits kept all his senses unperverted. . . .

John had a special work to do for God. He was to deal with the sins and follies of the people. In order to be fitted for this important public work, he must qualify himself in private by seeking heavenly knowledge. He must meditate and pray, and by studying become acquainted with the prophecies and the will of God. Away from the busy world, whose cares and alluring pleasures would divert his mind and pervert his thoughts and imaginings, he was shut up with God and nature. . . . By his strictly temperate habits he secured to himself physical, mental, and moral health. . . .

John accustomed himself to privations and hardships, that he might be able to stand among the people as unmoved by circumstances as the rocks and mountains of the wilderness that had surrounded him for thirty years. A great work was before him; and it was necessary that he should form a character that would not be swerved from right and duty by any surrounding influence. . . .

John was an example to . . . people in these last days, to whom have been committed important and solemn truths. God would have them temperate in all things. He would have them see the necessity for the denial of appetite, for keeping their passions under the control of reason. This is necessary that they may have mental strength and clearness to discern between right and wrong, between truth and error. There is work for every one . . . to do in the vineyard of the Lord, and He would have them fit themselves to act a useful part.—*Youth's Instructor,* Jan. 7, 1897.

A Voice in the Wilderness

This is he who was spoken of by the prophet Isaiah, saying:
"The voice of one crying in the wilderness: 'Prepare the way of the Lord;
make His paths straight.'" Matt. 3:3.

The preaching of John the Baptist created intense excitement. At the beginning of his ministry, religious interest was very low. Superstition, tradition, and fables had confused the minds of the people, and the right way was not understood. Zealous in securing worldly treasure and honor, the people had forgotten God. . . .

The teaching of John aroused in the hearts of many a great desire to have a part in the blessings that Christ was to bring, and they received the truth. These saw the need of reform. They must not only seek to enter in at the strait gate; they must strive and agonize in order to have the blessings of the gospel. Nothing save a vehement desire, a determined will, a fixedness of purpose, could resist the moral darkness that covered the earth as the pall of death. In order to obtain the blessings that it was their privilege to have, they must work earnestly, they must deny self.

The work of John the Baptist represents the work for these times. His work, and the work of those who go forth in the spirit and power of Elijah to arouse the people from their apathy, are the same in many respects. Christ is to come the second time to judge the world in righteousness. The messengers of God who bear the last message of warning to be given to the world are to prepare the way for Christ's second advent as John prepared the way for His first advent. If the kingdom of heaven suffered violence in the days of John, it suffers violence now; today the blessings of the gospel must be secured in the same way. If form and ceremony were of no avail then, a form of godliness without the power can be of no avail now.

Two powers are at work. On the one side Satan is working with all his forces to counterwork the influence of the work of God; on the other hand God is working through His servants to call sinners to repentance. Which will prevail? Satan, knowing that his time is short, has come down with great power and is working with all deceivableness of unrighteousness in them that perish. Every agent that he can employ, he is using to prevent souls from coming to the light. The victories we gain over self and sin are gained at the expense of the enemy, and he will not let us enjoy the blessings of God without making determined efforts to resist us.—*Youth's Instructor,* May 17, 1900.

Forerunner of Christ

He will also go before Him in the spirit and power of Elijah, "to turn the hearts of the fathers to the children," and the disobedient to the wisdom of the just, to make ready a people prepared for the Lord. Luke 1:17.

In John the Baptist God raised up a messenger to prepare the way of the Lord. He was to bear to the world an unflinching testimony, reproving and denouncing sin. . . . John had not been educated in the schools of the rabbis. He had obtained no human scholarship. . . .

To prepare the way before Christ, one was needed who, like the prophets of old, could summon the degenerate nation to repentance, and the voice of John was lifted up like a trumpet. His commission was "Shew my people their transgression, and the house of Jacob their sins." . . .

In this age, just prior to the second coming of Christ in the clouds of heaven, God calls for workers who will prepare a people to stand in the great day of the Lord. Just such a work as that of John is to be carried on in these last days. The Lord has given messages to His people, through the instruments He has chosen, and He would have all give heed to the admonitions and warnings He sends. The message preceding the public ministry of Christ was, Repent, publicans and sinners. Repent, Pharisees and Sadducees. Repent, "for the kingdom of heaven is at hand." Our message is not to be one of peace and safety. As a people who believe in Christ's soon appearing, we have a message to bear—"Prepare to meet thy God." We are to lift up the standard and bear the third angel's message. Our message must be as direct as was the message of John. He rebuked kings for their iniquity. Notwithstanding that his life was in peril, the truth did not languish upon his lips. And our work in this age must be as faithfully done. . . .

Look at the picture which the world presents today. Dishonesty, fraud, and bankruptcies, violence and bloodshed, exist on every hand. . . . Thus the discernment and sensibilities have become deadened as to what constitutes right principles. . . . The light given, calling to repentance, has been shut out by the thick cloud of unbelief and opposition brought in by human plans and human inventions. . . .

The prayerful, earnest appeals that come from the heart of the wholehearted messenger will create conviction. . . . All who know the only true and living God will know Jesus Christ, the only begotten of the Father, and they will preach Christ and Him crucified.—*Review and Herald*, Nov. 1, 1906.

As in the Days of Noah

Then the Lord saw that the wickedness of man was great in the earth.
Gen. 6:5.

The inhabitants of the world at this time are represented by the dwellers upon the earth at the time of the Flood. The wickedness of the antediluvians is plainly stated, "And God saw that the wickedness of man was great in the earth, and that every imagination of the thoughts of his heart was only evil continually." God became weary of this people whose thoughts were only of sinful pleasure and indulgence. They sought not the counsel of God who had created them, nor cared to do His will. The rebuke of God was upon them because they followed the imagination of their own hearts; and there was violence in the land. "And it repented the Lord that he had made man on the earth. . . ."

In His teachings Christ referred to this. "But as the days of Noe were," He said, "so shall also the coming of the Son of man be." . . .

The inhabitants of the antediluvian world had the warning given them prior to their overthrow, but the warning was not heeded. They refused to listen to the words of Noah; they mocked at his message. Righteous people lived in that generation. Before the destruction of the antediluvian world, Enoch bore his testimony unflinchingly. And in prophetic vision he saw the condition of the world at the present time. He said, "Behold, the Lord cometh with ten thousands of his saints, to execute judgment upon all, and to convince all that are ungodly among them of all their ungodly deeds which they have ungodly committed, and of all their hard speeches which ungodly sinners have spoken against him. These are murmurers, complainers, walking after their own lusts; and their mouth speaketh great swelling words, having men's persons in admiration because of advantage." . . .

It is living earnestness that God requires at this time. Ministers may have but little learning from books, but if they do the best they can with their talents; if they work as they have opportunity; if they clothe their utterances in the plainest and most simple language; if they walk in carefulness and humility, seeking for heavenly wisdom; if they work for God from the heart, actuated by love for Christ and the souls for whom Christ has died, they will be listened to by those of even superior ability and talents. There will be a charm in the simplicity of the truths they present.—*Review and Herald,* Nov. 1, 1906.

Build an Ark, Noah

Make yourself an ark of gopherwood. Gen. 6:14.

In how short a time from the first sin of Adam did sin increase and spread like the leprosy. It is the nature of sin to increase. From generation to generation sin has spread like a contagious disease. Hatred of God's law and—as the sure result—hatred of all goodness became universal. The world was in its infancy, yet after sin was first introduced, it soon became fearful in its proportions until it deluged the world. God, who created mankind and gave them with an unsparing hand the bounties of His providence, was slighted and despised by the recipients of His gifts. . . . But notwithstanding sinners forgot their benevolent Benefactor, God did not slight and turn away from them and leave them to perish in their violence and crime without setting before them their wickedness and the result of the transgression of His law. He sent them messages of warning and entreaty. . . .

God, whom men and women had slighted and dishonored and whose gracious love and benevolence they had abused, still pitied the race and in His love provided a refuge for all who would accept it. He directed Noah to build an ark and at the same time preach to the inhabitants of the world that God would bring a flood of waters upon the earth to destroy the wicked. If they would believe the message and prepare for that event by repentance and reformation, they should find pardon and be saved. God did not remove His Spirit from the human race without warning them of the sure result of their course in transgressing His law. . . .

The Spirit of God continued to strive with the rebellious until the time God had specified had nearly expired, when Noah and his family entered the ark and the hand of God closed the door of the ark. Mercy had stepped from the golden throne, no longer to intercede for mankind.

Notwithstanding God was working to draw sinners to Himself by the conviction of His Holy Spirit, they in their rebellion were drawing away from God and continually resisting the pleadings of infinite love. Noah stood up nobly in the midst of a world who were disregarding God and were indulging in all manner of extravagant dissipation which led to crimes and violence of every kind. . . . What a spectacle to the world as Noah stands forth connected with God by his obedience, in contrast to the world.—*Signs of the Times,* Dec. 20, 1877.

Noah's Unwavering Obedience

Noah was a just man, perfect in his generations. Noah walked with God. Gen. 6:9.

How simple and childlike amid the unbelief of the world was the faith of Noah.... His faith was perfected by his works. He gave to the world an example in believing just what God had said. He commenced under the directions of God to construct the ark, an immense boat, on dry ground. Multitudes came from every direction to see this strange sight . . . and to hear the earnest, fervent words of this singular man who seemed to believe every word he uttered.... A power attended the words of Noah, for it was the voice of God to the people through His servant. Some were deeply convicted and would have heeded the words of warning, but there were so many to jest and ridicule the message of entreaty and warning to repentance that they partook of the same spirit, resisted the invitations of mercy, . . . and were soon among the boldest and most defiant scoffers; for none are as reckless and will go to such lengths in sin as those who have once had light, who have been convicted and resisted the Spirit of God. Amid popular contempt and ridicule, amid universal wickedness and disobedience, Noah distinguished himself by his holy integrity and unwavering obedience.... He was one in the world, but not one of the world. Noah made himself the object of contempt and ridicule by his steadfast adherence to the words of God....

While the voice of God, through Noah, was making itself heard in entreaties and warnings in condemnation of sin and iniquity, Satan was not asleep; he was mustering his forces.... Noah was tested and proved. Opposition met him from the great men of the world, from philosophers and men of science, so-called, who tried to show him that his message could not be true, but his voice was not silenced; one hundred and twenty years the words of warning continued to be heard in earnest tones and were sustained by his energetic work upon the ark.... God's Spirit was striving with the people to lead them to accept and believe the truth, but Satan's suggestions were also heeded; their own wicked hearts were more inclined to harmonize with the sophistry of the father of lies than with the pleadings of infinite love. They manifested their indifference and contempt of the solemn warnings of God in doing the same as they had done before the warning had been given....

The days of Noah, Christ tells us, were as the days prior to His appearing in the clouds of heaven.—*Signs of the Times,* Dec. 20, 1877.

The End of Patience

And the Lord said, "My Spirit shall not strive with man forever."
Gen. 6:3.

In Noah's day all people were not in the fullest sense heathen idolaters. . . .
The class who professed a knowledge of God were the ones who had the
greatest influence and took the lead in making of none effect His word spoken
to them by Noah. They not only rejected the message of the faithful preacher
of righteousness themselves, but like their master the devil they sought every
means in their power to prevent others from believing and being obedient to
God. . . . While Noah was sounding the note of warning of the coming destruction of that generation, was their day of opportunity and privilege to become wise unto salvation. But they gave their minds to the control of Satan
rather than God, and he deceived them as he did our first parents. . . .

The world before the Flood reasoned that for centuries the laws of nature
had been fixed. The recurring seasons had come in their order. The rivers
and brooks had never yet passed their boundaries but had borne their waters safely to the proud sea. Fixed decrees had kept the waters from overflowing their banks. But these reasons did not recognize the Hand that had
stayed the waters, saying, thus far shalt thou go and no farther. . . . They reasoned then as people reason now, as though nature was above the God of
nature, and her ways were so fixed that God Himself could not change
them, thus making in the minds of the world God's messages of warning a
delusion, a grand deception, reasoning that if the message of Noah was correct, nature would be turned out of her course of order. . . .

Human nature in Noah's day, uninfluenced by the Spirit of God, is the
same in our age. Jesus in His assertions and representations recognizes Genesis
as the words of inspiration. Many admit the New Testament to be divine,
while they show no special regard for the Old Testament Scriptures; but these
two grand books cannot be divorced. Inspired apostles who wrote the New
Testament are continually carrying back the minds of the searchers of
Scriptures to the Old. Christ carries the minds of all generations, present and
future, to the Old Testament. He refers to Noah as a literal person who lived;
He refers to the Flood as a fact in history; He shows the specification of that
generation as characteristic of this age. The Truth and Life has anticipated the
questioning and doubts of men and women in regard to the Old Testament
by pronouncing it divine.—*Signs of the Times,* Dec. 20, 1877.

God's Sabbath

The seventh day is the Sabbath of the Lord your God. Ex. 20:10.

When God created the earth and placed human beings upon it, He divided time into seven periods. Six He gave to us for our own use, to employ in secular business; one He reserved for Himself. Having rested on the seventh day, He blessed and sanctified it. Henceforth, the seventh day was to be regarded as the Lord's rest day and to be sacredly observed as the memorial of His creative work. It was not the first, second, third, fourth, fifth, or sixth day that was sanctified, or set apart to a holy use; neither was it a seventh part of time and no day in particular; but it was the seventh day, the day upon which God had rested. . . .

When the law was given at Sinai, the Sabbath was placed in the midst of moral precepts, in the very bosom of the Decalogue. But the Sabbath institution was not then made known for the first time. The fourth commandment places its origin at Creation. The Creator's rest day was hallowed by Adam in holy Eden and by the people of God throughout the patriarchal ages. During Israel's long bondage in Egypt, under taskmasters that knew not God, they could not keep the Sabbath; therefore the Lord brought them out where they could remember His holy day. . . .

A threefold miracle was wrought in honor of the Sabbath, even before the law was given on Sinai. A double quantity of manna fell on the sixth day, none upon the Sabbath, and the portion needed for the Sabbath was preserved sweet and pure, when if any were kept over at any other time, it became unfit for food. Here is conclusive evidence that the Sabbath was instituted at Creation, when the foundations of the earth were laid, when the morning stars sang together, and all the sons of God shouted for joy. And its sacredness remains unchanged, and will so remain even to the close of time. From the Creation, every precept of the divine law has been obligatory on mankind and has been observed by those who fear the Lord. The doctrine that God's law has been abolished is one of Satan's devices to compass the ruin of the race. . . .

The holy oracles were especially committed to the Jews; not to be an Israelite was not to belong to the favored people of God. . . . Now the prophet declares that the stranger who will love and obey God shall enjoy the privileges that have belonged exclusively to the chosen people.—*Signs of the Times,* Feb. 28, 1884.

The Sabbath in the Gospel Dispensation

Blessed is the man . . . who keeps from defiling the Sabbath,
and keeps his hand from doing any evil. Isa. 56:2.

The prophet Isaiah, looking forward to the gospel dispensation, sets forth in the most impressive manner the obligation of the Sabbath and the blessings attending its observance. . . .

Hitherto, circumcision and a strict observance of the ceremonial law had been the conditions upon which Gentiles could be admitted to the congregation of Israel; but these distinctions were to be abolished by the gospel. "Every one that keepeth the Sabbath from polluting it, and taketh hold of my covenant; even them will I bring to my holy mountain, and make them joyful in my house of prayer: their burnt offerings and their sacrifices shall be accepted upon mine altar; for mine house shall be called a house of prayer for all people." . . .

Again, after rebuking the selfishness, violence, and oppression of Israel and exhorting them to works of righteousness and mercy, He declares, . . . "If thou turn away thy foot from the sabbath, from doing thy pleasure on my holy day and call the sabbath a delight, the holy of the Lord, honourable; and shalt honour him, not doing thine own ways, nor finding thine own pleasure, nor speaking thine own words: then shalt thou delight thyself in the Lord; and I will cause thee to ride upon the high places of the earth, and feed thee with the heritage of Jacob thy father: for the mouth of the Lord hath spoken it." . . .

This prophecy reaches down the centuries to the time when the man of sin attempted to make void one of the precepts of God's law, to trample underfoot the original Sabbath of Jehovah, and in its stead exalt one of his own creation. . . .

There were two institutions founded in Eden that were not lost in the Fall—the Sabbath and the marriage relation. These were carried by humanity beyond the gates of paradise. All who love and observe the Sabbath, and maintain the purity of the marriage institution, thereby prove themselves the friends of humanity and the friends of God. All who by precept or example lessen the obligation of these sacred institutions are the enemies of both God and humanity, and are using their influence and their God-given talents to bring in a state of confusion and moral corruption.—*Signs of the Times,* Feb. 28, 1884.

Biblical Foundation for the Sabbath

It is written, "Man shall not live by bread alone, but by every word that proceeds from the mouth of God." Matt. 4:4.

Christ resisted the temptations of the enemy with the only weapon that the soldier of the cross of Christ can successfully use—"It is written." Where? In the Old and New Testaments. With these words we are to defend ourselves and warn others, holding forth to them the Word of life.

Many have never understood that Sunday is not the Sabbath of the fourth commandment. In his subtlety, Satan has covered up this fact and has presented a common day as sacred, that the whole world may become guilty before God by transgression. Many are utterly ignorant that they are not keeping the fourth commandment. It is essential for all to seek for truth from the divine Guidebook, that they may decide what the Lord says on this question. People have said much, but we cannot build our faith on the words of any person. There are two sides to this question. The God of heaven presents His law, and Satan holds out his spurious sabbath. . . .

Sunday is a child of the Papacy. It has been nourished and cradled by the Protestant world as a genuine requirement of Jehovah; but it has no foundation in the Word of God. The Christian world is tested by their relation to this matter. God moves upon men and women to search the Scriptures for evidence to sustain Sunday. Those who search with a desire for truth will see that in the past they have been relying on tradition and have accepted an institution of the Papacy. . . .

We are accountable only for the light that shines upon us. The commandments of God and the faith of Jesus are testing us. If we are faithful and obedient, God will delight in us and bless us as His own chosen, peculiar people. When perfect faith and perfect love and obedience abound, working in the hearts of those who are Christ's followers, they will have a powerful influence. Light will emanate from them, dispelling the darkness around them, refining and elevating all who come within the sphere of their influence, and bringing to a knowledge of the truth all who are willing to be enlightened and to follow in the humble path of obedience.

Great blessings are promised to those who keep holy God's Sabbath.—*Review and Herald,* July 13, 1897.

What Is Lawful on the Sabbath?

Now it happened on another Sabbath, also, that He entered the synagogue
and taught. And a man was there whose right hand was withered.
Luke 6:6.

The scribes and Pharisees watched him, whether he would heal on the sabbath day; that they might find an accusation against him. But he knew their thoughts, and said to the man which had the withered hand, Rise up, and stand forth in the midst. And he arose and stood forth. Then said Jesus unto them, I will ask you one thing; Is it lawful on the sabbath days to do good, or to do evil? to save life, or to destroy it?" . . . Here Christ settled the question He had asked. He pronounced it right to perform a work of mercy and necessity. "It is lawful," He said, "to do well on the sabbath days." . . .

It had often been stated by the teachers of the people, and indeed was one of their maxims, that for them not to do good when they had opportunity was to do evil—that to refrain from saving life when it was in their power to do so was to make themselves guilty of murder. . . . They were following upon His track to find occasion for falsely accusing Him; they were hunting His life with bitter hatred and malice, while He was saving life and bringing happiness to many hearts. Was it better to slay on the Sabbath, as they were planning to do, than to heal the afflicted, as He had done? Was it more righteous to have murder in the heart upon God's holy day, than to have that love toward all people which finds expression in deeds of charity and mercy? . . .

The rulers communed one with another how they should rid themselves of this bold advocate of righteousness, whose words and works were drawing the people away from the teachers of Israel. Notwithstanding their counterinfluence, "the world," they declared, "is gone after him." But they thought that might and numbers would bring things as they wished; and they took counsel together how they might destroy Him.

We see this enacted today. Those who are themselves transgressing the law of God, making the commandments of God of none effect through their tradition, follow with reproach and accusations the servants whom God sends with a message to correct their evils. They determine to remove them, to still their voice forever, rather than forsake the sins that have called forth the rebuke of God.—*Review and Herald,* Aug. 10, 1897.

Preparation for Jesus' Coming

*Looking for the blessed hope and glorious appearing of our great
God and Savior Jesus Christ. Titus 2:13.*

Jesus is soon coming; and it is for us who believe this solemn truth to give the warning to the world. We should show by our dress, our conversation, and our actions, that our minds are fixed on something better than the business and pleasures of this short life. We are but pilgrims and strangers here and should give some evidence that we are ready and waiting for the appearing of our divine Lord. Let the world see that you are journeying from this to a better land, dear reader—to an immortal inheritance that passeth not away; that you cannot afford to devote your life to the things of this world, but that your concern is to prepare for the home that awaits you in the kingdom of God.

How shall we make this preparation? It is by bringing our appetites and passions into subjection to the will of God and showing in our lives the fruits of holiness. We must deal justly, love mercy, and walk humbly before God. We must let Christ into our hearts and homes. We must cultivate love, sympathy, and true courtesy one to another. . . .

Our lives should be consecrated to the good and happiness of others, as was our Savior's. This is the joy of angels, and the work in which they are ever engaged. The spirit of Christ's self-sacrificing love is the spirit that pervades heaven and is the source of its blessedness. And it must be our spirit, if we would be fitted to join the society of the angelic host. In proportion as the love of Christ fills our hearts and controls our lives, selfishness and love of ease will be overcome; it will be our pleasure to minister to others and to do the will of our Lord, whom we hope soon to see. . . .

We should do right because it is right, and not to avoid punishment, or for fear of some great calamity that may come upon us. I want to do right for the pleasure I have in righteousness. There is so much happiness to be found in doing good here; so much satisfaction in doing the will of God; so much pleasure in receiving His blessing. Then let us show that we are men and women of sound judgment, choosing our portion not in this world, but in that which is to come. Let us stand at our post, faithful in the discharge of every duty, having our lives hid with Christ in God, that when the chief Shepherd shall appear, we "shall receive a crown of glory that fadeth not away."—*Signs of the Times,* Nov. 10, 1887.

Present Duty

Not lagging in diligence, fervent in spirit, serving the Lord. Rom. 12:11.

The present duty of every true child of God is to wait patiently, to watch vigilantly, to work faithfully, until the coming of the Lord, that we may be prepared for the solemn event. The characteristics of the true follower of Christ, the perfect man and woman in Christ Jesus, will be manifested in working, watching, and waiting for the Lord. They will not be wholly given up to contemplation and meditation or be so engrossed in some busy works that they will neglect the exercise of personal piety; but in the symmetrical Christian, personal devotion will be blended with earnest work, and the followers of Christ will be "not slothful in business" but "fervent in spirit; serving the Lord." The lamps must be kept trimmed and burning, that they may send forth bright rays of light into the moral darkness of the world. . . .

The Lord is soon coming, and for this very reason we need our schools, not that we may be educated after the order of the world, but that our institutions of learning may be more like the schools of the prophets—places where we may learn the will of God and reach to the very highest branches of science, that we may better understand God and His works and the character of Jesus Christ whom He has sent. . . . The people of God must be gaining more and more skill and experience; for there will be increased work for all, and especially for those in positions of trust. As we near the end, Satan will be moved to make a desperate effort to overthrow all those who dispute his claim to supreme authority on earth, and the people of God must be prepared for the struggle. God requires the full exercise of all the ability He has given to men and women, that they may do to the extent of their natural and cultivated powers all that is possible for them to do. . . . The followers of Christ cannot leave their posts of duty without betraying sacred trusts, without endangering the salvation of their own souls and the souls of others. You are to be true to your entrusted work and not to be seeking after something new and strange.

As Christ opened before the disciples the great work that was to be done, and promised to them the gift of the Holy Spirit, they were anxious to know if they should then see the fulfillment of their long-cherished hope. They asked, "Wilt thou at this time restore again the kingdom to Israel?" The Lord rebuked their curiosity and said, "It is not for you to know the times or the seasons, which the Father hath put in his own power."—*General Conference Bulletin,* fourth quarter 1896, p. 764.

Reflectors of Christ

*It is not for you to know times or seasons which the Father has put in his
own authority. Acts 1:7.*

The disciples could not know the time of the second coming of Christ.]
There was one thing that they might understand, and that was that
they were to receive power after that the Holy Ghost should come upon
them, and that they were to be witnesses of Christ. All this itching curiosity
to know the set time is rebuked. This has not been given to us to know, and
we are not to feel anxious about these things which the Lord has never
committed to us but has kept in His own possession, unrevealed. But the
endowment of His Spirit is for us; this we may confidently expect and
freely receive; for we can do nothing for the salvation of souls without this
heavenly agency. Because of the shortness of human life, every event should
be made an occasion for enriching souls with the truths of the gospel.

As time is fast closing, we should keep before the mind the spirituality of
the law and the utter worthlessness of a formal, ceremonial obedience to
the commandments involved in a legal religion. The eternal principles of
truth should be extolled. The holy and paternal character of God should be
presented to all. Our obligation in our daily actions should be laid bare, that
we may understand our relation to God and to each other; for we are to
watch for souls as they who must give an account. We must present to the
people not the imaginations of men, not their schemes and conclusions, but
the grace of God in the gift of His only begotten Son, that whosoever believeth on Him should not perish, but have everlasting life. We are to lift up
Jesus, that He may draw men and women unto Himself. . . .

How hard for them to realize the necessity of constant prayer, of sincere
repentance, of attaining to more and more perfection of character, which is
the salt of Christian experience and the evidence of the operation of the
Holy Spirit on the heart. The Holy Spirit is to enlighten, renew, and sanctify the soul. . . .

Let all now do their duty, laboring actively with Jesus Christ. Represent Jesus
by your example of Christian piety, that the grace of Christ may appear as it
is—beautiful, attractive, harmonious, and always consistent. A life beautified
with holiness is not a life of idle contemplation, but a life filled up with earnest
work for the Master, whose light shineth more and more unto the perfect
day.—*General Conference Bulletin,* fourth quarter 1896, pp. 764, 765.

Decisive Action

Do business till I come. Luke 19:13.

As Seventh-day Adventists, we have a work to do in witnessing for Christi. . . . If the Lord is soon to come, begin to act decidedly and determinedly and with intense interest to increase the [institutional] facilities, that a great work may be done in a short time.

Those who have been allied to the world should heed the invitation of the Lord. He says, "Come out from among them, and be ye separate, saith the Lord, and touch not the unclean thing." . . . The bright beams of the Sun of Righteousness are to shine upon you, that you may be beautified with holiness.

Shall we now say there is no need of facilities? that faith is all we need? Genuine faith is a working principle, and works will appear as a proof of this agent in the soul. You should redouble your efforts, redouble your working forces. . . .

A great work must be done all through the world, and let none flatter themselves that because the end is near, there is no need of making special efforts to build up the various institutions as the cause shall demand. . . . All are to be workers, but the heaviest burden of responsibility rests upon those who have the greatest talent, the largest means, the most abundant opportunity. We are to be justified by faith and judged by our works.

When the Lord shall bid us to lay off the armor and to make no further effort to establish schools, to build institutions for the care of the sick, for the shelter of the orphans and the homeless and for the comfort of the worn-out ministers, it will be time to fold our hands and let the Lord close up the work, but now is our opportunity to show our zeal for God. . . .

Besides all this, God calls for home missionaries. Let every soul deny self, lift the cross, and expend far less means for the gratification of self, that there may be living, working agents in all the churches. A faith that comprehends less than this is one that denies the Christian character. The faith of the gospel is one whose power and grace are of divine authorship. Then let us make it manifest that Christ abides in us, by ceasing to expend money on dress and on needless things, when the cause of Christ is crippled for want of means, when debts are left unpaid on our meeting houses, and when the treasury is empty. "By their fruits ye shall know them." Shall we not follow the example of Him who for our sakes became poor, that we through His poverty might be made rich?—*General Conference Bulletin,* fourth quarter 1896, pp. 765-768.

Heaven-filled Lives

Blessed are those who do His commandments, that they may have the right to the tree of life, and may enter through the gates into the city. Rev. 22:14.

If we would enter heaven we should strive to bring all that we can of heaven into our lives on earth. The religion of Christ never degrades the receiver. It exerts a heavenly influence upon the minds and manners of men and women. When the Word of God finds access to the hearts of the rough and coarse, it commences a process of refining upon the character, and those who endure it become humble and teachable, like little children. . . . They are to be living stones in the temple of God, and are hewed, and squared, and chiseled, to fit them for God's building. Those who are naturally full of self-esteem become meek and lowly of heart. They have a change of character, and are transformed by the renewing of their minds and the regeneration of the Holy Spirit.

God said in the beginning, "Let us make man in our image, after our likeness," but sin has almost obliterated the moral image of God in humanity. This lamentable condition would have known no change or hope if Jesus had not come down to our world to be our Savior and Example. In the midst of a world's moral degradation He stands, a beautiful and spotless character, the one model for our imitation. We must study, and copy, and follow the Lord Jesus Christ; then we shall bring the loveliness of His character into our own life and weave His beauty into our daily words and actions. . . . Through Christ we may possess the spirit of love and obedience to the commands of God. Through His merits it may be restored in our fallen natures; and when the judgment shall sit and the books be opened, we may be the recipients of God's approval.

John saw the Holy City, the New Jerusalem, with its twelve gates of pearl and twelve foundations of precious stones, coming down from God out of heaven. . . . Everyone who shall enter those gates and walk those streets will here have been changed and purified by the power of the truth; and the crown of immortal glory will adorn the brow of the overcomer.

The nations that have kept the truth shall enter in, and the voice of the Son of God will pronounce the glad welcome, "Blessed are they that do his commandments, that they may have right to the tree of life."—*Signs of the Times,* Dec. 22, 1887.

Honor the Giver of Gifts

What have they seen in your house? 2 Kings 20:15.

Study the case of Hezekiah. He had been sick unto death. He had appealed to the Lord, and God had added to his life fifteen years. "At that time . . . [the] king of Babylon sent letters and a present to Hezekiah: for he had heard that he had been sick, and was recovered. And Hezekiah was glad of them, and shewed them the house of his precious things, the silver, and the gold, and the spices, and the precious ointment, and all the house of his armour, and all that was found in his treasures: there was nothing in his house, nor in all his dominion, that Hezekiah shewed them not. Then came Isaiah the prophet unto king Hezekiah, and said unto him, What said these men? and from whence came they unto thee? . . . What have they seen in thine house? And Hezekiah answered, All that is in mine house have they seen: there is nothing among my treasures that I have not shewed them. . . ."

The visit of the ambassadors to Hezekiah was a test of his gratitude and devotion. . . . God had raised him from a bed of death, giving him a new lease of life. The Babylonians had heard of his wonderful recovery. They marveled that the sun had been turned back ten degrees, as a sign that the word of the Lord should be fulfilled. They sent messengers to Hezekiah to congratulate him on his recovery. The visit of these messengers gave him an opportunity to extol the God of heaven. How easy it would have been to point them to the God of gods. But pride and vanity took possession of Hezekiah's heart, and in his self-exaltation he laid open to their covetous eyes the treasures with which God had enriched His people. . . . His indiscretion prepared the way for national disaster. The ambassadors carried to Babylon the report of Hezekiah's riches, and the king and his counselors planned to enrich Babylon with the treasures of Jerusalem.

Had Hezekiah improved the opportunity given him to bear witness to the power, the goodness, the compassion, of the God of Israel, the report of the ambassadors would have been as light piercing darkness. But he magnified himself above the Lord of hosts and failed to give God the glory. . . .

Oh, that those for whom God has done marvelous things would show forth His praises and tell of His mighty works. But how often those for whom God works are like Hezekiah—forgetful of the Giver of all their blessings.—*Signs of the Times,* Oct. 1, 1902.

Individually Responsible

Let a man examine himself. 1 Cor. 11:28.

This world is a training school, and the great object of life should be to obtain a fitness for those glorious mansions that Jesus has gone to prepare. Let us remember that this work of preparation is an individual work. We are not saved in groups. The purity and devotion of one will not offset the want of these qualities in another. Each case must bear individual inspection. Each of us must be tested and found without spot or wrinkle or any such thing.

We are living in the great antitypical day of atonement. Jesus is now in the heavenly sanctuary, making reconciliation for the sins of His people, and the judgment of the righteous dead has been going on almost forty years [written in May 1884]. How soon the cases of the living will come in review before this tribunal we know not; but we do know that we are living in the closing scenes of earth's history, standing, as it were, on the very borders of the eternal world. It is important that each of us inquire, How stands my case in the courts of heaven? Will my sins be blotted out? Am I defective in character, and so blinded to these defects by the customs and opinions of the world that sin does not appear to me to be as exceedingly offensive to God as it really is? It is no time now to allow our minds to be absorbed with the things of earth while we give only occasional thoughts to God and make but slight preparation for the country to which we are journeying.

In the typical Day of Atonement, all the people were required to afflict their souls before God. They were not to afflict the souls of others, but the work was between God and their own souls. The same work of self-examination and humiliation is required of each of us now. . . . Precious, golden moments which should be spent in seeking the inward adorning of a meek and quiet spirit are frittered away in adorning the dress and in other trifling matters not at all essential to comfort. . . .

We are living in an important and eventful age. We are almost home. Soon the many mansions that our Savior has gone to prepare will burst upon our sight. . . . We may now have in our hearts joy and peace that are unspeakable and full of glory; and soon, at the coming of Christ, the prize that lies at the end of the Christian race will be ours to enjoy throughout ceaseless ages.—*Signs of the Times,* May 29, 1884.

The Latter Rain

Ask the Lord for rain in the time of the latter rain. The Lord will make flashing clouds; He will give them showers of rain. Zech. 10:1.

In the East the former rain falls at the sowing time. It is necessary in order that the seed may germinate. Under the influence of the fertilizing showers, the tender shoot springs up. The latter rain, falling near the close of the season, ripens the grain, and prepares it for the sickle. The Lord employs these operations of nature to represent the work of the Holy Spirit. As the dew and the rain are given first to cause the seed to germinate and then to ripen the harvest, so the Holy Spirit is given to carry forward, from one stage to another, the process of spiritual growth. The ripening of the grain represents the completion of the work of God's grace in the soul. . . .

The latter rain, ripening earth's harvest, represents the spiritual grace that prepares the church for the coming of the Son of man. But unless the former rain has fallen, there will be no life; the green blade will not spring up. Unless the early showers have done their work, the latter rain can bring no seed to perfection. . . .

The work that God has begun in the human heart in giving His light and knowledge must be continually going forward. All of us must realize our own necessity. The heart must be emptied of every defilement and cleansed for the indwelling of the Spirit. It was by the confession and forsaking of sin, by earnest prayer and consecration of themselves to God, that the early disciples prepared for the outpouring of the Holy Spirit on the day of Pentecost. The same work, only in greater degree, must be done now. . . .

Only those who are living up to the light they have will receive greater light. Unless we are daily advancing in the exemplification of the active Christian virtues, we shall not recognize the manifestations of the Holy Spirit in the latter rain. It may be falling on hearts all around us, but we shall not discern or receive it.

At no point in our experience can we dispense with the assistance of that which enables us to make the first start. The blessings received under the former rain are needful to us to the end.—*Review and Herald,* Mar. 2, 1897.

Accept the Invitation

Go out into the highways and hedges, and compel them to come in,
that my house may be filled. Luke 14:23.

A man who had been invited to the feast with Christ in the house of one
of the chief Pharisees, and who heard Christ declare what was the duty
of those who had God's bounties, had exclaimed in self-satisfied compla-
cency, "Blessed is he that shall eat bread in the kingdom of God." He had
designed to draw away the minds of those at the feast from the subject of their
practical duty; but instead of this he furnished an occasion for the utterance
of a parable that had still deeper significance, and that more plainly opened
before the company the character and value of their present privileges. . . .

Christ had sent out an invitation to a feast that He had provided at great
cost. He had sent the Holy Spirit to move upon the minds of prophets and
holy men of old to invite His chosen people to the rich feast of the gospel.
. . . The man who had sought to divert the attention of the company spoke
with great assurance, as though he thought he would certainly eat bread in
the kingdom of God. But Jesus warned him and all present against the danger of rejecting the present invitation to the gospel feast. . . .

The Lord had first sent His invitation to His chosen people, but they had
slighted and rejected His messenger. How vain, how needless, were the excuses they offered; but are the excuses that men and women give in this age
any more sensible than those offered in the time of Christ?

Some who are invited exclaim, "I beg Thee have me excused. If I should
come, my neighbors would jest at and ridicule me, and I cannot bear their
scorn. I have lived among them a long time, and I do not want to displease
my neighbors." . . . Others are desirous of paying for their lands and of
building up their temporal interests, and the powers of mind and soul and
body are absorbed in their earthly affairs. . . .

The precious message has come to us in these last days. . . . The invitation
has been given, "Come; for all things are now ready." . . .

Christ has pledged His own life for the redemption of His people, and
He would have them consider their higher, eternal claims.—*Review and
Herald,* Nov. 5, 1895.

To All Nations

You shall be witnesses to Me in Jerusalem, and in all Judea and Samaria, and to the end of the earth. Acts 1:8.

Christ commissioned His disciples to do the work He had left in their hands, beginning at Jerusalem. Jerusalem had been the scene of His amazing condescension for the human race. There He had suffered, been rejected and condemned. The land of Judea was His birthplace. There, clad in the garb of humanity, He had walked with humanity, and few had discerned how near heaven came to earth when Jesus was among them. At Jerusalem the work of the disciples must begin.

But the work was not to stop here. It was to be extended to the earth's remotest bounds. To His disciples Christ said: You have been witnesses of My life of self-sacrifice in behalf of the world. You have witnessed My labors for Israel. Although they would not come unto Me that they might have life, although priests and rulers have done unto Me as they wished, although they have rejected Me as the Scripture foretold, they shall have still another opportunity of accepting the Son of God. You have seen that all who come to Me confessing their sins, I freely receive. He that cometh to Me I will in no wise cast out. All who will, may be reconciled to God and receive everlasting life. To you, My disciples, I commit this message of mercy. It is to be given to Israel first, and then to all nations, tongues, and peoples. . . .

Through the gift of the Holy Spirit the disciples were to receive a marvelous power. Their testimony was to be confirmed by signs and wonders. . . .

The disciples were to begin their work where they were. The hardest and most unpromising field was not to be passed by. So all of Christ's workers are to begin where they are. In our own families may be souls hungry for sympathy, starving for the bread of life. There may be children to be trained for Christ. There are heathen at our very doors. Let us do faithfully the work that is nearest. Then let our efforts be extended as far as God's hand may lead the way. The work of many may appear to be restricted by circumstances; but wherever it is, if performed with faith and diligence it will be felt to the uttermost parts of the earth. Christ's work when upon earth appeared to be confined to a narrow field, but multitudes from all lands heard His message.—*Review and Herald,* Oct. 9, 1913.

The First and Second Advent

And He will send His angels with a great sound of a trumpet, and they will gather together His elect from the four winds, from one end of heaven to the other. Matt. 24:31.

The leaders of the Jewish nation had the Old Testament Scriptures, which plainly foretold the manner of Christ's first advent. Through the prophet Isaiah God had described the appearance and mission of Christ, saying, "He is despised and rejected of men; a man of sorrows, and acquainted with grief." . . .

All the wonderful events clustering around His second coming, they looked for at His first. Therefore, when He came, they were not prepared to receive Him. . . .

Between the first and the second advent of Christ a wonderful contrast will be seen. No human language can portray the scenes of the second coming of the Son of man in the clouds of heaven. He is to come with His own glory and with the glory of the Father and of the holy angels. He will come clad in the robe of light, which He has worn from the days of eternity. Angels will accompany Him. . . . The sound of the trumpet will be heard, calling the sleeping dead from the grave. . . .

As they [the Jewish leaders] gaze upon His glory, there flashes before their minds the memory of the Son of man clad in the garb of humanity. They remember how they treated Him, how they refused Him and pressed close to the side of the great apostate. The scenes of Christ's life appear before them in all their clearness. All He did, all He said, the humiliation to which He descended to save them from the taint of sin, rises before them in condemnation. . . .

We are now amid the perils of the last days. The scenes of conflict are hastening on, and the day of days is just upon us. Are we prepared for the issue? . . .

The Son of man will bestow upon the righteous the crown of everlasting life, and they shall "serve him day and night in his temple: and he that sitteth on the throne shall dwell among them. They shall hunger no more, neither thirst any more; neither shall the sun light on them, nor any heat. For the Lamb which is in the midst of the throne shall feed them, and shall lead them unto living fountains of water: and God shall wipe away all tears from their eyes."—*Review and Herald,* Sept. 5, 1899

What a Christmas Present!

I will come again and receive you to Myself. John 14:3.

The time of Jesus' betrayal, suffering, and crucifixion was drawing near; and as the disciples gathered around Him, the Lord unfolded to them the mournful events that were about to take place, and their hearts were filled with sorrow. To comfort them He spoke these tender words: "Let not your heart be troubled. . . . I will come again, and receive you unto myself." He directed their minds away from the scenes of sorrow to the mansions of heaven and the time of reunion in the kingdom of God. . . . Though He must go from them and ascend to His Father, His work for those He loved would not be at an end. He was to prepare homes for those who, for His sake, were to be pilgrims and strangers on the earth. . . .

After His resurrection "he led them out as far as to Bethany, and he lifted up his hands, and blessed them. And it came to pass, while he blessed them, he was parted from them, and carried up into heaven." . . . Do you imagine as they went back to Jerusalem that they said to one another, "Well, the Lord has left us. What is now the use of trying to gain followers to Jesus? Let us return to our nets." . . . There is no record of any such conversation. Not a line is written or a hint given that they had a thought of leaving the service of their ascended Lord for the service of self and the world. The Savior's hand had been outstretched in blessing His disciples He had left behind as He ascended. They had seen His glory. He had gone to prepare mansions for them. Their salvation had been provided for, and if they were faithful in complying with the conditions, they would assuredly follow Him to the world of unending joy. Their hearts were filled with songs of rejoicing and praise.

We all have the same cause for thanksgiving. The resurrection and ascension of our Lord is a sure evidence of the triumph of the saints of God over death and the grave, and a pledge that heaven is open to those who wash their robes of character and make them white in the blood of the Lamb. Jesus ascended to the Father as a representative of the human race, and God will bring those who reflect His image to behold and share with Him His glory. . . .

Let us go forward together to reach the great reward and join in the song of the redeemed. If we ever sing the praises of God in heaven, we must first sing them here.—*Signs of the Times,* Jan. 27, 1888.

The Promise Fulfilled

Enter into the joy of your lord. Matt. 25:21.

Though the disciples had gazed far into the heaven until their Lord had vanished from their sight, they did not behold the angels that gathered around their beloved Commander. Jesus led a multitude of captives who had risen from the grave at His resurrection. As the glorious company approach the gates of the eternal city, the angels sing, "Lift up your heads, O ye gates; and be ye lifted up, ye everlasting doors; and the King of glory shall come in." And the angels guarding the gates respond, "Who is this King of glory?" The attendant angels reply, "The Lord of hosts, he is the King of glory." As the glorious train passes in, the angels are about to bow in adoration before the Lord of glory; but He waves them back. Before He will permit their homage He must know that His sacrifice for the fallen race has been accepted of the Father. He must know whether the price paid for the redemption of the lost has been sufficient to ransom them from the power of sin and the grave. . . . Amid the splendor of the courts of glory, amid ten thousand times ten thousand and thousands of thousands waiting to cast their crowns at His feet, He does not forget those that He has left on earth to bear opposition, reproach, and scorn. After the Father has assured Him that the ransom paid is accepted, still He has a request to offer for those who believe in Him and follow in His footsteps, "Father, I will that they also, whom thou hast given me, be with me where I am; that they may behold my glory, which thou hast given me: for thou lovedst me before the foundation of the world." He requested that His disciples might enter into His joy and share His glory, and at last the faithful servant of the Lord will hear the glad words, "Enter thou into the joy of thy lord."

When He had finished preferring His requests, the Father gave the command, "Let all the angels of God worship him." Then the song of joy and love swells through the heavenly courts, "Worthy, worthy, worthy, is the Lamb that was slain, and lives again, a triumphant conqueror." And this same Jesus, whom unnumbered hosts of angels delight to adore, is coming again to fulfill His promise and receive those who love Him unto Himself. Have we not great reason to rejoice? . . . The consummation of our hope is at hand; the faithful will soon enter into the joy of their Lord.—*Signs of the Times,* Jan. 27, 1888.

A Resolution

I will not let You go unless You bless me! Gen. 32:26.

There is need of earnest work, that we may have strength from God to resist the enemy when he shall come in like a flood. We must agonize in order to subdue self; for self-ease and self-indulgence are the most deceptive of sins, stupefying the conscience and blinding the understanding. . . . We need the earnest desire of the importunate widow and the Syrophenician woman—a determination that will not be repulsed.

Many, very many, are making a fatal mistake by failing to heed this lesson of God's providence. Peace and rest can be secured only by conflict. The powers of light and darkness are in array, and we must individually take a part in the struggle. Jacob wrestled all night with God before he gained the victory. As he pleaded with God in prayer, he felt a strong hand laid upon him, and thinking it to be the hand of an enemy, he put forth all his strength to resist Him. He wrestled for hours, but gained nothing over his Opponent, and he dared not relax his efforts for one moment, lest he should be overcome and lose his life. . . . Then the Stranger brought the conflict to a close. He touched the thigh of Jacob, and the wrestler's strength was paralyzed. It was not until then that Jacob learned who his Opponent really was, and, falling crippled and weeping on His neck, he pleaded for his life.

The Angel could easily have released Himself from the grasp of Jacob, but He did not do this. "Let me go," He pleaded, "for the day breaketh." But the answer came from the suffering but determined Jacob, "I will not let thee go, except thou bless me." The suppliant's tears and prayers gained for him what he struggled in vain to obtain. "What is thy name?" the Angel asked. "And he said, Jacob. And he said, Thy name shall be called no more Jacob, but Israel: for as a prince hast thou power with God and with men, and hast prevailed. . . . And he blessed him there." . . .

Resolution, self-denial, and consecrated effort are required for the work of preparation. . . . Only by earnest, determined effort and faith in the merits of Christ can we overcome and gain the kingdom of heaven. Our time for work is short. Christ is soon to come the second time.—*Youth's Instructor,* May 24, 1900.

Change in Raiment

I counsel you to buy from Me gold refined in the fire, that you may be rich;
and white garments, that you may be clothed. Rev. 3:18.

The Lord Jesus has sent a most solemn message to the Laodicean church. . . . In the counsel of the True Witness, He urges upon His people the necessity of being clothed in the white garment of His righteousness. Every guest accepted for the marriage supper of the Lamb will be arrayed in this spotless robe. But Satan is determined that those who have been sinners shall not wear this spotless garment, and he is seeking to obtain unlimited power over them. The controversy over those who have been purchased by the blood of Christ is pictured by the prophet. He says, "And he shewed me Joshua the high priest standing before the angel of the Lord, and Satan standing at his right hand to resist him. And the Lord said unto Satan, The Lord rebuke thee, O Satan; even the Lord that hath chosen Jerusalem rebuke thee: is not this a brand plucked out of the fire?"

Joshua represents those who are making a penitent plea at the throne of grace, and Satan stands as their adversary to accuse them before Christ. The prophet continues, "Now Joshua was clothed with filthy garments, and stood before the angel. And he answered and spake unto those that stood before him, saying, Take away the filthy garments from him. And unto him he said, Behold, I have caused thine iniquity to pass from thee, and I will clothe thee with change of raiment. . . ."

The wedding garment is the righteousness of Christ and represents the character of those who will be accepted as guests for the marriage supper of the Lamb. Those who have transgressed the law, who have committed sin, can find no saving quality in the law which condemns them, but Christ has become the sin bearer for the whole world. . . .

Those who receive Christ as their personal Savior yield up their way to His will and His way. They cast their sins upon Him and receive and rejoice in the imputed righteousness of Christ. They know what it means to have a change of raiment. . . . "He that believeth on the Son hath everlasting life."—*Youth's Instructor,* Oct. 21, 1897.

Use What You Have

And whatever you do, do it heartily, as to the Lord and not to men.
Col. 3:23.

Every individual, from the lowliest and most obscure to the greatest and most exalted, is a moral agent endowed with abilities for which each is accountable to God. . . .

Let the business man and woman do their business in a way that will glorify their Master because of their fidelity. Let them carry their religion into everything that is done, and reveal to others the spirit of Christ. Let the mechanic be a diligent and faithful representative of Him who toiled in the lowly walks of life in the cities of Judea. Let all who name the name of Christ so work that others, by seeing their good works, may be led to glorify their Creator and Redeemer. . . .

Those who have been blessed with superior talents should not depreciate the value of the services of those who are less gifted than themselves. The smallest trust is a trust from God. With the blessing of God, the one talent through diligent use will be doubled, and the two used in the service of Christ will be increased to four; and thus the humblest instrument may grow in power and usefulness. . . .

We are responsible only for the talents which God has bestowed upon us. The Lord does not reprove the servant who has doubled his talent, who has done according to his ability. Those who thus prove their fidelity can be commended and rewarded; but those who loiter in the vineyard, those who do nothing, or do negligently the Lord's work, make manifest their real attitude toward the work to which they have been called, by their works. They show that their hearts are not in the service for which they have been engaged. . . .

Let none mourn that they have not larger talents to use for the Master. . . . Thank God for the ability you have, and pray that you may be enabled to meet the responsibilities that have been placed upon you. If you desire greater usefulness, go to work and acquire what you mourn for. Go to work with steady patience, and do your very best, irrespective of what others are doing. . . . Let not your thought or your words be, Oh, that I had a larger work! Oh, that I were in this or that position! Do your duty where you are. Make the best investments possible with your entrusted gift in the very place where your work will count the most before God.—*Review and Herald,* Oct. 26, 1911.

The Blessed Hope

We should live soberly, righteously, and godly in the present age.
Titus 2:12.

We are exhorted to live soberly, righteously, and godly in this present world, and to look for the glorious appearing of the great God and our Savior Jesus Christ. Some have made an objection to my work, because I teach that it is our duty to be looking for Christ's personal appearing in the clouds of heaven. They have said, "You would think that the day of the Lord was right upon us to hear Mrs. White speak in reference to the coming of Christ; and she has been preaching on that same subject for the last forty years, and the Lord has not yet come." This very objection might have been brought against the words of Christ Himself. He said by the mouth of the beloved disciple, "Behold, I come quickly," and John responds, "Even so, come, Lord Jesus."

Jesus spoke these words as words of warning and encouragement to His people; and why should we not heed them? The Lord has said that it is the faithful who will be found watching and waiting for Him. It was the unfaithful servant who said, "My lord delayeth his coming," and began to smite his fellow servants and to eat and drink with the drunken.

The exact time of Christ's second coming is not revealed. Jesus said, "No man knoweth the day nor the hour." But He also gave signs of His coming, and said, "When ye shall see all these things, know that it is near, even at the doors." He bade them, as the signs of His coming should appear, "Look up, and lift up your heads; for your redemption draweth nigh." And in view of these things the apostle wrote, "Ye, brethren, are not in darkness, that that day should overtake you as a thief. Ye are all the children of light, and the children of the day." Since we know not the hour of Christ's coming, we must live soberly and godly in this present world, "looking for that blessed hope, and the glorious appearing of the great God and our Saviour Jesus Christ."

Christ gave Himself for us, that He might redeem us from all iniquity and purify unto Himself a peculiar people, zealous of good works. His people are to preserve their peculiar character as His representatives. There is work for every one of them to do. . . . Says the apostle, "We are not of the night, nor of darkness. Therefore let us not sleep, as do others; but let us watch and be sober."—*Signs of the Times,* June 24, 1889.

Preparing for Heaven

So they put a clean turban on his head, and they put the clothes on him.
Zech. 3:5.

As we approach the perils of the last days, the temptations of the enemy become stronger and more determined. Satan has come down in great power, knowing that his time is short; and he is working "with all deceivableness of unrighteousness in them that perish." The warning comes to us through God's Word that, if it were possible, he would deceive the very elect.

Wonderful events are soon to open before the world. The end of all things is at hand. The time of trouble is about to come upon the people of God. Then it is that the decree will go forth forbidding those who keep the Sabbath of the Lord to buy or sell, and threatening them with punishment, and even death, if they do not observe the first day of the week as the Sabbath. . . .

In the time of trouble, Satan stirs up the wicked, and they encircle the people of God to destroy them. But he does not know that "pardon" has been written opposite their names in the books of heaven. He does not know that the command has been given, "Take away the filthy garments" from them, clothe them with "change of raiment," and set "a fair mitre" upon their heads. . . .

While we speak of the necessity of separating from sin, remember that Christ came to our world to save sinners, and that "he is able also to save them to the uttermost that come unto God by him." It is our privilege to believe that His blood is able to cleanse us from every spot and stain of sin. We must not limit the power of the Holy One of Israel. He wants us to come to Him just as we are, sinful and polluted. His blood is efficacious. I entreat you not to grieve His Spirit by continuing in sin. If you fall under temptation, do not become discouraged. This promise comes ringing down along the line to our time, "If any man sin, we have an advocate with the Father, Jesus Christ the righteous." I feel that for this one promise a continual song of thanksgiving ought to go forth from the lips of mortals. Let us gather up these precious jewels of promise, and when Satan accuses us of our great sinfulness, and tempts us to doubt the power of God to save, let us repeat the words of Christ, "Him that cometh to me I will in no wise cast out."—*Review and Herald,* Nov. 19, 1908.

Heaven Below and Heaven Above

For whatever things were written before were written for our learning, that we through the patience and comfort of the Scriptures might have hope.
Rom. 15:4.

We have but one probation in which to form character, and our destiny depends upon the manner of character we form. Those who on earth have formed characters that through the grace of Christ bear the heavenly mold will be ripened through the gracious influence of the Holy Spirit for the eternal reward. They become partakers of the divine nature, having escaped the corruption that is in the world through lust. It is a realization of the fact that our characters are Christlike that calls forth the song of praise and thanksgiving to God and to the Lamb. Those who appreciate the goodness, mercy, and love of Christ, and by beholding Him become changed into His image, will be partakers of eternal life. The attributes of their character are like those of Christ, and they cannot fail of the rest that remains for the people of God. . . .

If we would see heaven, we must have heaven below. We must have a heaven to go to heaven in. We must have heaven in our families, through Christ continually approaching unto God. Christ is the great center of attraction, and the child of God hid in Christ meets with God, and is lost in the divine being. Prayer is the life of the soul; it is feeding on Christ; it is turning our faces fully toward the Sun of Righteousness. As we turn our faces toward Him, He turns His face toward us. . . .

By simple, earnest, contrite prayer, heavenly mindedness is greatly increased. No other means of grace can be substituted and healthiness of the soul be preserved. Prayer brings the soul into immediate contact with the wellspring of life and strengthens the spiritual sinew and muscle of our religious experience; for we live by faith, seeing Him who is invisible. . . .

The Word of God is a spiritual granary from whence the soul may receive that which will nourish its life. In perusing the Word of God we find doctrines, precepts, promises, admonitions, exhortations, and words of encouragement that will meet the case of emergency in every human mind. Here the man and woman of God may be thoroughly furnished unto all good works; for "all scripture is given by inspiration of God, and is profitable for doctrine, for reproof, for correction, for instruction in righteousness: that the man of God may be perfect, thoroughly furnished unto all good works."—*Signs of the Times,* July 31, 1893.

SCRIPTURE INDEX